GENET'S GENRES OF POLITICS

# LEGENDA

LEGENDA is the Modern Humanities Research Association's book imprint for new research in the Humanities. Founded in 1995 by Malcolm Bowie and others within the University of Oxford, Legenda has always been a collaborative publishing enterprise, directly governed by scholars. The Modern Humanities Research Association (MHRA) joined this collaboration in 1998, became half-owner in 2004, in partnership with Maney Publishing and then Routledge, and has since 2016 been sole owner. Titles range from medieval texts to contemporary cinema and form a widely comparative view of the modern humanities, including works on Arabic, Catalan, English, French, German, Greek, Italian, Portuguese, Russian, Spanish, and Yiddish literature. Editorial boards and committees of more than 60 leading academic specialists work in collaboration with bodies such as the Society for French Studies, the British Comparative Literature Association and the Association of Hispanists of Great Britain & Ireland.

The MHRA encourages and promotes advanced study and research in the field of the modern humanities, especially modern European languages and literature, including English, and also cinema. It aims to break down the barriers between scholars working in different disciplines and to maintain the unity of humanistic scholarship. The Association fulfils this purpose through the publication of journals, bibliographies, monographs, critical editions, and the MHRA Style Guide, and by making grants in support of research. Membership is open to all who work in the Humanities, whether independent or in a University post, and the participation of younger colleagues entering the field is especially welcomed.

### ALSO PUBLISHED BY THE ASSOCIATION

*Critical Texts*
*Tudor and Stuart Translations* • *New Translations* • *European Translations*
*MHRA Library of Medieval Welsh Literature*

*MHRA Bibliographies*
*Publications of the Modern Humanities Research Association*

*The Annual Bibliography of English Language & Literature*
*Austrian Studies*
*Modern Language Review*
*Portuguese Studies*
*The Slavonic and East European Review*
*Working Papers in the Humanities*
*The Yearbook of English Studies*

www.mhra.org.uk
www.legendabooks.com

# RESEARCH MONOGRAPHS IN FRENCH STUDIES

The *Research Monographs in French Studies* (RMFS) are selected, edited and supported by the Society for French Studies. The series seeks to publish the best new work in all areas of the literature, language, thought, history, politics, culture and film of the French-speaking world and to cover the full chronological range from the medieval period to the present day. Proposals are accepted for monographs of up to 85,000 words, while proposals for 'short' monographs (50,000–60,000 words), a traditional strength of the series, are still welcomed.

❖

# PUBLISHED IN THIS SERIES

www.rmfs.mhra.org.uk

# Genet's Genres of Politics

❖

MAIRÉAD HANRAHAN

*l*

# LEGENDA

Research Monographs in French Studies 50
Modern Humanities Research Association
2023

*Published by Legenda*
*an imprint of the Modern Humanities Research Association*
*Salisbury House, Station Road, Cambridge CB1 2LA*

*ISBN 978-1-78188-711-0 (HB)*
*ISBN 978-1-78188-438-6 (PB)*

*First published 2023*

*Copy-Editor: Charlotte Wathey*

# CONTENTS

❖

*Do Mháire, à Violette*

# ACKNOWLEDGEMENTS

❖

I wish to extend my appreciation to the team at the Institut mémoires de l'édition contemporaine, and in particular its Literary Director Albert Dichy, for their help during my visits to Caen to consult the Genet archive held at the Abbaye d'Ardenne.

Very special thanks are due to James Strachan for his help in sourcing the photo on the front cover. I would also like to acknowledge the kind permission to reproduce the image granted by Robert Carl Cohen.

Many people have contributed in a variety of ways to this book. I am grateful to Tom Baldwin, Graham Nelson and Charlotte Wathey at Legenda for their assistance and expertise and, especially, to Diana Knight for the grace and elegance of her editorial insights and wisdom. Finally, in addition to the two steadfast rocks in my life to whom this book is dedicated, I would like to express my particular thanks to Kate Conley, Ursula Fanning, Eoin Hanrahan, Róisín Hanrahan, Tadhg Ó hAnnracháin and Judith Still whose support was invaluable in helping me bring this endeavour to completion.

M.H., February 2023

# ABBREVIATIONS

❖

*Works by Jean Genet*

B       *The Balcony*, trans. by Barbara Writing and Terry Hands (London: Faber & Faber, 1991)

CA      *Un Captif amoureux* (Paris: Gallimard, 1986)

DE      *Jean Genet: The Declared Enemy, Texts and Interviews*, trans. by Jeff Fort (Stanford, CA: Stanford University Press, 2004)

ED      *L'Ennemi déclaré*, ed. by Albert Dichy (Paris: Gallimard, 1991)

FA      *Fragments of the Artwork*, trans. by Charlotte Mandell (Stanford, CA: Stanford University Press, 2003)

FR      *Funeral Rites*, trans. by Bernard Frechtman (London: Panther, 1971)

LRB     *Letters to Roger Blin*, trans. by Richard Seaver (New York: Grove Press, 1969)

M       *The Maids*, trans. by Bernard Frechtman [1953] (London: Faber & Faber, 2009)

MR      *Miracle of the Rose*, trans. by Bernard Frechtman (London: Penguin, 1971)

OC      *Œuvres complètes*, 6 vols (Paris: Gallimard, 1952–79)

OLF     *Our Lady of the Flowers*, trans. by Bernard Frechtman (London: Panther, 1966)

PL      *Prisoner of Love*, trans. by Barbara Bray (New York: New York Review Books, 2003)

RP      *Romans et poèmes*, ed. by Emmanuelle Lambert and Gilles Philippe with Albert Dichy (Paris: Gallimard/Pléiade, 2021)

TC      *Théâtre complet*, ed. by Michel Corvin and Albert Dichy (Paris: Gallimard/Pléiade, 2002)

TJ      *The Thief's Journal*, trans. by Bernard Frechtman (London: Penguin, 1967)

*Other Works*

BSJ     Éric Marty, *Bref séjour à Jérusalem* (Paris: Gallimard/L'Infini, 2003)

G       Jacques Derrida, *Glas: que reste-t-il du savoir absolu?* [1974] (Paris: Denoël, 1981)

GE      Jacques Derrida, *Glas*, trans. by John P. Leavey, Jr., and Richard Rand (Lincoln & London: University of Nebraska Press, 1986)

JGP     Éric Marty, *Jean Genet, post-scriptum* (Paris: Verdier, 2006)

VIJG    Ivan Jablonka, *Les Vérités inavouables de Jean Genet* (Paris: Seuil, 2004)

Unless specified otherwise, translations, including passages not featuring in the translations listed above, are mine; quotations from published translations have often been modified. Unless otherwise indicated, all italics in quotations mark an emphasis in the original.

# INTRODUCTION

❖

What are Genet's politics? Given his singular trajectory, it is scarcely surprising that this question has been central to debates about Genet since his death in 1986. His public renunciation of writing following the suicide of his lover Abdallah in 1964, together with his activism on behalf of the Black Panthers and the Palestinians from 1970 onwards, invited the perception of a shift that neatly opposed in the first instance the early 'work' to the later 'life' and, secondarily, the early 'literary' texts to the 'political' writings he produced in the years immediately before he died — a perception to which a number of Genet's own pronouncements undoubtedly contributed. Much of this book will be concerned with questioning the periodising narrative that thus distinguishes a late 'political' Genet from the early one. Yet even more than the problem of the continuity or discontinuity between his writing and his other forms of intervention, between the politics of his first texts and those of his last, Genet's case is of particular interest because it crystallises broader questions about the relationship between art and politics. At issue is not merely where to situate the writer on the political spectrum (left or right, revolutionary or reactionary) but the grounds on which we assess a writer's politics. *How* Genet is political is as important a question as *what* his politics are. Perhaps even more importantly, he exemplarily calls into question the very category of a 'political' writer.

Historically, the basis on which a writer was designated as 'political' was primarily at the level of his or her subject-matter: either the work dealt with unequivocally political material or the author took advantage of the platform afforded by literary renown to express political views unexplored in the work. The assumption that a political author is one who deals with political themes — either in the work or in otherwise public pronouncements — remains active today; for example, it appears to underpin the criteria for judging the Orwell Prize for Political Fiction, founded as recently as 2019, whose brief is to 'reward novels and short stories that illuminate major social and political themes, present or past, via the art of narrative'.[1] Similarly, the most periodising accounts of Genet situate the political at the level of thematic content. In *Le Dernier Genet*, Hadrien Laroche singles out 1968 as inaugurating 'la dernière période de l'écrivain, où l'homme a tenté une sortie politique par le seul moyen du poète: la langue' [the writer's last period, when the man attempted political action by the means the poet uses: language].[2] While this quotation might suggest that a poet's choice of form as well as topic has a political dimension, Laroche's book as a whole identifies the new political Genet it posits as one who gives priority to meaning, ending with the claim that Genet wanted at the end to be judged for his 'idées politiques' [political ideas].[3] Most others who identify a major watershed in Genet's trajectory date it substantially earlier.[4] The turning-point they privilege is an epiphanic encounter that Genet later describes as having taken place on a train in 1953 with a man in whom he was shocked to recognise 'une sorte d'identité universelle à tous les hommes' [a sort of universal identity shared by all men].[5] This encounter, deemed by the writer to have jolted him into the realisation that each man is defined or singularised not by what sets him apart from others but by the woundedness that is the condition common to all humanity, sparked an ethical transformation whose consequences can be traced in the politicisation of his subsequent writings. These interpretations of Genet's trajectory thus differ regarding both the date of the new departure and its origins. However, they share the basic assumption that Genet's life changed in such a way as to bring about a profound alteration in his work, moving it away from the focus on fantasy of his earliest texts towards an engagement with a 'reality' which is usually not defined as such but whose principal characteristic is assumed to be its independence from Genet's imagination. Implicit in the political 'turn' these critics identify in Genet's writing is thus a shift in priority towards the object of representation: the notion that politicisation involves a subordination of the text to the message it conveys.

The readings mentioned above share the further assumption that this shift was fundamentally progressive. I shall return below to the question of how the form as much as the meaning of Genet's writing might be politically determined. First, I want to note that the same years that saw this periodisation emerge also saw the emergence of very different, not to say opposing, readings of Genet as fascist sympathiser and antisemite. Chapters 1 and 4 engage with these in detail; it will be clear that I find those arguments unconvincing. But the point I want to highlight here is less that there have been such markedly divergent evaluations of Genet's politics than that, nearly forty years after his death, opinions still differ about whether he was a revolutionary or a reactionary. My aim is not to reconcile those divergences but rather to explore the implications of their irreconcilability. What might the dramatic lack of consensus about Genet's politics tell us about his politics? Is the difficulty of categorising him politically a reflection of an apolitical standpoint on his part or rather of a particular political configuration?

Views have in effect varied widely not only on what Genet's political position was, but on whether he had one. The incompatible readings above are ironically in agreement that politics looms large in Genet's work, an idea in marked contrast with the early reception of his work. The thrust of Sartre's reading in his hugely influential *Saint Genet: comédien et martyr* was to depoliticise Genet's writing as individual 'revolt' rather than 'revolution', a view which dominated critical opinion for many years.[6] My point of departure is the belief that Genet's writing has *always* been political. His first texts doubtless did not correspond to any conception of politics prevalent at the time, in that they engaged little with the socio-economic conflicts at either national or international level that were then alone considered to constitute the political domain. Yet from the outset his texts are profoundly concerned with power relations and power structures.[7] 'Weidmann vous apparut dans une édition de cinq heures' [Weidmann appeared before you in a five o'clock edition] (*RP*, 3; *OLF*, 55): in addressing his reader as 'vous' in the combative opening line of his very first novel he famously insists on the difference between them, and hence on the non-identity of interests without which there would be no need for any politics.[8] The shift from the erotic fantasies of the early texts to the Palestinians' struggle for emancipation in the posthumously published *Un Captif amoureux* incontestably marks a change in focus from the personal to the public. But from the very beginning Genet's work challenges the opposition that traditionally confined the political to the public sphere. Indeed, it played an important part in the intellectual developments that have made the notion of a sexual politics uncontroversial today; already in the 1970s Genet was a key reference for second-wave feminists and theorists of gender such as Hélène Cixous and Kate Millett.[9] Far in advance of his time in showing how the personal is political, his novels were ground-breaking in exploring how psychical structures — particular constructions of gender and sexuality — involve particular constructions of society. They specifically draw attention to the existence of a connection between the taboo or censored fantasies to which they give voice and the instances of power whose authority depends on the ability to project an objectivity unaffected by fantasy or desire. So, for example, the extraordinary representation at the end of *Miracle de la rose* of Harcamone's execution as a penetration of his body by the judge, lawyer, chaplain and executioner serves to highlight the repressed desire underpinning the system that condemned him to death.

Genet's early works thus trouble the idea of a clear dividing line between the realm of personal fantasy and the arena of impersonal 'political' intervention. Similarly, the later texts with a primary focus on more traditionally political questions, notably the pieces collected in *L'Ennemi déclaré* and *Un Captif amoureux*, repeatedly underscore the unacknowledged desires in operation in political activity, exposing the idea of politics as a fantasy-free zone as itself a fantasy. Hence, for example, Genet's insistence on the pleasure of the policemen at the 1968 Democratic Convention who segregate the black protesters from the white; or his critique of the notion of Frenchness that he detects at work in the Raymond Barre government's 1977 'Droit à la différence' [Right to Difference] policy, ostensibly aimed at revalorising manual labour but in effect excluding the immigrant labour on which Genet claims the accumulation of French capital — in particular (and most audaciously) French *cultural* capital — has historically depended.[10] Genet's work consistently probes in this way at the limits of the political, suggesting both that politics as habitually understood is intrinsically and unavoidably desirous, and that no sphere of human activity can be considered apolitical.

But Genet also probes at the limits of the political in another sense. Although his writing has always been political, it has never been *only* political. For a writer in whose work the analysis of power relations is exceptionally important, it is striking that, even during his period of greatest proximity to Sartre, Genet never seems to have been convinced or even tempted by the idea of a *littérature engagée* [engaged literature]. He has scant respect for writing as a way of effecting extra-textual change. But he also has scant respect for writing that suggests that extra-textual change is the benchmark of its value. For example, he comments dismissively that Rimbaud's iconic statement in the final chapter of *Une saison en enfer* that he has 'un devoir à chercher, et *la réalité rugueuse à étreindre*' [to seek some obligation, to *wrap gnarled reality in my arms*] is merely 'du politique' [politics].[11] As we shall see, in his interviews and other paratextual writings he repeatedly disputed the idea of an equivalence between a 'cultural' or artistic revolution and a 'political' one. Indeed, he has even suggested that writing is inherently conservative, looking back to a previous state rather than forward to a possible new one: 'Et créer c'est toujours parler de l'enfance. C'est toujours nostalgique' [And creating always means talking about childhood. It's always nostalgic] (*ED*, 277; *DE*, 239). My contention is that, for Genet, writing is both irreducibly political and irreducible to politics.

I would suggest, moreover, that readings of Genet's work as progressively more 'activist', more focused on effecting extratextual change, are in contradiction to the arc of his own activity. Rather than increasingly deploying his art towards political ends, it seems more probable to me that Genet suffered a disenchantment with the political potential of writing. The revelling in the productive, creative dimension of writing manifest in his early texts, especially his novels, conveys a confidence that writing is transformative and imbues them with a sense of political optimism. Conversely, his embrace of activism in the latter part of his life did not lead him to overturn his intervening rejection of literature (Chapter 3 explores in detail the reservations he felt about literature's revolutionary potential). And when he did return to writing towards the very end, it was explicitly in awareness of the futility of trying to instrumentalise writing as a means to a political end: *Un Captif amoureux* is profoundly haunted by his fear that his attempt to give voice to the Palestinian revolution serves on the contrary to silence it. I would argue that Genet's own famous 'silence' can in fact be interpreted as an effect of his writing. To borrow one of the politer bodily metaphors he uses to express what is at stake for him in writing, Genet initially believed he was spitting on France and its instances of authority. How disconcerting for him it must have been to find himself admired, 'canonised', appropriated by the very bourgeois audience he believed he was attacking and in effect transformed into a jewel in France's cultural crown. Genet was a writer who remained constant throughout his life in his opposition to hegemonic power structures; in a 1983 interview, he explicitly rejects the idea that the changes in his writing practice reflected an evolution in his beliefs or standpoints:

> Je ne vais pas vous demander de lire mes livres d'il y a trente ans, mais si vous voulez essayer, vous verrez que ce n'est pas la même écriture. Mais vous verrez aussi que c'est le même homme qui parle.

> [I won't ask you to read my books from thirty years ago, but if you want to try, you'll see that it's not the same writing. But you will also see that it's the same man who is speaking.] (*ED*, 278; *DE*, 240)

The most plausible explanation for his giving up writing over a long period is that he came to suspect his art would serve to shore up the very structures he unreservedly contests.

The focus of this book, then, is on the *tension* that I believe exists for Genet between the poetic and the political, a tension that makes his work such particularly rich terrain for exploring the relation between aesthetics and politics. If, for most of Western history, aesthetics and politics were seen as mutually exclusive, over the course of Genet's lifetime the relationship between them became a central issue in critical thought.[12] From Gramsci onwards, a range of thinkers was to theorise the role of culture as a factor in impeding or facilitating political change. Two broad trends emerged in relation to the economic determinism that was the key tenet of traditional Marxist theory (although many, notably Althusser, were to reject this idea as a simplification and to quote Engels to the effect that neither Marx nor he had believed that economics was the only driver of social activity). At issue in that tenet is the belief that relations between the means of production are the foundation on which society in its entirety is organised, and that cultural activity is only ever an effect of these. For figures such as Raymond Williams or Fredric Jameson who essentially maintain a belief in the primacy of the base over the superstructure, art is ultimately seen as an expression of a particular configuration of economic relations. Construed as a social function determined by economic forces, art constitutes an integral element of the dialectical movement by which classes relate to each other. Other thinkers, however, situate the political potential of art not in the enlightenment it can provide about the society in which it originates but as a productive process of its own, one fundamentally at odds with the production practices characteristic of capitalism, in which the process is subordinated to the product. Hence, for example, Theodor Adorno deems Beckett, or Julia Kristeva deems Lautréamont, subversive for what they do rather than for the message they convey. From such a perspective, it is primarily at the level of form rather than content that art offers resistance to the forces whose interest lies in maintaining hegemonic social structures.

The thinker in this regard whose work has most directly informed the approach I take in this book is Jacques Derrida. The idea that the meaning of writing, political or otherwise, is inseparable from the conditions of its production — that the 'what' is always a function of the 'how' — is itself a legacy of the insights of deconstruction that what a system excludes is what makes the system possible in the first place, and that the product cannot be thought without consideration of the process that generates it. In addition, Derrida of course himself elaborated on the relationship between aesthetics and politics specifically in Genet's work in *Glas: que reste-t-il du savoir absolu?*[13] While the reflection on aesthetics in this famously abstruse and elusive text, structured in two parallel columns on Hegel and on Genet, is evident from the beginning, its concern with politics is less immediately perceptible.[14] I shall defer a detailed discussion of its reading of Genet's (sexual) politics until Chapter 1, since the insights Derrida develops in greatest depth are most directly relevant to my analysis of Genet's novels. But *Glas* also gestures, usually aphoristically, towards certain other political implications of the works it studies. Derrida's choice not to elaborate a sustained argument in relation to them has its own logic. It is no accident that *Glas*, and in particular the column dealing with Genet, is one of Derrida's least thetic texts, one least interested in setting out and defending a clear thesis, since the book expressly seeks to avoid replicating the violence involved in Hegel's speculative dialectics that it investigates in the left-hand column, and from which it differentiates the undecidability established as the hallmark of Genet's writing in the right-hand column. It nonetheless bears restating here that the undecidable is what cannot be categorised: it is fundamentally a matter of class, of classification. As such, it is related to that most archetypal of political questions, class. *Glas* — both with and without a capital letter: the book so titled and the eponymous concept — is also about the different classes of class: class as categorisation and class as political sub-group. Years before Derrida overtly engaged with Marxism in *Spectres de Marx*, *Glas* addresses both the politics of class and the possibility of a different class of politics. The word *glas* even shares the same etymology as class, as Derrida develops in the passage that makes the largest claims for the concept:

> Le travail de deuil, est-ce un travail, une espèce de travail? [...] Tout travail n'est-il pas un travail de deuil? et du même coup d'appropriation du plus ou moins de perte, une opération *classique*? une opération violente de classe et de classification? une décollation de ce qui tient le singulier à lui-même? Ce travail de deuil *s'appelle* — glas. Il est toujours du nom propre. Le glas est d'abord (*clas, chiasso, classum, classicum*) le signal d'un trompette destiné à *appeler (calare)*, convoquer, rassembler en tant que telle, une *classe* du peuple romain. Il y a donc du glas dans la littérature classique, mais aussi dans la lutte des classes: classe [...] contre classe, glas des classes, ici même, ici maintenant. Sort du même nom toujours en jeu. Ça s'écrit avec détachement.

> [Is the work of mourning work, a kind of work? [...] Is not all work a work of mourning? And, by the same appropriative stroke of the more or less of loss, a *classic* operation? A violent operation of class and classification? A decollation, an ungluing, of what keeps the singular for itself? This work of mourning *is called* — glas. It is always for/of the proper name. The *glas* is first of all (*clas, chiasso, classum, classicum*) the signal of a trumpet destined to *call* (*calare*), convoke, gather together, reassemble as such, a *class* of the Roman people. There is given then *glas* in classical literature, but also in the class struggle: class [...] against class, *glas* of classes, even here, here and now. The lot of the same noun always in play, at stake. That is written (writes itself) with detachment.] (G, 120-37b; GE, 86-97b)

This passage does not merely make a link between mourning and class (the Roman elite); it proposes mourning itself as an 'operation of class and classification'. As Derrida would develop shortly afterwards in his preface to Torok and Abraham's study of Freud's 'Wolfman' case study, it conceives of mourning as an inherently violent exercise in appropriation, an attempt by the subject to reintegrate the loss of a singular (unclassifiable) otherness.[15] Furthermore, the quotation asks successively both if mourning is a subset of 'work' — a term which, unqualified, in the first instance calls to mind remunerated labour, mental or physical, as distinct from capital — and if 'work' is a subset of mourning. It is therefore impossible to decide which subsumes the other. *Glas*, in italics and in Roman, again both the book and the 'operation' it describes, is fundamentally concerned with how writing undermines the privilege awarded to any one kind of 'work' over others.

This includes the work of naming as well as the work of labour and the work of mourning. 'Ce travail de deuil *s'appelle* — glas': the discontinuous syntax suggests both that *glas* is the name of the 'violent operation of class and classification', and that the process of naming adds to and participates in the process of mourning. The name is part of what it names, one of a series of different classes of work none of which can be argued to fully contain or subsume all the others — a series of which the *work of class* also forms part. Naming, in other words, is both a supplement to and a substitute for the activity which was traditionally taken to comprise politics itself: the class struggle. It is written 'with detachment': far from representing *the* political conflict subsuming all others, the class struggle is one of a series of different political struggles that relay and substitute each other, each of which can successively detach itself as representative of political struggle in general. Politics is both specifically, irreducibly, a matter of the class struggle *and* irreducible to it:

> On ne touche pas au glas, donc, sans toucher à la classe. Ni à l'économie de l'anthérection sans lutte des classes. Mais le discours codé, policé, sur la lutte des classes, s'il forclôt la question du glas (tout ce qui s'y forge, tout ce sur quoi elle retentit, en particulier l'expropriation du nom partout où elle porte) manque au moins une révolution. Et qu'est-ce qu'une révolution qui ne s'attaque pas au nom propre? Mais aussi bien qu'est-ce que *la* révolution si le nom propre (effet de glassification) — *déjà* — s'anthérige, *commence* donc par tomber en ruine? Des révolutions.

> [One does not touch, tamper with the *glas,* then, without tampering with class. Nor with the economy of antherection without class struggle. But the coded, policed discourse on the class struggle, if it forecloses the question of *glas* (everything forged there, all that on which it reverberates, in particular, wherever it carries, the expropriation of the name) lacks at the least a revolution. And what is a revolution that does not attack the proper name? But then again what is *the* revolution if the proper name (glassification effect) — *already* — is antherected, then *begins* by falling in ruins? (Of) revolutions.] (G, 289b; *GE*, 207b)

To be truly revolutionary, Derrida suggests, *the* revolution must needs comprise of revolution*s*. Revolution is always a part revolution. Revolution is a revolving set of revolutions: just as there can be no revolution that does not reckon with the class struggle, there can be no revolution that does not 'attack the proper name'.[16] The extent to which Genet's practice of naming can be considered revolutionary is at stake as early as *Glas's* opening pages:

> Quand Genet donne à ses personnages des noms propres, des espèces de singularités qui sont des noms communs majusculés, que fait-il? Que donne-t-il à lire sous la cicatrice visible d'une émajusculation qui menace toujours de se rouvrir? S'il s'appelle Mimosa, Querelle, Yeux-Verts, Culafroy, Notre-Dame-des-Fleurs, Divers, [...] etc., arrache-t-il violemment une identité sociale, un droit de propriété absolue? Est-ce là l'opération politique la plus effective, la pratique révolutionnaire la plus signifiante?

> [When Genet gives his characters proper names, kinds of singularities that are capitalized common nouns, what is he doing? What does he give us to read beneath the visible cicatrix of a decapitalization that is forever threatening to

open up again? If he calls himself Mimosa, Quarrel, Green-Eyes, Culafroy, Our-Lady-of-the-Flowers, Divers, [...] and so on, does he violently uproot a social identity, a right to absolute proprietorship? Is that the most effective political operation, the most significant revolutionary practice?] (G, 9-11b; GE, 7-8b)

This quotation flags up the importance of antonomasia in Genet's writing, to which I will return in more detail in Chapter 1. Here, let me note that Derrida's own writing replicates the uncertainty that he highlights in the interchangeability of common noun and proper name in Genet's writing. Not only does he deem the capitalisation the site of a potential 'émajusculation' [decapitalisation] that would reverse it, but this French neologism evokes two more common paronyms, *émasculation* [emasculation] and *éjaculation* [ejaculation], which are in contradiction to each other insofar as that one involves a loss, the other an expression, of masculinity. Moreover, the quotation comprises a series of unanswered questions concerning how Genet's writing operates and how to interpret its operation politically; what is at stake here is both a question of undecidability and an undecided question. Above all, implicit in the French although more obvious in the English translation, is the potential of all the different meanings of 'capital' to make a political difference. What if, Derrida asks following Genet, 'the most effective political operation, the most significant revolutionary practice' involved a new relation to (capital) *letters* as much as a new relation between labour and capital?

*Glas*, then, is profoundly concerned with the political implications of the form of Genet's text. Taking Derrida's insights as its point of departure, my book too focuses on Genet's writing; even Chapter 3, which analyses his most overtly political interventions, adopts a primarily textual approach. In particular, I explore the political work carried out by the very aspects of his texts that undermine the possibility of identifying an unequivocal political position on Genet's part. My analysis notably gives pride of place to the widespread homonymisation and pervasive undecidability that more traditional political approaches dismiss as irrelevant, that is, as immaterial to the graver matters as privileged, for example, by dialectic materialism. Yet, as deconstruction has lengthily and repeatedly demonstrated, such an approach serves to widen rather than narrow the materialist focus by attending to the materiality of Genet's language, to language as body. Moreover, his work obliges us to reconsider the 'dialectic' as much as the 'materialism'. I explore also how Genet's writing relentlessly resists dialectisation, although with a very different emphasis from Derrida who casts the difference between Hegel and Genet as the difference between a dialectical operation (in which conflicts or contradictions are ideally reconciled in an overarching unity or generality) and an undecidable one (in which no such resolution emerges). My basic premiss is that the tension between the poetic and the political which is the principal focus of this book is a non-dialectical relationship in which neither is subordinated to the other.

Similarly, rather than attempting to identify a clear, let alone consistent, political position on the writer's part, I seek to understand the ambiguities and contradictions that characterise his trajectory, even when most active in support of the Black Panthers or the Palestinians. Not only is there no single political position that adequately encapsulates the whole of his work but, perhaps more importantly, it is a misunderstanding to view his trajectory as a linear movement between a series of clearly defined but mutually exclusive positions. One of Genet's greatest singularities is the ease with which he differs from himself, including politically. Dialectisation is intrinsically a process of totalisation, the integration of different parts into a whole. As such, it is also closely related to the question of generalisation, the extent to which the part is representative of the whole. What is fascinating about Genet's treatment of identity of all kinds is that no part is ever fully representative of the whole. Or, conversely, every part is partially representative of the whole.

The question of generalisation brings me to the question of genre and the title of my book. Genre is not just another word for class or category; it names a specifically literary classification and constitutes one of the principal literary institutions. Furthermore, genre is by no means the neutral phenomenon it is usually taken to be. Once a staple of literary criticism, today genre is rarely considered a fertile lens through which to approach texts, principally in my view because it continues to be considered a formal, uniquely aesthetic, consideration in a world where political concerns have increasingly come to dominate literary theory and criticism. It is noteworthy how little recent theoretical investigation there has been into genre, given how important a role the question played in debates about cultural politics at their emergence a century ago. Generic issues were at the very heart of the work of both Lukács and Bakhtin, for example; both *The Theory of the Novel* and *The Dialogic Imagination* placed genre at the very centre of their arguments in their reformulation of the relation between literature and extratextual reality. It is true, more recently, that much of Kristeva's major contribution draws on Bakhtin, yet she too downplays or minimises the specific question of genre by recasting his insights in broader arguments about intertextuality.[17] Of contemporary figures, Fredric Jameson is exceptional for the attention he has devoted to the politics associated with specific genres. For him, genre is inseparable from the question of periodisation; generic conventions offer the 'simplest and most accessible demonstration' of the dialectical workings of history, in that they project 'a formal conjuncture through which the "conjuncture" of coexisting modes of production at a given historical moment can be detected and allegorically articulated'.[18] Shifts in genre map the dialectical process itself; genre is an inherently periodising, and hence an inherently political, phenomenon. He thus conceives of genre in purely diachronic terms, in line with his strictly materialist perspective. Yet Jameson himself acknowledges that in his discussion of the ideology of form, '"form" is apprehended as content'.[19] In other words, he is interested in genre less for its formal characteristics than for its capacity to elucidate the ideology of an underlying socio-economic situation. It comes therefore as no surprise that the genre that has dominated his thinking is the novel, or that he devotes scant attention to poetry. The thinkers who situate the political potential of art in its capacity to express a particular socio-economic configuration have tended predominantly to focus on the novel, whereas those who situate it rather in its fundamental otherness to (capitalist) modes of production have typically been drawn to more poetic modes of composition. It is surely not incidental that those whose analysis has concentrated on the realist novel have been more likely to argue the (realist) position that art is a reflection of an extratextual reality, or that a focus on poetic texts has generated discourses privileging the productivity specific to language. In other words, the genres on which an argument is based are a major determinant directly shaping the ensuing argument; any generalisation about the politics of genre is necessarily limited by the genre(s) for which it seeks to account.

Hence, while my book is not a primarily theoretical enterprise seeking to elaborate a general argument about the politics of genre, it is nonetheless predicated on the intuition that genre is never merely an apolitical concern. Another decisive factor justifying my approach is that the most convincing periodisation of Genet's writing can in fact be identified at the level of genre. This remained the default option for many years: early Genet criticism was dominated by approaches to his work in terms of a generic succession (from poems to novels to plays). There are clear limitations to any overly categorical approach: as well as profoundly troubling the boundaries of the genres he practises, Genet also wrote texts that simply do not lend themselves easily to any generic categorisation (for example, *Fragments...*). Nonetheless, the fact remains that the writer on the whole explored different genres sequentially. Roughly speaking, the poetry and novels of his first creative outburst were followed by the plays (and screenplays). For a period Genet then turned away from literature, before writing most of the 'journalistic' pieces now collected in *L'Ennemi déclaré*. Finally, his posthumously published memoir, *Un Captif amoureux*, marks a return to literature at the very end of his life. The four chapters in this book deal respectively with his novels, his plays, his journalistic writing (published and unpublished) and his final memoir. Its generic approach does not attempt to account for the totality of his texts, but I believe it has the heuristic value of offering a partial account of his work. It is my contention that Genet's engagement with, and exploitation of, genre is bound up with the political dimensions of his writing. As we shall see, his practice of each genre is at odds with itself; the aim of this book is to explore the link between that insufficiency or inadequacy of generic identity and the fact that the poetic and the political are also always both linked and at variance with each other throughout his corpus.

This book is therefore absolutely not an attempt to offer a comprehensive study of Genet's politics. Not only would such an enterprise be both impossible and undesirable, but it would also necessarily involve revisiting already well-trodden ground to no obvious advantage. Given the overtly political subject-matter of many of Genet's texts — *Le Balcon, Les Nègres, Les Paravents, Un Captif amoureux* — it is only to be expected that a substantial proportion of the secondary literature devoted to them already foregrounds political questions. Similarly, the exponential growth in interest relating to identity politics over recent decades has found in Genet's work an immensely fertile terrain; many critics, including myself, have already lengthily explored questions relating to sexual or racial politics across the range of his corpus. In contrast, while hostility to the bourgeoisie may provide one of the motive forces for Genet's writing, he displays neither any desire to be integrated into it nor much sympathy for those outside it, with the result that there has to date been minimal discussion of the most common political paradigm, that of class. The reason this book devotes somewhat more attention to the question of class than to gender, sexuality or race is a reflection of that fact, not an indication that I consider the former a more political or more important issue than the latter. Indeed, one of the things I have found most amusing in writing this book was the realisation that, for once, the fact that the French word *genre* means 'gender' has not proven a source of particular significance for me. An indication, perhaps, of how thoroughly destabilising Genet's genres of politics turn out to be...

## Notes to the Introduction

1. See <https://www.orwellfoundation.com/the-orwell-prizes/about/about-the-prizes/> [accessed 8 June 2022].
2. Hadrien Laroche, *Le Dernier Genet* (Paris: Seuil, 1997), p. 9; *The Last Genet,* trans. by David Homel (Vancouver: Arsenal Pulp Press, 2010), p. 9.
3. Ibid., p. 256; p. 283.
4. See for example Carl Lavery, *The Politics of Jean Genet's Late Theatre: Spaces of Revolution* (Manchester: Manchester University Press, 2010); and Clare Finburgh, 'Genet and the Problem with Postmodernity', in *Jean Genet: Performance and Politics*, ed. by Clare Finburgh, Carl Lavery and Maria Shevtsova (Basingstoke & New York: Palgrave-Macmillan, 2006), pp. 78-102. For a discussion of Lavery's reading, see Chapter 2, n. 12.
5. Jean Genet, 'Ce qui est resté d'un Rembrandt déchiré en petits carrés bien réguliers, et foutu aux chiottes', in *OC*, IV, 22. Genet also evokes this experience in 'L'Atelier d'Alberto Giacometti', in *OC*, V, 50-51.
6. Jean-Paul Sartre, *Saint Genet: comédien et martyr* (Paris: Gallimard, 1952).
7. For a concise and cogent discussion of what is conceptually at stake in the use of the term 'power' and its inseparability from questions relating to the private domain (and in particular gender), see Anne Berger, *The Queer Turn in Feminism: Identities, Sexualities and the Theater of Gender*, trans. by Catherine Porter (New York: Fordham University Press, 2014), pp. 70-75.
8. See *ED*, 231; *DE*, 198.
9. Hélène Cixous, 'Le Rire de la méduse', *Arc*, 45 (1975), 39-54; 'The Laugh of the Medusa', trans. by Keith Cohen and Paula Cohen, *Signs*, 1.4 (Summer 1976), 875-93; Kate Millett, *Sexual Politics* [1969] (London: Virago, 1977).
10. See Jean Genet, 'Les Membres de l'Assemblée' [The Members of the Assembly] (*ED*, 309-19; *DE*, 267-75) and 'Cathédrale de Chartres: "Vue cavalière"' [Chartres Cathedral] (*ED*, 191-97; *DE*, 164-70).
11. Jean Genet, letter to Patrick Prado, Fonds Genet archive, IMEC.
12. There were of course exceptions before then, for example Shelley's pronouncement in 'A Defence of Poetry' that '[p]oets are the unacknowledged legislators of the world'.
13. Jacques Derrida, *Glas: que reste-t-il du savoir absolu?* [1974] (Paris: Denoël, 1981); *Glas*, trans. by John P. Leavey, Jr., and Richard Rand (Lincoln & London: University of Nebraska Press, 1986). Page and column references will henceforward be given in the text to these editions, preceded by *G* and *GE* respectively; I have frequently modified the translations.
14. Compared to Derrida's other works, *Glas* has received singularly little attention. Exceptions include Geoffrey Hartman, *Saving the Text* (Baltimore, MD: Johns Hopkins University Press, 1982); Leslie Hill, *Radical Indecision: Barthes, Blanchot, Derrida and the Future of Criticism* (Notre Dame, IN: University of Notre Dame Press, 2010); and *Resounding Glas*, ed. by Mairéad Hanrahan, Simon Morgan Wortham, Martin McQuillan (Edinburgh: Edinburgh University Press, 2016) (= special issue of *Paragraph*, 39.2 (2016)). Richard Beardsworth's *Derrida and the Political* (London: Routledge, 1996), is to my knowledge alone in examining the specifically political aspect of *Glas,* albeit only in relation to the Hegel column. For discussion of the inherently political dimension of deconstruction, see Geoffrey Bennington, *Legislations: The Politics of Deconstruction* (London: Verso, 1994); *The Politics of Deconstruction: Jacques Derrida and the*

*Other of Philosophy*, ed. by Martin McQuillan (London: Pluto, 2007), and *Derrida and the Time of the Political*, ed. by Pheng Cheah and Suzanne Gerlach (Durham, NC: Duke University Press, 2009).

15. Jacques Derrida, 'Fors: les mots angles de Nicolas Abraham et Maria Torok', in Nicolas Abraham and Maria Torok, *Cryptonymie: le verbier de l'homme aux loups* (Paris: Aubier Flammarion, 1976), pp. 9-73. Derrida's dialogue, in *Glas*, with their theory of mourning is clearly evident in the importance of the motif of the crypt throughout the text, for example: 'Ce que veut-dire la dialectique spéculative, c'est que la crypte peut encore être incorporée au système' [What speculative dialectics means (to say) is that the crypt can still be incorporated into the system] (G, 232; GE, 166a).

16. I differ here from Richard Beardsworth's argument that Derrida prioritises undecidability at the expense of any specific political determination: 'The Irony of Deconstruction and the Example of Marx', in *The Politics of Deconstruction*, ed. by McQuillan (London: Pluto Press, 2007), pp. 212-34.

17. See, for example, David Duff, 'Intertextuality versus Genre Theory: Bakhtin, Kristeva and the Question of Genre', *Paragraph*, 25.1 (2002), 54-73.

18. Fredric Jameson, *The Political Unconscious* [1981], Routledge Classics (Abingdon: Routledge, 2002), p. 85.

19. Ibid., p. 84.

# CHAPTER 1

❖

# A Novel Form of Politics?

Genet's first novel, *Notre-Dame-des-Fleurs*, initially published clandestinely in 1943, was his breakthrough work. While he had previously written a number of poems (and even published 'Le Condamné à mort' [The Condemned Man] at his own expense in 1942) which had won him some highly influential readers (notably Jean Cocteau), Genet became known primarily as an author of novels. His poems were later gathered together and published,[1] yet even today, notwithstanding the decades in which Genet's work has enjoyed a canonical position in French literature, they have rarely been the focus of critical attention.[2] Nor has there been much discussion of why the writer's novels should have resonated far more powerfully than his poems. Rather than simply substituting one genre for another, however, Genet's novel is an exceptionally heterogeneous form. This chapter seeks to explore the extent to which that heterogeneity explains the greater reach of Genet's early prose writing and, especially, the extent to which it constitutes a (new) political gesture. The shift to the novel does not merely mark a difference in terms of the intertextual collectivity to which the text belongs; what matters for Genet in the question of genre is also very much the specific relationship to the reader that different kinds of text invite. Genre, in other words, is in part a question of desire: different kinds of text engage differently with readerly expectations. Genet's novel is not at one with itself; similarly, reading it is an experience more likely to trouble or unsettle than to reassure its reader. Moreover, just as it leaves neither itself nor its reader intact, so too with the relationship it instigates with the outside world. Genet's novel suggests a relationship between art and politics that opens each to the other while subordinating neither.

*Notre-Dame-des-Fleurs*, then, is the first novel of an author who hitherto had written poems. Within the text, most of the metatextual comments on writing or literary creation concern poetry rather than novels. There are thirty-seven instances of the word *poétique* [poetic] and related terms such as *poésie, poète, poème* [poetry, poet, poem] etc., compared with only ten of the word *roman* [novel]. Furthermore, the references to the *roman* operate more to throw into question the genre of what Genet is creating in *Notre-Dame-des-Fleurs* than to consolidate it. The term that the narrator usually chooses when speaking about the text he is writing is *livre* [book], as on the first page when, having listed a number of famous murderers, he asserts: 'c'est en l'honneur de leurs crimes que j'écris mon livre' [And it is in honor of their crimes that I am writing my book] (*RP*, 3; *OLF*, 55). If a 'book' is what he writes, 'novels' appear to be what he reads: 'je vais le chercher à travers les lignes serrées des pages lourdes des romans-feuilletons' [I shall seek him throughout the close-packed lines of the heavy pages of adventure novels]; 'Je lis ce que je ne lirais jamais ailleurs (et j'y crois): les romans de Paul Féval' [I read things I would never read elsewhere (and I believe in them): the novels of Paul Féval]; 'les fumées de soufre qui montent, lentes, des pages chargées de romans populaires' [the fumes of sulphur that rise slowly from the charged pages of cheap novels]; 'Je continue la lecture de mes romans populaires' [I continue my reading of cheap novels]; 'Pour consentir à mêler dans sa vie de tous les jours [...] des aventures de roman policier, il faut avoir soi-même l'âme un peu fée' [Anyone who is willing to mix detective-story adventures into his daily life [...] has to be a bit fey himself]; 'Les contes naissaient du journal, comme les miens des romans populaires' [The stories were born of the newspaper, as mine are born of cheap novels] (*RP*, 45, 118, 134, 174, 177, 181; *OLF*, 100, 177, 194, 239, 242, 247). The novels that the narrator of *Notre-Dame-des-Fleurs* reads belong to the genre of *roman populaire*, novels addressed predominantly to a lower-middle-class or working-class audience of which the *roman policier*, or crime novel, was a privileged example. The narrator's practice mirrors that of the author, as vouchsafed years later in an interview when asked by Hubert Fichte which books had influenced him when he began to write: 'Des romans populaires. Des romans de Paul Féval' [Pulp novels. Novels by Paul Féval] (*ED*, 165; *DE*, 141). In a still later (1983) interview with Rüdiger Wischenbart and Layla Shahid Barrada, Genet elaborates on what the term 'novel' means for him, rejecting the idea that his text about the Palestinians 'Quatre heures à Chatila' could be deemed one:

> J'ai dit que ce n'est pas un roman parce que le mot roman pour moi renvoie presque immédiatement à la rêverie, à l'irréalité. *Madame Bovary*, c'est un roman. Dans la mesure où le mot roman est employé pour définir un genre littéraire, ce n'est pas un roman.

> [I said that it's not a novel because for me the word novel refers almost immediately to daydreaming, to unreality. *Madame Bovary* is a novel. To the extent that the word novel is used to define a literary genre, it is not a novel.] (*ED*, 278; *DE*, 240).

The choice of Flaubert's novel is somewhat surprising; Genet selects a work hailed as one of the masterpieces of French realism as an example of the 'daydreaming' and 'unreality' that for him are the defining features of the genre. The salient distinction here appears to lie not between realism and the fantastic, not between highbrow and popular culture, nor works that give priority to questions of style and those privileging the plot, but between fiction and non-fiction. This distinction maps onto Genet's own work insofar as, just prior to these comments on 'Quatre heures à Chatila', he had used the term *rêverie* to describe his novels:

> Quand j'ai écrit j'avais trente ans, quand j'ai commencé à écrire. Quand j'ai terminé l'écriture, j'avais trente-quatre ou trente-cinq ans. Mais c'était du rêve. C'était en tout cas une rêverie. J'avais écrit en prison. Une fois libre, j'étais perdu. Et je ne me suis retrouvé réellement, et dans le monde réel, qu'avec ces deux mouvements révolutionnaires, les Panthères noires et les Palestiniens. Et

alors je me soumettais au monde réel. C'est-à-dire [...] j'agissais en fonction du monde réel et plus en fonction du monde grammatical... Dans la mesure où on oppose le monde réel au monde de la rêverie. [...] Mais on sait qu'on peut agir sur la rêverie d'une façon presque illimitée. On ne peut pas agir sur le réel d'une façon illimitée.

[When I wrote I was thirty years old, when I started writing. When I was finished with writing, I was thirty-four, thirty-five years old. But that was a dream. It was in any case a daydream, a reverie. I wrote in prison. Once I became free, I was lost. And I didn't find myself again in reality, in the real world, until I was with those two revolutionary movements, the Black Panthers and the Palestinians. And so then I submitted myself to the real world. [...] I was acting in relation to the real world and no longer to the grammatical world... To the extent that you oppose the real world to the world of daydreaming. [...] But we also know that you can act upon dreams in a way that is almost unlimited. You cannot act upon the real in an unlimited way.] (*ED*, 277; *DE*, 239)

Genet thus implicitly casts the difference between his novels and his later work for the Panthers and the Palestinians as the difference between a 'daydream', in which anything is possible, and an activity constrained by the 'real world'. Looking back at them retrospectively, Genet does not consider his novels political, an assessment that chimes with his insistence to Fichte that in his early life he had no political or revolutionary awareness (*ED*, 170; *DE*, 146). But the difference he outlines between imaginative literature and a (political) writing that is subject to the need to bear witness to an external reality is not a simple opposition. The two are comparable in that he 'found himself' in both, supposedly unlike what had occupied him during the intervening period. His lexicon of presence posits them as different but equally truthful expressions, with the difference between them explicitly formulated as a matter of genre (the end of this chapter will explore how his novels suggest on the contrary that the 'world of daydreaming' is not simply opposed to the 'real world' as he (mis)remembers here).

Of course, Genet's views do not, and should not, dictate, how we receive his texts. The gap of thirty or so years between the writing of his novels and these comments advises us to treat the latter with caution. More broadly, so too does the general need to beware of the notion that an author's paratextual or theoretical pronouncements contain a privileged mode of access to the truth of artistic practice, a need strengthened in Genet's case by his insistence to the contrary that only in his art does he approach the truth (*ED*, 163; *DE*, 139). Given that I will frequently quote his interviews, as a methodological precaution I take this opportunity to register at the outset the warning he gave towards the end of his interview with Hubert Fichte:

H.F.:    *Est-ce que vous croyez quand même que l'interview donne une idée de ce que vous pensez réellement?*
G.:    Non.
H.F.:    *Qu'est-ce qu'il y manque?*
G.:    La vérité. Elle est possible si je suis tout seul. [...] J'ai essayé de répondre au plus près de vos questions. En fait, j'étais très loin. [...] Je ne peux rien dire à personne. Rien dire à d'autres que des mensonges. Si je suis tout seul, je parle peut-être un peu vrai.

> [H.F.:    Still, do you think that the interview gives an idea of what you really think?
> J.G.:    No.
> H.F.:    What's missing?
> J.G.:    The truth. It's possible when I'm alone. [...] I tried to answer your questions as closely as I could. In fact, I was very far away. [...] I can't say anything to anybody. To others, I can't say anything but lies. If I'm all alone, I speak a bit of the truth, perhaps.] (*ED*, 176; *DE*, 151)

At issue is a deemed inability to tell the truth, rather than an unwillingness to do so, an inability arising from the fact that words spoken in conversation function differently from the same words produced in a different context (for example in the solitude of writing a novel). Again, for Genet, to the extent that the context in which words appear affects their functioning, genre matters.

Whatever the pitfalls inherent in analysing Genet's early work in the light of his later pronouncements, this idea that truth is best found in unexpected places, and in particular in the manifestly untrue, is already a central theme in *Notre-Dame-des-Fleurs*: 'La vérité n'est pas mon fait. Mais "il faut mentir pour être vrai". Et même aller au-delà. De quelle vérité veux-je parler?' [Truth is not my strong point. But 'one must lie in order to be true.' And even go beyond. What truth do I want to talk about?] (*RP*, 140; *OLF*, 201). Genet's choice of fiction, as distinct from poetry, plausibly constitutes a similar attempt to engage with a truth he could not otherwise tell. We too can 'go beyond', and ask what kind of truth Genet's choice of the novel, and specifically of the *roman populaire*, makes possible. *Notre-Dame-des-Fleurs* itself echoes or doubles the *romans populaires* that the narrator evokes, most obviously in its parody of the detective novel. While its loose, non-linear plot is poles apart from the tight construction of crime fiction, elements of its structure play with the generic conventions of the crime novel, albeit acclaiming rather than censuring the threat posed by the criminal to social order. It begins with the praise of those murderers 'in honour of whose crimes' the narrator is writing his book and it reaches its climax not with the identification of Notre-Dame as the criminal — the standard moment at which the reader's desire for closure is satisfied and social order is reimposed — but with his condemnation and summary execution, underlining the criminal's humanity. It includes several ludic allusions to crime novels, such as the discussion of the best techniques of shoplifting in the passage describing Mignon's arrest for theft:

> Enfin, il fallait retrouver, comme un objet perdu, — ou mieux, comme un de ces personnages de devinettes dont les lignes sur les assiettes à dessert sont aussi celles des arbres et des nuages, — le détective. Trouvez le détective. C'est une femme.

> [Finally, you had to find, like a lost object — or better, like one of those picture-puzzle figures, the line of which on dessert plates are also those of trees and clouds — the detective. Find the detective. It's a woman.] (*RP*, 163; *OLF*, 228)

Instead of the stereotype of the detective saying 'Cherchez la femme', we are invited to find the detective — who *is* a woman! Genet's novel is in many respects a detective novel turned upside down.

The limitless freedom of the imagination that Genet later recalls as a feature of his early writing is doubtless a significant aspect of the attraction that the *roman populaire* holds for him. He certainly practises a freer version of the novel than the poem. Formally, whereas Genet's poems largely respect the constraints of traditional French prosody, his novels are much less bound by novelistic convention. In addition, by definition a novel, unlike poetry, involves the creation of a fictional diegetical universe. Genet takes liberties with a form that itself takes liberties with reality, that offers the reader a world different at least in some respect from the 'real' world. The opening postulate of this chapter is that that gap, and the relationship to the reader that it implies, are especially significant factors in Genet's shift to the novel in general and his borrowing from the *roman populaire* in particular. A further difference between poetry and popular novels is the question of readership; the latter were addressed predominantly to a lower-middle-class or working-class audience. Genet's novels neither addressed nor reached a similar readership; rather, I would contend that Genet 'found himself' in writing novels that infer a different reader from that of his poems. Whereas readers of poetry are typically both economically and culturally privileged, they are less likely to share *bourgeois* values. Genet's novels posit an addressee who belongs to the economic and cultural elite but espouses hegemonic values, one likely both to be aware of the high cultural status attached to poetry and to feel ashamed at finding popular novels alluring. As we shall see, *Notre-Dame-des-Fleurs* profoundly destabilises the boundary between poem and popular novel; it extols the poetic as it leaves the poem behind. But Genet's shift to the novel heralds an attack on more than merely literary hierarchy. His book posits a homology between literary and other forms of privilege, and throws a spotlight on the political implications of devaluing the aesthetic.

Genet explicitly attributes the attraction of the *roman populaire* to the fascination with transgression that it holds for the *bourgeois*. From the very outset, *Notre-Dame-des-Fleurs* addresses the *bourgeois*; Genet explicitly identifies the *vous* or formal 'you' to whom the evening newspaper famously revealed the murderer Weidmann's face as '[des] bourgeois attristés' [mirthless bourgeois] (*RP*, 3; *OLF*, 55). Used pejoratively, the term has both economic and cultural, or more specifically ideological, connotations: it categorises both the middle classes, and the proponents, across all classes, of values that serve and protect the interests of the dominant class. The first of these associations seems clearly subordinate to the second in his writing; the target he attacks is less the materially privileged than the materialistic values (especially to the detriment of any aesthetic considerations) and conventional attitudes that support and consolidate the status quo. Genet's originality in highlighting the interests at stake in matters of cultural/ideological privilege rather than in economic disparities situates the writer as a man at the vanguard of his epoch, insofar as the idea that culture was a political sphere was still a relatively recent development within Marxism. Notwithstanding Genet's own later view that he had had no political consciousness when he wrote his novels, and although there is no reason to believe he was at the time familiar with the debates in the West that later came to be labelled (mainly by the right) as 'cultural Marxism', by exploring how certain kinds of cultural/ideological divisions serve the interests of a particular section of society Genet was echoing the extension of the political from the uniquely economic to the cultural that was theorised by Gramsci and the Frankfurt School before World War II. Genet's attack on the *bourgeois* in *Notre-Dame-des-Fleurs* is an attack on the very structure of privilege. This includes literary privilege; the novel's challenge to hierarchies gives pride of place to undermining hierarchies of genre.

Genet's portrayal of the bourgeois fascination with transgression has to date been primarily explored in relation to the journalistic *fait divers*.[3] One passage of the novel elaborates in detail on the troubling lure of reports of violence:

> Ainsi, Adeline partait tout droit aux minuscules lignes des faits divers, qui sont — les meurtres, les vols, les viols, les agressions à main armée — les 'Barrios Chinos' des journaux. Elle en rêvait. Leur violence concise, leur précision ne laissaient pas au rêve le temps ni l'espace de s'infiltrer: elles la terrassaient. [...] Quand cette vague de fond s'était éteinte, elle lisait tous les titres des morceaux de musique de la rubrique de radio, mais elle n'aurait jamais toléré qu'un air de musique entrât dans sa chambre, tant la mélodie la plus légère corrode la poésie. Ainsi, les journaux furent inquiétants, comme s'ils n'eussent été remplis que de colonnes de faits divers, colonnes sanglantes et mutilées comme des poteaux de torture. Et, bien qu'au procès que nous lirons demain, la presse n'ait accordé que très parcimonieusement dix lignes, assez espacées pour laisser l'air circuler entre les mots trop violents, [...] ces dix lignes firent battre tous les cœurs des vieilles femmes et des enfants jaloux. Paris ne dormit pas. Elle espérait que, demain, Notre-Dame serait condamné à mort; elle le désirait.

> [In like manner, Ernestine went straight to the tiny lines of the short crime items, which are — the murders, robberies, rapes, armed assaults — the 'Barrios Chinos' of the newspapers. She dreamed about them. Their concise violence, their precision left the dream neither time nor space to filter in; they floored her. [...] When this tidal wave subsided, she would read all the titles of the musical selections listed in the radio column, but she would never have allowed a musical air to enter her room, for the slightest melody corrodes poetry. Thus, the newspapers were disturbing, as if they had been filled only with columns of crime news, columns as bloody and mutilated as torture stakes. And though the press has very parsimoniously given to the trial, which we shall read about tomorrow, only ten lines, widely enough spaced to let the air circulate between the overviolent words, [...] these ten lines quickened the hearts of the old women and jealous children. Paris did not sleep. She hoped that the following day Our Lady would be sentenced to death; she desired it.] (*RP*, 181-82; *OLF*, 248)

In French, this final sentence is a marvel of ambiguity in that both pronouns 'elle' and 'le' can refer to several antecedents: 'she' — Adeline, but also Paris — both desired Notre-Dame and desired his death.[4] *Notre-Dame-des-Fleurs* thus replicates the *fait divers* in catering to its readers' disavowed fascination with crime and the forbidden; however, rather than complicitly indulging their pleasure it uncomfortably places their illicit gratification under the spotlight. Moreover, Genet highlights the structural connection between their pleasurable horror at crime and his text's celebration of it. The narrator explicitly compares Adeline's reaction to what she read in the papers to his own story-telling, and specifically his borrowing from *romans populaires*:

> C'est bien pour elle, pour enchanter son crépuscule, que Notre-Dame avait tué un vieux. Depuis toujours qu'elle faisait des contes fatals ou des histoires d'une allure plate et banale, mais où certains mots explosifs crevaient la toile, et par ces accrocs, montrant, si l'on peut dire, un peu des coulisses, on comprenait pourquoi elle avait ainsi parlé. Elle avait la bouche pleine de contes, et l'on se demande comment ils pouvaient naître d'elle, qui ne lisait chaque soir qu'un fade journal: les contes naissaient du journal, comme les miens des romans populaires.

> [It was indeed for her, to enchant her twilight, that Our Lady had killed an old man. Ever since she had started making up fatal tales, or stories that seemed flat and trivial, but in which certain explosive words ripped the canvas, showing, through these gashes, a bit of what went on, as it were, behind the scenes, people understood why she had talked that way. Her mouth was full of stories and people wondered how they could be born of her, who every evening read only a dull newspaper; the stories were born of the newspaper, as mine are born of cheap novels.] (*RP*, 180-81; *OLF*, 247)

Just as Adeline finds a catalyst in the *fait divers*, so the narrator is inspired by the *romans populaires* (a form which itself originated in the press as the earlier-mentioned 'romans-feuilletons', often first serialised in the same papers that contained the *faits divers*). The dimension the *fait divers* and the *roman populaire* have in common with each other — that they make their reader dream of taboo pleasures — is clearly what they also share with *Notre-Dame-des-Fleurs* itself. Genet leaves his reader in no doubt as to the mediocrity of the original sources, the scornful attitude here towards the 'dull newspaper' echoing an earlier designation of the *romans populaires* as 'textes imbéciles' [imbecilic texts] (*RP*, 174; *OLF*, 240). The mediocre sources nonetheless inspire extremely powerful works. Adeline's 'enchantment' leads her to tell 'contes', tales of imaginary — in the case of fairy tales, even magical — events. At issue is a specifically narrative form with a dreamlike, unreal quality, generated by the 'explosive' eruption of words deemed to belong to one realm (the 'coulisses', or wings) into another.

This description of Adeline's story-telling offers a clear figure of what is at stake in Genet's own staging of forbidden desire. Displaying what was hitherto screened away out of sight, revealing onstage the reality relegated behind the scenes, is a typical, even stereotypical, trope of realism. But the effect of Genet's exposure of an unacknowledged reality is far from realist; on the contrary, revealing it adds a dreamlike element that emphasises the proximity between novel and fairy tale or poem. The novel he writes, like those he reads, is as much a way of liberating him from reality as of grounding him within it. When he mentions Paul Féval's novels, he explains that reading them is part of a process of detaching himself from the 'earthly' world: 'Ne rien faire de propre, d'hygiénique: la propreté et l'hygiène sont du monde terrestre. Il faut se nourrir de potins de tribunaux. Se nourrir de rêve' [Do nothing clean or hygienic: cleanliness and hygiene are of the earthly world.

I must feed on the gossip of the law courts. Must feed on dreams] (*RP*, 118; *OLF*, 177).

The novel's staging of the repressed thus expressly complicates the relation to the material world by supplementing it with an otherworldly or divine dimension (hence 'Divine', the name that the principal character chooses for herself in addition to the prosaic 'Louis Culafroy', encapsulates the wider functioning of *Notre-Dame-des-Fleurs* as a whole). To do this, it supplements itself with its own other, in this case poetic, dimension. Genet's novel is one where novel and poem cannot be disentangled. It is an irreducibly heterogeneous form, its identity troubled by the infiltrations of the poetic. Numerous passages attribute to the poetic a destabilising aspect, one that challenges the grip of the 'earthly world':

> [Divine] causait un trouble délicieux, quelque chose comme cette émotion que je ressens à la lecture d'une phrase, à la vue d'un tableau, à l'audition d'un motif musical, lorsque enfin je décèle un état poétique. C'est la solution élégante, soudaine, lumineuse, claire, d'un conflit dans mes profondeurs.

> [[Divine] caused a delightful agitation, something like the emotion I feel when I read a thrilling phrase or see a painting or hear a musical motif, in short, when I detect a poetic state. It is the elegant and sudden, the luminous and clear solution of a conflict in my depths.] (*RP*, 128-29; *OLF*, 189)

> Je repris pied sur ce fond solide qu'est la drôlerie, alors que le poème, toujours, fait le sol se dérober sous la plante de vos pieds et vous aspire dans le sein d'une merveilleuse nuit.

> [I regained my footing on the solid basis of joking, whereas poetry always pulls the ground away from under your feet and sucks you into the bosom of a wonderful night.] (*RP*, 161; *OLF*, 225)

> [La grandeur] est la magnificence vue du dehors. Misérable peut-être, vue du dedans, elle est alors poétique si vous voulez bien convenir que la poésie est la rupture (ou plutôt la rencontre au point de rupture) du visible et de l'invisible [...] un signe qui peut mettre en branle un monde, parce qu'il procède d'un monde dont le sens nombreux est inavouable.

> [[Greatness] is magnificence seen from without. Though it may be wretched when seen from within, it is then poetic, if you are willing to agree that poetry is the break (or rather the meeting at the breaking point) between the visible and the invisible [...] a sign that can set a world in motion because it issues from a world whose multifarious meaning is unavowable.] (*RP*, 194; *OLF*, 262)

The poetic is the mark of instability: it is the sign of trouble, stumbling, disruption; it indicates that some ground is shifting. However, another passage that returns to the question of attachment to the earthly world stresses a specifically political angle to that instability; the precarious life that Divine and Mignon live together is described as:

> Une vie magnifique et légère, qu'un souffle peut crever, — pensent les bourgeois, qui sentent bien la poésie des vies de créateurs de poésie: danseurs nègres, boxeurs, prostituées, soldats, mais qui ne voient pas que ces vies ont une attache terrestre, puisqu'elles sont grosses d'épouvantes.

[A splendid and casual life, a life that a breath might shatter — so think the bourgeois, who sense the poetry of the lives of creators of poetry — Negro dancers, boxers, prostitutes, soldiers — but who do not see that these lives have an earthly tie, since they are big with terror.] (*RP*, 107; *OLF*, 164)

Within the novel, the key political fault-line lies not between the classes but between different attitudes towards the poetic. The *bourgeois* register its charm but seek to keep it at a distance, without an 'earthly tie' or connection, separated off into a sphere unrelated to real lives. The contrast is striking with Divine's attitude to her dreaming: 'Elle pensa cela sans pourtant s'élever à, ou sombrer dans une poésie coupée du monde terrestre. L'expression poétique ne changera jamais son état. Elle restera toujours la fille préoccupée du gain' [That was what she thought, though without rising to, or sinking into, a poetry cut off from the terrestrial world. Poetic expression will never change her state of mind. She will always be the tart concerned with gain] (*RP*, 21; *OLF*, 75). The difference in how one responds to the poetic intersects with an economic difference. Genet thus relates the difference that Divine represents and the challenge it poses to society to the most classic of political questions, that of economic interest. The *bourgeois* are those whose interest lies in ensuring and maintaining a separation between the 'poetic' and the 'real'.

I shall return shortly to the question of the relative weights of these differences of genre, gender and economics. For the moment, it should be noted that in elaborating a link between them Genet challenges a line of thinking that dates back to Kant's formulation in the *Critique of Judgement* of the principle of the disinterestness of aesthetic judgements.[5] One of the messages conveyed most forcefully by Genet's early work is that all judgements are interested, in the sense of partial: affected by the judge's views/beliefs/practices in other domains. This point is accentuated at the climax of both his first two novels: Notre-Dame is condemned by a judge profoundly affected by the young criminal's words, and the poetic intensity of *Miracle de la rose* reaches its culmination when the execution of Harcamone is conveyed through the highly-sexualised image of the penetration of his body by the four figures of authority. In terms specifically of the aesthetic, Genet's emphasis is on the interested nature not so much of the judgement itself (what people define as poetic) as of the response provoked by an aesthetic experience. The diverse list of clients in the bar silenced by Divine's first appearance is exemplary in this respect, uniting categories defined by their markedly different economic or social status: 'banquiers, commerçants, gigolos pour dames, garçons, gérants, colonels, épouvantails' [bankers, shopkeepers, gigolos for ladies, waiters, managers, colonels, scarecrows] (*RP*, 19; *OLF*, 72). The poetic is no ivory tower: the salient dividing line is not between aesthetic and non-aesthetic considerations but rather between those who seek to enforce a strict division between them and those who do not.

If all works are interested, then, a novel that gives pride of place to the poetic is logically more aligned with the interests of those who look to generalise enchantment than those invested in keeping the earthly work 'pure' (of poetry/heaven). Within the diegetic universe of *Notre-Dame-des-Fleurs*, the narrator's sympathies clearly lie more with Divine, the character most open to the destabilisation the poetic involves, than with the *bourgeois*, wary of the threat it poses to their interests. Significantly, the magic she contributes involves an ongoing investment; it takes time. Creating her, he specifies, is a lengthy process: 'J'en ai pour toute la durée d'un livre, que je ne l'aie tirée de sa pétrification' [It will take me an entire book to draw her from her petrifaction] (*RP*, 20; *OLF*, 74). Similarly, for the narrator of *Miracle de la rose* the 'interest' of writing a novel is a question of magnitude: 'Si j'écrivais un roman, j'aurais quelque intérêt à m'étendre sur mes gestes d'alors' [If I were writing a novel, I would have an interest in describing the gestures I made] (*RP*, 244; *MR*, 27). Leaving aside the suggestion that *Miracle de la rose* might not be a novel, I want to highlight the association between extension, or expansion, and the novel. The difference between the *fait divers* and the novel, or between the poem and the novel, is a matter also of extension. Size appears to matter. This is evident in the earlier quotation about the *fait divers*, in which Adeline goes straight to its 'minuscules' [tiny] lines, ten paltry, widely-spaced lines whose 'concise violence' leaves neither time nor space for the dream to 's'infiltrer'. In contrast, the *romans populaires* are voluminous: the quotations at the beginning of this chapter stress the 'close-packed lines of the heavy pages of adventure novels', the 'charged pages of cheap novels', their 'typographie serrée, compacte comme un tas d'immondices, bourrée d'actes sanglants' [close print, compact as a pile of rubbish, crammed with acts as bloody as linens] (*RP*, 174; *OLF*, 240). Furthermore, the material difference in this respect between the first, tightly-printed clandestine edition of the novel and the more conventionally-spaced *Œuvres complètes* edition should not be overlooked. The reader of the first could not but relate those expressions back to what she or he was reading. For Genet, the novel is where the minute expands to occupy the space without ceasing to be minute, and in so doing enables the dream, the poetic, most effectively to 's'infiltrer': filter through but also infiltrate, a meaning with unmistakeable connotations of political activity.

This apparently minor question of minuscule writing, of enjoying minuscule writing, of making writing minuscule, is of major, indeed of capital interest in *Notre-Dame-des-Fleurs*. Writing a novel is a capital matter, a matter simultaneously of capitals and of capital. Genet makes repeated use of the word 'capital' throughout the text, deploying its several homonyms. At times, the meaning seems clear, as in an antanaclasis; in this book which, like *Miracle de la rose*, eulogises murderers condemned to be decapitated, both real and fictional, the signifier is regularly invoked in relation to the 'peine capitale' [capital punishment] that literally makes 'minuscule' prisoners even shorter:

> C'était dans une autre prison de France, où les couloirs aussi longs que ceux des palais royaux, avec leurs lignes droites, bâtissaient et tissaient des géométries où glissaient, minuscules à l'échelle des couloirs, sur des chaussons de feutre, des prisonniers tordus. En passant devant chaque porte, j'y lisais une étiquette qui indiquait la catégorie de son occupant. [...] 'Peine capitale'.

> [It was in another French prison, where the corridors and their straight lines, which were as long as those in a king's palace, wove and constructed geometrical patterns on which the gnarled prisoners, tiny in proportion to the scale of the corridors, glided by on felt slippers. As I passed each door, I would

read a label indicating the category of the occupant. [...] 'Capital Punishment'.]
(*RP*, 101; *OLF*, 158)

More usually, however, identifying which meaning of capital dominates the others, which capital is capital in the sense of most important, is by no means clear, as the writing of the scene where Notre-Dame is condemned exemplifies. The defendant's lawyer's attempt to argue for rehabilitation backfires:

> Enfin, comme avec une promptitude à discerner d'entre mille l'instant de dire le mot capital, Notre-Dame, doucement, comme toujours, fit une moue chagrine et dit sans le penser: 'Ah! la Corrida, non, pas la peine, j'aime mieux claquer tout de suite.' L'avocat resta stupide, puis vivement, d'un claquement de langue il rassembla ses esprits épars et bégaya: 'Mon enfant, voyons, mon enfant! Laissez-moi vous défendre.' [...] La cruauté du mot dénuda les juges et les laissa sans autre robe que leur seule splendeur. La foule racla sa gorge. Le Président ne savait pas qu'en argot, la Corrida c'est la maison de correction. [...] Notre-Dame était condamné à la peine capitale.

> [Finally, as with a promptness for sensing the one moment in a thousand for saying the capital word, Our Lady, gently as always, screwed up his face and said, though without thinking it: 'Ah no, not the Corrida, it ain't worth it. I'd rather croak right away.' The lawyer stood there dumbfounded; then quickly, with a cluck of his tongue, he gathered his scattered wits and stammered: 'Child, see here child! Let me defend you.' [...] The cruelty of the word stripped the judges and left them with no robe other than their splendour. The crowd cleared its throat. The presiding judge did not know that in slang the Corrida is the reformatory. [...] Our Lady was condemned to capital punishment.] (*RP*, 199; *OLF*, 268)

Which here *is* the 'mot capital', the capital or most important word? Logically it cannot refer to the only actual inscription of the word, the verdict of capital punishment which is pronounced by the court, not by the young criminal. The capital word is not the word 'capital'. It refers more reasonably to the highly visible, because capitalised, 'Corrida', that the narrator subsequently explains is slang for the reformatory. Yet, notwithstanding this narratorial direction, it seems more plausible that the 'mot capital' in question is actually 'claquer', also a slang word, one to which our attention is audibly rather than visibly drawn by its immediate repetition in 'claquement de langue' and whose brutal evocation of the harsh reality awaiting Notre-Dame is more likely to shock the audience in the circumstances. The 'mot capital' is not what it may most obviously appear to be. The passage offers a superb example of how Genet's writing undermines hierarchy in the very act of asserting it.

The challenge to hierarchies of privilege is developed even further in the paragraph containing the remaining other inscriptions of 'capital' in the novel, a paragraph which is also, not coincidentally, one of its most poetic passages:

> Des capitales surgissaient au milieu de son enfance sablonneuse. Des capitales comme des cactus sous le ciel. Des cactus comme des soleils verts, rayonnants de rayons aigus, trempés de curare. Son enfance, comme un sahara, tout minuscule ou immense — on ne sait — abrité par la lumière, le parfum et le flux de charme personnel d'un gigantesque magnolia fleuri qui montait dans

un ciel profond comme une grotte, par-dessus le soleil invisible et pourtant présent. Cette enfance séchait sur son sable brûlé, avec, en des instants rapides comme des traits, minces comme eux, minces comme ce paradis qu'on voit entre les paupières d'un Mongol, un aperçu sur le magnolia invisible et présent; ces instants étaient en tous points pareils à ceux que dit le poète:

> *J'ai vu dans le désert*
> *Ton ciel ouvert...*

[Capitals rose up from his sandy childood. Capitals like cactuses beneath the sky. Cactuses like green suns, radiating pointed rays and steeped in poison. His childhood, like a sahara, quite minuscule or immense — we don't know — a childhood sheltered by the light, the scent, and the flow of personal charm of a huge flowering magnolia that rose into a sky deep as a grotto above the invisible though present sun. This childhoood was withering on its broiling sand, with — in moments swift as pencil strokes and as thin, thin as the paradise one sees between the eyelids of a Mongol — a glimpse of the invisible and present magnolia. These moments were at all points like those of which the poet speaks:

> *I saw in the desert*
> *Your open sky...*] (*RP*, 78; *OLF*, 135)

From the very beginning, the undecidability of the word 'capitales' confronts the reader: capital cities or capital letters? The verb 'surgissaient' can apply to both, albeit on different metaphorical grounds (rapid development for the cities; upward movement for the letters). As we read on, the extended spatial metaphor that childhood is a desert, with the cactus, the pointed rays and the burning sand all combining to create a sense of arid harshness, invites us retrospectively to privilege the spatial meaning of 'capitales' as cities. However, this accelerates rather than resolves the uncertainty of meaning. A desert is a space inhospitable to life, whereas cities are spaces where life succeeds, even proliferates. Is a desert where cities grow still a desert? Is a city in a desert a space of nature or of culture? Or indeed of horticulture? The comparison of the capitals with the cacti can suggest that the cities were planted or designed as much as that they self-seeded across the desert (as their common initial phoneme repeats sporadically across the first sentences: 'capitales', 'comme', 'cactus', 'curare'). This initial comparison between capitals and cacti is only the first of a chain of similes: the latter in turn are like the sun (presumably because the prickly spines evoke the latter's 'pointed rays'). The verticality introduced by the verb 'surgissaient' paradoxically produces a markedly horizontal textual movement. But this syntagmatic shift is also mirrored along the paradigmatic axis. The second simile (cacti = suns) simultaneously extends the first and evokes an absent one, itself famous for troubling spatial relations; the analogy between plant and celestial body is reminiscent of Éluard's famous line 'La terre est bleue comme une orange' [The earth is blue like an orange] in *L'Amour la poésie*, published in 1929 only three years after his *Capitale de la douleur* and hence scarcely more than a decade before Genet wrote his novel. The disproportion of these comparisons becomes even more pronounced in what follows, when childhood is no longer a desert in which plants grow but a desert itself shaded by a 'huge flowering magnolia'.

On the one hand, writing thus has the power to minimise the mighty. 'Son enfance, comme un sahara, minuscule ou immense': the vast desert has not only shrunk but has lost its own capital (letter), the immense can become minuscule. On the other hand, the converse too is true: writing also magnifies the minuscule. This is evident both thematically in the enlargement of the magnolia into a Jack-and-the-Beanstalk-like growth of sufficient stature to provide shade for a desert, and at the level of the signifier in that the tree's very name evokes a magnification, or a magnificence, that echoes further in the apparent conjuring up of a capital M following a series of the letter in lower case: 'en des instants rapides comme des traits, *m*inces comme eux, *m*inces comme ce paradis qu'on voit entre les paupières d'un *M*ongol'. In this passage, Genet in effect proposes the image of a very unusual paradise or garden of Eden. It is a space of absolute undecidability where the line or 'trait' between big and small, up and down, high and deep (the magnolia climbs high in a sky 'deep as a grotto') is indeed so thin that a letter is enough to turn the one into the other. Or a facial feature, such as eyes; like the different meanings of 'capitales', those of 'traits' heave successively into view in this green desert, as if outlined by a kohl pencil. Genet's paradise can be seen 'entre les paupières', a magnificently ambiguous formulation: is the Mongol the one who sees or in whom paradise is seen? The question of visibility, or more specifically invisibility, dominates the end of the passage, most obviously in the shift from the 'invisible though present' sun to the later glimpse of the 'invisible and present' magnolia. But what is a glimpse of the invisible? Decades before deconstruction analysed the fundamental lack of identity to itself of a presence seemingly grounded in visibility, Genet here emphasises the momentariness of any visibility, evident thematically in the succession of one invisible thing after another, manifest also in the syntagmatic chain itself, in the sequence of words that give way to each other without any achieving dominance. This extraordinarily elusive passage both describes and inscribes a very particular vision of paradise, one characterised not by the absence of privilege but by the instability of any privilege awarded to any one thing, any one word, over another.

That vision is first and foremost a poetic vision. Not only is it inseparable from the language that articulates it, but what it glorifies, or magnifies, is above all the power of language. The power, specifically, of letters: this is a passage about (capital) letters, highlighting that letters make a capital difference. 'Minuscule or immense — you don't know': the undecidability that allows the minuscule to be magnificent, or a city to turn into a letter, is a potentiality of writing. Moreover, this passage about the overturning of privilege deals explicitly with the displacement of literary property. Genet specifies that the images he has proposed are 'at all points like those of which the poet speaks'. But in question here is no poetic giant. Google reveals that the lines *'J'ai vu dans le désert | Ton ciel ouvert...'* are from the French version of 'Nearer, my God, to Thee'. It is impossible to categorise which is 'poetic' here, the prose of Genet's writing or the extract from the 'poem'.[6] The impossibility of discriminating the minuscule from the immense is thus closely bound up for Genet with the blurring of the distinction between novel and poem, a difference that is itself a matter of capitals. A capital letter is so called because it is used at the head of a word either to signal that the word is a proper noun or to mark a new line in a poem. One of the differences between a poem and a novel is that the former has proportionately more capitals, and allocated to words grammatically too 'common' to merit one.

The distinction between novel and poem is thus no more secure than that between minuscule and immense, important and insignificant, proper noun and common noun or, for that matter, common noun and common noun. This passage exemplifies superbly how Genet's writing works systematically and at every level to challenge distinctions of all kinds: that is, not to abolish or homogenise them but rather to trouble the very possibility of identifying one thing, one word, as more important than another. Its concerted attack on property is, conjointly, an attack on privilege. Insofar as the (poetic) vision that pervades his writing concerns an upending of privilege, a redistribution of power, it is therefore also a political vision. In this paragraph, whose primary function seems to be to draw attention to the workings of his writing, the word Genet chooses to elaborate on is highly significant: in addition to its own homonymic meanings, in '(la) capitale' we cannot but also hear its homophone, '(le) capital'. Furthermore, a relation between its general destabilisation of hierarchy and the prototypal political question, that of a specifically economic privilege, is explicitly created by the abrupt shift to the next paragraph, which begins: 'Ernestine et son fils habitaient la seule maison du village qui fût, avec l'église, couverte d'ardoises' [Ernestine and her son lived in the only house in the village, except for the church, that had a slate roof] (*RP*, 78; *OLF*, 135). With Divine, the sexual intersects with the economic, her childhood experience making it impossible to situate her unequivocally in relation to privilege: she is both marginalised (as a transvestite homosexual) and privileged (economically).

This passage, then, clearly links the troubling of generic difference to a challenging of privilege of all sorts. Of course, some privileges are more obviously political than others. Few would contest that challenging privilege in certain domains counts as a political gesture, class being the quintessential example. Although, as discussed above, the *bourgeois* is Genet's enemy of choice, his novels are singularly uninterested in exploring class-related issues. In contrast, they are consistently invested in destabilising sexual privilege, in terms of both gender and sexuality, the aspect of his novels that has garnered the most political debate. In the next section, I develop the implications of Derrida's analysis of the writer's treatment of sexual questions. But first I want to dwell a moment on the politics of Genet's destabilisation of literary genre. How should we read the homology that Genet posits between challenging hierarchies of size, gender, economics, on the one hand, and troubling the distinction between novel and poem on the other? What are the political implications of the fact that, for Genet at this time, these challenges appear of equal importance? What kind of political gesture is it to challenge the hierarchy between novel and poem? *Is* it a political gesture to trouble hierarchy per se, including the hierarchy of different political questions?

From some ideological standpoints, the apparent equivalence in Genet's early work between attacking literary authority and attacking phallocentrism, homophobia or capitalism doubtless constitutes a frivolous and depoliticising gesture. Some may even judge that not discriminating between exposing economic exploitation and destabilising literary privilege constitutes less an apolitical than a rightwing stance. However, other perspectives exist which are less hostile to the idea that undermining literary institutions in itself constitutes a political gesture. The work of thinkers such as Kristeva, Derrida and more recently Jacques Rancière has consolidated an intellectual tradition arguing that the very act or fact of imagining a new configuration of relationships already anticipates change, already has a transformative potential.[7] Indeed, for Rancière 'la politique' [politics] is defined by this performative element that enacts change, as distinct from 'la police' [police] that oversees and regulates the status quo.[8] Much of the analysis of gender, sexuality or race in Genet is in fact predicated on the related assumption that (literary) representation is never neutral, and that imaginative originality has a political effect. But of what writer is this not true? While Genet's early texts may have an iconic status in terms of revolutionising the treatment of issues of identity that today are the subject of highly politicised debates, that does not make them 'more' political than others: the point I want to stress is that they lend themselves to political analysis in the same way as other works of literature. Reading his novels is an inescapably aesthetic experience, an engagement with their singular form; the fact that they also foreground the relationship between literature and its outside, between the aesthetic and the political, does not make them intrinsically more political than any other. Conversely, the attention Genet pays to questions of genre and of form and his lack of interest in theorising his own political position at this early stage of his trajectory, unlike in later years when his writing engaged explicitly in political discourse, do not make his texts apolitical. As an intervention in a public sphere, no literary work is ever neutral. Genet's novels' singular representation of the world and practice of writing channel a particular politics, that is, a particular vision of how the world is and should be. They exemplify a tension between a maximal exploitation of the possibilities specific to language and an equally fundamental engagement with language as a social phenomenon; however, far from constituting a new category of writing, this tension is inherent to the literary experience. Genet's novels are both intensely political and irreducible to politics: like literature, art, in general.

*　*　*　*　*

If Genet's texts are political in the way of all literature, the question, then, is how to assess their political impact. The preceding discussion has shown how *Notre-Dame-des-Fleurs* devotes considerable energy to destabilising the hierarchy that relegates the aesthetic to a subordinate position. It certainly differs radically from political approaches where only the 'earthly world' matters. At no point, however, does Genet suggest that *only* the aesthetic is of importance, or that the 'earthly world' does not matter: his revalorisation of the aesthetic cannot be accounted for by a purely formalist approach. As flagged up in the Introduction, the richest contribution to date to our understanding of these issues in Genet is that of Jacques

Derrida. *Glas* seeks most obviously to explore the philosophical implications of neglecting issues of style. However, in concerning itself with the structures of privilege that relegate aesthetic questions to a subordinate position and underpin the replication of hierarchy in other domains, it also throws a spotlight on the political implications of doing so.

The left-hand column of the text of *Glas* offers a lengthy meditation on how style has no place in the movement of the Hegelian dialectic. Style — and the related question of narrative space (and by extension that of genre) — is in fact what the work of conceptualisation leaves aside: 'Du point de vue conceptuel, qu'est-ce qu'une différence de style ou de rythme voire d'espace narratif? Il n'est pas insignifiant que le concept la réduise à rien' [From the conceptual perspective, what is a difference of style or rhythm, even of narrative space? Not insignificantly, the concept reduces the difference to nothing] (G, 60a; GE, 43a). But the insignificance attributed by Hegel in particular, and philosophy in general, to questions of style finds a parallel in dominant approaches to Genet's literature. Early in the right-hand column Derrida signals Sartre's avoidance in *Saint Genet: comédien et martyr* of what he calls 'la question de la fleur, la question anthologique' [the question of the flower, the anthological question] (G, 18b; GE, 13b), a question in which he includes both Genet's images of flowers and his use of the flowers of rhetoric. 'Anthology' is not alone in having a link, via its etymology, to the flower; as he points out, 'style' too has a specifically floral meaning: 'Quand une fleur "s'éclôt", les pétales s'écartent et se dresse alors ce qu'on appelle le *style*' [When a flower opens up, the petals part, and then there rises up what is called the *style*] (G, 29b; GE, 21b). The question of the flower *is* also the question of style.

Derrida, in contrast, places 'the question of the flower' centre-stage, approaching it via the lens of the signature, the mark of an individuality or singularity. Hegel is typical of philosophers in considering the philosophical work as fully detachable from its origin, as a logical, rational, conceptual output in which the singularities of the author have no place. From such a perspective, the philosopher's signature belongs outside the text proper, on the cover or in the publishing contract that appropriates the work by identifying it as produced by a proper name; it should not affect the text itself: 'Sa signature [...] enveloppera ce corpus mais n'y sera pas comprise' [His signature [...] will envelop this corpus, but no doubt will not be contained therein] (G, 2a; GE, 1a). Yet, as Derrida develops, various aspects of Hegel's work contradict that aspiration towards a signature-free work, a text that would bear no sign of its author.[9] Hegel's text is not neutral in a whole range of ways. Derrida notably brings out how Hegel's ideas are complicit with the genealogical system of filiation that has dominated Western history, in which the father's property and proper name are transmitted from father to son, when he glosses the earlier philosopher to the effect that Absolute Knowledge 's'impose un écart en se signant' [imposes a gap in signing itself] (G, 319a; GE, 229a). In French, *se signer* also means to make the sign of the cross, that is, to sign 'in the name of the Father and the Son and the Holy Spirit'. Insofar as Hegel seeks to keep his name apart from his work, to attain a universality free of any singularity, he signs not neutrally but in the name of the Father.

The right-hand column of *Glas* explores how Genet signs himself and his work differently from Hegel. Literature, of course, makes no claim to being impersonal; it is a space where it is not only accepted but expected that the work should bear the trace of its author. For Derrida, Genet's work is exemplary in endlessly reproducing the author's signature internally as well as externally:

> Genet, par un de ces mouvements en *ana*, aurait [...] silencieusement, laborieusement, minutieusement, obsessionnellement, compulsivement, avec les gestes d'un voleur dans la nuit, disposé ses signatures à la place de tous les objets manquants. Le matin, vous attendant à reconnaître les choses familières, vous retrouvez son nom partout, en grosses lettres, en petites lettres, en entier ou en morceaux, déformé ou recomposé. Il n'est plus là mais vous habitez son mausolée ou ses chiottes. Vous croyiez déchiffrer, dépister, poursuivre, vous êtes compris. Il a tout affecté de sa signature. Il a affecté sa signature. Il l'a affectée de tout. Il s'en est affecté (il se sera même, plus tard, attifé d'un accent circonflexe). Il a essayé d'écrire, lui, proprement, ce qui se passe entre l'affect et le seing.

> [Genet, by one of those movements in *ana*, would have [...] silently, laboriously, minutely, obsessionally, compulsively, and with the moves of a thief in the night, set his signatures in place of all the missing objects. In the morning, expecting to recognize familiar things, you find his name all over the place, in big letters, small letters, as a whole or in morsels deformed or recomposed. He is no longer there, but you live in his mausoleum or his latrines. You thought you were deciphering, tracking down, pursuing, you are included. He has affected everything with his signature. He has affected his signature. He has affected it with everything. He himself is affected by it (he will even be decked out, later on, with a circumflex). He has tried, he himself, properly, to write what happens between affect and the *seing*.] (*G*, 58b; *GE*, 41-42b)

Genet is exemplary for Derrida, then, not only for leaving signs of himself throughout his text (as do all great writers?), but for doing so in such a way as to trouble any possibility that his name can be taken as a secure guarantee or guarantor of property. His signature operates a displacement rather than an appropriation. Setting his signatures in place of the 'missing objects', he signs in the place of loss, a loss with specifically maternal connotations: the arcane term for signature, *seing*, is homophonous in French with both *saint* and *sein* [breast]. Being illegitimate, Genet bears his mother's surname. *Glas*'s Genet column in effect develops how signing in the name of the mother — a sexually different signature — involves a process other than deploying one's name as a guarantee of property. Signing with her proper name would merely set the mother up in opposition to the father, constitute her as an alternative identity that would efface the difference and ultimately amount to the same as signing with the father's name. In contrast, Genet's signature does not serve to consolidate property; he signs like a thief. Not only does Genet sign by leaving his signature behind (rather than taking something away), but his signature undermines rather than consolidates identity, leaving bits of his name all over the place. He signs even with bits that are not part of his name, notably the circumflex he adds to his surname. In a passage quoted extensively in *Glas* (*G*, 254b; *GE*, 182-83b), the statement by the narrator of *Journal du voleur* that his mother's name was Gabrielle Genet famously leads on to a development of the kinship he feels with the plant *genêt* [broom], and two footnotes then spell out the link between his surname and both the plant and the homophonous 'jennet' (*genet*) which he also (inappropriately) endows with a circumflex. Genet signs antonomastically, with a common noun instead of a proper name. That is, he signs improperly, with a replacement or inappropriate name. Furthermore, his signature goes even further in undermining identity. Derrida reads the insistent presence of words with the letters 'gl' throughout Genet's texts as remnants of his mother's first name, Gabrielle: *glaïeul, glaviaud, glaive, algues, galerie, aigle* and, of course, *glas*. The deathknell announced by the title is that of the proper name itself: 'glas du nom propre' [the *glas* of the proper name] (*G*, 27b; *GE*, 20b).

*Glas* thus emphasises how Genet's dissemination of proper names both is profoundly at odds with the practice of naming that shores up patriarchal structures and goes in tandem with a full-scale attack on the primacy of the referential function of language; to sign in the name of the mother is to sign undecidably, to challenge the very process of signification. The passage that elaborates most explicitly on the letters 'gl', a passage in the very middle of the book whose layout moreover visually places 'GL' at the centre of the right-hand column, states the impossibility of constituting it as a centre of meaning:

> GL
> je ne dis pas le signifiant GL, ni le phonème GL, ni le graphème GL. La marque ce serait mieux, si on entendait bien ce mot ou si on lui ouvrait les oreilles; ni même la marque donc.
>
> Il est aussi imprudent d'avancer ou de mettre en branle *le* ou *la* GL, de l'écrire ou de l'articuler en majuscules. Cela n'a pas d'identité, de sexe, de genre, ne fait pas de sens, ce n'est ni un tout défini, ni la partie détachée d'un tout
> gl reste gl.

> [GL
> I do not say either the signifier GL, or the phoneme GL, or the grapheme GL. Mark would be better, if the word were well understood, or if one's ears were open to it; not even mark then.
>
> It is similarly imprudent to advance or set GL swinging in the masculine or feminine, to write or to articulate it in capital letters. That has no identity, sex, gender, makes no sense, is neither a definite whole nor a part detached from a whole
> gl remains(s) gl.] (*G*, 167–68b; *GE*, 119b)

GL is undecidable to the point of having no attributable property: it is unclassifiable as either masculine or feminine, part or whole, capital or lower-case. The very distinctions that anchor a signifying system are 'set swinging', all placed in movement. Signing in the name of the mother means signing in a way that tolls the end of meaning itself:

> A *ne plus* signifier, la signature [...] n'est plus à l'ordre ou de l'ordre de la signification, du signifié ou du signifiant.
> Donc — ce qu'émet un coup de glas, c'est que la fleur, par exemple, en tant qu'elle signe, ne signifie plus rien.

[In *no longer* signifying, the signature [...] no longer belongs to or comes from the order of signification of the signified or the signifier.

   Thus what the tolling of the knell [*glas*] emits is the fact that the flower, for example, inasmuch as it signs, no longer signifies anything.] (*G*, 42-45b; *GE*, 31–32b)

Derrida thus highlights an unremitting attack on meaning as a key element to Genet's style. What is at stake, however, is not the promotion of meaninglessness, not an abolition of significant differences but rather a new (non-exclusive) relationship between them. To zoom out a little, here is where *Glas* offers a very different perspective from Sartre on the 'tourniquets' that the earlier philosopher had highlighted in Genet's writing, the ways he twists together opposites: good and evil, sainthood and criminality, activity and passivity, etc. For Sartre, Genet has a fundamentally Manicheistic view of the world; he inverts rather than undermines hierarchies in a way that ultimately leaves the opposition intact. For Derrida, the oscillating movement between binary poles that proliferates in Genet's writing — and in which his narrator declares his delight in a note on the very first page of *Journal du voleur*: 'Mon émoi, c'est l'oscillation des unes aux autres' [My excitement is the oscillation from one to the other] (*RP*, 1097; *TJ*, 5) — serves rather to render the opposition fundamentally unstable. He variously calls this operation the 'anthologique de l'indécidable' [anthologic of the undecidable] or the logic of the 'anthérection' [antherection] (*G*, 177b, 183b; *GE*, 126b, 130b). By adding a supernumerary 'h' (as here in 'anthérection'), Derrida signals that Genet's floral signature is at work; this 'antherection' is something other than an anti-erection. Later he will similarly add a 'h' to 'antonymy' to create a general category for the rhetorical ploys that disorganise categorical thinking in Genet's writing: he forges the word 'anthonymie' (*G*, 253b; *GE*, 181b) to describe Genet's signature rhetorical flourish (of which his play on his own name, the 'anthonomase' [anthonomasis] that troubles the distinction between proper name and common noun, offers a privileged example). At issue is a space where nothing can be detached from its opposite: the more from the less, the high from the low, good from evil, the significant (in all senses of the word) from the insignificant, strength from weakness, masculine from feminine.

   This evidently has adverse implications for structures of privilege: the stability of a hierarchy depends on the possibility of securely distinguishing between its constituent elements. Derrida explores this most comprehensively in relation to sexual difference, an area where Genet's exaggeration of gender-specific characteristics makes the idea of an equivalence between the sexes seem particularly counter-intuitive. He analyses a number of passages in *Journal du voleur* featuring Stilitano, the ostensibly hyper-masculine, one-armed bandit, drawing attention to the link between the character's name and the various meanings of style, and in particular the etymological link between style and cutting (*G*, 340b; *GE*, 244b). In effect, from the outset Genet associates Stilitano with a cut, but a cut that has nothing castratory about it: 'Quand un membre est enlevé, m'apprend-on, celui qui reste devient plus fort. Dans le sexe de Stilitano, j'espérais que la vigueur de son bras coupé s'était ramassée' [When a limb has been removed, the remaining one is said to grow stronger. I had hoped that the vigour of the arm which Stilitano had lost might be concentrated in his penis] (*RP*, 1088; *TJ*, 16). Cutting has the paradoxical effect of (also) increasing the whole it reduces. Conversely, the comical sexual prosthesis that Stilitano uses to tease men with the promise of exceptionally large genitalia serves less to enhance his virility than to throw it into question. The bunch of false grapes he pins inside his trouser crotch simultaneously emphasises the bulge at his groin and reveals it to be false; it later figures explicitly as a 'plaie postiche' [fake wound], and is compared to the 'rose d'étamine' [muslin rose] worn at a similar level by a Spanish prostitute 'pour remplacer sa fleur perdue' [to replace her lost flower] (*RP*, 1132, 1088; *TJ*, 43, 54). This rose is as undecidable as the grapes, in that the word *étamine* can refer both to a fabric and to a flower's male sexual organ (stamen). It is no more unequivocally feminine than the grapes are a sign of uncontrovertible masculinity.[10]

The point is not that the sexes are not different — of all literary universes, Genet's must surely figure as one that makes most place for sexual specificity — but that they are equivalent: they are of equal value, they displace and replace each other. In Genet's work, the more phallic a man appears to be, the more feminine (or castrated, in psychoanalytical parlance) he is too. As Derrida says, 'Ça n'érige pas *contre* ou *malgré* la castration, *en dépit* de la blessure ou de l'infirmité, en châtrant la castration. Ça bande, la castration' [It does not erect *against* or *inspite of* castration, *despite* the wound or infirmity, by castrating castration. Castration erects itself] (*G*, 193b; *GE*, 138b). Derrida posits the (sexual) difference between Hegel and Genet not as an opposition between phallus and castration but as the difference between sexual opposition and sexual undecidability. The series of explicitly homosexual, ithyphallic encounters which fill Genet's texts in effect stage a long succession of symbolically undecidable, substitutable sexes. Derrida brings out the successive component of Genet's writing: his texts form a long succession of successions in which it becomes impossible to determine a centre of any kind, a core more important than its surroundings, including, for example, 'le phallus dans une certaine organisation fantasmatique' [the phallus in a certain phantasmatic organization] (*G*, 292a; *GE*, 209a). The sexes are *apposed* rather than opposed: castration is an addition to an erection, not its negation.

This structure of apposition rather than opposition fundamentally undermines any system of privilege: by definition, a structure in which the different elements could replace each other would not be a hierarchy. But Derrida also explores the implications of substitutability in other ways pertinent for my argument in this chapter. He juxtaposes the question of the substitutability or apposability of the sexes — the fact that they relay and prolong each other — and the question of the fetish: 'Apposons ici la question du fétiche' [Let us appose here the question of the fetish] (*G*, 311b; *GE*, 222b). This is doubtless no accident; in psychoanalytical theory the fetish is itself a question of substitutability. For Freud, the fetish always signals a disavowal of sexual difference; he claims that the fetishist selects some detached object to set in place of the mother's missing penis whose absence is too unbearable to contemplate.[11] If Derrida integrates a discussion of fetishism into his analysis of sexual politics in Hegel and Genet, it is because fetishism intrinsically involves a relation between sexual difference and the question of representation. In the Hegel column (G, 288-95a; GE, 206-11a), he explores how for Freud the fetish — a word which shares the etymology of 'factitious' — functions as a substitute to posit the existence of something non-substitutable. It deploys a fiction to advance a clear opposition between fiction and truth.[12] The difference in the Genet column lies not in an alternative theory of fetishism but in the writer's embrace of the substitutability that fetishism seeks to disavow. In Genet's work, there are only substitutes; the manifestly artificial gives way not to a revealed truth but to a different artifice. Derrida's account thus proposes a link between the challenge Genet poses to phallic privilege and his celebration of overt fakeness: 'Dès lors que la chose même, en sa vérité dévoilée, se trouve déjà engagée, par le dévoilement même, dans le jeu de la différence supplémentaire, le fétiche n'a plus de statut rigoureusement décidable. Glas du phallogocentrisme' [As soon as the thing itself, in its unveiled truth, is already found engaged, by the very unveiling, in the play of supplementary difference the fetish no longer has any rigorously decidable status. Glas of phallogocentrism] (G, 315b; GE, 226b). Derrida's analysis does not merely emphasise that Genet's writing simultaneously undermines both phallocentrism and logocentrism; it also signals that his (sexual) politics cannot be thought without taking into consideration the impossibility of distinguishing categorically between truth and falseness — between truth and fiction — in his work.

★   ★   ★   ★   ★

The question of the distinction between truth and fiction is central to the controversy that enveloped Genet criticism three decades after the publication of Glas. Derrida's book had explored Genet's writings as sapping the foundations of any system of privilege or social hierarchy, and recognised in his writings at every level a sequential or revolving arrangement of parts that defied all integration into a unified totality. In stark contrast with Derrida's suggestion that Genet's thinking is revolutionary in offering a way to think the revolution in other than totalising terms, two critics proposed readings of Genet as a writer in thrall to totalitarianism. Ivan Jablonka's Les Vérités inavouables de Jean Genet argues that Genet was fascinated by Nazism and that his work displays deep affinities with Nazism and its French supporters.[13] Its publication was bookended by two different books by Éric Marty, which similarly seek to position Genet as a writer with right-wing authoritarian sympathies.[14] 'Jean Genet à Chatila', the section of Bref séjour à Jérusalem that deals with his work, alleges that the author was profoundly antisemitic and focuses principally on Genet's writings about the Palestinians; I examine its accusations in Chapter 4. Although it rests its case for Genet's racism on the assumption that Pompes funèbres displays its author's fascination with Hitler, it says very little about Genet's early works, in which Jews scarcely feature. It is only subsequently in Jean Genet, post-scriptum that Marty argues more broadly that Genet was in sympathy with Nazism.[15] My primary aim in what follows is not to defend Genet against these accusations, but rather to explore what their different approaches reveal about

Genet's work, especially with respect to the politics of its undecidability and the border it traces between fiction and truth.[16]

Jablonka, who presents his book as a reflection on a moment of 'literary history' (*VIJG*, 9, 373, 401), paints a picture of a Genet enthused by Nazi ideology and in tune with its French collaborationist supporters. The most damning evidence he adduces in support of his argument is Genet's frequentation, from 1942 until 1944, of people with overt fascist sympathies, notably Jean Turlais, Roland Laudenbach and François Sentein, through whom he was introduced to the figure who would provide him with an entry into Parisian literary and intellectual circles, Jean Cocteau, himself to prove a politically controversial figure after the war. For Jablonka, who entitles the section in which he discusses these contacts 'Les Amis de Genet' [Genet's Friends], this is proof of the writer's affinity with their fascist views (although he later recognises that the fascists of *Je suis partout*, for example, did not recognise Genet as one of them, *VIJG*, 286). Notwithstanding his book's ostensibly historical approach, he does not take into account the extent to which Genet's range of possible associates was determined by his social condition. As a petty thief, deserter and ex-prisoner without family, Genet had access only to a narrow circle of acquaintances; most of his contacts in Paris belonged on the margins of the criminal underworld, a sphere disproportionately disposed to collaboration with the German occupation, and also relatively uneducated. Jabonka does not consider the possibility that Genet was drawn to his (comparatively-cultured) companions because of their shared interest in literature rather than their political views. Nor does he deem it of significance that Genet did not maintain contact with these circles after the war, when other options for company became available to him; the idea that his most fundamental affinities were with these short-lived right-wing friendships is contradicted by his steady shift leftwards over the course of his life. Although Jablonka focuses on a 'moment' of literary history, he in fact generalises that particular moment as definitive of Genet's life in its entirety.

Beyond the bare fact of Genet's association with these figures, there is little evidence that he shared their views. Jablonka acknowledges in his conclusion that the writer is not 'foncièrement' [fundamentally] nazi and cannot plausibly be considered a real 'suppôt' [acolyte] of Hitler (*VIJG*, 388). He nonetheless argues that Genet's novels reflect his 'fascination avouée et assumée pour le fascisme italien et surtout pour le nazisme' (*VIJG*, 155) [avowed, recognised fascination for Italian fascism and especially for Nazism].[17] Genet's early texts, and *Pompes funèbres* in particular, are unquestionably both scandalous and offensive. I fully appreciate that they may inspire repugnance, especially on the part of those whose loved ones were innocent victims of atrocity. Nonetheless, to dismiss them as pro-fascist is both to misread them profoundly and to miss the opportunity of learning from the insights of a writer profoundly sensitive to his epoch. However outrageous Genet's ostensible celebration of Hitler's defeat of France may be, a blanket judgment that refuses to take account of the ways his work is fundamentally incompatible with totalitarian thinking is more likely to hinder than to advance understanding of the era — an era that unprecedentedly brought into new relief the relation between aesthetics and politics that constitutes the central focus of this book. As such, it is also therefore more likely to hinder rather than help the task of ensuring that such atrocities do not recur.

Jablonka claims that Genet's works in general, and not just *Pompes funèbres*, show the writer's unequivocal support for the fascist project. He rests his case on three elements of Genet's imagination that he claims are evidence of his positive and enthusiastic 'adhésion aux valeurs nazies' (*VIJG*, 171) [endorsement of nazi values]: 'la hiérarchisation d'un univers fragmenté entre demi-dieux et sous-hommes, une esthétique médiévale nourrie de rites féodaux, une contre-morale où les valeurs communes sont systématiquement renversées' (*VIJG*, 172) [a hierarchical universe split between demi-gods and subhumans, a medieval aesthetic drawing on feudal rites and a counter-morality that systematically overturns common values]. His argument is untenable in too many respects to enumerate fully. He interprets the mere fact that Genet has recourse to myth and feudal imagery in *Notre-Dame-des-Fleurs*, regardless of how he uses them, as proof in itself of his alignment with fascism, given that the Nazis deployed both in the service of their propaganda. Similarly, he sees in Genet's glorification of crime an endorsement of the lawlessness endemic within fascism and its overturning of social norms, notwithstanding Genet's stated unhappiness at discovering that his affirmation of everything society repudiated suddenly risked integrating him into the world rather than setting him apart from it. The most preposterous example in my opinion is the proposal that Si Slimane's return from the dead in *Les Paravents* is an example of black magic that corresponds to the Nazi cult of the occult, and is similar to the promotion of the irrational in works by fascist writers such as Drieu La Rochelle and Brasillach (*VIJG*, 196). Here as elsewhere, Jablonka isolates a detail in Genet's text to which he attributes a uniquely ideological resonance and presents it as evidence of Genet's alignment with the project of fascism, regardless of how he deploys it in context. For reasons of space, I will limit my remarks to the first of the three accusations listed above, since the question of Genet's treatment of hierarchy is central to the argument in this chapter.

Jablonka's argument that Genet presents a highly stratified world with a clear and rigid hierarchy of gods, supermen and subhumans, and as such is in harmony with the Nazi ideal of triumphant, brutal masculinity, depends entirely on discounting the working of Genet's rhetoric. It takes the writer's words literally, as a direct and transparent expression of his views. As such, it utterly fails to take into consideration both the discrepancies between what Genet says at different textual moments and, more importantly, the difference between the text's literal meaning and the overall effect it produces (or the related, more technical, difference between the *énoncé* and the *énonciation*, usually rendered in English as 'statement' and 'utterance'): that is, the difference between what the text 'says' and what it 'does'. Genet not only maximally exploits those differences throughout his writing, but repeatedly calls attention to the fact that he does so in both his fictional and non-fictional texts. For example, he begins one essay, 'Ce qui est resté d'un Rembrandt déchiré en petits carrés bien réguliers, et foutu aux chiottes', with the assertion that the work of art negates itself:

> C'est seulement ces sortes de vérités, celles qui ne sont pas démontrables et même qui sont '*fausses*', celles que l'on ne peut conduire sans absurdité jusqu'à leur extrémité sans aller à la négation d'elles et de soi, c'est celles-là qui doivent être exaltées par l'œuvre d'art.

> [It's only those kinds of truths, the ones that are not demonstrable and even '*false*,' the ones that one cannot without absurdity lead to their conclusion of them and of onself — those are the ones that must be exalted by the work of art.] (*OC*, IV, 21; *FA*, 91).

The first paragraph of another essay, 'Le Secret de Rembrandt', immediately casts doubt on the claim it has just proffered: 'Ça, ou bien l'inverse?' [Is that it, or just the opposite?] (*OC*, V, 31; *FA*, 84). In the essay 'L'Étrange Mot d'...' a reflection on language culminates in the statement 'je sais que je n'ai rien dit et que je ne dirai jamais rien: et les mots s'en foutent' [I know that I have said nothing and that I will never say anything: and the words couldn't care less] (*TC*, 888; *FA*, 111). Writing, for Genet, is not primarily a matter of conveying meaning; literature uses language for purposes other than signification. Derrida insisted on the same point in the earlier quotation that the flower 'ne signifie plus rien'. My analysis in the first section of this chapter shows how in practice Genet's text ceaselessly undercuts itself, destabilising distinctions of all kinds and challenging any attempt to pin down its meaning definitively. In both its discourse and its textual working, Genet's writing warns consistently against taking it at face value.

Jablonka, however, accepts what Genet says — *sometimes*. He believes his most outrageous statements, for example that the various murderers condemned to death, fictional and otherwise, that feature in his texts are God-like creatures; that cruel, brutal men are worthy of worship; that weaker men are vile and merit the abuse they receive. But he does not recognise how such statements are contradicted at other textual moments or how, in very Proustian fashion, a character viewed initially from one perspective appears differently in another. In *Notre-Dame-des-Fleurs*, for example, Divine, initially presented as a limp, passive, martyrised figure in thrall to her hard, macho pimp, later switches to a virile role: 'Divine alors endossa le corps d'un mâle; soudain forte et musclée, elle se voyait dure comme fer, les mains dans les poches, sifflotant' [Divine then donned the body of a male. Suddenly strong and muscular, she saw herself hard as nails, with her hands in her pockets, whistling] (*RP*, 93; *OLF*, 149). She *changes*; how she behaves varies from context to context or over time. *Miracle de la rose* elaborates still more systematically on the impossibility of definitively fixing any man's sexual role. Recalling the formative experience in Mettray when Villeroy, his 'marle' ('big shot' in Frechtman's translation), made him become a 'marle' for another boy, only to divulge that he in turn had his own 'marle', the narrator explains:

> Je fus encore terrassé par cette idée que chaque mâle avait son mâle admirable, que le monde de la beauté virile et de la force s'aimait ainsi, de maillon en maillon, formant une guirlande de fleurs musclées et tordues, ou rigides, épineuses. Je devinai un monde étonnant. Ces marlous n'en finissaient pas d'être femmes pour un autre plus fort et plus beau. Ils étaient femmes de moins en moins en s'éloignant de moi, jusqu'au marlou très pur, les dominant tous,

celui qui trônait sur sa galère, dont la verge si belle, grave et lointaine, sous forme de maçon, parcourait la Colonie. Harcamone!

[I was still astounded at the thought that each male had his own glorious male, that the world of force and manly beauty loved in that way within itself, from link to link, forming a garland of muscular and twisted or stiff and thorny flowers. Those pimps were always being women for someone stronger and handsomer than they. They were women less and less the further away they were from me, all the way to the very pure pimp who dominated them all, the one who lorded it over the galley, whose lovely penis, grave and distant, moved about the Colony in the form of a mason. Harcamone!] (*RP*, 451; *MR*, 213)

Far from a rigid hierarchy in which roles are the expression of an essential and inalterable identity, the structure of erotic relations in Genet's universe is that of a 'garland' of men attached together incrementally, each simultaneously 'mâle' for one partner and 'femme' for another, with the result that no individual can be defined as masculine or feminine, powerful or powerless.[18]

By neglecting to take account of the contradictions that Genet's writing systematically develops and their implications for his world view, Jablonka's argument thus relies on a simultaneously literal and selective reading of Genet's texts. It is also insensitive to the many discrepancies between the diegesis and the narrative and between the *énoncé* and the *énonciation*. While the novels indeed contain statements where the narrator or protagonist voices admiration for brutal, cruel men, the text as a whole systematically undermines that admiration. As well as countering such statements explicitly (for example, 'dès que j'acquis une virilité totale — ou, pour être plus exact, dès que je devins mâle — les voyous perdirent leur prestige' [as soon as I achieved total virility — or, to be more exact, as soon as I became a male — the thugs lost their glamour], *RP*, 241; *MR*, 25), Genet shows repeatedly how the hardness he professes to admire is a mask for weakness and cowardice. Scene after scene illustrates and reinforces the realisation reached by the narrator of *Miracle de la rose* that 'les marles les plus forts étaient des donneuses' [the strongest big shots were squealers] and that treachery was overwhelmingly to be found 'parmi les plus nobles, les plus durs' [among the noblest, the hardest] (*RP*, 492; *MR*, 248). In other words, the thrust of Genet's writing is its attack on authority: it consistently evokes codes based on degrees of social distinction only to undermine them, in the same way the narrator of *Miracle* fantasises being of royal lineage not in order to assume a position of authority but to violate the system itself: 'Je ne désirais que commettre un sacrilège, souiller la pureté d'une famille comme je souillerais la caste des marles en y faisant admettre le vautour que j'étais' [I desired only to commit a sacrilege, to soil the purity of a family, just as I would have soiled the caste of big shots by introducing among them the chicken that I was] (*RP*, 458; *MR*, 218). Jablonka overlooks this core question of the overall functioning of Genet's writing. Hence, for example, he misses the fact that *Notre-Dame-des-Fleurs* in effect constitutes a hymn not to Notre-Dame or Mignon or indeed Pilorge, but to Divine. The character raised to godly status by her name, to epic status by the devotion of a 'Saga' to her (*RP*, 18; *OLF*, 72), to the status of a tragic operatic heroine by the 'Divinarianes' that punctuate the book, is not a fascist brute but a complicated, contradictory transvestite. One of the most powerfully evocative moments of the text is a one-line paragraph in the final set of Divinarianes: 'Elle a passé sa vie à se précipiter du haut d'un rocher' [She has spent her life hurling herself from the top of a rock] (RP, 204; OLF, 273). The character whose praises Genet's writing sings is not a heartless, macho thug but an intense, Christlike figure who has suffered from her passions throughout her life.

Jablonka's argument that Genet's texts in general bear witness to a worship of triumphant brutality that aligns them with fascism and its supporters is thus highly dependent on reading his writing both reductively and selectively. The same is true of his discussion of *Pompes funèbres*, a text which at least on the surface provides some ammunition for allegations that the writer had fascistic tendencies. This novel is indubitably extremely troubling in its apparent affirmation of people who commit acts of gratuitous cruelty. But it can only be judged an unequivocal statement of support for Nazi atrocity by ignoring its complexity, and hence forclosing the possibility of learning from the insights it provides into its epoch. In *Journal du voleur*, the narrator comments that a Communist poem apparently castigating the fascists is in fact a song of praise to them: 'Écrit contre eux, c'est eux qu'il chante' [Though written against them, it actually hymns them] (RP, 1226; TJ, 143). The converse is true of *Pompes funèbres*: although on the face of it the novel lauds the Third Reich and the Milice française, to see it as channelling an 'admiration sans bornes pour l'œuvre de destruction nazie' (VIJG, 170) [limitless admiration for the nazi work of destruction] is to ignore the many ways in which Genet's target is the hypocrisy and cruelty of those who seek to situate evil uniquely elsewhere and, in so doing, replicate the very behaviour they judge. Genet himself certainly makes no claim to occupy the moral high ground; he shockingly praises the Nazis and their sympathisers for the moral depths to which they descend. Nevertheless, distasteful and offensive though it may be, the support Genet expresses in *Pompes funèbres* for Hitler and the Milice is highly equivocal. In what follows I seek to explore the significance of that equivocity. Whereas the charge of being equivocal is usually levelled against those who do not adhere to the moral values they claim to respect, in Genet's case it is rather the claim to absolute immorality that is doubtful. The novel undermines both its own endorsement of radical evil and its (French) reader's putative assumption of moral rectitude. It makes uncomfortable reading for anyone who wants to believe that the conflict between good and evil, oppressor and oppressed, was a straightforward combat between the Germans and the French in that it offers an astonishingly early reflection on what Henry Rousso would later term 'the Vichy syndrome': the legacy of French complicity with the Nazis.[19] More broadly, it engages with the still thornier question of the general attraction of evil. While it may be gratifying to reject evil as a monstrous pathology, it is also simplistic; as Georges Didi-Huberman states in a different context, 'on se simplifie la vie éthique en rejetant le "mal radical" du côté de l'"Autre absolu"' [it is a simplification of ethical life to reject 'radical evil' to the side of the 'absolute Other'].[20] Genet's refusal to do this does not situate him on the side of evil. Nor is it a valid reproach in itself that his work sought to engage with the attraction of evil. Fascism exerted widespread fascination, and not merely in Germany; the era in which Genet wrote his novel was unprecedented for its promotion, and normalisation, of evil, although revelation of the genocidal worst was yet to come when Genet was writing *Pompes funèbres*. Statements such as the following leave no doubt that Genet was impressed by the rhetorical efficacy of Nazi propaganda: 'La puissance du signe, c'est la puissance du rêve, et c'est dans le rêve aussi que le national-socialisme a été rechercher, par la grâce d'un explorateur des ténèbres, la croix gammée' [The potency of the sign is the potency of the dream, and it was likewise in the realm of dream that National Socialism went to search, thanks to an explorer of darkness, for the swastika] (*RP*, 419; *MR*, 181). That efficacy is not a matter of debate; acknowledging and investigating how evil is seductive is not the same as being in thrall to its seductions. Genet was not carried away or 'fascinated' by the Nazi rhetoric whose power he recognised. On the contrary, *Pompes funèbres* shines an uncomfortable but illuminating spotlight on the truth of a particularly horrifying historical moment.

A number of elements forcefully counter the idea that Genet was of a totalitarian mindset. Rather than a positive endorsement of Nazi monstrosity, the delight he expresses at Hitler's successes derives from his intense satisfaction at the French defeat, as the author articulated repeatedly in his interviews. With Fichte:

> Le fait que l'armée française, ce qu'il y avait de plus prestigieux au monde il y a trente ans, ait capitulé devant les troupes d'un caporal autrichien, eh bien ça m'a ravi. [...] je ne pouvais qu'adorer celui qui avait mis en œuvre l'humiliation de la France.

> [The fact that the French army, the most prestigious thing in the world thirty years ago, that they surrendered to the troops of an Austrian corporal, well, to me, that was absolutely thrilling. [...] I could only love someone who had so humiliated France.] (*ED*, 149; *DE*, 125)

With Bertrand Poirot-Delpech:

> Quand Hitler a fichu une raclée aux Français, eh bien oui! j'ai été heureux, j'ai été heureux de cette raclée. [...] Mais il s'agit de la France, il ne s'agit pas du peuple allemand ou du peuple juif, ou des peuples communistes qui pouvaient être massacrés par Hitler.

> [When Hitler gave a thrashing to the French, well yes! I was glad, this thrashing made me happy. [...] But what I'm talking about is France, not the German people or the Jewish people, or the communist people that Hitler massacred.] (*ED*, 232; *DE*, 200)

With Nigel Williams: 'Je détestais tellement, et encore maintenant, tellement la France, que j'étais ravi que l'armée française soit battue. Elle était battue par les Allemands, elle était battue par Hitler, j'étais très content' [I hated France so much — and still do — so much that I was utterly thrilled that the French army had been beaten. It was beaten by the Germans, it was beaten by Hitler, I was very happy] (*ED*, 301; *DE*, 260). The same vitriolic pleasure accompanies the rare mentions of the Occupation in the earliest novels, as when the narrator of *Notre-Dame-des-Fleurs* describes the 'bataillons de guerriers blonds qui nous enculèrent le 14 juin 1940' [battalions of blond warriors who on June 14, 1940, buggered us] (*RP*, 48; *OLF*, 103).

While one may consider it puerile for an adult thus to allow his personal feelings to dominate his view of the war, the emotion in question is clearly a vengeful delight at the downfall of French power, not a brutal exultation in the crushing of the weak.

The timing of *Pompes funèbres*, written over the last months of 1944, is also of crucial importance. Genet's earlier novels, written during the Occupation, rarely refer to the Nazis. Unlike writers with fascist sympathies such as Drieu la Rochelle or Brasillach, Genet only expressed admiration for Hitler after the Liberation. He wrote *Pompes funèbres* not when the Nazis were in the ascendant but when the roles had been reversed and the French were no longer in the position of underdog. His attack on the French is therefore consistent with the systematic assault on authority that I am arguing is characteristic of his writing. Working relentlessly to destabilise positions of privilege, it favours not domination but revolt; as the narrator of *Miracle de la rose* says: 'J'aime ceux que j'aime, qui sont toujours beaux et quelquefois opprimés mais debout dans la révolte' [I love those I love, who are always handsome and sometimes oppressed but who stand up and rebel] (*RP*, 477; *MR*, 236). Here lies in substance the fundamental difference between my reading of Genet and those of Jablonka and Marty, whose basic contention is that Genet eulogises power. Marty states categorically that 'la violence de Genet a pour objet paradoxal et pour point de départ l'être-victime de l'Autre' [the paradoxical object and departure point of Genet's violence is the victimhood of the Other] and develops a complicated argument that places Genet 'en position de Maître' [in the position of Master], arguing that his diegetic universe is governed by a 'seule hypothèse fantasmatique de relation humaine: celui de la domination' [single phantasmatic hypothesis of human relations: that of domination] (*JGP*, 35, 60, 69). He thus sees Genet as opposed not to the system that produces Master and victim but rather to the place of victim within that system — 'bouc émissaire' [scapegoat], 'pur et solitaire déchet' [pure and solitary waste-product] (*JGP*, 32) — where he risks finding himself because of his own marginal experience as a foundling and homosexual.[21] His perspective construes Genet's violence and hatred as directed towards the weak and powerless, rather than the figures of authority (judge, priest, policeman, etc.) who in fact consistently provide the direct target of his enmity throughout his work, in both his texts and paratexts.

To defend his thesis, Marty develops an argument that relies on interpreting Genet's words, not literally, like Jablonka, but as meaning the opposite of what they say. This is most obvious in relation to Genet's portrayal of Hitler in *Pompes funèbres,* a singularly controversial element of the text. At the midpoint of the novel, Genet imagines a scene of homosexual relations between Hitler and Paulo, a French hoodlum sent to Berlin as forced labour to work on the railways. The scene is sinister to the extent that it involves a huge power imbalance between 'l'homme le plus puissant de l'époque' [the most powerful man of the age] and the pale, young prisoner alert to the danger he faces in speaking in private 'avec les êtres de la nuit — nuit du cœur versée sur l'Europe — avec les monstres des cauchemars' [with the creatures of night — a night of the heart that was poured out over Europe — with the monsters of nightmares] (*RP*, 638, 646; *FR*, 92, 97). However, its most striking aspect is the equally huge discrepancy between Genet's representation of Hitler and usual images of the tyrant. The worship Hitler inspired was in part due to his success in projecting a public image of himself as celibate, outside the demands of a personal life and free to devote himself entirely to his mission as Führer of the Third Reich. The first mention of him in *Pompes funèbres* alludes to that image; he is described as standing aloof, watching a Nazi parade 'du fond de sa solitude. Sa castration l'avait coupé des humains. Ses joies ne sont pas les nôtres' [from the depths of his solitude. His castration had cut him off from human beings. His joys are not ours] (*RP*, 544; *FR*, 21). The reader, unprepared for the sudden eruption of Hitler at a Nazi rally into the text, may not immediately register the fact that the procession, which includes 'jeunes hitlériens en culottes courtes, mollets nus' [Hitler Youth in short pants, bare calves], takes place in his bedroom. In contrast, the scene with Paulo places the focus squarely on Hitler as sexual being.

The scene is iconoclastic in a variety of ways. It not only portrays as homosexual a leader known for his outright homophobia, but describes him engaging in a range of deviant practices: analingus, fellation, sodomy. Although Hitler controls the encounter and decides on the course it takes, sexually he is in the subordinate rather than dominant position in that he is sodomised rather than sodomiser and, unlike Paulo, he does/can not achieve orgasm. His subordination is moreover endowed with a wider political significance insofar as Paulo explicitly represents his penetration of Hitler as France's revenge: 'Çui-là, c'est la France qui te le met' (*RP*, 653) [that one is France sticking it to you]. The picture Genet paints of a 'petit homme chétif et ridicule' [puny, ridiculous little fellow], with a 'pauvre visage ridicule et bouffi' [poor puffy, ridiculous face] and the general figure 'd'une vieille tante, d'une "folle"' [of an old queen, a 'faggot'] (*RP*, 645, 646, 649-50; *FR*, 96, 97, 100), is thus a highly ironic image of Hitler that profoundly undermines his prestige, contrary to Marty's assertion (*JGP*, 91).[22] Although Marty acknowledges the burlesque nature of Genet's portrait of Hitler in the scene with Paulo, he proposes that overall the humour is 'tragic' rather than ironic because of Genet's insistence, in the sentence quoted earlier, on the castration that had 'cut Hitler off' from humans. He asserts:

> Loin d'être dévirilisante, la castration est au contraire la condition même de la puissance et du pouvoir [...]. Ainsi la castration n'est nullement, dans l'univers inversé de Genet, la marque de l'impuissance, le signe du manque ou celui du ridicule et de la dérision.

> [Far from being devirilisng, castration is on the contrary the very condition of potency and power [...]. Thus, in Genet's inverted universe, castration is not at all the mark of impotence, the sign of lack or ridicule or derision.] (*JGP*, 97)

Marty's argument is deeply flawed in a number of ways. Firstly, by sheer sleight of hand the ironic aspect of Genet's portrayal of Hitler that Marty acknowledged earlier entirely disappears: castration is now deemed 'nullement' a sign of weakness or ridicule, despite all the indications to the contrary not only in the scene with Paulo but in many other examples throughout Genet's writing (for example, as we shall later see, in *Le Balcon*). Secondly, the claim that Hitler's castration is not devirilising is equally unfounded; the comparison Genet explicitly makes, and Marty quotes, is with Jeanne d'Arc's genitals, and Hitler is moreover specifically designated as 'Madame' (*RP*, 652; *FR*, 101). Thirdly, the scene with Paulo contradicts the earlier claim that Hitler's castration isolates him in a realm of his own and hence marks an insurmountable gap between master and victim. The encounter with the young hoodlum is presented as breaking the isolation to which Hitler's castration condemns him. The scene as a whole is framed by a reflection on the randomness of the distinction between master and slave; Gérard, having spotted Paulo working on the railway while scouting youths for Hitler, is aware of the fact that:

> Il eût suffi d'un rien — la volonté de refuser le destin — pour qu'il ait au bout des bras deux mains pareillement sales, au bout des mains des rails de fer, dans les bras la fatigue de longs jours de travail, et avec elle l'humiliation d'être un esclave. (*RP*, 644)

> [It would have taken nothing — the will to refuse destiny — for he himself to have two similarly dirty hands at the end of his arms, railtracks at the end of his hands, the tiredness of long working days in his arms, along with the humiliation of being a slave.]

The scene is then punctuated by reminders, or revelations, of Hitler's humanness (and even, provocatively, his humanity), both on Hitler's part ('J'entourai Paulo de mon bras et me tournai de façon que nous nous trouvâmes face à face et je souris. J'étais un homme' [I put my arm around Paulo and turned my body so that we faced each other, and I smiled. I was a man], *RP*, 646; *FR*, 97) and on Paulo's ('Mais ce mec-là c'est qu'un petit vieux de cinquante berges, après tout' [But this bimbo's just a little old guy of fifty, after all], *RP*, 648; *FR*, 99), to the point where Hitler's most emblematic features (his moustache, the lock of hair on his forehead) 'prirent d'un seul coup les proportions humaines' [suddenly took on human proportions] and 'l'emblème fabuleux du peuple délégué par Satan descendit habiter cette simple demeure qu'est le corps chétif d'une vieille tante, d'une "folle"' [the fabulous emblem of Satan's chosen people descended to inhabit that simple dwelling, the puny body of an old queen, a 'faggot'] (*RP*, 649-50; *FR*, 100).

Genet's portrayal of Hitler is thus iconoclastic as much for its emphasis on the leader of the Third Reich and seat of ultimate authority as body, as for its depiction of him as a passive homosexual. This focus on Hitler as man rather than monster, or idol, is reinforced by one of the novel's most distinctive properties, the sporadic shifts in the first-person narration to refer to characters other than the narrator, including Hitler. By oscillating between the third and first persons to refer to him, Genet subjectifies Hitler, puncturing the aura of remote superiority that the real dictator had cultivated so successfully. A corollary of this is that the first person places the reader in the position of Hitler, obliging him/her to adopt the Nazi's viewpoint and to admit a transitory identity with him. In this way, the representation of Hitler feeds into the book's larger project of highlighting a similarity between the French and the Nazis at the very time France was claiming victory, both military and moral, over its enemy. From its opening paragraph stressing that the German police 'recrutait ses plus terribles tortionnaires parmi les

Français' [recruited its worst torturers from among the French] (*RP*, 529; *FR*, 7), Genet draws attention to the cruelty shown by the French. The novel challenges the emerging narrative that the war had been a battle between French heroism and German atrocity by emphasising the association — epitomised in the main subplot about the relations between Riton and Erik — between French collaborators and the German occupiers, and focusing on the cruelty of the former.[23] But Genet also calls into question the morality of those most vociferously opposed to the Milice. The narrator elects Riton as imaginary hero when he sees newsreel coverage of a young militiaman, weary and defeated, being captured and beaten by a Free French soldier, to the intense pleasure of the audience in the cinema who gloat frenziedly at the sight of the boy's suffering. The picture he paints of a crowd 'aux yeux féroces' [with fierce eyes], filled with vindictive hatred and revelling in the humiliation of a sad, trembling child (*RP*, 562-63; *FR*, 39), suggests a moral equivalence between those French spectators and the crowds at mass National Socialist rallies who, in images that had recently aired in those same cinemas, had similarly given indulgence to their unbridled passions. In contrast, the narrator's behaviour sets him apart from them. Imagining that the boy was the militiaman who had killed Jean Decarnin, his lover who had been a member of the Resistance, he decides to turn his hatred into love, and to affirm the existence of the person he has most cause to consider his enemy. *Pompes funèbres* thus presents, brazenly and perversely, its celebration of the militia in terms of a gesture of forgiveness, an act of charity. Just as the cinema audience's intolerant behaviour belies their claim to righteousness, so the narrator's forbearance contradicts his ostensible praise for cruelty.

What both Jablonka and Marty overlook is that *Pompes funèbres* is a paean of praise primarily to those who refuse to follow the crowd. The single comment where Genet directly affirms admiration for the Nazi project ironically situates that admiration as a feature that distinguishes the narrator from those around him: 'Il est naturel que cette piraterie, le banditisme le plus fou qu'était l'Allemagne hitlérienne provoque la haine des braves gens, mais en moi l'admiration profonde et la sympathie' [It is natural for the piracy, the ultra-mad banditry of Hitler's adventure, to arouse hatred in decent people but deep admiration and sympathy in me] (*RP*, 628; *FR*, 84). (The admiration, however, is not unequivocal; the narrator immediately goes on to explore the contradiction involved in simultaneously feeling shame at seeing 'partir en chantant pour le front russe les premiers volontaires français sous l'uniforme allemand' [the first French volunteers set off in German uniform for the Russian front].) Other passages specify a powerful resistance on his part to the fascist imperative to merge one's individual will with that of the crowd. The narrator distances himself from the communal promotion of evil, speaking of his shame at having mistakenly believed 'que les domaines du mal étaient moins fréquents que les domaines du bien, et qu['il] y serai[t] seul' [that realms of evil were fewer than those of good and that [he] would be alone there] (*RP*, 679; *FR*, 122). A few pages later he develops further the horror he feels at discovering that the pursuit of evil he had undertaken in order to detach himself from a 'monde social et moral' [social and moral world] governed by virtue was no longer a guarantee of (im)moral solitude, but rather something he had in common with many around him. Reflecting on his own relation to his 'époque' [age], he elaborates on how the German occupying forces (and then General Kœnig) had legalised and generalised denunciation to such an extent that betrayal had emerged as the attitude most characteristic of the time. To his great chagrin, the immense effort he had spent on cutting his ties to the social order now ran the danger of integrating him into it:

> Je me suis voulu traître, voleur, pillard, délateur, haineux, destructeur, méprisant, lâche. A coup de hache et de cris, je coupais les cordes qui me retenaient au monde de l'habituelle morale, parfois j'en défaisais méthodiquement les nœuds. Monstrueusement, je m'éloignais de vous, de votre monde, de vos villes, de vos institutions. Après avoir connu votre interdiction de séjour, vos prisons, votre ban, j'ai découvert des régions plus désertes où mon orgueil se sentait plus à l'aise. Après ce travail — encore à moitié fait — qui m'a coûté tant de sacrifices, m'obstinant toujours plus dans la sublimation d'un monde qui est l'envers du vôtre, voici que j'ai la honte de me voir aborder avec peine, éclopé, saignant, sur un rivage plus peuplé que la Mort elle-même. Et les gens que j'y rencontre y sont venus facilement, sans danger, sans avoir rien coupé. Ils sont dans l'infamie comme un poisson dans l'eau, et je n'ai plus, pour gagner la solitude, qu'à faire marche arrière et me parer des vertus de vos livres.
>
> [I chose to be a traitor, thief, looter, informer, hater, destroyer, despiser, coward. With ax and cries I cut the bonds that held me to the world of customary morality. At times I undid the knots methodically. I monstrously departed from you, your world, your towns, your institutions. After being subjected to your legal banishment, your prisons, your interdicts I discovered more forsaken regions where my pride felt more at ease. After that labor — still only half-finished — which required so many sacrifices as I persisted more and more in the sublimation of a world that is the underside of yours, I now know the shame of being approached painfully, by people lame and bleeding, on a shore more populous than Death. And the people I meet there came easily, without danger, without cutting anything. They are as at home in infamy as a fish is in water, and all I can do to attain solitude is turn back and adorn myself with the virtues of your books.] (*RP*, 683; *FR*, 124)

This lament is central to an understanding of *Pompes funèbres* for the very reasons Genet gives in *Journal du voleur* (in passages that neither Jablonka nor Marty quote) for his rejection of the Third Reich. Far from revelling in its generalised lawlessness, his narrator muses over the unease it instilled in him:

> À l'Europe entière l'Allemagne hitlérienne inspirait la terreur, elle était devenue, surtout à mes yeux, le symbole de la cruauté. Déjà elle était hors la loi. Même Unter den Linden j'avais le sentiment de me promener dans un camp organisé par des bandits. Je croyais le cerveau du plus scrupuleux bourgeois berlinois recéler des trésors de duplicité, de haine, de méchanceté, de cruauté, de convoitise. J'étais ému d'être libre au milieu d'un peuple entier mis à l'index. Sans doute y volai-je comme ailleurs mais j'en éprouvais une sorte de gêne car ce qui commandait cette activité et ce qui résultait d'elle — cette attitude morale particulière érigée en vertu civique — toute une nation le connaissait et le dirigeait contre les autres.
>
> 'C'est un peuple de voleurs, sentais-je en moi-même. Si je vole ici je n'accomplis aucune action singulière et qui puisse me réaliser mieux: j'obéis à

l'ordre habituel. Je ne le détruis pas. Je ne commets pas le mal, je ne dérange rien. Le scandale est impossible. Je vole à vide.'

J'éprouvais une sorte de malaise après que j'avais volé. Il me semblait que les dieux présidant aux lois ne se révoltassent pas, simplement ils s'étonnaient. J'avais honte. Mais surtout je désirais rentrer dans un pays où les lois de la morale courante font l'objet d'un culte, sur lesquelles se fonde la vie.

[Germany terrified all of Europe; it had become, particularly to me, the symbol of cruelty. It was already outside the law. Even on Unter den Linden I had the feeling that I was strolling about in a camp organized by bandits. I thought that the brain of the most scrupulous bourgeois concealed treasures of duplicity, hatred, meanness, cruelty and lust. I was excited at being free amidst an entire people that had been placed on the index. Probably I stole there as elsewhere, but I felt a certain constraint, for what governed this activity and what resulted from it — this particular moral attitude set up as a civic virtue — was being experienced by a whole nation which directed it against others.

'It's a race of thieves,' I thought to myself. 'If I steal here, I perform no singular deed that might fulfil me. I obey the customary order; I do not destroy it. I am not committing evil. I am not upsetting anything. The outrageous is impossible. I'm stealing in the void.'

I would feel a kind of uneasiness after stealing. It seemed to me that the gods who govern the laws were not revolted. They were merely surprised. I was ashamed. But what I desired above all was to return to a country where the laws of ordinary morality were revered, were laws on which life was based.] (*RP*, 1186; *TJ*, 102)

He could not live in Hitler's Germany not because he dissents from the regime but rather, he claims provocatively, because he would not be a dissenter there. He dissents from a regime in which there is no dissent. However perverse and puerile his reasoning may seem, however repugnant his refusal to castigate Nazi disregard for a law-based order, he is manifestly not enthralled by its totalitarian regime. Far from whole-heartedly endorsing the fascist promotion of evil, Genet distances himself, literally, from it.

Similarly, his admiration for the Milice is not based on the destructive cruelty for which they are infamous; their attraction for him derives from their social pariahdom. Their principal quality in his eyes is that they are 'haïe des bourgeois' [hated by the bourgeois] (*RP*, 719; *FR*, 148) and traitors to France: 'La Milice était une organisation de gars armés dont l'Allemagne avait permis en France la création, à condition qu'elle fût dévouée au gouvernement français imposé par l'Allemagne et d'abord dévouée à l'Allemagne' [The Militia was an organisation of armed guys that Germany had allowed be set up in France, on condition that it be devoted to the French government imposed by Germany and firstly devoted to Germany] (*RP*, 585). He describes them not as the 'élite révolutionnaire' to which Jablonka attributes their seductive power (*VIJG*, 164), but as a 'stupéfiante association de voyous, lâches presque toujours, menés au pillage' [astounding association of hoodlums, who were almost always cowardly and indulged in looting] (*RP*, 724; *FR*, 153) whose attraction for him lies in their situation as object of the most extreme vilification and exclusion:

> Je veux dire quelques mots de l'admirable solitude qui accompagna les miliciens dans leurs rapports avec les Français et avec leurs camarades et finalement dans la mort. Ils furent plus réprouvés que les filles, plus que les voleurs et les vidangeurs, les sorciers, les pédérastes, plus qu'un homme qui, par inadvertance, ou par goût, aurait mangé de la chair humaine. Ils ne furent pas seulement haïs, mais vomis. Je les aime.

> [I want to say a few words about the admirable solitude that accompanied the militiamen in their relations with Frenchmen and with each other and finally in death. They were considered to be worse than whores, worse than thieves and scavengers, sorcerers, homosexuals, worse than a man who, inadvertently or out of choice, ate human flesh. They were not only hated, but loathed. I love them.] (*RP*, 585; *FR*, 55)

'Admirable solitude': what Genet professes to admire most in the Milice is their acceptance of the position of outcast, deriving from their infringement of moral norms. He applauds them for daring to free themselves of social convention, even if murder is the way they choose to assert their freedom:

> Jusqu'à la dernière fraction de seconde il m'est cher qu'il [Riton] continue par la destruction, le meurtre — bref le mal selon vous — d'épuiser pour et dans une exaltation — qui veut dire élévation — toujours plus grande à mesure, l'être social ou gangue d'où surgira le plus éclatant diamant; la solitude, ou sainteté, c'est-à-dire le jeu incontrôlable, étincelant, insupportable de sa liberté.

> [I am keen on his continuing until the last fraction of a second, by destruction, murder — in short, evil according to you — to exhaust, and for an ever greater exaltation — which means elevation — the social being or gangue from which the most glittering diamond will emerge; solitude, or saintliness, which is also to say the unverifiable, sparkling, unbearable play of his freedom.] (*RP*, 673; *FR*, 116)

Here we approach one of the most original and thought-provoking aspects of this perturbing book. Genet neither justifies Riton's actions by suggesting that cruelty and destructiveness are in themselves behaviours to be admired, nor does he condemn them; he displaces the question of inhumanity away from a judgment of good and evil towards an investigation into the difference between the moral and the human, or what he later terms the distinction between 'le comportement moral' and 'le comportement vital' (*RP*, 740) [moral and vital behaviour]. As a figure of the lowest of the low, the Milice are another instance of the chain of abjectly reprehensible characters throughout Genet's works who incarnate the mismatch between the human and the moral, beginning with Alberto in *Notre-Dame-des-Fleurs*: 'On peut dire d'un homme pourri de vices: Tout n'est pas perdu tant qu'il n'a pas "celui-là". Or, Alberto avait *celui-là*' [we may say of a man who is full of vices: All is not lost so long as he doesn't have 'that one.' But Alberto did have *that* one] (*RP*, 186; *OLF*, 253). Throughout his work, Genet relentlessly highlights that the morally abject are nonetheless human. His emphasis on the fine line that separates society from those it excludes as irredeemable has the opposite effect of fascism's espousal of social hierarchy. His writing systematically challenges rather than consolidates the very principle underpinning the fascist world view, according to which some people are deemed less worthy of being human than others.

Monstrosity, then, is part of what it is to be human. Yet Genet's insistence in 1944 on the commonality of evil does not involve a relativisation that in the final analysis abolishes or dismisses the distinction between good and evil. Rather, *Pompes funèbres* elaborates his own idiosyncratic — perverse? outrageous? — reformulation of the distinction. In the previous quotation, the narrator admires Riton not for being destructive but for having found a way to realise himself, a path towards 'solitude'. He admires him for being destructive creatively. In the French, the same paragraph opens with a distinction between different kinds of evil that appears to situate the decisive difference not between people who follow their destructive impulses and those who do not, but between people who use their destructive impulses creatively and those who do not:

> Mon art consistant à exploiter le mal, puisque je suis poète, on ne peut s'étonner que je m'occupe de ces choses, des conflits par quoi se caractérise la plus pathétique des époques. Le poète s'occupe du mal. C'est son rôle de voir la beauté qui s'y trouve, de l'en extraire (ou d'y mettre celle qu'il désire, par orgueil?) et de l'utiliser. [...] La poésie, ou l'art d'utiliser les restes. D'utiliser la merde et de vous la faire bouffer. Par mal, j'entends ici le péché contre les lois sociales ou religieuses (de la religion d'État) alors que le Mal n'existe réellement que dans le fait de donner la mort, ou d'empêcher la vie. (*RP*, 672-73)

> [As my art consists of exploiting evil, since I am a poet, it should come as no surprise that I deal with the things, the conflicts characteristic of the most moving of eras. The poet deals with evil. His role is to see the beauty in it, to extract it (or to add in the beauty he desires, out of pride?) and to use it. [...] Poetry, or the art of using remains. Using shit and making you eat it. By evil, here I mean sinning against social or religious (of the State religion) laws, whereas Evil only really exists in giving death, or preventing life.]

The distinction Genet makes here is highly provocative; while his assertion that poetry draws on the forces of evil calls for reading in the context of a French tradition that includes Baudelaire as one of its highpoints, his notion that poetry identifies beauty in the most unlikely of places, excrement and murder, remains extremely troubling. Although the distinction between 'evil' (that the narrator embraces as contrary to good) and 'Evil' with a capital letter (that he rejects as contrary to life) initially seems to situate actual, literal murder beyond the pale, it is neither transparent nor stable: the passage (and the book as a whole) goes on to praise the sparkling 'solitude' Riton creates out of murder. Similarly, if killing can be life-giving, poetry — a quintessentially creative enterprise: its Greek etymon, *poiesis*, meant 'making' — can be a form of destruction; force-feeding with excrement is unquestionably a violent, aggressive gesture, calculated to disgust the reader. Nothing is simply what it seems; Genet's writing systematically troubles the distinction between destruction and creation, between giving life and giving death. This is reflected at every level throughout the novel. For example, Riton's career of murder originates in an attempt to assuage hunger; the description of how, starving, he captures and eats a cat (a violation of (Western) social convention that connects with the narrator's taboo fantasies of cannibalising his lover) is followed by the information that the following day he joined the Milice (*RP*, 674; *FR*, 118).

His destructiveness ('evil according to you') and the struggle for survival, for life, are presented as different manifestations — or facets, to pick up on the extended play on the diamond or 'solitaire' instanced above — of the same life force. A later passage declares even more explicitly that the distinction between 'evil' and 'Evil' is not between lesser forms of harm and (unjustifiable) murder: 'Tuer un homme est le symbole du Mal. Tuer sans que rien ne compense cette perte de vie, c'est le Mal. C'est le Mal absolu' [Killing a man is the symbol of Evil. Killing without anything compensating for that loss of life is Evil, absolute Evil] (RP, 735; FR, 162). The difference lies not between one category of act and another, but between an evil that nonetheless creates something and absolute destructiveness.

This difference is something that distinguishes the narrator from the Nazis. In another untranslated passage, Hitler is described as uniquely destructive:

> Poète il savait se servir du mal. Il serait fou de croire qu'il n'a pas vu que la morale selon les principes du cœur, des religions et des mœurs, n'est pas du côté d'un communisme plus ou moins égalitariste. Il détruisait pour détruire, il tuait pour tuer. L'institution nazie ne cherchait qu'à se dresser orgueilleusement dans le mal, ériger le mal en système et hausser tout un peuple, et soi-même au sommet de ce peuple, jusqu'à la solitude la plus austère. Hitler tirait des effets magnifiques par un truquage de l'orgueil que l'on nomme l'art. (RP, 693)

> [As a poet he knew how to use evil. It would be crazy to think that he didn't see that morality in line with the principles of heart, religions and mores is not on the side of a more or less egalitarian communism. He destroyed in order to destroy, killed in order to kill. The Nazi institution only sought to set itself up in evil, to erect evil into a system and to raise an entire people, and itself at the summit of that people, to the most austere solitude. Hitler created magnificent effects by a rigging of pride named art.]

In highlighting the artistic component of Hitler's success, Genet clearly recognises the aestheticisation of politics that only a decade earlier Walter Benjamin had identified as key to the success of fascism. However, his emphasis here is that Hitler deploys his art solely to destroy: 'He destroyed in order to destroy, killed in order to kill'. In contrast, the narrator presents his book as an attempt to create life out of death. A few pages after asserting the association between poetry and evil, he muses:

> Pourtant, si je me complais dans la vue de tant de laideurs que j'enlaidis encore quand j'en écris, dans ce que m'inspire la mort de Jean existe cet ordre de ne rien faire de mal. Est-ce parce que la vie m'ordonne de compenser une mort par une vie, c'est-à-dire par le bien (mot également employé dans son sens habituel), la mort par la vie? Mais si je me délecte dans l'examen du mal et des choses mortes ou mourantes, comment pourrais-je faire œuvre de vie?

> [Yet, though I take pleasure in the sight of so many ugly things which I make even uglier by writing about them, in that which Jean's death inspires me to write, there is an order to do no evil. Is it because life orders me to set off a death with a life, that is, with good (a word also employed in its usual sense), to balance death with life? But if I delight in examining evil and dead or dying things, how could I be making a work of life?] (RP, 679; FR, 122)

The narrator casts his book explicitly as an attempt to follow in the steps not of Hitler but of his Resistance lover, working to wrench some good out of the evil of his loss, to make a 'work of life' (as distinct from a work of art?). Similarly, he later situates himself on the side of good:

> Mais si je montre tant de passion pour sortir du bien, c'est que je suis lié passionnément au bien. Et si le mal suscite une telle passion c'est qu'il est lui-même un bien puisque l'on ne peut aimer que ce qui est bien, c'est-à-dire vivant.

> [But if I display such passion in discarding good, it's because I'm passionately attached to it. And if evil arouses such passion, it's because it itself is a good, since one can love only what is good, that is, alive.] (*RP*, 728; *FR*, 155)

Far from a panegyric on the unbridled lust for power, the narrator declares *Pompes funèbres* an attempt to give life rather than death. Notwithstanding its declaration of love for the Milice, he presents the book as the opposite of Nazism: whereas Hitler draws on art to give death, it draws on evil to create life.

Of course, we may be tempted not to take Genet seriously here. He himself anticipates, and parries, a reaction of that kind: 'Ce livre est sincère et c'est une blague' [This book is true and it's bunk] (*RP*, 676; *FR*, 119). There simply is no logical or internally coherent basis for determining that some parts, or which parts, of the text are sincere and others not. There is no rationale for prioritising only some elements of the text as worthy of being taken at face value. The challenge *Pompes funèbres* poses its reader is not to separate the sincere from the false, the good from the bad, but to grapple with the disconcerting relationship the text posits between them. Most importantly, there are many other aspects to the text that support the view that Genet is not just flippantly diluting or contradicting his putatively 'genuine' views to present a more socially acceptable image of himself (as the defenders of the thesis that he revelled in destructiveness would presumably believe). To return, for example, to his violent image of poetry as feeding the reader with excrement: as well as a violent act, the metaphor makes of poetry a space where the excremental, the unassimilable becomes nourishment, serves life rather than death, just as eating the cat kept Riton from starving to death. Above all, however outrageous and preposterous the idea of mourning Jean Decarnin by imagining an amorous relationship between the traitor who killed him and his German enemy may strike us, the strength of Genet's own poetic achievement is such that the book nonetheless powerfully conveys the impression that its writing is indeed rooted in a deep grief for his lover and constitutes an attempt to wrench something positive and 'vital' from his brutal murder.[24]

This impossibility of distinguishing clearly between truth and fabrication, good and bad, life and death, extends into an uncertainty specifically between political enemy and friend. Far from an unequivocal endorsement of Nazi brutality and its supporters, *Pompes funèbres* expresses a fundamental ambivalence with regard to them. Riton figures this within the diegesis. The young *milicien* stands with the Germans against the French, fighting at their side; but he also rejects them and kills Erik for that very reason: 'les Allemands lui parurent ce qu'ils étaient: des monstres.

[...] Tout en eux était monstrueux, c'est-à-dire s'opposait à la joie des Français' [the Germans seemed to him to be what they were: monsters. [...] Everything about them was monstrous, that is, was opposed to the joy of the French] (*RP*, 744; *FR*, 170). Similarly, Genet's narrator elevates or embellishes the Germans despite or against himself:

> Les Boches — voici ce qui montre bien que la douleur invente toute une symbolique par quoi l'on espère agir mystiquement; j'ai hésité à mettre un B majuscule au mot Boche, par mépris, pour en faire un nom *commun* (les Boches et les Miliciens ont tué Jean que je vénère et c'est selon moi la plus belle histoire de Boche et de Milicien que j'offre à sa mémoire).

> [The Boches — the word clearly shows that grief invents a whole symbolism whereby one hopes to act mystically: I hesitated to write the word Boche with a capital B, out of contempt, in order to make it a *common* noun — the Boches and the Militiamen killed Jean, whom I revere, and as I see it this is the finest story of Boche and Militiaman, which I offer up to his memory.) (*RP*, 743; *FR*, 168)

Genet *hesitates*. About whether to capitalise, and thus dignify, the Germans who killed Decarnin; and hence about whether to engage in an endeavour in profound contradiction with his love for Jean and his respect for what the Resistance fighter stood for. But he also hesitates more broadly between the proper and the common. Elsewhere he even describes hesitation as his proper condition:

> Ma situation est inconfortable *mais elle est propre*. Elle est propre tant que je peux dire ou ne pas dire, encore que durant cette hésitation j'aie choisi de ne pas dire puisque je ne dis pas et pourtant que je ne dise pas n'a pas la stabilité du fait, le 'je ne dis pas' est encore mourant, tremblant: 'je peux dire'. (*RP*, 627)[25]

> [My situation is uncomfortable *but it is right*. It is right as long as I can still say or not say, even though during that hesitation I have chosen not to say since I do not say, and yet my not saying has not the stability of a fact, the 'I do not say' is still dying, trembling: 'I can say'.]

As we saw with the earlier discussion of *Glas*, what is 'proper' to Genet's narrator, his defining characteristic, is above all his attack on property, his challenge to the conventional signifying practices that make the appropriation of meaning possible. While he here reports hesitating by not speaking, as we have seen his writing primarily practises hesitation by speaking in such a way that saying one thing does not exclude its opposite.

The quotation about the Boches is of particular relevance because it links the weightiest of political questions — the narrator's stance towards the German occupier — with a specifically literary question, a question of a letter. Again, many may consider it frivolous to consider the two together. But, as we saw in relation to *Notre-Dame-des-Fleurs*, what is considered frivolous and what serious is itself a political question. I have chosen to end this chapter with a discussion of *Pompes funèbres* precisely because the book directly explores not just the political ambivalences that it identifies at work at the time of writing, but also a tension between the political and the aesthetic. It does so especially forcefully in a key scene, one that the narrator deems 'la clef qui ouvre le tabernacle et montre enfin le pain' [the key that opens the tabernacle and reveals the Host] (*RP*, 568; *FR*, 43), recounting the first time he and Jean Decarnin make love. Afterwards, piqued at Decarnin's calm and the absence of any sign of 'cette peur légère qui fait toujours le fond de la vision poétique' (*RP*, 570) [the slight fear always underpinning poetic vision], the narrator, 'afin de ramener un peu d'émotion parmi nous, ou peut-être par cruauté, pour me venger de sa lucidité' [in order to bring a little emotion back between us, or perhaps out of cruelty, to revenge myself for his lucidity], dips his finger in their 'mingled' blood, and with a smile traces 'sur sa joue droite une faucille avec un marteau rudimentaire, et sur sa joue gauche une croix gammée' (*RP*, 571) [on his right check a sickle with a rudimentary hammer, and on his left cheek a swastika]. The provocative element of the gesture is obvious: the narrator offends his lover by suggesting an equivalence between communism and fascism, accentuated by situating the hammer and sickle on the right and the swastika on the left. But it also brings his own position into view: he differs from Decarnin not because he espouses a different ideological standpoint, but because his trembling 'poetic vision' is at odds with his lover's political certainty and 'lucidity'.

The scene goes on to suggest that that difference is itself inherently political. Surprisingly, the text next recites a poem that Decarnin 'brought' the narrator a few days later:

> *La paume de mes mains refusant tous ces dons*
> *La nuit dansera seule au bord de notre tombe*
> *Une danse arrachée aux objets les plus pauvres*
> *Le pas du sel, du blé, la pavane du plâtre*
>
> *Et des cristaux de soufre. Accroupi dans la mousse...*
> *Quoi, le malheur me tue et me parle d'un pâtre!*
> *Laisse-moi me vêtir pour gagner tes misères*
> *Ces reposoirs de sel des marches souterraines*
>
> *Les bosquets de sapins, puissance des ténèbres*
> *Ton œil. A voir dans les minutes entr'ouvertes*
> *Immobile un galop s'échapper sous tes pieds*
> *A remettre à tes doigts mes armes dangereuses*
>
> *Je te reconnais juste et sainte dans le sang*
> *Beau jeune homme au poignet de qui cent roses tintent*
> *Cette faucille est endormie dans l'herbe noire*
> *Chantant, chantant la mort, les morts de la victoire.* (*RP*, 571)

[*The palm of my hands refusing all these gifts* | *Night will dance alone at the edge of our tomb* | *A dance ripped out of the very poorest things* | *The step of salt, of wheat, the strutting of plaster* || *And sulphur crystals. Crouched down in the moss...* | *What, unhappiness kills me, speaks of a pastor!* | *Let me get dressed to gain your wretched ground* | *These altars of salt from underground steps* || *The thickets of pine, power of darkness* | *Your eye. On seeing, still, in the half-open minutes,* | *A gallop escape from under your feet* | *On replacing my dangerous arms on your fingers* || *I recognise you just and holy in blood* | *Beautiful youth from whose wrist roses chime* | *This sickle is asleep in the dark grass* | *Singing, singing of the death, the deaths of victory.*]

This poem, one of two in the novel that interrupt the narrative, thus appears to be Decarnin's answer to the narrator's reproach that he is overly rational and lacking in poetic sensitivity, especially as the latter goes on to explain that saying aloud 'les mots qu'il prononçait, ses phrases, les poèmes maladroits qu'il écrivit, risquerait de lui donner corps en mon corps' (*RP*, 572) [the words he pronounced, his sentences, the clumsy poems he wrote, would run the risk of his taking form in my body]. The reference in particular to the sickle at the end of the poem reinforces the assumption that the insertion of the poem into the text constitutes an attempt by the narrator to give voice to his (Communist) lover. The reader may nonetheless note that the poem shares some striking similarities with Genet's own writing both in terms of content (the emphasis on the body, the link between men and flowers, the priority given to death) and of form (the somewhat conventional use of the alexandrine, the occasional enjambement, the religious imagery etc.). It also remains unclear if reproducing Decarnin's words in writing is equivalent to reciting them aloud, and if this poem counts as one of his 'clumsy' creations. The narrator himself emphatically declines to pronounce on the poem's artistic merit:

> Le poème, était-il beau, je ne peux y répondre honnêtement ne sachant ce qu'est la beauté. Les mots 'beaux' et 'beauté' dans ce livre (et les autres) ont un pouvoir qui tient à leur matière même. Ils ne signifient plus rien d'intelligible. Je les emploie comme on met un diamant sur telle indifférente partie d'une robe et non pour qu'il serve de bouton. Le poème était autre chose. (*RP*, 572)

> [I cannot honestly answer if the poem was beautiful, as I don't know what beauty is. The words 'beautiful' and 'beauty' in this book (and others) have a power deriving from their very matter. They no longer mean anything intelligible. I use them as one places a diamond on some indifferent part of a dress, not so that it will act as a button. The poem was something else.]

What is at stake in the poem is 'autre chose', but is that to be understood as something other than beauty or something other than a judgment of beauty, something other than a categorical use of language aiming to distinguish what is beautiful from what is not? The narrator specifies explicitly that he uses such words not instrumentally, in order to convey meaning, but as a (beautiful) ornament, a 'diamond' that makes the 'indifferent' — undistinguished? usually unremarked? less privileged? — part of a dress glitter. The poem certainly poses a severe challenge to unambiguous certainty; not only does its meaning incontestably elude any immediate understanding, but the narrator's subsequent elaboration accentuates its uncertainty in several unexpected respects:

> Ces quatre vers, j'ai voulu les mêler à douze autres (comme son sang s'était mêlé au mien. Je sais que ces jeux sont puérils, mais pas plus que les cérémonies de la signature d'un traité entre grandes puissances, pas plus que les solennités de la purification au carrefour de Rethondes, pas plus que le jeu des initiales entrelacées dans l'écorce, pas plus...) ces quatre vers sortant par la bouche de Jean (je tiens au mot) un (un corps ou une âme?) révélaient une âme irisée, mais de tons nocturnes ou très vifs, riches en paysages avec des acteurs aux gestes étincelants. (*RP*, 572)

[I wanted to mingle these four lines with twelve others (as his blood had mingled with mine. I know these games are childish, but no more than the ceremonies of signing a treaty between great powers, no more than the purifying solemnities at Rethondes, no more than the game of intertwined initials in bark, no more...) those four lines coming out of Jean's mouth (I need that word) a (a body or a soul?) revealed an iridescent soul, but one with nocturnal or very vivid shades, rich in landscapes with actors making sparkling gestures.]

The poem is astonishingly declared to be an expression not of Genet's lost lover, but of the lovers' mingling. A mingled expression of their mingling, in which it is impossible to decide which lines are of which Jean. Or indeed if it is an expression of life or of death: the four 'vers' coming out of Jean's mouth could mean worms decomposing his dead body as well as the verse in which his 'soul' lives on. Significantly, Genet situates the mingling on the same level as the decisive actions of 'great powers', including Hitler's insistence that the French surrender take place at the same spot the Armistice was signed in 1918. German triumph mingles inseparably with French victory, but the puerile also mingles with the solemn, personal eroticism with international treaties, playing with language with winning wars.

Genet himself thus proposes an equivalence between power relations at their most portentous and a playful or poetic use of language. But what are the politics of such an equivalence, one which simultaneously and equally aestheticises politics and politicises aesthetics? Nothing in *Pompes funèbres* justifies privileging either of these gestures over the other, respectively deemed characteristic of fascism and communism. There lies in large part the interest of this scene: the narrator marks his distance from both the swastika and the sickle not just in his refusal of any ideological certainty but in his recognition that, rather than either being subordinate to the other, art and politics are different but equivalent.

It is significant, moreover, that he asserts this equivalence in a scene that very emphatically foregrounds the question of genre. As exemplified in previous quotations, the narrator of *Pompes funèbres* presents himself as a poet rather than a novelist (his metatextual comments are even more skewed in favour of poetry than in *Notre-Dame-des-Fleurs*, with only one mention of the word *roman*). But here the poem's insertion into the text makes the difference between narrative and poem highly visible; the poem sparkles in the novel like a diamond in a piece of jewellery or on a dress. Furthermore, the question of generic difference is at issue in how the scene evolves. The context in which the minglings noted above emerge is very clearly the mingling of novel and poem.

Genet explicitly alerts us in his narrative to the fact that he may not be answering 'honestly'. If what is at stake in the poem is something other than categorical intelligibility, what is at stake in the novel is therefore something other than honesty. Unlike a poem, a novel tells fictions. 'This book is sincere and it's a joke': the fictions Genet's novel tells specifically place the relation between truth and fiction in question. If his novel borrows from the poem in glittering undecidably (beautifully), it intensifies that undecidability in embedding it in a further one. He alerts the reader to the fact that *Pompes funèbres* both is and is not a truthful account of reality, while making it impossible to determine which elements of it are 'sincere'. But the relation to reality is the classic domain of politics. By signalling that the novel is *unreliably* grounded in the extratextual world, he calls attention both to its political dimension and to its irreducibility to its political dimension. Genet's choice of the novel is imbued with political significance insofar as his writing at the time presents the form's defining feature as the uncertainty of its relation to reality (and not by the opposition to the 'real world' that he later retrospectively posited). This scene clearly implicates the difference between novel and poem in the relationship it proposes between the political and the aesthetic: the novel is specifically a form at odds with the (political) reality it involves.

Genet's early writing, then, affirms an irresolvable tension between art and politics. Refusing all ideological positions equally, it does not position itself on the political spectrum, but nor does it present itself as separable from political issues or practice. On the contrary, as this chapter has sought to demonstrate, issues of power are the stuff of its dreaming. And his dreaming was an exercise in power. In an archive document held in the Fonds Genet in the Institut Mémoires de l'édition contemporaine (IMEC) and most likely written in the 1970s, he looks back to the time of his beginning to write as one when he was headily discovering 'l'écriture et le pouvoir poétique des mots' [writing and the poetic power of words].[26] The phrase conveys the memory of a real sense of being intoxicated by the early experience of writing; in the throes of the extraordinary creative outburst that saw him produce five novels and two plays in just over five years, he was indisputably more taken up with the excitement of practising his new powers than with thinking through their political implications. The notion of 'poetic power' is nonetheless revealing. The sheer energy, palpable in the passages analysed above, that Genet's writing devotes to troubling hierarchies is itself a piece of evidence that needs to be taken into consideration. His work during this early period is imbued with an extraordinary sense of its own power, with an immense confidence in its own transformative potential. In my view, far from developing a new faith in the real-world impact of the contribution he could make, as time went on his confidence that writing makes a difference was rather shaken. As Chapter 2 now explores, his theatre is haunted above all by the question of recuperation.

## Notes to Chapter 1

1. Jean Genet, *Poèmes* (Décines: Marc Barbezat/L'Arbalète, 1948).
2. Élise Nottet-Chedeville's 'Les Poèmes de Jean Genet: la subversion comme style?' (unpublished doctoral thesis, Sorbonne Université, 2020) constitutes a signal exception to this general rule.
3. See notably David Walker, *Outrage and Insight: Modern French Writers and the Fait Divers* (Oxford & Washington, DC: Berg, 1995).
4. The recent Pléiade edition of the novels restored the 'Adeline' of the earliest Arbalète edition of the novel, whereas Genet had changed the name to that of Divine's mother, 'Ernestine', in the later Gallimard editions on which the English translation is based.
5. Immanuel Kant, *Critique of Judgement*, trans. by James Creed Meredith, rev. and ed. by Nicholas Walker (Oxford: Oxford University Press, 2007).

6. Éluard is of course by no means the only poet whose work resonates in Genet's prose here. Echoes of Baudelaire, Rimbaud, Nerval, etc. enrich its dense texture.

7. This idea can in fact be traced back to William Blake's affirmation in *The Marriage of Heaven and Hell* that poets believe that 'a firm persuasion that a thing is so, make[s] it so'. Hélène Cixous famously pays tribute to Blake for that reason in 'Sorties': 'Tous les poètes savent ça: ce qui est pensable est réel, voilà ce que William Blake avance aussi' (Hélène Cixous and Catherine Clément, *La Jeune Née* (Paris: 10/18, 1975), p. 143).

8. See for example Jacques Rancière, *La Mésentente: politique et philosophie* (Paris: Galilée, 1995).

9. For a more developed discussion of this point, and of how *Glas* countersigns both Hegel and Genet, see my 'Double Signature', in *Resounding Glas*, ed. by Hanrahan, McQuillan and Wortham, pp. 165-86.

10. For an analysis of the link between the grapes and the flower, see my 'Espèces de travestissements et travestissement de l'espèce dans l'écriture de Genet', *Modern Language Notes*, 128.4 (September 2013), 917-34.

11. Sigmund Freud, 'Fetishism' [1927], in *Collected Papers*, 5 vols (London: Hogarth Press & Institute of Psycho-Analysis, 1924-50), V, 198-204.

12. Derrida recalls how Freud's theory is predicated on the assumption that the fetish stands in fundamental opposition to what it represents: 'la chose même en tant que centre et source d'être, origine de la présence, la chose même par excellence, Dieu ou le principe, l'archonte, ce qui occupe la fonction de centre dans un système, par exemple le phallus dans une certaine organisation fantasmatique' [the thing itself as center and source of being, the origin of presence, the thing itself par excellence, God or the principle, the archon, what occupies the center function in a system, for example the phallus in a certain phantasmatic organization]. It is a substitute for the truth: 'Si le fétiche se substitue à la chose même dans sa présence manifeste, dans sa vérité, il ne devrait plus y avoir de fétiche dès qu'il y a vérité, présentation de la chose même dans son essence' [If the fetish substitutes itself for the thing itself in its manifest presence, in its truth, there should no longer be any fetish as soon as there is truth, the presentation of the thing itself in its essence]. As such, it assumes a distinct demarcation between substitute and non-substitute: 'Quelque chose — la chose — n'est plus elle-même un substitut, il y a du non-substitut, voilà ce qui construit le concept de fétiche' [Something — the thing — is no longer itself a substitute; there is the nonsubstitute, that is what constructs the concept fetish] (G, 292a; GE, 209a). However, in classic deconstructive mode Derrida points out that Freud himself already grapples with the limitations of this categorical definition of the fetish. To the extent that he recognises that the fetish is both a token of triumph over the threat of castration and a protection against it, and stresses the contradiction involved in signifying that women both are and are not castrated, Freud registers that in certain respects the fetish is profoundly indeterminable. In order to accommodate this indeterminability, he needs to posit a category of fetishism in which the categorical opposition between substitute and non-substitute no longer holds. As such, his argument constitutes 'une *spéculation* économique sur l'indécidable. Elle n'est pas dialectique mais joue avec la dialectique' [an economic *speculation* on the undecidable. This speculation is not dialectical, but plays with the dialectical] (G, 294a; GE, 210a). Derrida's focus in the Hegel column is thus on how fetishism is fundamentally incompatible with metaphysics: 'Tant qu'on critiquera le fétichisme [...] aura-t-on touché à l'économie de la métaphysique, à la philosophie-de-la-religion?' [As long as fetishism will be criticized [...] will the economy of metaphysics, the philosophy-of-religion have been tampered with?] (G, 289a; GE, 206-07a). The fetish is irreconcilable with the notion of truth as revelation.

13. Ivan Jablonka, *Les Vérités inavouables de Jean Genet* (Paris: Seuil, 2004) (hereafter referenced as *VIJG*).

14. Éric Marty, *Bref séjour à Jérusalem* (Paris: Gallimard/L'Infini, 2003) (hereafter referenced as *BSJ*); and *Jean Genet, post-scriptum* (Paris: Verdier, 2006) (hereafter referenced as *JGP*). Harry E. Stewart and Rob Roy MacGregor, *Jean Genet: From Fascism to Nihilism* (New York & Berlin: Lang, 1993).

15. Most of the discussion subsequently generated by these publications focused on the allegations of antisemitism (see Chapter 4, n. 3); there has been less debate about the claims that Genet had fascistic sympathies.

16. Neither critic engages in depth with *Glas,* notwithstanding its status as a major work concerned with the relation between aesthetics and power in Genet's work by one of France's leading intellectual figures. In the four pages Marty devotes to it (*BSJ*, 183-86), he characterises it as 'tant d'enfantillages', and summarily suggests that Derrida's childhood experience as an 'enfant juif' finds expression in an identification with Genet. Notwithstanding his overall suggestion that the name 'Hitler' is alone for Genet in not having any homonym, he does not engage with Derrida's analysis of the proper name in Genet's writing.

17. This statement is particularly perplexing in that, to my knowledge, Genet makes no reference anywhere to Mussolini or his regime.

18. See my *Lire Genet: une poétique de la différence* (Montréal: Presses de l'Université de Montréal; Lyon: Presses Universitaires de Lyon, 1997) for a more developed discussion of Genet's destabilisation of identity in terms of both gender and sexuality. But of course I am by no means alone in having explored how his writing unsettles identities of all kinds. Particular recent highlights include Michael Lucey, 'Genet's *Notre-Dame-des-Fleurs*: Fantasy and Sexual Identity,' in *Genet: In the Language of the Enemy*, ed. by Scott Durham (= special issue of *Yale French Studies*, 91 (1997)), 80-102, and his chapter on Genet in *Someone: The Pragmatics of Misfit Sexualities, from Colette to Hervé Guibert* (Chicago & London: University of Chicago Press, 2019), pp. 85-108; and Elizabeth Stephens, *Queer Writing: Homoeroticism in Jean Genet's Fiction* (Basingstoke: Palgrave Macmillan, 2009).

19. Henry Rousso, *Le Syndrome de Vichy* (Paris: Seuil, 1987).

20. Georges Didi-Huberman, *Images malgré tout* (Paris: Minuit, 2003), p. 193. See also Tsvetan Todorov, *Face à l'extrême* (Paris: Points, 1994), pp. 131-70, for a related discussion.

21. Marty bases his idea that Genet is antisemitic on the grounds that the Jew is a figure of the victim that he is terrified of being.

22. Similarly, according to Jablonka, 'la figure d'Hitler est invariablement magnifiée' (*VIJG*, 165) [the figure of Hitler is invariably magnified].

23. The book in fact contains little direct representation of Nazi monstrosity. An example highlighting the horrors committed by the Milice is when Pierrot, a youth arrested by the militia on suspicion of belonging to the Resistance and under the threat of losing his own life, denounces twenty-eight people. The first ten he identified were real *maquisards* but then, as he realises more names are expected and he assumes, wrongly, that the Milice would surely not execute that many people, he picks out prisoners whose face he doesn't like; his random malice is then compounded by the indifference of the militia captain who realises that the accusations may have no basis but has all twenty-eight shot anyway (*RP*, 712; *FR*, 142). Riton of course also betrays Erik at the climax of the novel.

24. I have discussed this question in more detail in 'Une écriture retorse: la réponse de Genet à ses juges', *French Studies*, 68.4 (October 2014), 510-25.

25. This hesitation echoes in the repeated use of the image of the swing to evoke the moment of instability where an oscillating movement is at its zenith (*RP*, 680, 759; *FR*, 183).

26. Fonds Genet, IMEC, GNT 6.17 (all such IMEC references hereafter given with the GNT number only).

CHAPTER 2

❖

# Revolting Theatre

Before debating the political significance of Genet's shift to theatre, it is necessary first to consider the extent to which a clearly discernible shift to theatre can convincingly be argued to have taken place. The fact that Genet's plays were published after his novels led to the emergence of a narrative which dominated criticism of his work for many years, according to which Genet followed a linear trajectory from fiction to theatre. In contrast, it is now generally accepted that Genet experimented with writing for the stage from very early in his writing career, even before *Notre-Dame-des-Fleurs* was published; the first contract he signed, with Paul Morihien, included a commitment to publish five plays.[1] The idea of a 'turn' to theatre is not supported by the historical evidence; indeed, Michel Corvin and Albert Dichy make a plausible case in the 'Notice' to *Les Bonnes* in the Pléïade edition of Genet's theatre that Jouvet's 1947 production of the play marked the author's 'entrée officielle en littérature' [official entry into literature].[2] There is a further complicating factor to the idea of a clear break between Genet's fiction and his drama. Genet's rhythm of production is undoubtedly discontinuous, yet the most obvious break — the period of silence that separates *Le Balcon*, *Les Nègres* and *Les Paravents* from his earlier texts — is temporal rather than generic. This is reflected in the number of readings that identify a salient shift but situate it rather within his theatrical production. In proposing the existence of a substantive rupture in Genet's writing between his early plays and what he sees as the 'trilogy' of the last three, Carl Lavery is the most explicit and vocal proponent of this view.[3] However, he is by no means alone in treating these three later plays as clearly distinguishable, in practice if not in theory, from Genet's early writings.[4]

Chronologically, there was thus no single turning-point at which theatre replaced fiction. As a characterisation of Genet's trajectory, it is more accurate to propose that, when he began writing again in the late fifties after his period of silence during the first half of that decade, theatre emerged in a dominant position. This generic dominance is what is new: the contrast is striking with the period of the extraordinary creative outburst in the 1940s in which he had produced poems, five novels, four plays, a ballet and a film. The very word 'dominance' implies a power relationship. How significant should we consider the promotion of theatre to a privileged position within Genet's *œuvre*? Especially, what are its links with the questioning of political power that thereby emerged as the dominant theme of his writing? Genet's last three plays are all explicitly concerned with revolution: the action in *Le Balcon* takes place during an insurrection; the action in *Les Nègres* is finally revealed to have been a distraction from the offstage execution of a traitor in the struggle for black emancipation from white power; *Les Paravents* stages a revolution highly evocative of the Algerian War of Independence, ongoing while Genet was writing the first draft of the play. However, in *Le Balcon* the old order prevails; *Les Nègres* warns of the difficulty of inventing a new language, indispensable to creating a new value system; the revolution in *Les Paravents* turns into a copy of the order it overthrows. More than a representation of revolution, these plays are primarily concerned with the possibility of revolution, and in particular the power of theatre to bring it about. Yet this question of theatre's ability to effect 'real' change, to transform power structures and power relations, is already a central concern in *Les Bonnes*.

Genet's plays, then, are indisputably concerned with politics, and with the politics of theatre. Less clearcut, however, is what they say about either. There is a remarkable absence of critical consensus about their interpretation that dates back to the very earliest studies. Martin Esslin's seminal characterisation of Genet as a dramatist of the Absurd and his theatre as 'a world of fantasy about a world of fantasy' sparked a series of approaches that typically regarded Genet's reflection on reality as a negligible, relatively unimportant aspect of his work.[5] For example, Richard Coe sees the plays' thematic focus on revolution as an illusion, a sleight-of-hand; he goes so far as to assert categorically that *Le Balcon*, *Les Nègres* and *Les Paravents* 'are not political plays'.[6] Contrary to this perspective, Lucien Goldmann argued that it is for their sociological insights, as works of realism in a profound rather than superficial sense, that Genet's theatre is of greatest consequence.[7] In the same year as Coe's study, Philip Thody recognised the importance of the plays' political dimension although, unlike Goldmann, he viewed Genet as 'unremittingly pessimistic in things political'.[8] More recent criticism has questioned this categorical assumption, with a number of studies arguing for progressive readings of the late plays in particular. This is the case with respect not only to *Les Nègres* and *Les Paravents*, whose overt thematisation of issues relating to decolonisation has meant that critical approaches have unsurprisingly tended to adopt a political focus,[9] but also to *Le Balcon*, the play most often cited in support of the view that, for Genet, revolution is doomed to failure because it inevitably ends up replicating the symbolic order it seeks to overthrow.[10] And the debate continues: the two most extensive studies of Genet's theatre in recent years both highlight its political dimension, yet adopt strikingly different positions. Lavery believes that Genet's three last plays mark a radical political departure catalysed by an experience in the early 1950s that forced on the author a sense of the connectedness of all humanity, and made it imperative that he forge a new ethical relation to the world. Taking issue with 'the common view that sees Genet's theatre as politicised without, necessarily, being committed', Lavery claims that the plays written after the first period of silence reflect a shift on Genet's part towards collective practices of revolution.[11] He reads them as specifically involving an attempt to undermine the notion of 'Frenchness' that emerged in response to the movements of decolonisation, and hence to ensure a fairer future for those it sought to exclude.[12] In sharp contrast, Olivier Neveux declares himself unconvinced by such 'lectures unilatéralement progressistes' [unilaterally progressive readings] of Genet's theatre and situates the plays ultimately on the side of the negative, although his study recognises the complexity of the political questions underpinning them.[13]

It is scarcely surprising that opinions should be divided about the extent to which Genet's theatre is political and the kind of politics it involves (anarchic or progressive), given the contradictory positions espoused by the author himself on numerous occasions, in addition to the ambiguity of the plays themselves. On the one hand, his famous comment that *Les Bonnes* is not a 'plaidoyer sur le sort des domestiques' (*TC*, 127) [plea about the fate of servants]; on the other, his acknowledgement in his interview with José Monleón that, even if he was lacking in 'conscience politique' (political awareness) when he wrote the play, 'probablement, la pièce accède à cette dimension' (*TC*, 968) [the play probably makes room for that dimension]. Similarly, his protestation on the one hand that *Le Balcon* is the 'glorification de l'Image et du Reflet' [glorification of the Image and the Reflection] (*TC*, 260; *B*, xiii), and on the other, his concession that, '[s]i Victor Garcia retrouve dans mes pièces écrites il y a 20 ans des préoccupations politiques, c'est qu'elles y sont' [if Victor Garcia finds political concerns in my plays written twenty years so, it is because they are there].[14] In one context, he insists that *Les Paravents* must be read as a fable, not as a commentary on Algeria:

> Le vrai sujet ne peut pas être la guerre d'Algérie. Ma position politique ou morale relativement à cette guerre n'a que peu d'intérêt. Et la fin de cette pièce, c'est-à-dire sa signification morale comme œuvre d'art ne relève pas de la morale courante (dont les fins sont sociales). [...] C'est ma seule sensibilité qui doit me permettre de mettre au point une œuvre ayant sa morale et son esthétique et ne se raccordant que très indirectement à ce qui en fut le prétexte: cette guerre d'Algérie. [...] nous ne devons pas chercher à tirer la pièce vers une signification politique trop nette.[15]

> [The true subject cannot be the Algerian War. My political or moral position in relation to that war is of little interest. And the end of the play, that is its moral meaning as a work of art is not a matter of usual morality (whose ends are social). [...] Only my sensibility can enable me to develop a work with its own moral and aesthetic and only very indirectly relating to what was its pretext: the Algerian War. [...] we should not seek to force the play into too clear a political meaning.]

In a different context, he nonetheless claims that the play 'ne fut qu'une longue méditation sur la guerre d'Algérie' [was nothing but a long mediation on the Algerian War] (*ED*, 41; *DE*, 28). His comments about the political dimension of theatre in general are equally difficult to reconcile, since sometimes he accentuates the unbreachable gap, sometimes the inextricable links, between theatre and (extratheatrical) reality. In the 'Avertissement' that preceded the second edition of *Le Balcon* in 1960, the author declares that theatre makes the actions or experiences that it stages less likely, since staging them 'nous dispense généralement de tenter de les accomplir sur le plan réel et en nous-mêmes' [usually relieves us of the obligation of attempting to perform or undergo them ourselves, and in reality], and that 'l'artiste n'a pas — ou le poète — pour fonction de trouver la solution pratique des problèmes du mal' [it is not the function of the artist or the poet to find a practical solution to the problems of evil] (*TC*, 261; *B*, xiv). Theatre's concerns are not the practical concerns of the social order. Yet just two years earlier he fulminates in a letter to Bernard Frechtman against the 'ramassis de conneries' [ragbag of crap] as reported in *L'Observateur* of a round table (including luminaries such as Jean-Paul Sartre, Michel Butor and Arthur Adamov) on the question 'Le théâtre peut-il aborder l'actualité politique?' [Can theatre treat of political reality?]:

> Ainsi cinq ou six cons se sont mis à table pour décider comment on doit traiter une pièce d'actualité. Comme si on devait forcément utiliser les méthodes de l'autre, et tous une méthode générale! D'abord, sauf de rares exceptions, *toutes les pièces sont d'actualité*. Il n'y a pas un auteur qui ne se préoccupe de ce qui le préoccupe, et c'est lié à l'actualité. Sauf Montherlant, et encore! (*TC*, 919)

> [So five or six twats sat around a table to decide how a topical play should be treated. As if one should necessarily use someone else's methods, and all a general method! Firstly, with rare exceptions, *all plays are topical*. There is no such thing as an author who isn't concerned with what concerns him, and it's linked to today's world. Except for Montherlant, and even there!]

And, in the 'Préface' to *Les Nègres* that he wrote in 1955 but never published during his lifetime, he signals even more emphatically the close connection between art and reality:

> L'art [...] ne peut avoir de vigueur que dans la mesure où il s'appuie sur la réalité d'où il est sorti et témoigne pour elle. [...] L'art est le refuge le moins vil des esclaves. Mais il ne faut pas qu'il demeure désintéressé et destiné seulement à amuser les repos du seigneur. Il se justifie s'il incite à la révolte active, ou, à tout le moins, s'il introduit dans l'âme de l'oppresseur le doute et le malaise de sa propre injustice. (*TC*, 837)

> [Art is vigorous only insofar as it draws on the reality from which it came and bears witness to it. [...] Art is the least vile refuge of slaves. But it must not remain disinterested and destined only to amuse lords at their leisure. It is justified if it incites active revolt or, at the very least, if it introduces doubt and uneasiness at his own injustice into the soul of the oppressor.]

Art is not only inextricably grounded in reality but should be valued according to the effect it produces ('if it incites revolt'). Yet this too appears to contradict Genet's stance in the 'Avertissement', where he takes his distance from artists who 'chantent le Peuple, la Liberté, la Révolution' [sing of the People, Freedom, Revolution] on the grounds that 'Écrits, parfois somptueusement, ils deviennent les signes constitutifs d'un poème, la poésie étant nostalgie et le chant détruisant son prétexte, nos poètes tuent ce qu'ils voulaient faire vivre' (*TC*, 262) [When written, sometimes sumptuously, they become the constituent signs of a poem, but poetry being nostalgia and song destroying its pretext, our poets kill what they wanted to make live]. And the contrast is in turn striking between this dismissal of overt protestation and the excoriating attack in the unpublished 'Préface' on Catherine Dunham's ballets for the total lack of any such protestation. Genet berates the latter's aesthetic for ignoring the material hardship of black lives, with the result that the reality of the blacks' condition 'toujours plus s'irréalise' [becomes ever more unreal], and continues:

> Je ne sais pas si j'aurai l'audace de prétendre que tout acte — et tout geste — nés dans l'humiliation doivent se colorer de révolte, mais il faut tenir pour piètre et misérable un art né dans l'humiliation, la domestication, et qui refuse de rendre compte de la misère. (*TC*, 836)

> [I don't know if I have the audacity to claim that every act — and every gesture — born out of humiliation should take on the hue of revolt, but we must consider pathetic and miserable an art born out of humiliation and domestication that refuses to give an account of poverty.]

These contradictory stances are not wholly incompatible: art can of course convey something of an appalling reality without necessarily proposing a solution; a play can be tinged with revolt without automatically imagining a revolution; Genet's criticisms of utopian revolutionary dreamers on the one hand and of the absence of any revolutionary fervour in Dunham's ballets on the other can be reconciled as different aspects of a single critique of aestheticisation, and so on. Indeed, Genet himself provides pointers for ways of reconciling some of the contradictions. His tirade above that all plays deal somehow with the world to which they belong leads him to the following development:

> Quant à cette notion de transposition, ça me fait rire. La transposition (comme ils l'entendent) ne suffit pas à rendre compte du phénomène poétique ni théâtral. Ma méthode de transposition ne peut être celle de Sartre, par exemple. Mais écrire une pièce étant choisir un fait réel et le métamorphoser en fait imaginaire (dès qu'un fait est représenté, c'est cela. Il n'est plus que sa propre métaphore), c'est donc transposer. Quant aux procédés de transposition, ils varient avec notre psychologie, notre tempérament, etc. Nous désirons tous *l'efficacité*. (*TC*, 919)

> [As for the notion of transposition, that makes me laugh. Transposition (as they mean it) cannot account for the poetic or theatrical phenomenon. My method of transposition could not be Sartre's, for example. But as writing a play involves choosing a real fact and transforming into into an imaginary fact (as soon as a fact is represented, that is what happens. It is no longer anything but its own metaphor), it means transposing. As for the procedures of transposition, they vary with our psychology, our temperament, etc. We all desire *efficiency*.]

Defined thus as the metamorphosis of a 'real fact' into an 'imaginary' one, art unavoidably both has a connection with reality and marks a break with it. The variations in Genet's political pronouncements often depend on whether at any moment he wishes to stress the former or the latter. His comments in an interview towards the end of his life help to elucidate his contradictory position:

> Toutes mes pièces à commencer par *Les Bonnes* jusqu'aux *Paravents* sont quand même, d'une certaine façon — du moins j'ai la faiblesse de le croire — tout de même un peu politiques, dans ce sens qu'elles abordent la politique obliquement. Elles ne sont pas neutres politiquement. [...] Donc c'était une façon un peu oblique d'aborder la politique. Pas la politique en tant que telle, telle qu'elle est faite par les hommes politiques. Aborder les situations sociales qui provoqueront une politique.

[All my plays, from *The Maids* to *The Screens*, are after all, in a certain way — at least I'd like to think so — they are after all somewhat political, in the sense that they address politics obliquely. They are not politically neutral. [...] So this was a more indirect way for me to address political issues. Not politics as such, as it's practiced by politicians, but to address social situations that would provoke a politics.] (*ED*, 284-85; *DE*, 246)

Genet's plays are 'obliquely' political: they are both political and non-political in that they constitute a political gesture (they are not politically neutral) at the same time as they refuse to propose a politics. (I shall return later to the question of time: as the future tense of this last sentence of this quotation suggests, they are also both political and pre-political.) The image of the oblique stresses the disjointedness of the relation, the impossibility of eliminating the difference.[16] Genet's plays are at an angle to politics: although his theatre and politics intersect, they are incongruent.

The idea that Genet's theatre is 'obliquely political' may in fact offer the simplest possible formulation of Genet's politics, a politics that simply isn't simple.[17] There is no single unified political position to which he subscribes. He positions himself at an angle, with a divergent focus that sometimes looks backwards to the reality in which art originates, at others looks forwards to what it makes possible; sometimes stresses the power of the imagination, at other times deplores its inability to realise change (or, even worse, its capacity to work against the change that it imagines: his art, obliquely political, is also politically oblique). In other words, his stance is inherently divergent. The swings in Genet's position point not to an evolution in his thinking, not to an attempt to find a standpoint at which the contradictions could be reconciled, but rather to shifts in focus depending on whether it is what art can do or what it cannot do that is of uppermost priority at any one time. They indicate an oscillation rather than a linear development: the 'Préface', which is the text that insists the most on the political grounding of art (in a first version it even hails the effectiveness of the 'engagements de l'action directe' (*TC*, 837) [commitments of direct action]), predates the 'Avertissement' by five years, countering any notion that Genet followed a trajectory of increasing politicisation of his theatre.

I want to argue that these contradictions are central, not incidental, to Genet's practice and conception of theatre. It verges on the axiomatic for him that art is a fundamentally political gesture. But the evidence also suggests that over time he became more rather than less sceptical about its political effectiveness (as the above quotation from Frechtman shows, 'l'efficacité', which he elsewhere defines as the capacity to 'agir profondément sur l'âme' [to move souls deeply] (*ED*, 119; *DE*, 98) is his ultimate desideratum). The question of revolution emerges in his theatre along with the question of recuperation; it emerges *as* a question of recuperation, at a point in Genet's life when his extraordinary earlier success had inevitably alerted him to the danger that his work could be recuperated by a social order he unambiguously opposed. But why theatre? The hypothesis I explore in this chapter is that the emergence of theatre as a dominant form in the late fifties reflects not a shift from a focus on an individual struggle to a collective one — as we shall see, theatre is in fact for Genet no less solitary an art in many ways than fiction — but rather a new focus on the link between an individual struggle and a collective one.

Many critics have noted that the revolution happens outside or beyond the theatre in Genet's plays. In beckoning to a revolution that takes place offstage, Genet for the first time also probes the relationship between his own work and the outside world. The collective dimension of theatre is indeed a key factor in why it became dominant at that time: not because it allows him to explore a commonality of interests, but rather because it enables him to confront the tensions that set the artistic project at odds with itself. To explore these questions, I will first examine how these tensions are manifest in Genet's views about the singularity of theatre and its difference from other genres, before turning to analyse their traces in some of the plays themselves.

★   ★   ★   ★   ★

Given Genet's general reluctance to discuss his work, his willingness to vouchsafe his opinion about the difference between his fiction and his plays is in itself remarkable. The reason I begin with his views rather than the works themselves is not to suggest either that his observations, mostly expressed years after he had stopped writing plays, automatically correspond to his own practice, or that his plays are best examined through the lens they provide. What interests me is that, notwithstanding the apparent clarity of the positions they propose, they lay bare an internal conflict concerning the political dimension of theatre that will guide my subsequent analysis of the plays. Two texts in particular focus on the specificity of theatre, one an interview and the other an essay.

In his 1969 interview with Monleón, Genet responded to the question 'Que signifie le théâtre par rapport à vos romans autobiographiques?' as follows:

> J'ai essayé ensuite de rendre objectif tout cela qui jusqu'alors avait été subjectif, en le retraduisant devant un public visible. Ma position d'écrivain fut changé dès lors, car quand j'écrivais en prison, je le faisais pour des lecteurs solitaires; quand je me suis mis au théâtre, j'ai dû écrire pour des spectateurs solidaires. Il fallait changer de technique mentale et savoir que j'écrivais pour un public qui serait chaque fois visible et nombreux, tandis que le lecteur de romans, spécialement des miens, est un lecteur invisible et qui parfois se cache. [...] Les gens n'osent pas trop demander mes livres dans une librairie, ils se cachent un peu pour les acheter et pour les lire; en revanche, pour voir mes œuvres, il n'y a pas d'autre solution que de se laisser voir. Mon attitude mentale pour écrire était dès lors différente. (*TC*, 967)

> [I then tried to make objective everything that until then had been subjective, in retranslating it for a visible audience. My position as a writer changed from then on, for when I wrote in prison, I did it for solitary readers; when I took to the theatre, I had to write for spectators in solidarity. I had to change mental technique and realise that I was writing for an audience who each time would be visible and numerous, whereas the reader of novels, especially of mine, is an invisible reader who moreover sometimes hides. [...] People don't really dare to ask for my books in a bookshop, they hide a little to buy and read them; in contrast, to see my works the only solution is to let oneself be seen. My mental attitude in writing them was therefore different.]

Genet's reply to the question is manifestly determined by the play of the paronyms *solitaire* and *solidaire*, situating the difference between his plays and his preceding texts above all at the level of reception. Whereas the reader of the novels reads alone, free to relate to the text without needing to acknowledge or take account of the social context, the spectator's relation to the play is triangulated by the other members of the audience. The tiny variation between the two words generates an oppositional schema composed of a series of binaries: subjective/objective, invisible/visible, single/plural. However, the antithetical relationship that Genet thus develops between fiction and drama is by no means as unequivocal as it initially appears. Especially, the robustness of the distinction between *solitaire* and *solidaire* on which it is founded remains opaque. Is the solidarity shared by the spectators produced by the play, or does it precede the experience? Why would the feeling generated by the spectator's consciousness of being in the presence of the other members of the audience necessarily be one of solidarity? An argument could perhaps plausibly be made that Genet seeks to achieve a feeling of solidarity among the spectators in *Les Paravents*; when revising the play for the *Œuvres complètes*, he even scribbled a handwritten note to the effect that 'Cette pièce doit être jouée devant des gens déshérités mais qui veulent vivre' (*TC*, 1247) [This play should be played before people who are dispossessed but want to live]. In contrast, Genet asserts in 'Comment jouer *Les Bonnes*' that the aim of that play was 'd'établir une espèce de malaise dans la salle' (*TC*, 126) [to establish a kind of uneasiness in the theatre]. And it is impossible to see how the single most conspicuous example of Genet's factoring the physical presence of the spectator into his shaping of a play, his insistence that there be at least one white person present at every performance of *Les Nègres* (*TC*, 475), could be designed with 'solidaires' spectators in mind, if the term is to be understood in its usual sense of denoting the support that members of a group show for each other, arising from their common interest. Furthermore, given the fact that the members of a theatrical audience are considerably more likely to belong to the same class as the mistress rather than the maids of *Les Bonnes*, not to mention the outrage caused by the farting scene of *Les Paravents*, it seems more credible to suggest that, rather than a feeling of solidarity, one of antagonism or discord among the audience or between the play and the audience is the response Genet's theatre sought to provoke.[18] Genet may well have adapted his writing technique in some way to suit the generic requirements of theatre, but it is not evident that it involved a change in his 'mental attitude': his relationship to his spectator is no less hostile or inimical than his relationship to the reader of his novels.[19]

Similarly, the idea that Genet passed from subjectivity to objectivity in writing drama simply does not bear scrutiny. Genet emphasises in text after text that the spectator's response is a profoundly personal, individual one; however public the context of the theatrical performance, the play addresses each person separately, 'alone'. 'Comment jouer *Les Bonnes*' places solitude at the core of the theatrical experience:

> Je vais au théâtre afin de me voir, sur la scène (restitué en un seul personnage ou à l'aide d'un personnage multiple et sous forme de conte), tel que je ne saurais — ou n'oserais — me voir ou me rêver, et tel pourtant que je me sais être. Les comédiens ont donc pour fonction d'endosser des gestes et des accoutrements

qui leur permettront de me montrer à moi-même, et de me montrer nu, dans
la solitude et son allégresse. (*TC*, 127)

[I go to the theatre to see myself on stage (reconstituted as a single character
or with the help of a multiple character in the form of a fairytale), such as I
could not — or would not dare — see or dream of myself, and yet such as I
know myself to be. The function of the actors is thus to take on the gestures
and paraphernalia that will enable them to show me to myself, and to show me
naked, in my solitude and its joy.]

In a letter to his translator and agent, Bernard Frechtman, Genet specifies that theatre
is a journey inwards rather than outwards: 'Que le spectateur aille à la rencontre
de lui-même et non de péripéties extérieures. Le remue-ménage anecdotique est
là pour masquer la pauvreté du dramaturge' (*TC*, 928) [The spectator should go to
discover himself, not external adventures. Anecdotal commotion is there to mask
the playwright's impoverishment]. In the *Lettres à Roger Blin*, he explicitly highlights
the distinction between the collectivity of the audience and the individuality of
the spectator when he calls on the actor to 'découvrir une beauté que chaque
spectateur — *non le public, mais chaque spectateur* — pourrait retrouver d'une façon un
peu hésitante, en lui-même, enfoui, mais capable de remonter à sa propre surface'
[discover a beauty that each spectator — *not the audience, but each spectator* — could
find a little hesitantly, in himself, buried deep but capable of coming back to the
surface] (*TC*, 877; *LRB*, 72; my emphasis).

Far from transparent, therefore, the 'solidarity' that the interview with Monleón
attributes to the audience raises more questions than it resolves. A key aspect of
the term of relevance to this discussion is that the word has specifically political
connotations, as the *OED* definition exemplifies: 'The fact or quality, on the part
of communities, etc., of being perfectly united or at one in some respect, esp. in
interests, sympathies, or aspirations: *spec.* with reference to the aspirations or actions
of trade-union members'. In the light of this definition, it is interesting to recall that
the acerbic affirmation that *Les Bonnes* is not a 'plaidoyer sur le sort des domestiques'
is followed by the sentence: 'Je suppose qu'il existe un syndicat des gens de maison
— cela ne nous regarde pas' (*TC*, 127) [I suppose domestic servants have a trade
union — that does not concern us]. Apparently, writing for the theatre both is
and is not concerned with political issues; it simultaneously involves and does not
involve a shared political response to the dramas it stages. The fact that theatre
brings people together literally — physically, in the same space — is clearly central
to Genet's conception of the genre. Whether, or how, it brings them together in
any other way is a much trickier question. In the 'Lettre à Jean-Jacques Pauvert', the
playwright laments the absence of contemporary plays 'qui lient, fût-ce pour une
heure, les spectateurs' [that unite the spectators, even for an hour] (*TC*, 818; *FA*,
39). But what kind of bond is at stake? The etymological link between the verb *lier*
and religion is manifestly relevant, given that Genet voices this regret immediately
after the often-quoted declaration that the consecration of the host in the Mass is a
superb example of theatre:

Sur une scène presque semblable aux nôtres, sur une estrade, il s'agissait de
reconstituer la fin d'un repas. À partir de cette seule donnée qu'on y retrouve à

peine, le plus haut drame moderne s'est exprimé pendant deux mille ans et tous les jours dans le sacrifice de la messe. [...] Sous les apparences les plus familières — une croûte de pain — on y dévore un dieu. Théâtralement, je ne sais rien de plus efficace que l'élévation.

[On a stage almost the same as our own, on a dais, imagine recreating the end of a meal. Starting from this single elusive fact, the greatest modern drama has been expressed for two thousand years, every day, in the sacrifice of the Mass. [...] Under the most familiar appearance — a crust of bread — we devour a god. Theatrically speaking, I know nothing more effective than the Elevation of the Host.] (*TC*, 817; *FA*, 38)

Discussions of the relationship between religion and theatre in Genet's work have shown how the comparison works in both directions: in addition to the emphasis in this quotation on how religious ceremony owes its impact to its theatricality, numerous studies have explored the ritualistic dimension to his plays.[20] However, these are usually predicated on the assumption that the religiosity of Genet's writing is the element that offers greatest resistance to a political reading. To consider the extent to which the 'communion' (*TC*, 818) he urges theatre should create among the audience may have political implications, I shall now turn to 'L'Étrange Mot d'...', the short essay first published in *Tel Quel* in 1967 which contains not only Genet's most sustained reflection on the singularity of theatre but also his most thorough treatment of theatre's hieratic appeal.

Genet ends one of the sections into which 'L'Étrange Mot d'...' is divided by asking: 'Que perdrait-on si l'on perdait le théâtre?' [What would we lose if we lost the theatre?] (*TC*, 886; *FA*, 109).[21] Left hanging in this way, the question emphasises the refusal of this highly dense, enigmatic text to propose any straightforward answer, in contrast with Genet's categorical, albeit erratic, responses in the interview discussed above. Moreover, the disconcerting expatiation in the essay's two-page final section on the impossibility of ever elaborating a coherent discourse undermines any confidence we may have at that point that we have grasped the import of the text we have just read:[22]

Pas plus mal vécue que n'importe quelle autre mais cette langue comme les autres permet que se chevauchent les mots comme des bêtes en chaleur et ce qui sort de notre bouche c'est une partouze de mots qui s'accouplent, innocemment ou non, et qui donnent au discours français l'air salubre d'une campagne forestière où toutes les bêtes égarées s'emmanchent. Écrivant dans une telle langue — ou la parlant — on ne dit rien. [...] Moi, devant ce troupeau enragé, encagé dans le dictionnaire, je sais que je n'ai rien dit et que je ne dirai jamais rien: et les mots s'en foutent.

[Living no more poorly than any other, yet this language, like others, allows words to overlap each other like animals in heat, and what comes out of our mouth is an orgy of words that mate, innocently or not, and that give French discourse the salubrious air of a forested country where all the wandering animals are screwing. Writing in such a language — or speaking it — one says nothing. [...] Facing this enraged herd caged in the dictionary, I know that I have said nothing and that I will never say anything: and the words couldn't care less.] (*TC*, 887-88; *FA*, 110-11)

Taken in isolation (as it often is), this final section of 'L'Étrange Mot d'...' reads as a comment on language in general, as a generalisable reminder that we are never in control of the message our words convey, that language speaks us more than we speak it (a message that the reader of *Tel Quel* in 1967 was disproportionately well placed to receive). Taken in the context of the text as a whole, however, this final section calls for reading as a comment specifically on theatre. It is framed at beginning and end by the evocation of an ancient Roman 'mime funèbre' [funeral mime] introduced as having the role of leading the funeral procession, being 'chargé de mimer les faits plus importants qui avaient composé la vie du mort quand il — le mort — était vivant' [supposed to mime the most important deeds that made up the life of the dead man when he — the dead man — was alive] (*TC*, 887; *FA*, 110). The mime gestures, acts, but does not speak. Is theatre to be considered as part of language, as an example of linguistic activity more generally? Or is language on the contrary only one element of theatre? In what sense for Genet is the mime emblematic of theatre?

The mime recapitulates a number of the motifs that Genet had advanced earlier in the text. Temporally, the reference to ancient Rome situates the mime outside the Christian era; similarly, theatrical time is defined for Genet by the fact that it 'n'appartient à aucun calendrier répertorié. Il échappe à l'ère chrétienne comme à l'ère révolutionnaire' [does not belong to any identifiable calendar. It eludes the Christian era as well as the Revolutionary era] (*TC*, 880; *FA*, 104). The mime's funeral role picks up on the spatial association between theatre and cemetery which is the text's most developed conceit: Genet asserts that theatre will thrive only in an urban environment that keeps its cemetery in the centre of the city (rather than displaced to the margins), and furthermore keeps it 'vivant', alive, in the sense that new burials continue to be made there.[23] In addition, in 'les villes actuelles' [today's cities], the cemetery itself is deemed the only auspicious site for a new theatre: 'Qu'on songe à ce que serait la sortie des spectateurs après le *Don Juan* de Mozart, s'en allant parmi les morts couchés dans la terre, avant de rentrer dans la vie profane' [Think of the spectators' exit after Mozart's *Don Giovanni*, leaving amid the dead lying underground, before returning to secular life] (*TC*, 884; *FA*, 108). This spatial rhetoric places a relationship to the dead at the very core of theatre. For Genet, the advent of film and television should have the effect of casting the 'fonction essentielle' [essential function] of theatre into relief, in the same way that the technical advances of photography made evident in contradistinction 'ce qu'était encore la peinture' [what painting still was]. Unable to compete with cinema's superior ability to represent the world realistically, 'les écrivains de théâtre découvriront les vertus propres au théâtre, et qui, peut-être, ne relèvent que du mythe' [writers for the theater will discover the virtues unique to the theater, which, perhaps, have to do only with myth] (*TC*, 882; *FA*, 106). Theatre is fundamentally mythical: 'solennel' [solemn], 'spirituel' [spiritual] and 'sacerdotal' [priestly] (*TC*, 879, 881; *FA*, 103, 105), it connects the spectator with the dimension of existence furthest removed from everyday concerns.

The funeral mime thus functions in the essay above all as the figure of an alternative space-time to Christianity, both a reminder of what came before and a promise of what might follow. He is an incarnation of theatre's ability to 'nous faire échapper au temps, que l'on dit historique, mais qui est théologique' [make us escape time, which we call historical, but which is theological] (*TC*, 880; *FA*, 104). By making available a different experience of time that 'chaque spectateur vit pleinement' [each spectator lives fully], however, theatre offers more than a merely spiritual alternative to Christianity. Significantly, Genet describes this interruption of 'theological' time in unequivocally political terms, as a liberation:

> Il fait sauter les conventions historiques nécessitées par la vie sociale, du coup il fait sauter aussi les conventions sociales et ce n'est pas au profit de n'importe quel désordre mais à celui d'une libération [...], c'est au profit d'une libération vertigineuse.

> [It overturns the historical conventions necessitated by social life; suddenly, it also overturns social conventions, and not just for any random chaos, but for that of liberation [...] — it is for a breathtaking liberation.] (*TC*, 880; *FA*, 104)

The liberation is moreover described in unmistakably anti-imperial terms: at issue is the possibility of escaping Christianity's colonisation of both time and space. Theatre has the emancipatory potential to challenge the 'coup du calendrier' [calendar trick] by which, having succeeded 'impérialistement' [imperialistically] in imposing the 'hypothétique Incarnation' [hypothetical Incarnation] as the origin of an era, 'l'Occident chrétien' [the Christian West] now threatens to extend its control of time worldwide. Hence the urgent need to 'multiplier les "Avènements"' [multiply the 'Advents'], to find events other than the 'Très Contestable Nativité' [Very Questionable Nativity] that can serve to count or name time (*TC*, 880-81; *FA*, 104-05). As this sudden proliferation of capital letters exemplifies, what is at stake is literally a question of naming: Christianity's dominance is reflected in its ability to impose its version of history, to name events as it chooses. In this context, it is impossible to overlook the political implications of the marked change of fontsize in the lines that immediately follow:

> Le théâtre...
> LE THÉÂTRE?
> LE THÉÂTRE. (*TC*, 881)

The progressive capitalisation — from lowercase to smallcaps to uppercase — does not just call attention to theatre. Coming just after the quixotic string of proper nouns, it emphasises theatre's power to capitalise, its ability to direct attention, to determine what is important. Genet's text makes very clear here that, insofar as theatre offers an alternative representation of history, articulates a different set of priorities from that of the 'Christian West,' it is intrinsically political.

Theatre's political potential therefore pertains to what Genet deems its very essence: its mythical dimension (which in a previous era might have been called its capacity to touch the human soul — itself a word used surprisingly often by Genet himself — or, today, its capacity to tap into the unconscious). The more profoundly disruptive the theatrical experience, the more it opens up an alternative space to historical reality. In other words, the greater its theatrical 'efficacité', the greater its political impact. Theatre has its greatest political charge when it is theatre at its purest, that is, theatre purified of the mundane or profane considerations that pollute it — the first of which, paradoxically, is politics itself: 'La politique, l'histoire, les démonstrations psychologiques classiques, le divertissement du soir lui-même devront céder la place à quelque chose de plus je ne sais comment dire mais peut-être de plus étincelant. Tout ce fumier, tout ce purin seront évacués' [Politics, history, classic psychological demonstrations, evening entertainment itself will have to give way to something more, I don't know how to say it, but maybe more sparkling. All that shit, all that manure will be eliminated] (TC, 882; FA, 106). As the first term in this enumeration of elements to be eliminated from theatre, politics is itself in the place of the mime, at the head of a procession. I shall return shortly to this privileged position.

Pure theatre, then, is (political) theatre pure of politics. Another paradox: theatrical purity contains impurities. Genet immediately specifies that a theatre free of 'fumier' and 'purin' may include numerous references to them:

> On aura compris que les mots un peu chauds ne sont ni fumier ni purin. Je noterai d'ailleurs que ces mots et les situations qu'ils appellent sont dans mon théâtre si nombreux parce qu'on les a 'oubliés' dans la plupart des pièces: mots et situations qu'on dit grossiers se sont pressés, réfugiés chez moi, dans mes pièces, où ils ont reçu un droit d'asile. Si mon théâtre pue c'est parce que l'autre sent bon.

> [You'll understand that the slightly controversial words are not shit or manure. I will remark, moreover, that these words and the situations they summon are so numerous in my theater because they have been 'forgotten' in most plays: words and situations regarded as coarse have crowded into and taken refuge in my work, my plays, where they have received the right of asylum. If my theater stinks, it's because the other kind smells nice.] (TC, 882-83; FA, 106-07)

Genet's pure theatre stinks. It is anathema both to those who want to preserve traditional boundaries (and it is significant that Genet uses another politically-charged term, 'droit d'asile,' to describe the functioning of his supposedly politics-free theatre) and to those for whom politics is unambiguously a process of achieving the good, eliminating the evil. It revolts those who want no revolt and those for whom the purpose of theatre is revolt. The homonymy in English of the word 'revolting' serendipitously renders an undecidability intrinsic to Genet's theatre: it is both revolting (in the sense of fetid, repugnant) and not revolting (it does not prioritise political objectives), revolting also because not revolting, or not revolting because revolting. Genet's pure theatre is theatre profoundly at odds with itself.

To return to the funeral mime, 'L'Étrange Mot d'...' closes with the affirmation that the mime must 'découvrir, et oser les dire, ces mots dialectophages qui, devant le public, boufferont la vie et la mort du mort' [discover, and dare to say them, those dialectophage words that in front of the audience will devour the life and death of the dead man] (TC, 888; FA, 112). As Samuel Weber has pointed out, this in effect means celebrating his own funeral; a mime who dares to speak is no longer a mime.[24] Weber's main focus is the idea of language as mimicry, as theatricality; he is above all interested in how 'acting' and 'writing' mirror each other. Yet, as indicated earlier, the final section about the mime suggests both that theatre features as a subset of linguistic activity, and that theatre has some particularity that sets it apart. Following the recognition that language never says anything, Genet differentiates explicitly between words and acts in the very process of comparing them: 'Les actes ne sont guère plus dociles. Comme pour la langue, il y a une grammaire de l'action' [Deeds are scarcely more docile. As in the case of language, there is a grammar of action] (*TC*, 888; *FA*, 111). Is theatre like language in being at odds with itself, yet different in some other way? It is noteworthy that in this text Genet never uses the epithet *poétique* [poetic] to describe the *acte théâtral* [theatrical act], as distinct for example from the unpublished 'Préface' to *Les Nègres* or the letter to Frechtman cited earlier where he uses the terms interchangeably.[25] While his emphasis on the hieratic aspect of theatre (mythical, solemn, spiritual, etc.) unquestionably associates it with the resources of the poetic that we analysed in Chapter 1, 'L'Étrange Mot d'...' presents itself as concerned with the singularity of theatre, not its commonality with other creative practices or forms of writing.

This singularity invites reading in relation to the irresolvable contradiction between, on the one hand, its unavoidably political status — as a public intervention, as the actualisation of an experience that inherently contests the norms and conventions that prolong and maintain the established order — and, on the other hand, its inability to achieve political objectives, the inevitability that any attempt to make a political statement will backfire or be recuperated. The 'efficacité' or power that makes theatre a political gesture in the first place is also what deprives it of any political efficacity. Earlier, we saw Genet specify that theatrical time offers an escape not only from the Christian era but from 'l'ère révolutionnaire', historically the principal other recent instance of an attempt to reorder time via a new calendar. Theatre also offers an alternative to revolution in a further sense: 'Il est possible que l'art théâtral disparaisse un jour. Il faut en accepter l'idée. *Si un jour l'activité des hommes était jour après jour révolutionnaire, le théâtre n'aurait pas sa place dans la vie*' [It is possible that the art of the theater may someday disappear. We must accept the notion. *If one day the activity of men were revolutionary dary after day, the theatre would have lost its place in life*] (*TC*, 886; *FA*, 109). Two mutually exclusive readings of this quotation are possible. One is that theatre is a prelude to revolution, an activity that will make itself redundant in giving way to revolution (just as the mime who speaks ceases to be a mime). The other is that theatre is a substitute for revolution: rather than contributing to revolutionary activity, theatre takes its place.[26] One suggests that theatre is conducive to revolution; the other suggests the contrary. Both, however, stress the asynchronicity of the relationship between the two terms: theatre and revolution do not belong to the same time. Theatre is incompatible with revolutionary time as well as with Christian time. Yet there is a striking contrast in Genet's attitude to the two discrepancies, just as there is a difference in his attitude to the various elements of the list of pollutants of theatre in which politics comes first: 'La politique, l'histoire, les démonstrations psychologiques classiques, le divertissement du soir...'. Nowhere in all the paratextual material is there any evidence to suggest that Genet was in any way exercised by the existence of plays that prioritised psychological dramas, or sought merely to entertain. In contrast with his myriad observations on the association between theatre and politics, such plays seem to have bored him, or at best left him indifferent, whereas politics is a constant irritant. Or a constant temptation? It seems that for Genet politics is *the* privileged contaminant of the purity of theatre. Theatre is primarily at odds with itself in being at odds with its own political dimension.

Is this for Genet the substance of theatrical specificity? Is this why theatre, rather than fiction or poetry, emerges as the genre of choice to tackle questions of revolution? Fiction and poetry are also at odds with themselves; yet for Genet they serve best to explore how the human condition is one of being at odds with oneself at an individual level. He calls on them to expose the splits in subjectivity that undermine any pretention to psychical consistency, that endow the forbidden and the taboo with such a potent charm. Theatre becomes preponderant in his work when his concern shifts to the mismatch or misalignment between the individual and the collective, between the gesture of protest inherent in imagining something that does not exist and the understanding that such a gesture may impede rather than assist the process of bringing something new into existence. The interview with Monleón claims that theatre necessitated a change in 'mental attitude' on Genet's part to take account of spectators who were conscious of others around them. But can we be sure which is cause, which effect? It seems plausible to suggest that Genet's newfound awareness of others' awareness is a factor in his privileging of theatre. It is no coincidence that theatre prevailed as Genet himself became newly conscious of others around, that is, conscious of the effects produced by his art, conscious above all that the effects produced by his art are not necessarily those he would have liked to produce.

In his 1964 interview with Madeleine Gobeil, Genet muses that '[i]l se pourrait que j'aie écrit ces pièces contre moi-même' [it could be that I wrote these plays against myself] (*ED*, 23; *DE*, 13), a view he repeats in the *Lettres à Roger Blin*, reminding the director that his plays

> étaient écrits contre moi-même. [...] Et si je ne réussis pas, par mon seul texte, à m'exposer, il faudrait m'aider. Contre moi-même, contre nous-mêmes, alors que ces représentations nous placent de je ne sais quel bon côté par où la poésie n'arrive pas.

> [were written against myself. [...] And if I do not succeed, by my text alone, in revealing myself, you have to help me. Against myself, against ourselves, whereas these representations take us I don't know where, to some side, somewhere that doesn't allow poetry in.] (*TC*, 874; *LRB*, 69)

'Against myself, against ourselves': both individual and collective are split. To the extent that theatre involves a shift from the individual to the collective, the focus in Genet's case has shifted from a divided individual to a divided collective, and especially to the links between the divided individual and the divided collective. Significantly, the interview with Gobeil (which took place before he renounced literature, while he still saw himself writing more plays) suggests that the split between Genet and society so prominent in his earlier work is no longer a focus for him: 'Maintenant je ne suis ni pour vous ni contre vous, je suis en même temps que vous et mon problème n'est plus de m'opposer à vous mais de faire quelque chose où nous soyons pris ensemble, vous comme moi' [Now I am neither for you nor against you, I am here at the same time as you are and my problem is not to oppose myself to you but to make something in which we are caught up together, you as well as me] (*ED*, 17; *DE*, 8).[27] Genet dreams, then, of a collective, even perhaps a 'communion' (to borrow the term used in the letter to Pauvert). But the collective is always already divided, the communion a discordant one that punctures the dream of revolution even as it invokes it. Genet's theatre brings (divided) people together in a divided collective.

To recapitulate, I am in effect arguing that Genet's theatre is itself divided by his own desire for revolution. His theatrical trajectory reflects an increasing pessimism about the possibility of a transformative politics. Already implicitly inscribed in *Les Bonnes*, the tensions between the political gesture involved in an imaginary perspective that differs from (and contests) the existing social order, and the political change that such an imagination can produce, come to the fore in the latter plays. I shall now explore how these tensions can be traced in two of the works themselves, taking into account the evidence provided by different drafts and editions. It is logical that the places where the text did not remain identical to itself are often those where the tensions which interest me are most visible, making a genetic approach particularly fruitful.

★   ★   ★   ★   ★

From very early on, Genet associates the origin of his theatre with a divergence. In the 'Lettre à Jean-Jacques Pauvert', the author presents *Les Bonnes* as an attempt 'd'obtenir un décalage qui, permettant un ton déclamatoire, porterait le théâtre sur le théâtre' [achieve a distancing that, allowing a declamatory tone, would devote the theater to theater]. His theatre about theatre is one that rejects a 'théâtre qui reflète trop exactement le monde visible, les actions des hommes, et non les dieux' [theater that too exactly reflects the visible world, the actions of men, and not of gods] (*TC*, 816; *FA*, 37). It thus opens up a gap within theatre that calls for analysis in light of the play's own lacunary ending: the uncertainty created by the abrupt stopping of the play when Claire, back in the role of Madame, drinks the poisoned tea prepared for her mistress. This dramatic climax owes its impact not to any vagueness over the diegetic consequences of the 'révolte des bonnes' [maids' rebellion] (*TC*, 134; *M*, 12); Solange's final tirade and Claire's closing instructions to her leave little doubt that Solange will be condemned either to life imprisonment in Guyana or to death for murdering her sister. What remains supremely enigmatic is the meaning Genet invites us to attach to Claire's death, and hence what the play suggests about the power of theatre to transform the world.

Today, decades after the play was written and first performed, there is still no consensus about this final question with respect to *Les Bonnes*. There is a strong strand of criticism that argues for a reading of the play as subversive. Theoretically-informed approaches such as those by Jeannette Savona and Cynthia Running-Johnson, inspired in the first case by Foucault, in the second by Cixous and Irigaray, see Genet's transgressive treatment of sexuality and identity respectively as socially transformative.[28] In contrast, another line of inquiry places the emphasis rather on the ways in which the play points to the failure to achieve any such transformation. For example, in Philip Thody's view *Les Bonnes* reflects 'the failure of the socialist revolution forecast so confidently as one of the results of the Second World War'.[29] Christopher Lane too disagrees with readings of the play as emancipatory; he argues that no Hegelian dialectic can be identified at work in the play and he disputes the idea that Genet is in any way concerned with achieving freedom for his characters.[30] Similarly, Marie-Chantal Killeen considers the implications of the violence of the maids' affect at an individual rather than social level.[31] However, while many of these and other studies explore different aspects of the play as theatre about power, there is relatively little direct focus on the message it conveys about the power of theatre.

A useful starting-point for any discussion of what *Les Bonnes* implies for the transformative potential of theatre is the play's own thematisation of this question. To what extent does the maids' play-acting constitute a liberation for Claire, for Solange, or for anyone else? As noted above, Genet ends the play on this question without providing any answer. Viewed from a realistic perspective, Claire's death ultimately represents a suicide that in political terms achieves nothing. Even if the sisters' subsequent state, dead or in prison, is preferable to the humiliation of their situation as maids (especially when exposed as incompetent plotters to bring about Monsieur's downfall), even if it can thereby be construed to some extent as a 'deliverance', the only change achieved is at an individual level.[32] Read realistically, therefore, the play's message is that theatre is impotent to affect power relations. However, as we have seen, Genet insistently demarcates his theatre in general and this play in particular from realist theatre. Especially, such a reading fails to take into consideration the jubilant note on which this extremely unusual 'tragedy' ends.[33] Since there is no counter-voice within the play to bring the spectators back to reality, in dramatic terms the ending leaves unchallenged the maids' viewpoint that their action is a way for them to become 'belles, libres et joyeuses' (*TC*, 163) [beautiful, joyous and free].

In addition, it is important to consider that the ending is itself an outcome of theatre. It is Solange who initiates the 'ceremony' for a second time and who first envisages pursuing it beyond its usual limits. She imagines actually killing Claire-as-Madame (rather than merely acting it); furthermore, she moves to furnish the ceremony with an audience: it is precisely at the point where Solange exceptionally interrupts the customary course of action and opens the window to 'parler au monde' that Claire becomes scared and calls for help: 'Tu vas trop loin' (*TC*, 159) [You are going too far]; 'Solange! Solange! Au secours!' (*TC*, 160) [Solange! Solange! Help!]. Still the dominant sister, Solange ignores her and launches into the long tirade where she imagines a glorious future awaiting her once she has killed her sister: 'seule' [alone], the equal of Madame and Monsieur, acclaimed by all the domestics of the neighbourhood, able to insist on being addressed as 'Mademoiselle Solange Lemercier'. Importantly, her flight of fancy climaxes and then falls away without any intervention by Claire: 'Maintenant, nous sommes Mlle Solange Lemercier. La femme Lemercier. La Lemercier. La fameuse criminelle. (*Lasse.*) Claire, nous sommes perdues' [Now, we are Mademoiselle Solange Lemercier, that Lemercier woman. The famous criminal. (*Tiredly.*) Claire, we are lost] (*TC*, 162; *M*, 40). Solange is not convinced by her own acting, does not believe in the future she has envisioned. But it has convinced Claire, who takes the initiative and commands Solange to give her the poisoned drink. In other words, although Solange herself loses belief in her fantasy, her performance alters Claire's behaviour. Within the diegesis, theatre produces very real effects, transforms the context in which it takes place. As such, *Les Bonnes* suggests that imagining a revolution itself does not merely announce a revolution; it already constitutes a revolutionary act.

Further evidence in support of the idea that in *Les Bonnes* theatre is politically as well as theatrically 'effective' can be found in the fact that the ceremony leaves traces. Some of these are material: Madame notes the makeup that Claire has not had time to clean away, the kitchen gloves and clock out of place in the *salon*, the telephone left off the hook in Claire's disarray after Monsieur's phone call. While these could realistically be seen as an insufficient attention on the part of the maids to the mechanics of staging the ceremony (that is, as a failure of theatre rather than its consequence), Claire interprets them differently: 'Tu sais bien que les objets nous abandonnent' (*TC*, 156) [You know perfectly well that the objects are abandoning us]. She endows the accessories, and thus theatre itself, with an independent force or agency that again suggests a capacity to influence the turn of events. More significantly, theatre also leaves immaterial traces: 'Tout va parler, Claire. Tout nous accusera. Les rideaux marqués par tes épaules, les miroirs par mon visage, la lumière qui avait l'habitude de nos folies, la lumière va tout avouer' (*TC*, 143) [Everything will talk, Claire. Everything will accuse us. The curtains marked by your shoulders, the mirrors by my face, the light that was used to our craziness, the light will admit it all]. Genet's play presents a view of reality in which a theatrical performance alters the world in which it arises, although not according to any programme: the consequences expressly escape the control of those who bring it about.[34]

*Les Bonnes* suggests, then, that theatre changes the world. This does not in itself make it subversive: all changes are not politically equivalent. The play nonetheless hints at the direction it would like the change to take. One of the play's most influential insights, now become a critical orthodoxy due to the work of Judith Butler, is that all identity is fundamentally performative; the fact that Solange plays Claire in the ceremony emphasises that being a maid is as much a role for the sisters as being a mistress. The maids' frustration derives from the limitations of the role available to them in their daily life as much as to any economic disparity. The ceremony is designed to offer the actress playing the maid the chance to revolt, as when Claire tells Solange: 'Tu sens approcher l'instant où tu quittes ton rôle [...] Tu sens approcher l'instant où tu ne seras plus la bonne. Tu vas te venger' [You feel the time coming when you change role [...] the time coming when, no longer a maid, you become vengeance itself] (*TC*, 133; *M*, 11). Solange will change role not because it will be her turn to play Madame but rather because by revolting she will no longer be playing a maid: a maid who revolts is not a maid. Likewise, when deciding actually to kill Madame rather than merely act it, new identities open up for them: 'Solange, à nous deux, nous serons ce couple éternel, du criminel et de la sainte. Nous serons sauvées, Solange, je te le jure, sauvées!' [We shall be that eternal couple, Solange, the two of us, the eternal couple of the criminal and the saint. We'll be saved, Solange, saved, I swear to you] (*TC*, 145; *M*, 22). These roles are further behind Solange's subsequent dream of forging a new identity for herself as 'l'étrangleuse' [the strangler] (*TC*, 161; *M*, 38), and Claire's persuasion that her dying is not a sacrifice but a path to a free existence. The point I wish to stress is that the maids do not dream of being Madame. Indeed, numerous critics have pointed out that the maids and Madame share the same fantasy; before she learns of Monsieur's release from prison, the latter exclaims in words that closely recall Claire's: 'Je l'accompagnerais jusqu'à la Guyane, jusqu'en Sibérie. [...] D'un bonheur monstrueux! Monsieur n'est pas coupable mais s'il l'était, avec quelle joie j'accepterais de porter sa croix!' [I'd accompany him to Devil's Island, to Siberia. [...] With a monstrous happiness. Monsieur is not guilty, but if he were, I would bear his cross with such joy] (*TC*, 148; *M*, 24). The roles of criminal and saint are thus repeatedly valorised within the play. In contrast, Solange explicitly criticises Claire at one point for dreaming of being rich and powerful:

> J'ai aimé la mansarde parce que sa pauvreté m'obligeait à de pauvres gestes. [...] Rien ne nous forçait à un geste trop beau. Mais rassure-toi, tu pourras continuer en prison à faire ta souveraine, ta Marie-Antoinette, te promener la nuit dans l'appartement [...]. Enveloppée dans les rideaux ou le couvre-lit de dentelle, n'est-ce pas ? Se contemplant dans les miroirs, se pavanant au balcon et saluant à 2 heures du matin le peuple accouru défiler sous ses fenêtres.

> [I like the garret because it was plain and I didn't have to put on a show. [...] Nothing forced us to make pretty gestures. Don't worry, you'll be able to go on playing queen, playing at Marie-Antoinette, strolling about the apartment at night. [...] Wrapped in the curtains or the lace bedcover. Oh no! Looking at herself in the mirrors, strutting on the balcony at two in the morning, and greeting the populace which has turned out to parade beneath her windows.] (*TC*, 137-38; *M*, 15)[35]

The play therefore contains its own hierarchy of fantasy in that it presents some fantasies as more desirable than others. Identifying with privilege (and thus leaving the social hierarchy intact) is represented as shameful, whereas the roles of criminal and saint, both of which can be argued to contest the social order (*ED*, 20; *DE*, 10), are endorsed several times.

Evidence from the first version of *Les Bonnes* published in 1947 and from other genetic material available for consultation suggests that Genet's reworking of the play progressively de-emphasised this element of explicit social criticism attacking the existent social order. Fragments of typescripts dating back to Jouvet's first production, containing versions of the scene between Claire and Madame when Solange has gone to call a taxi, and the final scene between the two maids, are particularly revealing. They emphasise the power dynamic between the maids and Madame more overtly than in the definitive edition. The disparity of condition is intensified in that Madame specifies that the two sisters had been 'des pauvres filles de l'Assistance publique' (*TC*, 201) [poor girls fostered by social services], the only recorded mention of the Assistance publique in Genet's works, other than the famous paragraph about his birth in *Journal du voleur*. Madame is also painted as more needy of the maids' gratitude and more invested in accentuating the gap between them in that she obliges Claire to recite the full litany of her own 'bontés' [kindnesses] that in the final version Claire only recites bitterly after her departure (*TC*, 207). The fragments are also notable for their use of expressions or themes that Genet will later explicitly repudiate. Most strikingly, and in sharp contrast with his comments in 'Comment jouer *Les Bonnes*', they specifically reference trade-union activity: 'Quand, le mois dernier, les gens de maison décidèrent de présenter une pétition pour l'augmentation des gages, il n'y eut que deux bonnes pour refuser, ma sœur et moi' (*TC*, 208) [Last month, when domestic staff decided to present a petition for better wages, only two maids refused: my sister and I]. Genet's later trenchant dismissal of any dimension of social advocacy in his play may be an indication that he was not always so wholly persuaded of its irrelevance as he would have us believe.

The fragments also directly propose an instrumentalisation of theatre that disappears in the later versions. It is Claire rather than Solange who has the idea of relaunching the ceremony:

> CLAIRE:    Nous n'avons plus de chance qu'en nous-mêmes.
> SOLANGE:    Des mots! Ce ne sont que des mots.
> C:    Des mots. Mais terribles et qui vont nous mener par-delà la honte. Solange, nous serons plus fortes que les tribunaux. Nous nous embourberons nous-mêmes...
> S:    Que veux-tu? Précise.
> C:    Une scène. Je veux une scène, Solange. La dernière.
> S:    Mais tu es folle! À quoi peut-elle nous mener? Hein? Claire? À quoi peut-elle nous servir maintenant?
> C:    Je ne sais pas. J'avoue ne pas le savoir au juste, mais je suis sûre d'y trouver des indications pour notre sort. [...]
> S:    Je te le demande, où cela peut-il nous conduire? Vers quelle solution? Il serait plus simple de nous tuer tout de suite toutes les deux ou fuir...
> C:    Tu te trompes, Solange. Nous devons d'abord survivre à notre défaite.
> S:    Pourquoi? Le bateau...
> C:    Pourquoi? Je ne sais pas. Pour avoir accompli une belle chose peut-être.
> (*TC*, 209-10)

> [C:    Our only chance now is in ourselves.
> S:    Words! That's only words.
> C:    Words. But terrible ones, that will lead us out of shame. Solange, we will be stronger than the courts. We will sink ourselves in the mud...
> S:    What do you want? Be more clear.
> C:    A scene. I want one more scene, Solange. The last one.
> S:    You are mad! Where would that bring us? Hah? Claire? What good would that do us now?
> C:    I don't know. I admit I don't know precisely, but I'm sure it would give us a clue for our fate. [...]

s:    I ask you, where would that lead us? To what solution? It would be
easier just to kill ourselves immediately or to flee...
    c:    You are mistaken, Solange. First we have to survive our defeat.
    s:    Why? The boat...
    c:    Why? I don't know. To have done something beautiful perhaps.]

Acting, 'une scène', is depicted here as a sure way of escape, a step towards an as-yet-unknown but promising 'solution'. In other words, Genet here openly deploys the idea that theatre serves an end other than itself, an idea that remains only implicit in the final version where the focus shifts rather to the beauty of the thing itself, leaving its consequences a matter of conjecture. In the fragment, the ceremony is adopted with a teleological objective (that of providing a 'solution'), rather than the 'solution' emerging as a possibility from the ceremony.

The version published in 1947 marks a step closer in this respect to the definitive edition. Solange escorts Claire offstage prior to her long tirade, with the result that the audience does not know whether she is imagining having killed Claire or has really done so. As in the final edition, Solange's soliloquy proves determining insofar as it convinces Claire to drink the poisoned tea. However, it is only towards the end of the soliloquy that Claire's reappearance onstage dissolves the audience's uncertainty as to whether she is alive or dead. As a result, the focus is inevitably more on the difficulty of deciding between falsehood and truth, life and death, and correspondingly less on the agency of theatre. This is compounded at the very end of the play, as Claire drinks the tea, by Solange delivering another soliloquy in which she imagines Madame's return home:

Madame monte en voiture. À l'oreille, Monsieur lui chuchote des mots d'amour. Elle voudrait sourire, mais elle est morte. [...] Madame monte l'escalier. Elle entre chez elle: or, Madame est morte. Ses deux bonnes sont vivantes: elles viennent de surgir, délivrées de la forme glacée de Madame. Auprès d'elles toutes les bonnes furent présentes — non elles-mêmes, mais plutôt l'angoisse infernale de leurs noms. Sauf qu'il ne reste d'elles, pour flotter autour du cadavre léger de Madame, que le délicat parfum des saintes filles qu'elles furent en secret. Nous sommes belles, libres, ivres et joyeuses!

[Madame steps into the car. Monsieur is whispering sweet nothings into her ear. She would like to smile, but she is dead. [...] Madame goes up the stairs. She enters her flat — but, Madame is dead. Her two maids are alive: they've just risen up, free from Madame's icy form. All the maids were present at her side — not they themselves, but rather the hellish agony of their names. And all that remains of them to float about Madame's airy corpse is the delicate perfume of the holy maidens which they were in secret. We are beautiful, joyous, drunk and free!] (TC, 199; M, 42)

The 1947 edition thus concludes on a more decisive, less ambiguous, note than the definitive version; only the last sentence of this quotation survives in the latter, uttered earlier by Claire as she instructs her sister how to proceed following her death. This final speech not only projects a signally better future for the individual maids but also articulates the symbolic consequences of their acting/actions that the later edition precisely leaves unspecified. In particular, the repeated statement that

'Madame is dead' amounts to asserting that the maids have succeeded in modifying the social order. However one interprets the passage, it suggests that the ceremony has produced effects that reach far beyond it. Whether one reads the subjects of the two iterations of the statement as the same or different, whether one takes the claim that Madame is dead literally or figuratively, the text proposes a blurring of the distinction between the imaginary 'Madame' and the 'real' one that later disappears, and hence suggests more forcefully than the definitive edition that the real is vulnerable to the imaginary, that the figurative affects what happens literally, that the maids have achieved not only their own emancipation but a step in the wider symbolic liberation of 'toutes les bonnes'.

The earlier stages of *Les Bonnes* consequently support the idea of an a priori assumption on Genet's part that theatre can have a subversive impact on the outside world. While the final version still leaves this possibility open, his revisions show a shift in focus: the emphasis is placed less on the solution to which theatre might lead and more on the act of fantasising liberation; less on theatre as an instrument of liberation and more on theatre as an end in itself. His pruning away in the definitive edition of any clear indication that the outcome of the ceremony fulfils the maids' ambitions indicates a deepening awareness of the complexities in the relationship between art and politics that will come to the fore in his next published text, *Le Balcon*. As noted earlier, this play thematises revolution for the first time in Genet's work; insurrectionary activity provides the frame for the action in both *Le Balcon* and *Les Nègres*, written concurrently although published with a two-year gap between them. If *Le Balcon* remains the single work by Genet about which opinions are most divided, it is because its exploration of the complex relations between the brothel, the social order and revolution is exceptionally ambiguous.[36] But analysis suggests that it is also because Genet himself was torn: both tempted by revolution and sceptical that it could ever be achieved.

As in *Les Bonnes*, much hinges on the interpretation of the play's final attack on authority. The concluding scene is generally accepted as marking the consolidation of the grip on power of the forces upholding the status quo when Roger, the principal insurrectionary figure, becomes the first client of the brothel to request to play the role of Chief of Police, enabling the (real) Chief of Police to declare: 'Messieurs, j'appartiens à la Nomenclature' [Gentlemen, I belong to the Nomenclature] (*TC*, 340; *B*, 94).[37] It is not only the Chief of Police whose status has changed to equal that of the Évêque, the Juge and the Général, whose symbolic power is established in the play's opening scenes in clients' willingness to pay to play those roles. The Chief's elevation within the system changes the system itself: unlike the earlier two instances of the word ('je ne vais pas vous énumérer la nomenclature' (*TC*, 287) [I'm not going to list the nomenclature for you], 'la nomenclature des bordels' (*TC*, 388) [the nomenclature of brothels]), the capital letter of 'Nomenclature' marks a shift in the status of the very system of naming. An order in which the Chief of Police exercises a fascination or seduction equal to that of older figures of power is qualitatively different from the regime it restores.[38] As such, the attempt at revolution has strengthened rather than weakened the order it sought to overturn.

However, the concluding scene also stages a (renewed) opposition to the power it consolidates; the establishment of the new figure of power simultaneously opens him to attack. As numerous critics have recognised, Roger's castration of himself in the role of Chief of Police is analogous in many respects to Claire's drinking the poison in *Les Bonnes*. Unlike the earlier play, *Le Balcon* gives a pointer to the impact of the gesture when the Chief checks his own genitals and asks: 'Alors, qui de nous deux est foutu? Lui ou moi? Et si, dans chaque bordel du monde entier, mon image était châtrée, moi, je reste intact' (*TC*, 347) [So which of us is done for? Him or me? Even if, in every brothel of the whole world, my image is castrated, I remain intact]. The interpretation of this scene remains supremely ambiguous; nonetheless, one thing it clearly proposes is a separation between the 'real' Chief and the image of him that henceforward circulates. This indubitably lends support to the reading that the counter-revolution has triumphed insofar as Roger's action succeeds only in paying tribute to the powerful attraction exerted by the figure of the Chief of Police; it does not impede the ability of the police to impose order as they wish. His attack on the image of the police can be read as a figure of both the impotence of revolution and the power of the police, especially in the light of Genet's description of the play at the end of 'Comment jouer *Le Balcon*' as the 'glorification de l'Image et du Reflet' [glorification of the Image and the Reflection] (*TC*, 260; *B*, xiii).[39] This description commonly serves as a starting-point to explore the complex net of relations staged in the play as a set of mirrors that, endlessly reflecting each other, not only make it impossible to separate reality from appearance but also present different aspects of reality as figures of each other: the brothel is a reflection of society as a whole; reality outside the Balcony is as theatrical as the 'maison d'illusions', as the brothel is called; the social order and the revolution are mirror images of each other, etc. Chantal is exemplary in this respect: an ex-prostitute who 'incarne' [incarnates] the revolution (*TC*, 312) and figures a saint in ways that explicitly parallel the Immaculate Conception played by Carmen in the Balcony (Roger protests that she 'échappe et grimpe au ciel' (*TC*, 311) [escapes and ascends into the sky]), her ability to inspire the revolutionaries derives directly from the brothel: 'Le bordel m'aura au moins servi, car c'est lui qui m'a enseigné l'art de feindre et de jouer' (*TC*, 314) [The brothel will at least have been some use to me, for it taught me how to pretend and play]. When the insurgents come to take her away from Roger to motivate their fighters, they present it as a financial transaction: 'Si on l'emmène, on la loue' [If we take her away, we will hire her] (*TC*, 311; *B*, 56). Their proposal to 'pay' Roger for her services by offering him a hundred women in exchange makes him equivalent to Irma, who as brothel-owner reaps benefit from the sale of women's bodies. The signal this gives that women function as objects of exchange for the revolutionaries in the same way as in the order they seek to overturn echoes comically in the difference of perspective between Chantal and the two men:

> ROGER:    Chantal appartient...
> CHANTAL:    À personne!
> ROGER:    ...à ma section.
> L'HOMME:    À l'insurrection!

[ROGER:   Chantal belongs...
CHANTAL:    To nobody!
ROGER:   ...to my section.
MAN:   To the insurrection!] (*TC*, 311; *B*, 55)

As well as the language and the images of the brothel, the revolutionaries replicate its commodification of women's bodies.

This scene with the revolutionaries (scene 6) is by a substantial margin the scene that underwent the most modifications over the course of writing the play, an indication that the relation of the brothel/theatre to its revolutionary outside (scene 6 alone is set outside the 'maison d'illusions') was not a question easily settled for Genet. In the definitive 1968 version, it is predominantly a love scene between Roger and Chantal, with a focus mainly on the conflict of interest between their love and the demands of the revolutionary struggle. Roger resents the use of Chantal as a political emblem: 'Elle n'est plus une femme. [...] C'est pour lutter contre une image que Chantal s'est figée en image. La lutte ne se passe plus dans la réalité, mais en champ clos' (*TC*, 312) [She is no longer a woman. [...] To fight against an image, Chantal set into an image. The struggle no longer takes place in reality, but in a closed field]. This version channels a pessimistic view of the revolution on two counts: the needs of the individual are at odds with those of the collective; and the revolution is presented as subject to the law of eternal recurrence, so that the attempt to combat the social order with its own weapons can only fail to achieve social transformation. Earlier versions were more complex, developing substantial contradictions both on the part of Roger as an individual and between him and the other revolutionaries. In addition to Roger's jealousy at the revolution taking Chantal away from him, the genetic material available explores an inconsistency between what he claims to believe and his actions. In all the versions, Roger is the character most suspicious of the image. Yet a dialogue in the earliest manuscript draft has Henri (who becomes 'L'Homme' in subsequent versions) claim that this is because he is all too susceptible to its appeal: 'Ce n'est pas contre la misère que tu te révoltes, n'est-ce pas? C'est contre l'image. Parce que tu y es sensible. Si la Reine t'apparaissait, ici, toi personnellement, tu saluerais' [It's not poverty you're revolting against, is it? It's the image. Because you are susceptible to it. If the Queen appeared here to you personally, you would bow].[40] And he later alleges, in a comment that adumbrates the description of the image of the Chief of Police as 'Hero', that, notwithstanding his mistrust of the image, Roger too assumes a pose: 'Tu t'es fixé dans une attitude héroïque, selon une image de toi que tu dis chérir, et, en moins de dix secondes, tu as proposé à l'officier une définition sublime de toi-même' (*TC*, 441) [You took on a fixed heroic attitude, with an image of yourself that you claim to love and, in less than ten seconds, you proposed a sublime definition of yourself to the officer].

Interestingly, these complexities disappear in the 1956 edition only to reappear more strongly in the version of the scene in the 1960 edition, before being cut again in 1962. In the 1960 scene, over twice the length of its previous (and later) iterations, Genet increases the number of revolutionaries to ten, and expands at length on the differences between them. Roger, 'type du chef prolo' (*TC*, 422) [typical prolo chief], is in conflict with his comrades not only because he is opposed to using Chantal as an emblem, but also because he disapproves of the pleasure they patently take in the struggle itself: 'Si par malheur on prenait du plaisir à tirer dans les bouteilles et dans les hommes, adieu l'esprit révolutionnaire' (*TC*, 425) [If unfortunately we took pleasure in shooting at bottles and men, it would be goodbye to the revolutionary spirit]. This repressive element — a vestige of which survives in the definitive edition in Irma's dismissal of the revolutionaries as 'des ouvriers. Sans imagination. Prudes, et peut-être chastes' [workers. With no imagination. Prudes, and possibly even chaste] (*TC*, 295; *B*, 38) — inclines Roger towards a utilitarian rationalism:

> ROGER, *pédant*:    Si on se conduit comme ceux d'en face, on est ceux d'en face. Au lieu de changer le monde on ne réussira que le reflet de celui qu'on veut détruire.
> GEORGETTE, *même ton*:    Tout doit être dirigé vers l'utilité.
> ROGER:    En nous servant de la séduction, on risque d'être soi-même happé par celle qu'exercent les autres. Il vaut mieux rester immobile et silencieux, plutôt que dire une phrase ou faire un geste qui ne seraient pas utilisables...
> GEORGETTE, *même ton*:    ... en fonction de la révolution.

> [ROGER, *pedantically*:    If we behave like the other side, then we *are* the other side. Instead of changing the world, all we'll achieve is a reflection of the one we want to destroy.
> GEORGETTE, *in the same tone*:    Everything must be aimed at utility.
> ROGER:    If we use seduction, we risk being caught ourselves by that exercise by others. It's better to remain silent and motionless than to say or do anything that can't be utilized...
> GEORGETTE, *in the same tone*:    ...for the revolution.] (*TC*, 426; *B*, 53)

From this perspective, the revolutionary struggle must not only resist the seduction of the social order, but indeed resist seduction per se: 'Il ne faut plus séduire mais servir' (*TC*, 429) [We must no longer be seductive but useful]. Not only is politics separable from art (and all associated with it: image, song, etc.), but for the revolution to be effective, they must remain separate. As one of the other revolutionaries points out, Roger's fantasy is that a fantasy-free revolution is possible: 'Tu rêves. D'une révolution impossible, qui se passerait dans la froide raison. Tu es fasciné par elle comme ceux d'en face par d'autres jeux' (*TC*, 433) [You are dreaming. Of an impossible revolution, one that would take only in cold reason. You are fascinated by it just as those across the way are fascinated by other games].

The 1960 version thus elaborates in detail on two opposing revolutionary positions. On the one hand, the utilitarian, rationalist one of Roger and Georgette (whose espousal of Roger's positions is later suggested ironically to be due not to his rational argument but to the attraction she feels for him); on the other, the position exemplified by Marc's declaration: 'À leur carnaval, nous allons opposer le nôtre' [We must counter their carnival with our own] (*TC*, 431; *B*, 56). Whereas the latter believes that the revolution needs to find a different image, or 'chant' [song], from those underpinning the social order, the former believes that recourse to any image is inconsistent with the 'revolutionary spirit' and liable to be recuperated. Genet's choice of names accentuates this division. Georgette's name links her with the Chief of Police, Georges, a name largely anagrammatised in Roger. Of the others, Henri and Louis bear the names of French kings, Marc and Luc those of Evangelists (like Jean), associating them rather with the old-established powers of the monarchy and church. Whereas the thrust of the definitive edition is to signal that the revolution will replicate the order it contests, in this earlier version a split between the revolutionaries mirrors the division between the older and newer figures of the 'Nomenclature'.

Significantly, Chantal has reservations about both positions: 'Il s'en faut d'un cheveu que je ne sois plus des vôtres. Pourtant, je ne peux pas non plus être de l'autre côté, et moi je veux chanter' (*TC*, 429) [I'm coming within an inch of no longer being with you. However, I can't either be on the other side, and I want to sing]. I would suggest that her stance invites reading as a figure of the author's, a suggestion that finds further support in the Chief of Police's statement in scene 7 that, 'comme moi, elle n'a ni père ni mère' (*TC*, 322) [like me, she has neither father nor mother]. The conflicting directions taken in Genet's reworking of the scene with the revolutionaries — developing positions he had previously removed, only to excise them again later — suggest that it posed particular challenges for him. His revisions lead to the inference that, while ultimately unwilling to sacrifice the desire to sing, he was unwilling also to sacrifice the possibility that singing may serve a revolutionary purpose. Significantly, the last paragraph in the 'Avertissement' quoted earlier is a truncated version of Marc's final speech in this 1960 version, which ends with a positive injunction to prepare 'des poèmes et des images, non qui comblent mais qui énervent' (*TC*, 435) [poems and pictures which leave us worked up rather than satisfied]. In another draft of the scene, Roger is hostile not to the image per se but to the images presented by his enemies: 'ceux que je vise de plus en plus se confondent avec des images de bordel, au point qu'on ne sait plus où l'on est' (*TC*, 438) [those I'm targeting more and more are confused with the images of the brothel, to such a point that we no longer know where we are]. When his comrade points out that the same is true of the revolution, Chantal having become a symbol of the 'Colère majuscule' [capital letter Anger] into which the people, 'dans sa révolte, a grossi sa colère' (*TC*, 438) [in its revolt amplified its anger], Roger tries to differentiate between poems that serve the revolution and those that do not:

> ROGER:   ...d'abord il y a des poèmes qui entraînent à la révolte. Quand ils ont servi on les déchire...
> L'HOMME:   S'ils sont en papier, oui. Mais s'ils continuent de vivre?... Tu ne réponds pas. Eh bien, s'ils continuent de vivre, ils se dégradent. Ils perdent les forces révolutionnaires. Ils deviennent ornement s'ils sont écrits: s'ils sont vécus, ils deviennent personnages de bordel...
> ROGER:   Tu veux dire?
> L'HOMME:   Rien du tout. Je te laisse penser ce que tu veux. (*TC*, 438)

> [ROGER:   ...first there are poems that incite revolt. When they've served their purpose they can be torn up...

MAN:    If they're in paper, yes. But if they go on living?... You don't answer.
Well, if they go on living, they get worse. They lose their revolutionary power.
If written, they just become ornament: if lived, they become characters in a
brothel...
ROGER:    You mean?
MAN:    Nothing at all. I'll let you think what you want.]

Here, while Roger conceives of an (instrumental) role for art in the revolutionary
purity for which he hankers, it is the other man who figures a more pessimistic
position, bringing Roger back to reality by insisting that the only potent image
is a compromised one. The different drafts show Genet trying out different
configurations of views, in which the idea that art constitutes a revolutionary force
stubbornly recurs.

This question of the potency of the image aptly returns us to the play's final
scene, which also underwent extensive modification. In the 1956 edition, Carmen
briefly narrates Roger's request to play the Chief of Police and subsequent self-
castration, whereas this is staged at length in the final version. The earlier edition
was the text of the play discussed by Jacques Lacan shortly after its publication,
in his 1957-58 seminar; his reading provides a useful framework for considering
the implications of Genet's later changes.[41] The psychoanalyst admires Genet for
differentiating between the other figures of authority and the Chief of Police in
terms of the symbolic power they wield: the demand to play the Bishop, Judge and
General in the brothel is an indication of the 'érotisation du rapport symbolique'
[eroticisation of the relation to the symbolic] (or, in less Lacanian language, a
perverse pleasure taken by the subject in acknowledging his/her own alienation; a
paradoxical transformation of the (unpleasurable) powerlessness that is the human
condition itself into a source of pleasure), whereas the power that consists in
maintaining order (the police) has no such appeal to the unconscious. For Lacan,
the value of the play lies above all in the insight it offers into how this difference
may evolve at moments of social crisis (and it must be recalled that when Genet was
writing the play France was in the throes of the Algerian War, with the emergence
of a Francoist-style regime perfectly conceivable). What happens when the threat
of social disorder makes the police preeminent? Lacan specifically makes the link
between the Chief's effective supremacy while the insurgency rages and recent
European history, seeing in the figure of the dictator 'ce type de personnage qui
offre à la communauté politique une identification unique et facile' [the type of
character offering the political community a single, easy identification].[42] His
account then picks out two ways the end of the play posits that police supremacy
could attain a symbolic status. The first is the outrageous proposal that the Chief
should appear 'sous la forme d'un phallus géant, d'un chibre de taille' [as a giant
phallus, a man-sized prick] (TC, 418 (332 in the final version); B, 85); the second,
which immediately follows the first in the 1956 edition but not in the final version,
is Roger's self-castration in the role of Chief. For Lacan, the second renders the first
nugatory. The conclusion he goes on to draw — one that corresponds closely to his
own theory — is that the play stages the fundamental role that castration plays in
underpinning the social order:

Ce sujet, celui qui représente le désir simple qu'a l'homme de rejoindre de façon authentique et assumée sa propre existence et sa propre pensée, une valeur qui ne soit pas distincte de sa chair, ce sujet qui est là représentant l'homme, celui qui a combattu pour que quelque chose que nous avons appelé jusqu'à présent le bordel retrouve une assiette, une norme, un état qui puisse être accepté comme pleinement humain, celui-là ne s'y réintègre, une fois l'épreuve passée, qu'à la condition de se castrer.[43]

[The subject, representing man's simple desire to assume authentically and reconnect with his own existence and his own thinking, a value that would not be separable from his flesh, this subject representing man, having fought so that something we have hitherto been calling the brothel could again ground itself in a norm, a state that could be accepted as fully human, can only be again integrated into it, once the ordeal has passed, on condition of being castrated.]

Accepting castration — recognising the lack that is integral to the human condition, the impossibility of a subject identical to itself — is the condition of 'normal' social relations. Lacan does not explicitly articulate the relationship between the enormous phallic symbol and the image of castration; however, in passing directly from one to the other, he appears to consider them alternatives. The choice is between an order predicated on a (totalitarian) fantasy of phallic unity or an order, like the previous regime, in which the condition for exercising power is the impossibility of personifying it (in the language of *Le Séminaire V*, an order in which the phallus is again 'promu à l'état de signifiant' [promoted to the state of signifier]).[44] In this perspective, the play ends with the success of the counter-revolution, but the suggestion is that this constitutes the only possible political outcome other than the authoritarian order to which Roger's revolutionary desire for plenitude, for identity, would otherwise have led.[45]

Lacan's reading thus gives pride of place to the immediate juxtaposition in the 1956 edition of the image of the giant phallus and Carmen's account of Roger's adoption and castration of the Chief's image. Genet's later revisions to the scene, more than doubling it in length, considerably attenuate the impact of this contrast; a five-page discussion of the differences between the Chief and the other figures of authority separates the phallic image from Roger's arrival, and Carmen's page-long account is developed into a six-page direct representation of him playing the role of Chief of Police. The stark alternative analysed by Lacan therefore gives way to a substantially more complex treatment of the implications of the Chief's entry into the 'Nomenclature'. Especially, whereas Lacan's reading ultimately implies that the Chief's status ends up as equivalent to that of the Bishop, Judge and General, in the definitive edition it is less clear if the castration institutes that equivalence or interrupts it. Insofar as Roger's entry into the brothel marks a shift from one position to its opposite, it merely replicates the old network of relations: he now seeks to have a slave, rather than fight an oppressive authority; he wants to be served, rather than to serve; he pays, rather than is paid (*TC*, 341; *B*, 88). As such, he continues the series of clients in the play's opening scenes. Yet in other ways the final scenario differs significantly from the initial series. It is unique in that Roger's partner is neither an employee of the brothel — the 'slave' is the client who plays the beggar in scene 4 — nor a woman. Unlike in the 1956 edition, when Carmen described Roger as her client ('il en est venu un pour moi' (*TC*, 420) [One came for me]), the action is scheduled to take place 'entre hommes' [between men].[46] But there is no hint not only of any homosexual dimension to the scenario as scripted, but of any sexual dimension whatever. Carmen stays only at Roger's request: 'Tout se passe toujours en présence d'une femme. C'est pour que le visage d'une femme soit témoin, que, d'habitude' [Everything always happens in the presence of a woman. It's to have a woman's face as witness that people usually] (*TC*, 343; *B*, 90). This contrasts with the opening scenes where, far from guaranteeing the truth (the role of witness), the role of the women is to lie. For example, having repeatedly obtained reassurance that the (capital) sins confessed were genuine, the Bishop continues:

> L'ÉVÊQUE:    Mais notre sainteté n'est faite que de pouvoir vous pardonner vos péchés. Furent-ils joués?
> LA FEMME, *soudain coquette*:    Et si mes péchés étaient vrais?
> L'ÉVÊQUE, *d'un ton différent, moins théâtral*:    Tu es folle! J'espère que tu n'as pas réellement fait tout cela?
>
> [BISHOP:    And all our sanctity was created for that very reason, that we might forgive her those very sins. Even if they were phoney.
> WOMAN (*suddenly flirtatious*):    And what if my sins were real?
> BISHOP (*in a different, less theatrical tone of voice*):    You must be out of your mind! You didn't really do all that, I hope?] (*TC*, 267; *B*, 4)

What the Bishop wants is for the sinner to pretend that her sins are true. Similarly, Irma explains in scene 5 that there is always a false detail in the decor — 'Ils veulent tous que tout soit le plus vrai possible... Moins quelque chose d'indéfinissable, qui fera que ce n'est pas vrai' [They all want everything to be as real as possible... Minus an indefinable something, so that it's not really real] (*TC*, 293; *B*, 30) — a detail which for the Bishop is always the same: 'dentelles noires sous la jupe de bure' [black lace under the homespun skirt] (*TC*, 292; *B*, 29). In contrast, Roger appears unequivocally to want everything to be true: 'Il n'y a vraiment rien qui cloche?' [Is everything exactly right?] (*TC*, 342; *B*, 89). In his case there is no mention of any false detail equivalent to the black lace. Above all, unlike the uncertainty in the earlier scenes as to whether the screams emanating from adjacent rooms are genuine or feigned, the castration is presented diegetically as definitely taking place. Indeed, the Chief of Police dismisses it on the grounds that '[c]e plombier ne savait pas jouer, voilà tout' (the plumber just didn't understand his role — that's all] (*TC*, 347; *B*, 94). Roger brings into the realm of fantasy the fantasy that everything to do with fantasy (sex, playing, etc.) can be excluded.

Is the castration Roger's rejection of fantasy, then, or the climax of his fantasy? Is Roger's fantasy substantively different from those of the opening scenes in its desire to leave fantasy behind, or does it resemble them to the extent that it, too, seeks to maintain the distinction between true and false? In fact, to what extent can the final scenario even be considered an enactment of his fantasy? The other salons respond to desires expressed by the client, as Irma makes clear in scene 5: 'je n'en suis que la directrice et chacun, quand il sonne, entre, y apporte son scénario parfaitement réglé' [I'm only the director, and everyone, when he rings my bell, comes in with his own carefully worked out, ready-made script] (*TC*, 293; *B*, 30).[47] In contrast, Roger inaugurates a salon furnished by Irma in the anticipation that someone will ask for it. Yet she manifestly fails to predict how he will act: 'Sur mes tapis! Sur la moquette neuve! C'est un dément!' [On my rugs! On my carpet! He's a maniac!] (*TC*, 347; *B*, 94). Does the difference between fantasising playing a non-castrated Chief and fantasising castrating him merely map onto Lacan's alternative of giant phallus or castration, or could the ending herald a liberatory event as theorised for example by Derrida (or even Badiou, according to whose reading *Le Balcon* precisely rules out the possibility of an emancipatory event)? In other words, just as Roger asks questions 'qui ne sont pas prévues dans le scénario' [that aren't in the script] (*TC*, 344; *B*, 91), might his actions reveal the possibility of an event that would not follow logically, programmatically, from the conditions in which it arose? A fantasy substantively different from those of the opening scenes? Might the castration signal the possibility of a fissure in the cultural hegemony, a visible non-adherence to social values and norms (including norms of desire), and not merely the normalisation of Roger's desire?

If the play evokes the possibility of a transformative gesture, it is certainly not by representing one. Any positive image serves only to propose a further illusion of plenitude (a further disavowal of castration). Lacan is surely correct that the political attraction of any 'identification unique et facile' is that of totalitarianism (whether fascist or Zhdanovian). But what interests me is that he limits himself to stating the alternative between totalitarian identification and castration as though the choice between them, and hence the interpretation of the play, was merely a matter of personal taste for the spectator: 'Est-ce blasphématoire? Est-ce comique? Nous pouvons porter l'accent à notre gré' [Is it blasphematory? Comical? We can place the emphasis where we want].[48] But what about Genet? Does *Le Balcon* suggest that he is indifferent to the choice between these outcomes? We saw above that Chantal bears interpretation as a figure of the author precisely insofar as she cannot be situated clearly on one side. There is no position to which the author can be said to subscribe; Genet's revisions show him constantly displacing the political viewpoint. But that is not to say that the play does not have a position of enunciation. The play's position of enunciation is one that is in constant displacement, that is, one that is not identical to itself.

What do Genet's revisions reveal about the play's perspective on the castration it stages, itself an unmistakable figure of non-identity? Relative to the earlier version on which Lacan based his analysis of the castration as condition of symbolic entry, the definitive edition draws attention to the castration as wound, a shift encapsulated in the replacement of the 'vivante' [living] image (*TC*, 421; *B*, 95) of himself that the 1956 Chief of Police predicts will follow from Roger's action by a 'châtrée' [castrated], 'mutilée' [mutilated] one (*TC*, 347, 348). Staging rather than narrating Roger's action inevitably makes its impact more violent for the audience: the spectator is forced to confront the assault on the body that is part and parcel of Roger's falling into line. Furthermore, the literal castration echoes symbolically: the final version highlights in several respects that power is assumed

at a cost to the body. Although unharmed by Roger's attack, the Chief too pays
a cost in that his previous life — if not his life — ends with his elevation to the
'Nomenclature'. To the dismay of Irma who, 'encore vivante' [still alive], still loves
him, he declares himself 'plus mort que mort' [deader than dead], with 'plus rien
à faire' [nothing more to do] on earth, and descends into the tomb that was the
scene in which Roger assumed his image (*TC*, 348). Earlier, when Roger asks if
the space where he finds himself is his 'tombeau' [tomb], Carmen corrects him:
'Mausolée' [Mausoleum] (*TC*, 342; *B*, 89). The word serves to emphasise the link
to the 'Vallée de los Caídos' mentioned just afterwards, the monument to the dead
of the Spanish Civil War officially inaugurated in 1959. But it is significant also
that the term 'mausoleum' is a common noun that derives from a proper name. Just
as Mausolus was eclipsed by the tomb built in his honour by his widow Artemisia
at Halicarnassus, one of the Seven Wonders of the Ancient World, the condition
for the Chief of Police's entry into the 'Nomenclature' is that the man himself
disappears as such. A line cut from the 1962 edition expresses the Chief's awareness
of the cost of attaining the status of an abstraction: 'je veux que mon image soit à
la fois légendaire et humaine. Qu'elle participe sans doute des principes éternels,
mais qu'on y reconnaisse ma gueule' (*TC*, 1173, n. 94) [I want my image to be both
legendary and human. For it to partake without doubt in eternal principles, but for
my mug to be recognisable in it].

In the definitive edition, the Chief does not voice this regret at the sacrifice
involved in becoming legendary. However, earlier in the scene the other figures
elaborate on the loss entailed in playing their roles in public rather than in private:
'Une situation de tout repos: [...] nous pouvions être juge, général, évêque, jusqu'à
la perfection et jusqu'à la jouissance! De cet état adorable, sans malheur, vous nous
avez tirés brutalement' [We were in a state of grace: [...] we could be Judge, General,
Bishop to the point of perfection — and paroxysm! You dragged us brutally out
of that marvellous enviable, blessed state] (*TC*, 334; *B*, 82). They are henceforward
torn between the demands of their individual, embodied life and the abstract
function they are called on to represent, as Irma recognises:

> LA REINE: Je ne serai donc jamais qui je suis?
> L'ENVOYÉ: Jamais plus.
> LA REINE:  Chaque événement de ma vie: mon sang qui perle si je
> m'égratigne...
> L'ENVOYÉ:  Tout s'écrira pour vous avec une majuscule.
> LA REINE:  Mais c'est la Mort?
> L'ENVOYÉ:  C'est Elle. (*TC*, 336)

> [QUEEN:   So I will never again be who I am?
> ENVOY:   Never.
> QUEEN:   Each event of my life: my blood seeping out if I scratch myself...
> ENVOY:   Everything will be written with a capital letter for you.
> QUEEN:   But it's Death?
> ENVOY:   It's Death.]

Embodying power is dependent on an abnegation of the body. Life as a symbol,
a 'fascinante image' (*TC*, 331) [fascinating image], involves a form of death. This

deathly survival is rendered literally in the Chief of Police's withdrawal into the mausoleum, with 'pour deux mille ans de boustifaille' [enough grub for two thousand years] (*TC*, 348; *B*, 94). The need for food suggests he is alive; the idea that he would need it for two thousand years suggests rather he has attained a (Christlike) eternity. He both is and is not alive, like Schrödinger's cat, just as earlier the (real) Queen 'brode et elle ne brode pas' [is embroidering and isn't embroidering], 'ronfle et elle ne ronfle pas' [snores and doesn't snore] (*TC*, 317; *B*, 59-60). Above all, however, being the object of someone else's fantasy comes at the price of renouncing one's own. In the Bishop's words:

> Tant que nous étions dans une chambre de bordel, nous appartenions à notre propre fantaisie: de l'avoir exposée, de l'avoir nommée, de l'avoir publiée, nous voici liés avec les hommes, liés à vous, et contraints de continuer cette aventure selon les lois de la visibilité.

> [So long as we were in a room in a brothel we belonged to our own fantasies. But since we've exposed them, given them a name and made them public, there has been a bond between us and other men, between us and you, and now we've no alternative but to carry on with this adventure according to the laws of visibility.] (*TC*, 333; *B*, 81)

Henceforward, the only pleasure he can envisage is that of returning secretly to the brothel to play at being a ballerina (*TC*, 334).[49] The General does not even anticipate that possibility: 'Il ne rêve plus' [He doesn't dream any more] (*TC*, 334; *B*, 82).

Diegetically, the castration is thus the climax of the restoration of order, but a climax that satisfies nobody, one in fact that signals the impossibility of satisfaction. Whereas the traditional theatrical denouement typically re-establishes closure, the end of *Le Balcon* does the opposite: it cogently exposes the dissatisfaction that underpins any social order, the price that maintaining a social function imposes on the living — that is, dreaming — body. Its denial to the audience of any illusory identification supports Goldmann's view of *Le Balcon* as a Brechtian play. Yet in my view the reasons why Genet disliked Brecht's work, and what they throw into relief about his own practice, offer a more valuable insight into the end of the play than Goldmann's comparison. Interestingly, Brecht is the artistic figure whom Genet judges most harshly in his interviews. He claims to Michèle Manceaux that 'Brecht n'a rien fait pour le communisme' [Brecht didn't do anything for communism] (*ED*, 62; *DE*, 48). When asked by José Monleón for his opinion about the German, he replies: 'Il ne me plaît pas. Il explique tout parce qu'il est didactique. Au lieu de montrer les choses de manière oblique, il les explique comme un maître de l'école laïque' (*TC*, 970) [I don't like him. He explains everything, because he is didactic. Instead of showing things obliquely, he explains them like a lay schoolteacher]. And when pushed by Hubert Fichte as to why he likes Strindberg but not Brecht, he explains: 'Rien de ce que dit Strindberg ne peut être dit autrement que poétiquement et tout ce que dit Brecht peut être dit et finalement a été dit prosaïquement. [...] il ne s'agit pas seulement de distanciation, mais d'absence de sensibilité' [Nothing Strindberg says could be said in any other way than poetically, and everything

Brecht says can be said and in fact has been said prosaically. [...] it's not simply a question of distancing, but of a lack of sensibility] (*ED*, 145-46; *DE*, 122). These comments show clearly that Genet's dismissal of Brecht is tied up with the latter's intellectualism. The view that his plays do not engage his audience emotionally is a judgement not only on their artistic quality (a lack of 'sensibilité') but on their political efficacity: they do not advance the cause they claim to support.

For Genet, the problem is thus not Brecht's jamming of the audience's identification with the characters but rather the attempt to foreclose any emotional response. Like Brecht, Genet's theatre draws attention to the fundamental alienation of the human condition. But Genet aims to promote dreaming, not to stop it. Far from distancing the audience emotionally, he seeks to invent a 'féerie', a space of magic or wonderland, as he writes in 1969 to Antoine Bourseiller, who was directing *Le Balcon* at the time:

> Toute représentation théâtrale, tout spectacle est une féerie. La féerie dont je parle n'a pas besoin de miroirs, d'étoffes somptueuses, de meubles baroques: elle est dans une voix qui se casse sur un mot — alors qu'elle devrait se casser sur un autre — mais il faut trouver le mot et la voix; elle est (la féerie) dans un geste qui n'est pas à sa place à cet instant [...].
>
> J'aurais voulu que mon texte soit en porte à faux, et qu'une féerie naisse de lui. (*TC*, 903-04)

> [Every theatrical representation, every spectacle is an enchantment. The enchantment I'm talking of doesn't need mirrors, sumptuous fabrics, baroque furniture: it lies in a voice breaking over a word — when it ought to break over another — but you have to find the word and the voice; the enchantment is in a gesture out of place at that moment [...].
>
> I would like my text to be at odds with itself, and for enchantment to be born of it.]

The magic lies in the gap between one word and another, in a breakage ('une voix qui se casse'), a displacement ('un geste qui n'est pas à sa place'). The enchantment derives from the very contrary of a fairy-tale illusion of wholeness: an unanticipated discrepancy, a discordance created by a text 'en porte à faux', at variance with itself. Here, non-identity is not a matter of the failure or rupture of fantasy, but rather its origin. At the heart of theatre for Genet is an experience that already invites the question with which Derridean deconstruction in general — and the notion of *différance* in particular — was soon after *Le Balcon* to transform the theoretical landscape: the impossibility for a being/entity/essence to be fully present to itself, and hence the inadequacy of any attempt to fully re-present it.

To return to the ending of *Le Balcon*: the play in no way suggests that Roger's actions, or those of any other character, exemplify a transformative way forward. His castration is consonant with Lacanian theory in that it epitomises not only the failure of the revolutionary dream, but the incompatibility of dreaming with reality. But, precisely, the castration is not the whole of it. The play as a whole is at odds with the scene it represents. (The text, in other words, is not a consistent whole: it conveys different meanings at different levels.) Genet's reworking of the final scene bears witness to the fact that, even if the castration signals the end of Roger's dream, dreaming nonetheless continues. As the Chief of Police disappears into the mausoleum, the fighting resumes:

> LA REINE:    Qui est-ce?... Les nôtres... ou des révoltés?... ou?...
> L'ENVOYÉ:    Quelqu'un qui rêve, madame...
> LA REINE:    ...Irma. Appelez-moi madame Irma, et rentrez chez vous. Bonsoir monsieur.
> L'ENVOYÉ:    Bonsoir, madame Irma.

> [QUEEN:    Who is that?... Our side ... or the rebels?... or what?...
> ENVOY:    Someone dreaming, Ma'am ...
> QUEEN:    ...Irma. Call me Irma, and go home. Goodnight.
> ENVOY:    Goodnight, Madam Irma.] (*TC*, 349; *B*, 95)

The 1956 version's certainty that the counter-revolution had triumphed gives way to the possibility that the revolution is not yet over, a possibility explicitly linked with someone dreaming. For the Envoy, the dreaming is presumably a signal of impotence. Yet it is difficult not to interpret its resurgence at the end of the play as a sign also of the perennial attraction of the revolutionary dream. The dreamer patently exceeds the binary of Irma's question; as a category, it contains both 'our' side and the rebels, beckoning once more towards the mirroring of the proponents and the opponents of the social order. But whereas most analysis of this mirroring posits that the revolution will replicate the order it contests, here it is clear that the mirroring works both ways: the counter-revolution has won, but in winning it ensures the continuation of its own contestation.

'Someone dreaming': this unidentified dreamer emerges at the very moment, in the same sentence, as Irma reverts to her identity as brothel-owner rather than queen. As she closes down the lights, and dismisses the audience with the same words she had just used to send the other figures home, 'où tout, n'en doutez pas, sera encore plus faux qu'ici' [where nothing will be any more real than it is here] (*TC*, 350; *B*, 96), the normal state of events appears to have been securely reinstated. Yet the indeterminate dreamer/fighter is not the only sign that the threat to its functioning has not fully been contained. Another trace of the night's events remains: she switches back on the lights in the mausoleum where the Chief of Police had withdrawn, remembering that 'il a besoin de lumière pour deux mille ans!... Et pour deux mille ans de nourriture... [...] la gloire c'est de descendre au tombeau avec des tonnes de mangeaille!' [he's going to want light for the next two thousand years! ... And food... [...] Glory consists of descending to the grave with tons of grub] (*TC*, 349; *B*, 96). Nothing dispels the undecidability of the Chief's condition of being both alive and eternal. Taken literally, it throws a spanner in the works of any realistic interpretation of the play. Yet Irma's reaction also makes it impossible to dismiss as merely a metaphor. The text is indeed 'en porte à faux', its constitutive pieces impossible to reconcile from any single standpoint.

This undecidability within the play mirrors the difficulty of ascertaining its overall position of enunciation; a fundamental unknowability emerges at the end of the written play just as was the case with the writing process. We saw earlier that when, in one draft, Roger asks his revolutionary interlocutor what he means, he receives the reply: 'Rien du tout. Je te laisse penser ce que tu veux'. Similarly, Genet's revisions systematically move away from telling the audience what to think. There is no writer less like the didactic schoolmaster that he reproaches Brecht for being, as the malicious final sentence of the 'Avertissement' highlights: 'Je me fais mal comprendre, peut-être?' [Maybe I'm not making myself clear?] (*TC*, 262; *B*, xiv). As in *Les Bonnes*, the final version of *Le Balcon* is much less directive than the earlier drafts. Especially, Genet's reworking of the play prunes away most of the discourse about revolution, specifically anything that pointed too clearly to a path that should be followed. *Le Balcon*, with some effort, avoids making any political statement that might recommend a political action. Genet ends up crafting a play about revolution that paradoxically avoids endorsing any political position.

This undecidability of the play's political stance is mirrored not only in the diegetic undecidability of the conclusion but in the contradictory readings it has elicited. There is clearly a case for arguing that the undecidability *is* the play's political stance. As we have seen, both within the play and in numerous paratexts Genet insistently highlights that a play is not the same as what it says or shows. In closing with an allusion to an offstage unidentified dreamer who may, or may not, be motivated by a desire for revolution, *Le Balcon* calls attention not only to the gap between what we see on stage and events elsewhere, but also to the possible existence of a dream in excess of the action we have just witnessed. However, the play resolutely refuses to define or identify where the difference might lie. The dream at best relates to the play 'obliquely', to use the word Genet prefers, or 'à côté' [beside itself]. The letter in which Genet expresses his wish for his text to be at odds with itself continues, 'Je ne sais pas grand-chose, sauf peut-être celle-ci: il faut se tromper. Je veux dire: jouer un peu à côté' (*TC*, 904) [I don't know much, except perhaps this: you have to be wrong. I mean: act a little on the side]. This last somewhat gnomic statement scarcely provides the clarification it promises. It is of course possible to align his playing 'à côté' with Chantal's performance, as when she stated that the brothel had been useful in teaching her 'l'art de feindre et de jouer' [the art of feigning or acting], or indeed that of Roger whose castration, proof for the Chief that he 'ne savait pas jouer' [didn't know how to act], could be held to constitute the acme of playing/acting when viewed from another perspective (*TC*, 314, 347). Except that, as I hope this chapter has shown, theatre for Genet is precisely a space of non-alignment, a space where words that say one thing may also say the opposite, where words and images matter less than the gaps between them, where the text is fundamentally at variance with any sense it makes. Above all, theatre is a space of political non-alignment. The evidence shows that Genet moved away from endorsing any political stance, both in his revisions to each of *Les Bonnes* and *Le Balcon*, and in the passage from one play to the other. But theatre did not only enable him to approach politics 'obliquely'; it was the space where obliqueness itself acquires a political tinge. Or, phrased differently, his theatre is political insofar as it is not just political: that is, not a utilitarian, instrumental, rational use of language and images in order to convey a clearly defined message, but an exploitation to the full of the inevitability of saying something other than you mean to say and above all a recognition that this shared experience of contradiction, non-alignment, non-identity is what gives theatre its 'efficacity'.

*Le Balcon* is at odds with itself in being a play about the defeat of a revolution that confronts its audience with a disruptive experience. Genet was impatient with suggestions that this made it an instrument of revolution. Yet it is fascinating that it is when he gives up writing that he articulates the idea that art can nonetheless prove transformational, as we shall now explore in Chapter 3.

## Notes to Chapter 2

1. Edmund White, *Genet* (London: Chatto & Windus, 1993), p. 233.
2. 'Notice', in *Les Bonnes* (*TC*, 1041).
3. Lavery, *The Politics of Jean Genet's Late Theatre*.
4. For instance, there are numerous comparative analyses of Genet's last three plays, although few that explore links between these and his earlier plays. See for example Albert C. Chesneau, 'Idée de révolution et principe de réversibilité dans *Le Balcon* et *Les Nègres* de Jean Genet,' *PMLA*, 88.5 (1973), 1137-45; or W. F. Sohlich, 'Genet's *The Blacks* and *The Screens*: Dialectic of Refusal and Revolutionary Consciousness', *Comparative Drama*, 10.3 (1976), 216-34.
5. Martin Esslin, *The Theatre of the Absurd* (New York: Anchor Books, 1971), p. 166.
6. Richard Coe, *The Vision of Jean Genet* (London: Owen, 1968), p. 258.
7. Lucien Goldmann, 'Une pièce réaliste: *Le Balcon* de Jean Genet', *Les Temps modernes*, 171 (1960), 1885-96, and 'Le Théâtre de Genet: essai d'étude sociologique', in *Structures mentales et création culturelle* (Paris: Anthropos, 1970), pp. 267-302.
8. Philip Thody, *Jean Genet: A Study of His Novels and Plays* [1968] (New York: Stein & Day, 1970), p. 195.
9. For a particularly insightful discussion of the productive contribution that Genet's work, and especially *Les Nègres*, can make to debates about racial politics, see Frieda Ekotto, *Race and Sex Across the French Atlantic: The Color of Black in Literary, Philosophical and Theater Discourse* (Lanham, MD: Lexington Books, 2011).
10. *Le Balcon* is in fact the play about which opinions have been most divided. Yet Goldmann early acclaimed it as the first great Brechtian play of French literature ('Une pièce réaliste'). David Walker's reading of the play's 'radicalisation' of form as an attempt to promote revolutionary activity ('Revolution and Revisions in Genet's *Le Balcon*', *Modern Language Review*, 79.4 (1984), 817-30) was the first to argue for a progressive interpretation of the play; and Claire Finburgh strikes an even more affirmative note, drawing on speech-act theory to claim that the play's undermining of the teleological causality between words and action can itself be read as a subversive act ('Speech Without Acts: Politics and Speech-Act Theory in Genet's *The Balcony*,' *Paragraph*, 27.2 (2004), 113-29).
11. Lavery, *The Politics of Jean Genet's Late Theatre*, p. 8.
12. Lavery's periodisation of Genet's work thus rests on primarily biographical grounds. Believing that the staging of collective struggles in the last three plays reflects an 'æsthetico-political' shift, he attributes its origin to an experience described by the author in 'Ce qui est resté d'un Rembrandt déchiré en petits carrés bien réguliers, et foutu aux chiottes...'. Genet there narrates how he was profoundly destabilised by an encounter in a train that jolted him into the realisation that the value of each man lies not in what sets him apart, but rather in a secret wound common to all humanity. Genet proposes that this human failing is what makes all men not merely equivalent — that is, equal in value — but identical to each other; and moreover that it is that identity 'qui permettait à tout homme d'être aimé, *ni plus ni moins*, que tout autre, et qui permettait que soit aimée, c'est-à-dire prise en charge et reconnue — chérie — jusqu'à la plus immonde apparence' [this identity that allowed every man to be loved, *neither more nor less* than any other, and that allowed even the most revolting appearance to be loved, that is to say, taken charge of and recognized, cherished] (*OC*, IV, 24; *FA*, 94). Lavery posits that this

revelation led to a transformation in Genet's practice evident in the way the late plays 'wound' his spectators, disorientating them by exposing the fault-lines that put the certainties on which they base their sense of themselves at risk. Theatre wounds them by confronting them with a 'wound in community' (*The Politics of Jean Genet's Late Theatre*, pp. 106, 136). While Lavery's audacious and unashamedly utopian reading of Genet's work as an 'oblique model of committed theater' (p. 5) has the very real value of paying close attention to the ways Genet puts the concrete historical context to work within the three plays, it nonetheless relies on a number of questionable assumptions. The biographism on which it is based is problematic not only in terms of the reservations about the relationship between life and text that a poststructuralist critique might foreground, as the critic himself acknowledges, but also because of the failure to recognise that the 'recourse to biography' (p. 50) in question is in fact a recourse to autobiography: the only access we have to the event is via Genet's own account of it. An account, moreover, which is so highly crafted, so textually dense, that its meaning is by no means as transparent as Lavery posits. A second, even more problematic, assumption is that the revelation of the wound was a watershed in Genet's work. The critic acknowledges various continuities between the early and late work; nonetheless, his argument fundamentally depends on the idea of a profoundly transformative break in relation to the wound. The problem is that the early work abounds in examples of the wound as Lavery seems to interpret it. For example, he sees in the void a figure of the wound; yet there is a very substantial body of criticism highlighting how from the very beginning Genet's work systematically, even compulsively, points to a void: the central episode in *Notre-Dame-des-Fleurs* of Culafroy's profaning the host only to find that no miracle took place is just one of many examples. There are also cogent reasons for relating the secret wound to the psychoanalytical notion of castration; and numerous studies of the novels have shown how the Genetian subject is always subject to castration. Similarly, the desire to wound is scarcely new to the plays; the adversarial relation that the narrator of the novels creates with the reader is one of the orthodoxies of Genetian criticism. Finally, there is a logical problem with the causal leap involved in proposing that Genet's discovery of a wound integral to the human condition resulted in plays that wound the spectator, insofar as the argument necessarily presupposes the possibility of a hitherto unwounded spectator, the very possibility that 'Ce qui est resté...' explicitly precludes. For these reasons, the periodisation on which *The Politics of Jean Genet's Late Theatre* is predicated remains unconvincing.

13. Olivier Neveux, *Le Théâtre de Jean Genet* (Lausanne: Ides et Calendes, 2016), p. 50.
14. Unpaginated document headed 'Espagne' (GNT 6.18).
15. Jean Genet, letter to Roger Blin, in *La Bataille des Paravents*, ed. by Albert Dichy and Lynda Bellity Peskine (Paris: Théâtre de l'Odéon, 1986), pp. 16-17. While a hint of this position echoes in the earlier *Lettres à Roger Blin* ('Ma pièce n'est pas l'apologie de la trahison. Elle se passe dans un domaine où la morale est remplacée par l'esthétique de la scène' [My play is not an apology for betrayal. It takes place in a sphere where morality is replaced by the aesthetics of the stage] (*TC*, 851; *LRB*, 13)), it is interesting that Genet chose not to include this letter elaborating his position in greater detail in the selection of letters first published. Barrault goes so far as to call *Les Paravents* 'anti-politique' [anti-political] (*La Bataille des Paravents*, p. 75).
16. An *oblique* is also something that is not *droite* which in French means both 'straight' and the (political) 'right'. It could be argued that Genet's oblique politics are at an angle to right-wing politics: opposed to them but not their straightforward (left-wing) opposite. In the letter to Roger Blin cited in n. 15 above, he specifies: 'Je ne suis pas un type de droite (ou alors quelle incohérence!) il faudrait que je reconnaisse le nationalisme, le chauvinisme, les valeurs officielles, etc... | Je ne suis pas un type de gauche. C'est-à-dire que je ne peux pas accepter une morale donnée, déjà élaborée, aussi généreuse soit-elle. Je reste un voyou c'est-à-dire un artiste, qui doit se démerder avec lui-même pour mettre au point une œuvre et une vie avec si possible, une morale éclairant les deux. Ça ne se fait pas du jour au lendemain, ni en termes clairs' [I am not a right-wing guy (or else the incoherence!) I would need to recognise nationalism, chauvinism, official values, etc... | I am not a left-wing guy. That is, I cannot accept an already given, formulated morality, however generous it may be. I remain a rogue, that is, an artist, who has to cope by himself to develop a work and a life and, if possible, a morality illuminating both.

That doesn't happen from one day to the next, nor in clear terms] (*La Bataille des Paravents*, ed. by Dichy and Peskine, p. 17). For a related although different discussion of obliquity in Genet's writing, see Joanne Brueton, *Geometry and Jean Genet: Shaping the Subject* (Cambridge: Legenda, 2022), pp. 99-119.

17. Is it mere chance that one of the earliest edited volumes about Genet's theatre was a special issue of the journal *Obliques* (2, 1972)?

18. For an argument that Genet's theatre aims to rouse hatred, see Raymond Federman, 'Jean Genet ou le théâtre de la haine', *Esprit*, n.s. 391.4 (1970), 697-713. Moreover, Genet's protestation, in his interview with Madeleine Gobeil merely five years prior to the interview with Monléon, that he himself had 'aucune solidarité' [no solidarity] (*ED*, 14; *DE*, 5) with anybody at all further undermines his new-found praise for the notion.

19. Less pertinently for my focus in this chapter, the solitude of the reader of the novels is also limited. As we saw in Chapter 1, Genet's novels derive much of their impact from the spotlight they shine on their inferred reader's desire to indulge fantasies that are deemed socially unacceptable. While the highlighting of a social context to the reader's furtive pleasure does not actually make it impossible for the reader (unlike the spectator) to read furtively, it is nonetheless analogous in some respects to the way the spectator is forced to recognise a social dimension to his/her relationship to the play. Interestingly, the first word of *Comment jouer Les Bonnes* is 'Furtif' [furtive] (*TC*, 125), a term whose etymology (from the Latin *furtum*, or theft) doubtless attracted Genet. Genet's first performed play is more similar than dissimilar to his novels in that it stages clandestine behaviour, and reveals what would remain invisible for all to see.

20. Richard Webb offers an interesting historicisation of the criticism, arguing that the view of Genet's theatre as ritualistic emerged only after *Les Nègres*: 'Ritual, Theatre and Jean Genet's *The Blacks*', *Theatre Journal*, 31.4 (1979), 443-59. For more recent accounts of the ritualistic in his work, see Gene A. Plunka, *The Rites of Passage of Jean Genet: The Art and Aesthetics of Risk Taking* (Rutherford, NJ: Fairleigh Dickinson University Press; London: Associated University Presses, 1992); and Marie-Chantal Killeen, 'Pour une lecture girardienne des *Bonnes* de Genet', *French Studies*, 58.4 (2004), 485-98.

21. For an exploration of Genet's notion of theatre as rupture or detachment in this text, see Samuel Weber, 'Double Take: Acting and Writing in Genet's "L'Étrange Mot de..."', in *Genet*, ed. by Durham, pp. 28-48. The question of what would be lost if theatre was lost forms the guiding thread in Neveux's *Le Théâtre de Jean Genet*.

22. This self-problematisation is a recurrent, even compulsive, feature in Genet's essays. For example, the final sentence of the first paragraph of 'Le Secret de Rembrandt' — 'Ça, ou bien l'inverse?' [Is that it, or just the opposite?] (*OC*, v, 31; *FA*, 84) — similarly undercuts the text the reader in this case is preparing to read. It raises the question of the extent to which the essay form counts for Genet as 'art', the sole sphere in which he can tell the truth according to the interview with Fichte previously cited. While the manifestly 'written' quality of 'L'Étrange Mot d'...' sets it apart from the responses necessarily produced hastily in an oral interview, the paramountcy of the regime of meaning in an essay distinguishes it from genres such as fiction or theatre. Is it because an attempt to convey some idea or message is fundamentally at the heart of the essay that Genet feels compelled to signal the limits of what the text can say?

23. As Jean-Bernard Moraly points out, this passage is, literally, central to the text: 'Exactement au centre. Dix morceaux le précèdent et dix le suivent' (*Le Maître fou* (Paris: Nizet, 2009), p. 154).

24. Weber, 'Double Take', p. 48.

25. See for example *TC*, 838-39 and 919.

26. Support for both readings can be found in Genet's other interventions. The first fits with his statement in his interview with Rüdiger Wischenbart and Layla Shahid Barrada as quoted earlier that art is obliquely political because it prepares the ground for political activity in the future by addressing social situations in such a way as to provoke a politics. The other chimes with the idea in the 'Avertissement' to *Le Balcon* that plays about revolution 'kill what they want to make live'.

27. Many years later, however, when pushed by Bernard Poirot-Delpech on his assertion that 'les comptes ont été réglées' [his accounts were settled] with society, Genet admits: 'Oh! Je l'affirme

d'une façon si péremptoire, si vivace que je me demande si, réellement, c'est sans colère et sans drame. Là vous venez de toucher quelque chose. Je crois que je mourrai encore avec de la colère contre vous' [Oh! I'm saying this in such a peremptory and spontaneous way that I wonder if it really is without anger or drama. You're touching on something there. I believe that I will die still with some anger directed at you] (*ED*, 233; *DE*, 199-200).

28. See Jeannette Savona, *Jean Genet* (New York: Grove Press, 1983), and Cynthia Running-Johnson, 'Genet's "Excessive" Double: Reading *Les Bonnes* through Irigaray and Cixous', *French Review*, 63.6 (1990), 959-66.

29. Thody, *Jean Genet*, p. 167.

30. Christopher Lane, 'The Voided Role: On Genet', *Modern Language Notes*, 112.5 (1997), 876-908.

31. Marie-Chantal Killeen, 'Pour une lecture girardienne des *Bonnes* de Genet', *French Studies*, 58.4 (2004), 485-98.

32. For Thody, Solange's final speech 'proclaims that they have now achieved their final deliverance' (*Jean Genet*, p. 164). It is not clear if Thody endorses Solange's optimism or not.

33. The question of theatrical genre is highly relevant. We know that a preliminary title of the play was 'La Tragédie des confidentes' (see *TC*, 1048) and, as Oreste Puccini established in a seminal early contribution to the criticism, *Les Bonnes* draws on classical theatrical conventions in numerous respects: respect for the three unities, division into five (informal rather than formal) sections, etc. ('Tragedy, Genet and *The Maids*', *Tulane Drama Review*, 7.3 (1963), 42-59). Yet, while the ceremonious, hieratic dimension to the play certainly aligns it with tragedy, analyses of different productions do not suggest that it is usually experienced by the spectator as tragic. This is doubtless related to the total absence of any final summation by a choir-figure or other character to hammer home the message or lesson to be learned. Since the most classically tragic aspect of the action — the death of the central character — is embraced by the character herself as a cause for celebration, it is understandable that amazement or bewilderment is a more common response to the ending than pity or terror. The play's political undecidability is inextricably linked to its generic unclassifiability.

34. This unpredictability provides another reason for rejecting readings of the play as focused on the need to ameliorate the lot of domestic servants: even if, contrary to what he says in the 'Avertissement' to *Le Balcon*, Genet may not have been entirely averse at this early stage to the idea that theatre could serve to find a 'solution pratique' to social problems, any temptation to instrumentalise art for political purposes would be countered by his awareness of the gap between staging a fantasy and its later implementation.

35. A little later, Claire in turn censures Solange for the pleasure her sister took as Madame the previous evening: 'J'ai inventé les pires histoires et les plus belles dont tu profitais. Hier soir, quand tu faisais Madame dans la robe blanche, tu jubilais, tu jubilais, tu te voyais déjà montant en cachette sur le bateau des déportés' [I invented the most fantastic stories and you used them for your own purposes. Yesterday, when you were Madame, I could see how delighted you were at the chance they gave you to stow away on the *Lamartinière*]. However, the role in question is not that of Madame herself, but of Madame-as-saint, a role she then concedes she went on to invent herself, 'mais avec moins de violence' [but with less violence] (*TC*, 139; *M*, 17).

36. See n. 10 above.

37. As with *Les Bonnes,* the published translations do not follow the definitive version. Citations in English are to the version with most translations of the lines analysed in French.

38. *Le Balcon*, whose draft title was 'España', is unmistakably informed by a reflection on Francoist Spain, as becomes explicit in the definitive version's comparison of the Chief of Police's tomb with the 'Vallée de Los Caídos' (*TC*, 342), the vast monument which took eighteen years to construct before opening with great fanfare in 1959.

39. Albert Bermel reads the castration as an inverted homage to the Chief of Police: 'His image will be enshrined in history as a man so potent that somebody felt it necessary to castrate him in effigy' ('Society as a Brothel: Genet's Satire in *The Balcony*', *Modern Drama*, 19.3 (1976), 265-80 (p. 278)).

40. 1955 manuscript held in the Fonds Genet, 80. The sentence 'Parce que tu y es sensible' is missing from the later typescripts and the published version of this scene in *TC*, 440.

41. Jacques Lacan, *Le Séminaire Livre V: Les Formations de l'inconscient*, ed. by Jacques-Alain Miller (Paris: Seuil, 1998), pp. 251-68.

42. Ibid., p. 267.

43. Ibid., p. 268.

44. Ibid.

45. For other engagements with Lacan's reading, see Lorenzo Chiesa, 'The First Gram of *Jouissance*: Lacan on Genet's *Le Balcon*', *The Comparatist*, 39 (2015), 6-21; and James Penney, 'The Phallus Unveiled: Lacan, Badiou and the Comedic Moment in Genet's *The Balcony*', *Paragraph*, 42.2 (2019), 170-87. While both present the castration as implying the restoration of the old order, they each use Lacan's reading as a springboard to suggest ways in which the message of Genet's play is not conservative.

46. Within the play, Irma uses the expression *entre hommes* to refer to Chantal and herself (*TC*, 295), producing a comedic effect that derives from the impossibility of knowing if she uses it ironically or metaphorically. In 1956, the expression is similarly used to include Carmen when the Chief of Police asks her to recount in full what has happened with Roger (*TC*, 420). Space does not allow me here to develop how relations between men are structured by a relationship to the femininity they exclude.

47. Hence, for example, Irma's instruction to Carmen to procure a pink rather than white apron for a scene scripted by a 'garçon de restaurant' [waiter] who 'exige une vraie révolte' [insists on a real revolt], or a green feather-duster for the 'employé de la S.N.C.F.' [railwayman] (*TC*, 293; *B*, 30).

48. Lacan, *Le Séminaire V*, p. 268.

49. Is this another difference between Roger and the other figures of authority? There is a case for reading the client playing the bishop, specified in an earlier draft as an 'employé d'une compagnie du gaz' [gas man] (*TC*, 405), as the plumber — 'le vrai' [the real one], 'celui qui répare les robinets' [the one who mends the taps] (*TC*, 290; *B*, 27) — mentioned in Scene 5 as leaving the brothel; we learn from cuts made to Scene 7 in 1962 that, having left the brothel, all the 'Grandes Figures' had returned to take refuge there.

# CHAPTER 3

❖

# Genres of Activism

Following the suicide of his lover Abdallah Bentaga in 1964, Genet tore up his unpublished manuscripts and declared that he would write no more literature. He was indeed to publish no further major work during his lifetime. However, as early as 1966 Paule Thévenin was able to persuade him to publish the *Lettres à Roger Blin*, which she deemed an important step forward in his being able to recognise that there was worth to what he had written and to 'renou[er] avec l'écriture' [reconnect with literature].[1] The publication in 1991 of *L'Ennemi déclaré*, a substantial collection of interviews and shorter texts that had for the most part appeared in various journalistic outlets from 1964 onwards, demonstrated that Genet had in fact continued both to write and to publish in the twenty years prior to his death. The considerable archive of unpublished material held in the Fonds Jean Genet in IMEC provides further evidence that writing remained a vital part of his experience right throughout the years of 'silence'. These documents take all kinds of form — letters, notes, speeches, projects clearly undertaken with a view to publication — and are at diverse stages of completion, ranging from off-the-cuff comments clearly scribbled in an immediate reaction to something that affected him, to substantial texts whose evolution can be followed over successive drafts. They provide incontestable evidence that Genet's 'silence' in the last two decades of his life was by no means a straightforward rejection of writing.

The period from which the majority of this documentation, both published and unpublished, dates (the late 1960s and early-to-mid 1970s) is often described as the period of Genet's activism. Genet's efforts on behalf of the Black Panthers and the Palestinians indubitably qualify as activism under any definition of the term, most commonly understood as mobilising in order to bring about a particular political or social change. In both cases, he travelled long distances and placed himself at some personal risk in order to show support for their respective causes. In 1970, he responded to the Black Panthers' request for help by travelling immediately to the US, where he spent two months and spoke at many different rallies and events.[2] The primary purpose of the trip was to campaign on behalf of Bobby Seale, one of the organisation's cofounders and a member of the 'Chicago Eight' imprisoned for conspiring to riot at the Democratic Convention of 1968, who was shortly due to go on trial again, in the context of the New Haven Black Panther trials, for kidnapping and murder. In October of that same year, briefed by the Palestinian Liberation Organisation (PLO) representative in Paris, Mahmoud El Hamchari, on the plight of the Palestinians in the wake of civil war in Jordan and the death of President Nasser of Egypt, the leader most supportive of their cause, he journeyed to Jordan. He intended to make a short visit but in the end stayed for nearly two years, during which time he not only travelled to the refugee camps but spent time with the Fedayeen in the hills. By any criteria, Genet's readiness to devote his time and energies to these political struggles amounts to an example of political commitment.

The question this chapter will examine is whether this political commitment reflects a significant shift away from Genet's earlier stance as explored in Chapter 2, a stance dismissive of the idea that his work should or could serve as an instrument to further any specific programme. To do this, we need to consider three different but related issues. The first concerns the evolution in Genet's political thinking. In contrast with his earlier statement that he was neither a 'type de droite' [right-wing guy] nor a 'type de gauche' [left-wing guy], he increasingly came to espouse left-wing positions in general, and notably to adopt a much more positive view of revolution than that reflected in his ambivalent portrayal of the insurrection in *Le Balcon*. The second issue is whether his growing interest in, and support for, revolutionary politics changed his views about the work of art and consequently the relationship between aesthetics and politics. Finally, and most importantly, the part played specifically by writing in Genet's activism during this period deserves careful investigation. While Genet's high symbolic status as an artist was the reason both the Panthers and the Palestinians appealed to him for help, his contribution in the examples of political commitment cited above involved lending them his name (and his bodily presence) more than it involved writing in their cause. The question therefore arises of the extent to which the texts he produced during the period in question function as activism. The fact that, when published, they appeared in predominantly journalistic fora is an unquestionable change; however, whether this reflects effect or cause of a transformation on Genet's part, and especially whether it marks a shift towards a more instrumental view of writing, is less sure. The vast majority of the pieces collected together in *L'Ennemi déclaré* are not only political in subject but openly promote a political cause. But this is also the case with most of the unpublished material from this time available for consultation in the IMEC archives. Much of this remains unpublished in accordance with Genet's own wishes; my aim is to explore what this implies for Genet's conception of the relationship between politics and aesthetics, and the contribution he felt his art could make to changing the world.

⋆　⋆　⋆　⋆　⋆

A major shift in Genet's political positioning can be inferred from his reaction to the events of May 1968. He had declined to sign the 'Manifeste des 121' in 1960, notwithstanding his support for the cause — 'j'approuve tout à fait les rebelles, et je les approuve en tout' [I entirely approve of the rebels, and I approve of them in everything] — citing the need to 'conserve[r] en moi cette complexe et difficile ambiguité' (*TC*, 940) [maintain this complex, difficult ambiguity in me]. Four years later, he had asserted in his interview with Madeleine Gobeil that he felt 'aucune' [no] solidarity even with those in situations comparable to his own, even though the only bond he felt was paradoxically with those who knew no bond: 'Je suis avec tout homme seul. Mais j'ai beau être, comment vous le dire, moralement, avec tout homme seul, les hommes seuls restent seuls' [I am for every man who is alone. But no matter how much I am — how shall I put it? — morally in favor of every man who is alone, such men remain alone] (*ED*, 14-15; *DE*, 5). In contrast, Genet appears to have experienced a deep and unreserved political connection with the students and workers of May '68. The delight he felt at the destabilising effect the protests had on Paris is evident in a short text he published in *Le Nouvel observateur* as early as 30 May 1968:

> Cohn-Bendit est l'origine, poétique ou calculée, d'un mouvement qui est en voie de détruire, en tout cas de secouer, l'appareil bourgeois et, grâce à lui, le voyageur qui traverse Paris connaît la douceur et l'élégance d'une ville qui se révolte. Les autos, qui sont sa graisse, ont disparu, Paris devient enfin une ville maigre, elle perd quelques kilos, et pour la première fois de sa vie, le voyageur a comme l'allégresse, en rentrant en France, et la joie de revoir des visages qu'il a connus ternes, enfin joyeux et beaux.

> [Cohn-Bendit is the originator, whether poetically or through calculation, of a movement that is going to destroy, or at least shake up, the bourgeois apparatus, and thanks to him, the traveler who makes his way through Paris knows the sweetness and elegance of a city in revolt. The cars, which are its fat, have disappeared, and Paris is finally becoming a lean city, it's losing a few pounds; and for the first time in his life, the traveler has a sense of exhilaration in returning to France, and he feels the joy of seeing the familiar grim faces now turned joyous and beautiful.] (*ED*, 31; *DE*, 20)

This piece is Genet's first foray into journalism; published at the very height of the upheaval, it shows him unambiguously celebrating the revolting students. This new willingness to align himself politically goes along with a new recourse to political terminology: his approval for the student movement's attempt to destroy the 'bourgeois apparatus' echoes an endorsement on the previous page of a 'jeunesse vraiment révolutionnaire' [truly revolutionary youth], the first time Genet uses the word revolutionary as an unequivocally positive term.[3] However, the text is scarcely a conventional piece of journalism. It is notable for the poetic register created by the metaphor of the city losing weight and by the persona of the 'voyageur': one who comes, we are told in the first line of the piece, 'de l'étranger, par exemple du Maroc' [from abroad, from Morocco for example] (*ED*, 29; *DE*, 18), as Genet himself had just done. The use of the third person to describe the traveller rejoicing at seeing familiar others cast in a new light suggests that the events had a destabilising effect on Genet himself as well as on Paris — although what has changed is not that he feels like an outsider within France, but rather that this new, strange, foreign France is one that does not alienate him.

Jacques Derrida, whose friendship with Genet was greatest at that time, recalled walking through the streets of Paris with him, delighted at the turmoil wrought by the riots.[4] However, Genet's enthusiasm was shortlived; he very soon became disillusioned with the students. Seven years later, when asked by Fichte if he found them revolutionary, he contrasted the violent sense of disruption he had experienced on his first visit to the Théâtre de l'Odéon occupied by the students with the order that had been re-established when he returned there, and suggested that the very decision to occupy a theatre (rather than the Palais de Justice, for example) showed a lack of seriousness on their part:

> Qu'est-ce que c'est qu'un théâtre? D'abord qu'est-ce que c'est que le pouvoir? Il me semble que le pouvoir ne peut se passer de théâtralité. Jamais. [...] Il y a un endroit au monde où la théâtralité ne cache aucun pouvoir, c'est le théâtre. [...] C'est absolument sans danger. En Mai 68, les étudiants ont occupé un théâtre, c'est-à-dire un lieu d'où est chassé tout pouvoir, où la théâtralité, seule, subsiste sans danger.

> [What is a theater? First of all, what is power? It seems to me that power can never do without theatricality. Never. [...] There is one place in the world where theatricality does not hide power, and that's in the theater. [...] There is absolutely no danger. In May '68, the students occupied a theater, that is, a place from which power has been evacuated, where theatricality remains on its own, without danger.] (*ED*, 155; *DE*, 131-32)[5]

Notwithstanding this disparaging assessment, May 1968 remained for years a touchstone for revolution in Genet's eyes. In 1970, when speaking at a debate organised by the Black Panthers at MIT, in Cambridge, MA, he evoked the atmosphere of the time as a model he would strive to recreate:

> En mai 68, je m'apercevais que j'étais tout à fait du côté des contestataires étudiants et ouvriers. En mai, la France que j'ai tant haïe n'existait plus, mais seulement, pendant un mois, un monde soudain libéré du nationalisme, un monde souriant, d'une extrême élégance, si vous voulez.
> Et mai a été saccagé par le retour en force du gaullisme et de la réaction.
> Je peux donc dire qu'en juin 68, ma tristesse et ma colère me firent comprendre que dorénavant je n'aurais de cesse que se retrouve, en France ou ailleurs, l'esprit de mai à Paris.

> [In May '68, I realized that I was completely and effortlessly on the side of the protesting students and workers. In May, the France that I so hated no longer existed; rather, for one month, there was a world suddenly liberated from nationalism, a smiling world, an extremely elegant world, you could say.
> And May was wrecked by the dramatic return of Gaullism and reaction.
> So I can tell you that in June 1968, my sadness and anger made me understand that from now on I would not rest until the spirit of that May in Paris returned, in France or elsewhere.] (*ED*, 41; *DE*, 28)

However fleeting its transformative effect may have been, May '68 represents a turning-point in Genet's political trajectory for the experience that it gave him of solidarity with the students and workers. We can note that here too, as in *Le Nouvel observateur*, he couches a political event in specifically aesthetic terms ('extremely elegant'). Genet's turn to active political engagement is motivated not by ideas but by beauty; at its origin, his commitment to revolution is above all an affective response. The reason he feels close to the Black Panthers is not because they have suffered injustice but because their struggle reawakens in him the 'grandes émotions de mai' [powerful emotions of May]: 'c'est ce movement révolutionnaire qui est le plus capable de provoquer, quand il réussira, une explosion de joie et de libération, en quelque sorte déjà préfigurée par mai en France' [this revolutionary movement is the most capable, when it succeeds, of provoking an explosion of joy and liberation, an explosion already prefigured in some ways by the events of May in France] (*ED*, 42; *DE*, 29). Similarly, he will later relate the depth of his connection to the Palestinians to the mixture of revolt and exultation that reminded him of May '68:

> Ce qui se passait dans les montagnes boisées de Jerash ressemblait un peu à ce que fut le mois de mai 68 à Paris, avec cette différence, mais importante, que les feddayin étaient armés. Comme à Paris, certains jours, il y avait sur les bases et sur les routes ou les chemins reliant les bases, une allégresse proche de l'effusion.
>
> [What happened in the wooded mountains of Jerash resembled in some ways the month of May '68 in Paris, with the important difference that the fedayeen were armed. As in Paris, on certain days, there was on the bases and on the roads or paths connecting the bases an elation bordering on effusion.] (*ED*, 92; *DE*, 74)

Genet's political engagement following May '68 thus appears tightly associated with an aesthetics of revolt. In the 1964 interview with Michèle Manceaux, he had claimed, 'Dans toute esthétique, il y a une morale' [In every æsthetics, there is a morality] (*ED*, 16; *DE*, 6). But the converse is also true. While he had never been a proponent of 'art for art', and would probably have agreed that an aesthetics necessarily implies a politics as well as an ethics, in the student riots he appears to have discovered a politics that appealed to him aesthetically. For the first time he felt solidarity with a collective as distinct from an individual revolt against society ('I was completely and effortlessly on the side of the protesting students and workers'). The contrast is striking between his 1964 claim to be 'avec tout homme seul' and his speech at MIT:

> Aussi bien, où que je me trouverai, je me sentirai lié toujours au mouvement qui provoquera la libération des hommes. Aujourd'hui et ici, c'est le Black Panther Party, et je suis auprès d'eux parce que je suis avec eux. [...] Je suis avec les Black Panthers.
>
> [Therefore, wherever I am, I will always feel connected to any movement that will provoke the liberation of men. Here and now, it is the Black Panther Party, and I am here by their side because I am on their side. [...] I am with the Black Panthers.] (*ED*, 42; *DE*, 29)

The idea of a specifically revolutionary beauty remained a major preoccupation for the rest of Genet's life. In *Miracle de la rose*, he had written: 'J'aime ceux que j'aime, qui sont toujours beaux et quelquefois opprimés mais debout dans la révolte' [I love those I love, who are always handsome and sometimes oppressed but who are upright in revolt] (*RP*, 477; *MR*, 236). In the latter part of his life, it appears that he found revolutionaries beautiful *because* they were 'upright in revolt'. In 'Quatre heures à Chatila', the text in which he develops his most sustained reflection on the 'beauté propre aux révolutionnaires' [beauty peculiar to revolutionaries] (*ED*, 251;

*DE*, 216), he affirms that revolution makes those who engage in it beautiful:

> Avant la guerre d'Algérie, en France, les Arabes n'étaient pas beaux [...]. Il fallait accepter l'évidence: ils s'étaient libérés politiquement pour apparaître tels qu'il fallait les voir, très beaux. De la même façon, [...] les feddayin étaient très beaux; et comme cette beauté était nouvelle, c'est-à-dire neuve, c'est-à-dire naïve, elle était fraîche, si vive qu'elle découvrait immédiatement ce qui la mettait en accord avec toutes les beautés du monde s'arrachant à la honte.

> [In France, before the Algerian War, the Arabs were not beautiful. [...] We had to admit the obvious: they had liberated themselves politically in order to appear as they had to be seen: very beautiful. In the same way, [...] the fedayeen were very beautiful; and since this beauty was new, or we could say novel, or naive, it was fresh, so alive that it immediately revealed its attunement with all the beauties of the world that have been freed from shame.] (*ED*, 261; *DE*, 225)

This production of beauty is framed here as a renewal, even a renaissance. Drawing our attention to the form of the word, the paronomastic shift from 'neuve' to 'naïve', and from 'naïve' to 'vive', reminds us that 'naïve' is etymologically linked to 'native': this beauty is a rebirth. In fact, Genet goes so far as to propose that revolution is liberatory insofar as it has this effect; the aim of revolution is beauty:

> Il faudrait peut-être reconnaître que les révolutions ou les libérations se donnent — obscurément — pour fin de trouver ou retrouver la beauté, c'est-à-dire l'impalpable, innommable autrement que par ce vocable. Ou plutôt non: par la beauté entendons une insolence rieuse que narguent la misère passée, les systèmes et les hommes responsables de la misère et de la honte, mais insolence rieuse qui s'aperçoit que l'éclatement, hors de la honte, était facile.
>
> Mais, dans cette page, il devait être question surtout de ceci: une révolution en est-elle une quand elle n'a pas fait tomber des visages et des corps la peau morte qui les avachissait. Je ne parle pas d'une beauté académique, mais de l'impalpable — innommable — joie des corps, des visages, des cris, des paroles qui cessent d'être mortes, je veux dire une joie sensuelle et si forte qu'elle veut chasser tout érotisme.

> [Perhaps we ought to recognize that the end pursued — obscurely — by revolutions or liberations is the discovery or rediscovery of beauty, that is something that is impalpable and unnamable except by this word. Or rather, no: by beauty we should understand a laughing insolence spurred by past misery, by the systems and men responsible for misery and shame, but a laughing insolence which realizes that, when shame has been left behind, the bursting forth of new life is easy.
>
> But on this page the question should also, and above all, be the following: is a revolution a revolution if it has not removed from faces and bodies the dead skin that distorted them? I'm not talking about an academic beauty, but rather the impalpable — unnamable — joy of bodies, faces, shouts, words that are no longer dead, I mean a sensual joy so strong that it tends to drive away all eroticism.] (*ED*, 261-62; *DE*, 225)

Revolutionary beauty is proof for Genet that those deadened by poverty and humiliation have been revitalised, their 'dead skin' replaced with joyful, living bodies. To be worthy of the name, a revolution must bring people alive. For him, the success of a revolution is ultimately to be judged not by whether it redresses injustice but by the beauty it produces.

Genet's distancing of the revolutionary 'sensual joy' of the body from eroticism at the end of this passage calls for analysis in the light of his view, as expressed in his interview with Fichte, that an intense erotic attraction was a crucial element in his support for the Panthers and the Palestinians:

> Je me demande si j'aurais pu adhérer à des mouvements révolutionnaires qui soient aussi justes que — je les trouve très justes, le mouvement des Panthers et le mouvement des Palestiniens — mais cette adhésion, cette sympathie, est-ce qu'elle n'est pas commandée en même temps par la charge érotique que représente le monde arabe dans sa totalité ou le monde noir américain, pour moi, pour ma sexualité?

> [I wonder whether I could have adhered to other revolutionary movements that are equally as just — I find these movements very just, the Panthers and the Palestinians — but isn't this adherence, this sympathy, also driven by the erotic charge that the whole Arab world or the Black American world represents for me, for my own sexuality?] (*ED*, 156; *DE*, 132)

Later in the interview, however, he elaborates: 'je ne faisais pas de distinction entre les Panthers, je les aimais tous, je n'étais pas attiré par un plutôt que par un autre. J'aimais le phénomène Black Panthers. J'en étais amoureux' [I didn't make any distinctions between the Panthers, I loved them all, I wasn't attracted by one rather than another. I loved the phenomenon of the Black Panthers. I was in love with that] (*ED*, 174; *DE*, 149). He will later reassert a link between his politics and his erotics in *Un Captif amoureux*, again with the nuance that the attraction he felt for both these groups was for the collective rather than any individual. Recalling the dynamic of a group of young black students listening to the Black Panther David Hilliard, Genet explains:

> Ces rapports étaient politiques et pourtant ce n'est pas le seul intérêt politique qui obtenait cette cohésion, mais un très subtil et très fort érotisme. Si fort, et à la fois si évident et discret, que je n'eus jamais de désir pour quelqu'un : je n'étais que désir pour ce groupe et mon désir était comblé par le fait que le groupe existait.

> [The links between them all were political, but that was not the explanation of their solidarity: also present was a very subtle but very strong eroticism. It was so strong, so evident yet so discreet, that while I never desired any particular person, I was all desire for the group as a whole. But my desire was satisfied by the fact that they existed.] (*CA*, 352; *PL*, 300)

Similarly, the Palestinian fedayeen strike him so strongly as the realisation of his desires that they paradoxically preclude any desire on his part. Their very existence satisfies him:

> Les deux premiers feddayin étaient si beaux que je m'étonnai moi-même de n'avoir aucun désir pour eux [...] chacun paraissait non seulement la transfiguration de mes fantasmes mais leur matérialisation m'attendant là [...]. Le seul trouble que j'éprouvais : que cette absence de désir correspondît avec la

*'matérialisation'* de mes propres désirs amoureux, à moins, comme je l'ai dit, que cette *'réalité-là'* rendît vaine la *'réalité en moi'* des fantasmes.

[The first two fedayeen were so handsome I was surprised at myself for not feeling any desire for them [...] each seemed not merely a transfiguration but also a materialization of my fantasies. And apparently at my disposal. [...] The only thing that disturbed me was the thought that this lack of desire coincided with the *'materialization'* of my own amorous desires — unless, as I said, the outward reality made the inner one superfluous.] (*CA*, 244; *PL*, 205)

Genet's investment in the political causes that attracted him thus pertains, in different ways, to both an erotics and an aesthetics. Whatever the role of the erotic in his initial agreement to become involved, insofar as the effect of the Panthers and Palestinians on Genet was to generate an absence of desire rather than to arouse him, his response is most accurately described as aesthetic.[6] It is also inspired as much by women as by men. In 'Quatre heures à Chatila', the writer explicitly differentiates between the beauty of the young male fighters, 'diffuse dans une forêt animée par la liberté des feddayin' [diffuse in a forest enlivened by the freedom of the fedayeen] and that of the Palestinian women in the camps: 'Plus encore que les hommes, plus que les feddayin au combat, les palestiniennes paraissaient assez fortes pour soutenir la résistance et accepter les nouveautés d'une révolution' [Even more than the men, more than the fedayeen in combat, the Palestinian women appeared strong enough to maintain resistance and to accept the changes brought by a revolution] (*ED*, 252; *DE*, 216). The beauty that for him is the manifestation of genuinely revolutionary activity has nothing to do with a conventional 'academic beauty'; when pushed by Rüdiger Wischenbart to elaborate on it, he clarifies:

Je n'ai jamais vu de banquier qui soit beau. Et je me demande si la beauté dont vous parlez [...] n'est pas venue du fait que les révoltés ont retrouvé une liberté qu'ils avaient perdue. [...] La beauté des révolutionnaires est visible par une espèce de désinvolture et même d'insolence à l'égard du peuple qui les a humiliés. [...] Tout naturellement j'ai été vers les peuples révoltés qui m'ont demandé mon adhésion. Cette beauté dont je parle [...] réside dans le fait que d'anciens esclaves se débarrassent de l'esclavage, de la soumission, de la servitude pour acquérir une liberté vis-à-vis de la France ou pour les Noirs, de l'Amérique, ou pour les Palestiniens, je dirais du monde arabe en général.

[I've never seen a banker who I thought was beautiful. And I wonder whether this beauty you're speaking of [...] doesn't come from the fact that those who revolt have regained a freedom they had lost. [...] The beauty of revolutionaries is visible in a sort of casualness and even insolence in relation to the people who have humiliated them. [...] Quite naturally, I was drawn toward people in revolt who asked me to join up with them. This beauty I'm speaking of [...] lies in the fact that former slaves have gotten rid of slavery, submission and servitude and have acquired a freedom in relation to France or, for the blacks, America, or for the Palestinians, I would say the Arab world in general.] (*ED*, 273-74; *DE*, 236)

It is as subjects, not objects, that he finds beauty in the revolutionaries. The beauty that attracts him is a matter not of their physical appearance but of a practice of the body; it is a lived sensuality rather than a visual ideal. What affects Genet so deeply is the sign of a physical enjoyment, a sense of bodily fulfilment generated by the very act of revolt against an oppressor.

There is thus an immense distance between Genet's ironic depiction of the rational, prudish revolutionary of *Le Balcon* and the sensual, joyful explosion that he found thrilling in May 1968 and that he subsequently recognised as a determining feature of all the movements he espoused. If, from 1968 onwards, he embraced the idea of revolution, it was not due to an ideological conversion but rather because he had an aesthetic, affective experience of collective action; his political commitment was passionate rather than intellectual in origin.[7] However, following his contact with revolutionary movements he became more interested in, and sympathetic to, revolutionary ideas. This is most evident in his adoption of the discourse of class politics, suggesting that the demands of the workers in May '68 had resonated with him, as well as the exuberance of the students. 'Français, encore un effort!', an article published in the leftwing *L'Idiot international* in March 1970 in defence of Roland Castro, imprisoned after the protests following the death of five African immigrants in appalling living conditions in Aubervilliers, is the first published indication of a shift in this direction. Genet structures his presentation of the context of Castro's trial as a conflict not between the French and the Africans but specifically between 'le patronat français' [French employers] and the 'main-d'œuvre pour Citroën, Simca, les mines et les usines' [manual labor for Citroën, Simca, the mines, and the factories] and accuses the authorities in the immigrants' countries of origin of complicity in allowing 'la mort d'un ouvrier noir, noir ou blanc' [the death of a black worker, black or white for that matter] to go unnoticed (*ED*, 37; *DE*, 25). The attention paid to class as much as to race is an indication of a new priority on Genet's part. In contrast with his longstanding sympathy for anti-imperialist struggles, as evidenced in his plays (and in the two earlier pieces he had written about the US), the writer had historically shown conspicuously little interest in the fate of the working class.[8]

A number of unpublished documents conserved in the IMEC archives show that Genet even went so far as to contemplate aligning himself publicly with socialism in the wake of May '68. Two folders in particular (GNT 6.17 and GNT 6.18), in all likelihood part of the one project, are fascinating in this regard. Consisting respectively of seven and eight pages, they contain a mostly unpaginated, rough copy discussion of ideas about politics, including Genet's intention imminently to make a public declaration of his conversion to socialism. The place and time of writing are explicitly given within the text as Spain and 1970; the absence of any mention of either the Black Panthers or the Palestinians suggests that it precedes his involvement with these movements. In the text, Genet variously addresses both a 'tu' who remains unidentified (Patrick Prado?) and a 'vous' that at times appears to refer to the Spanish nation as a whole; the document reads very much as a draft of the declaration that it announces. He presents the decision to make his declaration in that country as a gesture of solidarity with 'ce grand people qui tremble' [this great trembling people]:

> Une autre affirmation: j'ai choisi l'Espagne comme lieu de cette déclaration: ma décision était prise depuis longtemps où j'ai choisi le socialisme. Pour le déclarer

j'ai voulu attendre mon passage par l'Espagne, et m'y voici. Ma déclaration, sans
m'être imposée par personne ici, — je t'en remets le texte ainsi qu'à dix-sept
autres intellectuels — ne sera toutefois communiquée qu'en langue espagnole,
ce qui signifie que par [le moyen de] cette langue je me place au milieu des
Espagnols. (GNT 6.18)

[Another affirmation: I have chosen Spain as the place to make this declaration:
my decision was taken a long time ago when I opted for socialism. I wanted to
wait to be in Spain to declare it, and here I am. My declaration, although not
out of pressure from anyone here — I'm giving the text to you and to seventeen
other intellectuals — will nonetheless be delivered only in Spanish, to show [by
means of] that language that I am placing myself amidst the Spanish.]

While much of the text is a discussion of Spain, and especially of the power wielded
by Opus Dei (the reactionary Catholic organisation whose members, including Luís
Carrero Blanco, dominated the highest echelons of Franco's administration), it also
contains a narrative of Genet's own trajectory. He warns against seeing his embrace
of socialism as a rupture rather than a continuity:

Revenons encore au socialisme. Ne croyez pas non plus que je n'y songe que
depuis aujourd'hui. Les étudiants français de mai 68 (des gosses) m'ont obligé à
le vouloir plutôt que son contraire ou que ses faux-semblants. Si Victor García
retrouve dans mes pièces écrites il y a 20 ans des préoccupations politiques, c'est
qu'elles y sont. (GNT 6.18)

[Let us come back again to socialism. Don't think either that I've only been
thinking about it today. The French students of May '68 (all kids) obliged me to
want it rather than its opposite or its look-alikes. If Victor García finds political
concerns in the plays I wrote 20 years ago, it's because they are there.]

What has changed for him is not that he has developed a political awareness of the
ills of economic inequalities but rather that he is no longer held back from giving
voice to it by the more pressing need to find his own artistic voice. His political
position is no longer in conflict with the demands of writing:

Mon éducation n'est pas seule responsable de mon peu d'empressement à
rejoindre les mouvements socialistes: puisque je [disais] écrire j'étais obligé
de faire, solitairement, l'apprentissage de l'écriture. Et, de la même façon que
vous-mêmes, au bout d'un certain temps de répression vous en êtes venus à
vous affoler devant l'ombre de l'ombre d'un risque, ma solitude obligée m'avait
rendu frileux, et je craignais de me confronter avec d'autres hommes. Mais
depuis très longtemps je savais, mais sans le dire clairement, que les pouvoirs de
l'argent, et les sortilèges qu'il suscitait, et les sortilèges de la domination d'un
homme — ou de plusieurs — sur les autres, n'est pas seulement injuste: c'est
imbécile. (GNT 6.18)

[My education alone is not responsible for my lack of urgency in joining socialist
movements: since I [claimed] to write I had to do my solitary apprenticeship
of writing. And, in the same way that you, after a certain period of repression,
became anguished before the shadow of the shadow of a risk, my enforced
solitude had made me nervous, and I was afraid of confrontation with other
men. But for a very long time I knew, without saying so clearly, that the powers
of money, and the spells it casts, and the spells of a man's — or several men's —
domination over others, are not merely unjust: they are stupid.]

At the same time, however, he insists that even if he had never adopted a public political stance, he had been active in promoting challenges to the status quo of the kind he now commits himself to undertaking:

> Sans oser le déclarer publiquement, j'agissais et je parlais autour de moi de telle façon que ceux avec qui je vivais puissent à leur tour contester ces fausses valeurs, ces fausses grandeurs. Aujourd'hui, pour la première fois, et en termes clairs, je vous le dis, et c'est en Espagne. Je n'ai pas la folie de croire que je vais faire votre révolution: j'entreprends la mienne qui, comme je vous l'ai dit, me remettra un jour face au fait poétique et me replacera dans la solitude.
> Ce qu'il y a d'imprécis dans cette formulation, je suis prêt à le corriger pour l'exposé d'une méthode capable de réussir. Je ne la ferai pas ici, cette fois, mais je me tiens disponible pour te préciser les moyens d'aboutir, aux abords tout au moins, d'un tel socialisme. Il ne s'agit pas du reste, tu t'en doutes, de mettre au point une théorie, mais de reprendre quelques arguments de Mao-Tse-Tong, et, naturellement, de les appliquer. (GNT 6.18)

> [Without daring to declare so publicly, I acted and spoke in such a way that those I lived with could in turn contest those false values, false magnitudes. Today, for the first time, and clearly, I say it to you, and in Spain. I'm not mad enough to think that I can make your revolution: I'm undertaking my own which, as I said, will one day bring me back face to face with the poetic element and replace me in solitude.
> I am ready to correct whatever may be vague in this formulation to set out a method capable of success. I won't do that here, this time, but I am at your disposal to make clearer how such a socialism could succeed, at least roughly. As you can imagine, the issue is not to refine a theory but to take up some of Mao-Tse-Tong's arguments and, naturally, apply them.]

The document thus posits a mutually exclusive relationship between writing and speaking: writing is a solitary activity as distinct from actions and words deployed in order to achieve an aim. But how does the document itself fit into the schema it proposes? As an announcement 'in clear terms', it appears to mark a rejection, or more exactly a deferral, of poetry in favour of a more programmatic, theoretical, even scientific use of language.[9] The text's final words are 'élaborer une dialectique' [to elaborate a dialectic]: this astonishing document shows Genet not only contemplating declaring an unequivocal political position but adopting the language of dialectical materialism and attempting to develop a set of arguments that, however much he may disavow the idea, are difficult to distinguish from a theory.

The principal tenet of this rudimentary theory is that the freedom at which socialism should aim is subjective rather than economic. Genet repeatedly stresses the importance of creativity: 'il existe dans chaque homme des facultés ludiques, créatrices, poétiques, et qu'elles ont besoin de s'exercer. À tous les niveaux, dans toutes les situations, l'homme veut jouer et découvrir, découvrir le monde et se découvrir' [there exists in every man playful, creative, poetic capacities that need to be put in practice. At every level, in every situation, man wants to play and to discover, discover the world and discover himself]. And again: 'La liberté n'existe qu'à l'intérieur du jeu créatif individuel' [Liberty exists only within individual creative play]. As such, a playful inventiveness is the real hallmark of a revolution:

> Il faut prendre garde peut-être à ceci: que l'esprit révolutionnaire doit être total, et s'il ne s'exerçait qu'au profit de la seule politique, s'il n'avait pour but que la destruction du mode capitaliste, il est trop évident qu'en conservant la phraséologie qui permet à ce mode de se maintenir, une fois accomplie cette révolution, l'esprit qui l'a voulu ira se dégradant toujours plus jusqu'à reconstituer un mode tout aussi monstrueux d'asservissement. Autrement dit — et d'ailleurs tout aussi mal dit — la révolution aura lieu si elle permet à chacun d'exercer sa liberté, et la liberté complète ne peut se vérifier qu'à l'intérieur d'un jeu dont les règles sont à la fois observées et à la fois dépassées sans qu'il y ait tricherie. (GNT 6.17)

> [We need perhaps to be aware of the following: that the revolutionary spirit must be total, and if it is deployed on behalf of politics alone, if its only aim is to destroy capitalism, it's only too obvious that by keeping the phrasing that enables that world to keep on, once that revolution is achieved, the spirit that sought it will get worse and worse until it establishes just as appalling a mode of servitude. In other words — and indeed said just as badly — the revolution will take place only if it allows everyone to practise their freedom, and complete freedom can only be verified within a game whose rules are both respected and exceeded, but without there being any cheating.]

Genet places this idea in the lineage of Saint-Just's affirmation that 'le bonheur est une idée neuve en Europe' [happiness is a new idea in Europe]:

> Je dirai donc, ici, que le bonheur est une idée neuve en Espagne. Il serait temps d'en finir avec les résidus de la morale évangélique qui voudraient que le travail productif — la sueur de mon front, le cal de mes mains! — vont rester pour l'éternité une vertu. Le travail m'emmerde. (GNT 6.18)

> [So I say, here, that happiness is a new idea in Spain. It is time to bring to an end the residues of the evangelical morality according to which productive work — the sweat of my brow, the callouses on my hands! — is eternally deemed a virtue. Work pisses me off!]

He thus marks his distance from the moralising emphasis placed on productivity that had come to dominate the Marxist-Leninist regimes of Eastern Europe. The socialism he proposes is more holistic, arguably closer to the ideas of Marx himself, who theorised four different types of alienation of the working class: not only from the product of their labour but from the process of production, their own humanity and other workers. Genet explicitly calls for a reconceptualisation of the socialist ideal:

> Pour ce qu'il en est du socialisme, je crois qu'il faut le concevoir non comme les pays de l'Est ni comme [mot illisible] technocrate: d'une part le travail, d'autre part les loisirs. Cette sorte de dichotomie qui tranche l'homme en deux moitiés inégales, ne peut que lui causer un malaise qui peut le conduire au suicide. Pas plus loin, évidemment. [Mais] pensons à un socialisme où le travail est un bonheur, et je ne crains pas de dire que la révolution se fera sous les deux signes d'égales grandeur, le rouge et le noir. (GNT 6.17)

[As for socialism, I believe it needs to be conceived of not as the Eastern countries do, nor the technocrats: work on one side, leisure on the other. That sort of dichotomy splitting man into two unequal halves can only create an unease that may lead to suicide. No further, obviously. [But] let's think of a socialism where work is happiness, and I'm not afraid to say that revolution will take place under two signs of equal magnitude, the red and the black.]

The freedom not to work is in effect a freedom that challenges the opposition between work and play, effort and pleasure. The hallmark of socialism for Genet is the collective freedom to take pleasure in one's work, to do only work that gives one pleasure. But the corollary of this is that playing will be productive; people will be creative in all aspects of their lives. He explicitly formulates the goal of revolution as:

'Un socialisme qui chante', je ne veux pas dire un état d'idiots, peuplé d'anges qui s'embrassent: je parle au contraire de socialisme très dure, difficile à gagner, qui tiendra compte des luttes contre soi-même et contre les autres, et des luttes des autres contre soi-même, un socialisme aussi qui refusera l'ancienne et absurde malédiction: 'Tu gagneras ton pain à la sueur de ton front'. J'écrirai plutôt: 'Tu gagneras ton chant à la sueur de ton front' et je vous le jure mes amis, ce sera plus difficile et l'entreprise sera plus grave. (GNT 6.18)

['A singing socialism', I don't mean a state of idiots, peopled with angels kissing each other: I'm speaking rather of a very difficult socialism, one hard to earn, that will take into consideration the struggle within man and between men, and the struggles of others against oneself, a socialism that will also refuse the old, ridiculous condemnation: 'You will earn your bread by the sweat of your brow'. I would rather write: 'You will earn your song by the sweat of your brow' and I promise you, my friends, it will be more difficult and the project more serious.]

Genet's prioritisation of creativity over the class struggle here is even more reminiscent of Marcuse than of Marx. Marcuse's ideas had played an immensely influential role on the hippie movement in the US during the 1960s, and were increasingly available in French translation from the 1950s onwards; the French version of *Eros and Civilisation* was published in 1963.[10] However, while Genet's focus on pleasure and creativity chimes with that of the philosopher, his insistence on the difficulty of the struggle to attain a 'singing socialism' — and indeed on the centrality of conflict in the struggle — strikes a divergent note from the other's utopianism. The attention he pays to conflict both between humans and within the self suggests a sceptical attitude towards the Marcusian notion of a society that would be based on a minimal repression of the instincts.

Echoes of Marcuse are also in evidence in another substantive aspect of Genet's theory. The interest the writer takes in rethinking the lumpenproletariat suggests an awareness of the philosopher's belief that the revolutionary vanguard was located not in the working class but in the socially marginalised of all kinds. Genet does little more than mention the 'déplacement de la notion de lumpenprolétariat' [displacement of the notion of the lumpenproletariat] in the two documents identified above, but considers the question in surprising detail in another document written at approximately the same time:

> Un peu trop négligemment Marx parle du lumpenprolétariat pour le considérer comme un facteur réactionnaire. Marx va trop vite, et trop loin. Le lumpen n'est pas une classe homogène, avec ses critères de classe. Il est composé d'individus qui tous en fait ou l'autre, d'une ou de l'autre façon, se sont révoltés contre l'ordre établi, si bien que cet ordre les a [bannis]. Le bannissement, prison, bagnes, maison de redressement, certains 'milieux' les a réunis mais de telle sorte que personne ne peut s'y sentir solidaire des autres, même s'il s'agissait de défendre des intérêts communs là où il n'existe que des intérêts individuels.
>
> Pourtant, les régimes totalitaires ont su manipuler le lumpen, et pour une grande part, se servir de lui en le servant. Il faut peut-être en retirer ceci: c'est que les régimes totalitaires utilisant le lumpen ne sont pas *totalement* bourgeois. Je ne les défends pas. Je dis seulement que le moralisme de la bourgeoisie n'a pas [tant] d'importance à leurs yeux. Par certains côtés, le crapuleux, ils peuvent rassurer le lumpen.
>
> Il y a encore autre chose: chaque membre du lumpen a moins accepté une situation déterminée, qu'il n'a voulu la sienne, singulière quant au choix primordial, même si cette situation devait, par le bannissement des 'honnêtes gens' les coaguler tous dans ce qu'on croit à tort être une classe. Chaque individu a son originalité propre. Je n'en vois faire qu'une catégorie qui commande la solidarité de groupe sinon de classe, c'est les maquereaux. Je parle des proxénètes designés, [*mot illisible*] ou plus souvent absous par la justice.
>
> Mais tous les autres: voleurs, escrocs, vagabonds, drogués, etc... peuvent être utilisés un moment par la droite, et eux-mêmes séduits par elle, mais il faudra peu de temps pour que d'un côté comme de l'autre on se méfie: les voleurs deviennent voleurs à l'intérieur du moment réactionnaire, la droite se fait répressive à leur égard, comme la bourgeoisie classique. (GNT 6.24)

[Marx speaks a little too carelessly of the lumpenprolétariat in considering it a reactionary element. Marx goes too quickly, and too far. The lumpen is not a homogeneous class, with class criteria. It is made up of individuals who all, one way or another, rebelled against the established order, finding themselves excluded as a result. Banishment, prison, jails of different sorts, certain 'environments' may have brought them together but in such a way that nobody could feel in solidarity with others there, even if it was a matter of defending their common interests where there were only individual interests.

However, the totalitarian regimes were able to manipulate the lumpen, and in large part use it for their purposes while claiming to serve it. We should perhaps draw the following message: the totalitarian regimes using the lumpen are not *totally* bourgeois. I am not defending them. I am only saying that bourgeois morality is not so important in their eyes. In certain (heinous) ways, they reassure the lumpen.

There is something else: it is less that each member of the lumpen accepted a given situation than that he chose his own, made a singular choice, even if that situation, by excluding them from the ranks of the 'honest people', was to combine them all in what one would wrongly believe to be a class. Each individual has his own originality. The only category I see as developing a solidarity of group if not of class is that of the pimps. I'm talking of those clearly identified as pimps, [*illegible*] or more often absolved by justice.

But all the others: thieves, crooks, tramps, drug-addicts, etc... can be used for a while by the right, and themselves seduced by the right, but before long both sides will beware: the thieves become thieves within the reactionary moment, the right becomes repressive towards them, like the classic bourgeoisie.]

Here Genet appears to agree with Marcuse against Marx that the lumpenproletariat's lack of integration within the capitalist system affords it revolutionary potential, although he builds on this to complicate the system on the side of the oppressors as well as the oppressed, pointing up a heterogeneity within the totalitarian regimes that exploit the marginalised. Yet, leaving the content aside, by a considerable margin the most striking aspect of this text is the neutral, detached standpoint that Genet adopts to discuss the very questions that he had approached from an intensely personal perspective in his novels. At issue is the question whether a set of individuals defined by the very characteristics he had previously used to set himself apart from any community — individuals in revolt against the social order, including thieves and vagabonds, professing no allegiance to any group or class — can be grouped (lumped) together in a collective. At no moment, however, does he relate their case to his own. Does the external viewpoint of political theorist that he assumes in talking about them reflect the fact that he now sees himself as someone who feels solidarity with others? Or, given that the other question explored here is the extent to which the right makes use of these marginals to serve its own purposes, does it translate a reservation or anxiety on his part that it was not during his own time as a thief and outcast but rather at this later time of writing, when the financial dividend of his earlier success assured him the liberty to live his life as he pleased, that he was in danger of serving right-wing interests?

Other documents that specifically invoke Genet's personal circumstances convey a more equivocal attitude towards the social struggle endorsed so unambiguously in the documents cited above. Unfortunately, the date on which they were written cannot be ascertained, so we cannot say whether they bear witness to a later evolution in his thinking or a more complex position than he wished to acknowledge at the time of his public 'declaration'. One sheet of paper contains a series of notes in which he muses over his distance from the working class:

> Je ne suis peut-être pas de droite mais pas de gauche puisqu'elle est reven-diquée par les travailleurs. Je les aime pas, ni le travail.
> [*Biffé:*] 'La liberté — selon Pericles — c'est le courage de s'opposer au pouvoir.' [...]
> Plus je m'oppose au pouvoir plus je suis libre = à la limite je suis le pouvoir.
> La majorité des hommes travaille pour vivre sans doute mais produisent. Si leur travail est indispensable à leur vie il sert la mienne. On peut dire qu'une majorité d'hommes se fatigue pour mon seul luxe: écrire ou ne rien foutre. (GNT 6.66)

> [I may not be on the right, but I'm not on the left either as it's claimed by workers. I don't like workers, or work.
> [*Crossed out:*] 'Freedom — according to Pericles — is the courage to oppose power.' [...]
> The more I oppose power, the more I am free = one could even say that I am power.

Most men surely work to live but they produce. While their work is indispensable for their life, it serves mine. We could say that a majority of men tire themselves out to give me the luxury: of writing or doing nothing.]

Genet recognises his own position of relative privilege as a statement of fact, with no attempt either to justify or, crucially, to apologise for it. Far from the primary position it holds in a Marxist perspective, economic inequality is not the dominant motivation by which Genet models his conduct.[11] An accompanying document suggests that any regret he feels about his relative affluence derives not from a sense of injustice but rather from a feeling of betrayal that helps to explain the importance of the theme of betrayal throughout his work from *Journal du voleur* onwards:

> Selon une ligne qui semblait incassable j'aurais dû continuer dans la misère, le vol au moins, peut-être l'assassinat et peut-être aussi la prison à perpétuité — ou mieux. Cette ligne paraît s'être cassée. Or c'est cela qui m'a fait perdre toute innocence. J'ai commis ce crime d'échapper au crime, d'échapper aux pouvoirs et à leurs risques. J'ai dit qui j'étais au lieu de me vivre, et disant qui j'étais je ne l'étais plus.
>
> Cette désolation d'avoir cédé au monde renvoie peut-être à un supposé moral. Ce n'est pas certain. Une esthétique, c'est plus juste, a été ravagée. (GNT 6.65)

> [Following a line that seemed unbreakable, I should have continued my path of poverty, theft at least, perhaps murder and perhaps also life in prison — or better. That line seems to have broken. That has made me lose all innocence. I committed the crime of escaping from crime, escaping from powers and their risks. I said who I was instead of living it and, saying who I was, I was that no longer.
>
> The desolation of having given in to the world may possibly be related back to my morale. It is not certain. It is more accurate to say that an aesthetic was devastated.]

The 'crime' he reproaches himself with — of having escaped from crime and poverty, of no longer disobeying the rules of the social order — is explicitly aesthetic in nature rather than economic. It may have been vital (in the sense of the word meaning 'indispensable for life') in that it enabled him to live a life worth living. It may even have had some political effect; as he proceeds to elaborate, 'les cas de survie dans les interstices' [cases of survival in the interstices] can enable 'disjonctions institutionnelles' [institutional shifts], bring about a 'nouveau métabolisme social' [new social metabolism], although such displacements of the status quo 'ne sont pas encore révolutionnaires' [are not yet revolutionary]. Significantly, however, the text ends with the question 'Mais faut-il être révolutionnaire?' [But should we be revolutionary?] The sympathy for revolutionary activity that he indubitably developed in the years following May '68 did not equate to any certainty that a revolutionary position was an ideal that should necessarily be adopted or that redressing economic injustice should automatically take priority over all other issues.

The unpublished documents thus point to a more conflicted attitude towards the class struggle and issues of economic inequality than Genet expresses in the pieces he published during this period. It is interesting that the draft sections he crossed out pertain disproportionately to his own individual circumstances; this genetic material shows clearly that he achieved his 'neutral', theoretical tone literally by excising elements with a more personal focus. Yet it is equally significant that he never aired publicly the rather arid theoretical reflections he thereby formulated, let alone actually make his Spanish declaration. While the pieces he published do incontrovertibly indicate a new interest in class politics, it is evident from these private musings that he did not unambiguously endorse any clear ideological position and that his reluctance to espouse one publicly was bound up with his own particular, personal positioning in relation to class.

Similarly, the views he expressed in public about the intersection of class and race do not correspond fully to those he explores in the archival material. In the public interventions he made in public in support of the Black Panthers, he repeatedly relates race to class. Speaking at the University of Connecticut on 18 March 1970, he praised the Panthers' elaboration of a 'réflexion politique originale' [original political reflection] and proclaimed: 'L'origine du racisme est socio-économique. Nous devons en avoir bien précisément conscience car là est le point de départ de notre solidarité avec les Noirs et le parti des Black Panthers' [The origins of racism are socio-economic. We need to be very precisely aware of this, for it is the point of departure for our solidarity with blacks and the Black Panther Party] (*ED*, 44-45; *DE*, 30-32). His 'May Day Speech', delivered at Yale University a few weeks later, defines revolutionary action in uncharacteristically unambiguous and instrumental terms as 'tout acte capable de rompre brusquement l'ordre bourgeois en vue d'accomplir un ordre socialiste' [every act capable of abruptly breaking down the bourgeois order with the aim of creating a socialist order] (*ED*, 50; *DE*, 37). In the interview Genet gave on his return to France to promote awareness of the Panthers' cause, he similarly emphasises the economic dimension of their struggle: 'Ils voient dans leur combat un combat de classe. Leur but est une révolution de style marxiste' [They see their struggle as a class struggle. Their goal is a Marxist-style revolution] (*ED*, 59; *DE*, 46). The pieces he wrote in support of George Jackson again endorse the same message: 'Racisme et lutte de classe sont la même chose' [Racism and class struggle are the same thing] (*ED*, 103; *DE*, 83).

This new insistence on the impossibility of separating racial from economic injustice derives from the priorities of the Panthers themselves. The party differentiated itself from black 'cultural nationalism' such as propounded by LeRoi Jones by emphasising the links between racism and other oppressive power structures. In Bobby Seale's words, the fight for black liberation 'is a class struggle and not a race struggle'.[12] The Panthers thus broke new ground in adopting an explicitly revolutionary, anti-capitalist and anti-imperialist platform. They were not the first to see racial politics in the US as a form of colonialism; Stokely Carmichael and Charles Hamilton had drawn heavily on Fanon's *Les Damnés de la terre* to analyse the situation of Black Americans in terms of that of colonial subjects in their 1967 *Black Power: The Politics of Liberation*.[13] A reference by Genet (in an unpublished text kept in the 'Black Panthers' file of the Fonds Genet, and thus probably written during or shortly after his visit to the US) to this last book precisely as a precursor of the Black Panthers suggests that Genet had already read it prior to 1970:

> Il existe d'abord une littérature noire préfigurant celle des Panthères: Frederic[k] Douglass, du Bois, Richard Wright, Malcolm X. Mais les Panthères je suppose accepteraient aussi le beau livre de Le Roi Jones sur la musique noire et l'essai de Carmichael et Charles Hamilton sur le Black Power.
>
> Si j'ai parlé de ces écrivains, c'est qu'il est aussi dans la ligne d'une très longue révolte et de projets révolutionnaires. Volontairement j'en retranche Fanon ou d'autres révolutionnaires (Kim Il Sang) ayant influencé les Panthères. (GNT 6.2)[14]

> [A black literature prefiguring that of the Panthers already existed: Frederick Douglass, du Bois, Richard Wright, Malcolm X. But I suppose the Panthers would also accept LeRoi Jones's great book about black music, and the essay about Black Power by Carmichael and Charles Hamilton.
>
> If I've spoken of those writers, it's because they continue a long line of revolt and of revolutionary projects. I'm deliberately not including Fanon or other revolutionaries (Kim Il Sang) who influenced the Panthers.]

Genet was manifestly both convinced and enthused by *Black Power*'s argument about the colonial origins of black oppression, although by the time of his involvement with the Panthers in 1970 Carmichael had already left the Party (rejecting their anti-separatist perspective). Interestingly, after the split in the Panthers that emerged in 1971 between those who sought to prioritise the anti-imperialist dimension of the struggle for black liberation (notably Algeria-based Eldridge Cleaver) and those who believed the focus should be on redressing the socio-economic deprivation of US black communities (Huey Newton in California), Genet was to side with the latter.

Given the Panthers' systematic emphasis on the socio-economic roots of racism, it is fascinating to note the care Genet nonetheless takes not to subordinate race to class. He prefaces his 'May Day Speech' with a warning of the danger of overlooking the differences between him and the Panthers:

> Ma façon de vivre, ici et ailleurs, est celle d'un vagabond et non d'un révolutionnaire, mes mœurs même sont inusuelles, de sorte que je dois faire très attention quand je parle au nom du Black Panther Party [...]. Je veux dire que, dans mes interventions, aucune irréalité ne doit se glisser, car elle serait préjudiciable au Black Panther Party, et à Bobby Seale, qui est bel et bien dans une prison réelle, de pierre, de ciment et d'acier.

> [Here and elsewhere, I live like a vagabond, not like a revolutionary; my habits and behavior are themselves unusual, so that I must be very careful when I speak in the name of the Black Panther Party [...]. What I mean to say is that no unreality should slip into my interventions, for that would be detrimental to the Black Panther Party, and to Bobby Seale, who is in a very real prison, made of stone and cement and steel.] (ED, 47; DE, 34)

He then goes on to extend this need to be conscious of differences more generally, arguing that it was the duty of whites — and specifically the 'radicaux blancs' [white radicals] of whom the audience he was addressing was presumably composed — to bring 'une dimension nouvelle en politique' [bring a new dimension into politics]. He characterises this as a 'délicatesse du cœur' [delicacy of heart], as revealed in 'un comportement qui tendrait à effacer leurs privilèges' [behavior that would tend to erase their privileges] (*ED*, 48-49; *DE*, 35). As is the case in nearly all of the texts examined in this chapter, his use of *nous* [us] includes himself with other whites, as distinct from the blacks: 'Nous, nous vivons peut-être dans une démocratie libérale, mais les Noirs vivent, bel et bien, sous un régime autoritaire, impérialiste, dominateur' [As for us, perhaps we live in a liberal democracy, but blacks live, really and truly, under an authoritarian, imperialist regime of domination] (*ED*, 52; *DE*, 38).

Genet's awareness of the importance of not usurping the black voice is a recurrent motif in the unpublished material conserved in IMEC. The documents dealing with the Black Panthers, the vast majority of which are photocopies rather than originals, are very diverse. Most are contained in a folder entitled 'Dossier Black Panthers' (GNT 6.1-6.16). While few are explicitly dated, some were undoubtedly written during Genet's two-month stay in the US, as they contain drafts of responses to questions he could be asked about the Panthers and the reasons for his involvement with them. The status and dating of others are more difficult to decide. Some are written on American-size paper; however, this does not necessarily mean that they were written in America. Several of the more substantial documents of ten pages or more appear to be drafts of work intended to be published, with pages varying from scribbled notes to a series of paragraphs elaborating a sustained, coherent reflection. One of the most developed, a thirteen-page piece entitled 'Les Panthères sont des hommes' [The Panthers are Men] and filed in a different folder from the other documents devoted to the Panthers, refers to itself as an 'article' (GNT 5.4). Another (GNT 6.6) is headed 'ıer Chapitre', suggesting it was to form part of a longer project, presumably the book about the Black Panthers that he had promised David Hilliard he would write.[15] In addition, the IMEC archives contain the photocopy of an unpublished manuscript of approximately 15,000 words, labelled by someone other than Genet as an 'Ouvrage inédit sur les Black Panthers' [Unpublished work about the Black Panthers]. With very few corrections or revisions, it has clearly been copied out from an earlier draft or drafts and is at a much later stage of development than the other material, very little of which it repeats. The fact that the original was hand-written in two French copybooks is an indication that it post-dates Genet's journey to America, and a reference at one point to 1972 suggests that this *récit*, or narrative, is a relatively advanced version of the book about the Panthers and the Palestinians that Genet was working on during the early seventies, first commissioned by Yasser Arafat as early as November 1970.[16]

Throughout these documents, Genet's concern to respect the difference between himself and black people is unmistakable. The first extended text, consisting of ten pages entitled 'Situation actuelle: le mouvement des Panthères Noires', begins as follows:

> Il paraît évident qu'un blanc ne peut comprendre les noirs. Les preuves de l'imagination, l'amitié ni même l'affection ne le sauraient. Ni même l'amour, le plus souvent.

> La seule méthode qui permettra peut-être à un blanc de comprendre le peuple noir, c'est la lutte, quotidienne, et pour un même combat, avec les noirs. Mais à peine cela est-il formulé qu'il faut vite le corriger par ceci: l'initiative, quant à la forme du combat, doit être laissée au noir. (GNT 6.2)

> [It seems obvious that a white cannot understand the blacks. The achievements of imagination, friendship, even affection, could not do it. Not even love, most often.
>
> The only way a white could perhaps understand black people is by a daily struggle, for the same motivations, at their side. But no sooner have I formulated that than I need immediately to correct it by this: the initiative as to the form of the struggle must be left to the black.]

Again, the influence of *Black Power* can be perceived; Carmichael and Hamilton had argued that while there is a place for whites in the struggle for racial equity, '[t]heir function is not to lead or to set policy or to attempt to define black people to black people. Their role is supportive'.[17] Genet appears to have taken this view on board; it is clearly a priority for him to show loyalty to the Panthers and to respect their wishes, a loyalty all the more striking given the importance that betrayal had assumed in his later texts. In several texts he asserts that the way for whites to help the blacks is unreservedly to support the implementation of the Panthers' ten-point programme, the policy platform developed by Newton and Seale in 1966. He praises David Hilliard for being wary that Genet's desire to help could change into control:

> Il ne voulait pas que j'aie une seule idée originale, craignant que je ne me serve d'elle pour faire acte d'autoritarisme. Il avait raison. Le blanc a pour lui au[x] USA une masse qui lui tiendrait lieu de raison, et de servir à la civilisation occidentale lui offre un système de référence si compact, qu'il peut y puiser comme il veut, n'importe quel argument. (GNT 6.2)

> [He didn't want me to propose a single original idea, fearing that I might use it in an authoritarian way. He was right. In the USA the white's predominance means he doesn't have to be right, and being in the service of western civilisation gives him such a compact system of reference that he can draw any argument he likes from it.]

He reflects that only 'l'action directe' [direct action] as determined by the Panthers and 'sous leurs directives' [under their orders] can help their cause; whites have to set their own judgement aside and model their actions entirely on the Panthers:

> De telle façon que les buts, les réussites, les échecs, les espoirs, les deuils des Panthères sont les buts, les réussites, les échecs, les espoirs, les deuils des blancs. L'imagination la plus généreuse, la générosité la plus offerte dont on ne savait se délivrer, ferait moins que l'acte le plus discret, s'il est fait avec eux. (GNT 6.6)

> [In such a way that the goals, successes, failures, hopes, losses of the Panthers are the goals, successes, failures, hopes and losses of the whites. Even the most generous imagination, the most prodigious generosity that could not be escaped, would do less than the most discreet act if done with them.]

Genet, then, takes particular care not to speak *for* blacks or to prescribe the direction they should take.[18] There is indubitably an identificatory element to his support for them, expressed most clearly in his interview with Fichte: 'je ne pouvais me retrouver que dans les opprimés de couleur et dans les opprimés révoltés contre le Blanc. Je suis peut-être un Noir qui a les couleurs blanches ou roses, mais un Noir' [I could only place myself among the oppressed people of color and among the oppressed revolting against the whites. Perhaps I'm a Black whose color is white or pink, but a Black] (*ED*, 149; *DE*, 126). He was also undoubtedly affected by the fact that the Panthers' theoretical rejection of identitarian politics translated in practice into a genuine openness to his involvement and acceptance of him: 'Hilliard ni Masai [Ray 'Masai' Hewitt, the Panthers' Minister of Education] ne m'ont fait sentir que j'étais un étranger parmi eux' (GNT 5.4) [Hilliard and Masai never made me feel I was a stranger among them]. Nonetheless, he stresses repeatedly that racial difference always risks resurfacing as a danger for black people, however sympathetic and supportive a white may be. He situates this danger above all at the level of the unconscious, as a matter of fantasy or desire, not as a rational or logical position. In one document, he meditates on the limits of his own involvement in the black revolution:

> Dans la révolution noire, aucun blanc ne pourra imposer une stratégie révolutionnaire, parce qu'à certains moments il pourrait dériver, et demeurer sans contrôle, ni de lui ni des noirs. [...]
> Je ne suis pas blanc parce que j'ai la peau blanche, mais parce que mes souvenirs d'enfance m'ont préparé à une insertion dans le monde blanc.
> Arrivé à un certain âge, après des expériences plus que pourrissants, tout me porte vers la libération des noirs. Tout? Pas tout à fait. Mes phantasmes ne sont pas ceux d'un noir, ma vie nocturne ne l'est pas. (GNT 6.10)

> [In the black revolution, no white can impose a revolutionary strategy because at certain times he could drift off, and go out of control, either of himself or of the blacks. [...]
> I am not white because I have white skin, but because my memories of childhood prepared me to be part of the white world.
> At the age I have reached, after experiences that were more than putrefying, everything moves me towards the liberation of the blacks. Everything? Not quite. My fantasies are not those of a black, nor is my nocturnal life.]

The example he gives in this text is the difference between David Hilliard's enjoyment at seeing the French being killed in *La Bataille d'Alger* and his own; although ostensibly similar, Genet muses that their responses, deriving from different personal histories, could separate them rather than bring them together:

> Nous nous rencontrions, David et moi, dans le rire, mais n'étant pas provoqué par les mêmes motifs, il n'était pas le même. S'il n'était pas le même, à un certain moment il aurait pu cesser (si pour moi, par exemple, sa cause cessait). (GNT 6.10)

> [David and I came together in laughter, but as the laughter wasn't in response to the same grounds, it wasn't the same. If it wasn't the same, at a certain moment it could have stopped (if, for example, its cause for me stopped)].

Another example is the divergence of connotation attached to something as simple as a tree. As he recounts in his interview with Antoine Bourseiller, when he asks

David if he will accompany them to Stony-Brook, where Genet was to speak:

> David ne répond rien. Mais enfin il a fait quand même cette réponse: 'Non, il
> y a encore trop d'arbres.' C'est une réponse que seul un Noir américain pouvait
> faire. Pour lui, un arbre, c'était d'abord une plante à la branche de laquelle on
> pendait autrefois des Nègres.
>
> [David doesn't answer. But he finally did answer: 'No, there are still too many
> trees.' Only a black American could give that answer. For him, a tree was first
> of all a plant with branches from which black people had been hung.] (*ED*, 222;
> *DE*, 190)

The resonance this story held for Genet can be gleaned from the fact that he returns
to rework it in at least four separate texts.[19] In writing, he is drawn to engage with
the affective and psychical effect of centuries of injustice on the black communities,
as concretised in this image, more than with the socio-economic conditions in
which they live.

Notwithstanding Genet's growing interest in socialist theory and the Black
Panthers' own emphasis on the economic origins of racism, the need to transform
the material conditions of the Black community (as set out in the ten-point programme that he dutifully publicised when he spoke) is thus by no means the writer's
highest priority from the period of his involvement with the party onwards.[20] In
his unpublished writings, he places the emphasis squarely on the need to abolish
injustice by transforming intersubjective relations between people. One document
in particular, curated as dating from between 1971 and 1976, comprises a sustained
reflection on the insufficiency of revolutionary thinking that considered the
removal of economic inequality as the path to liberation. For Genet, economic
hierarchies are just one manifestation of a broader structure that for him is the
overarching problem, and as such should be the principal target of revolutionaries.
It opens on a surprisingly lyrical note:

> À qui peut servir une révolution si elle ne permet pas les changements des
> rapports entre les hommes, au niveau le plus humble, si elle n'a pas pour but
> principal que chaque rencontre, nouvelle ou non, entre des gens qui ne se
> connaissent ou qui s'ignoraient, ne soit une source d'émerveillements? Il faudra
> que tombent beaucoup de masques et que [s]'élabore une politesse — jamais
> codifiée, toujours inventée — qui, au lieu 'd'arracher' de nous un sourire nous
> mette si à l'aise qu'elle nous enveloppera d'un sourire. L'éclat de rire serait
> toujours imminent et les hommes pourraient s'aborder — en souriant sans
> doute — mais chacun posant à l'autre cette question 'Qu'avez-vous appris,
> depuis hier, de certain sur l'existence de Dieu?' (GNT 6.20)
>
> [Whom does a revolution serve if it doesn't bring about a change in the relations
> between men, at the most humble level? If its main aim is not for every
> encounter, new or otherwise, between people who do not know each other
> or know much about each other to be a source of wonder? Many masks would
> have to fall and a politeness — never programmatically, always inventively —
> would have to emerge that, instead of 'wrenching' a smile from us, would set
> us so much at our ease that it would wrap us in a smile. Laughter would always
> be imminent and men could approach each other — doubtless smiling — with

each asking the other 'What have you learned with certainty since yesterday about the existence of God?']

Genet's revolutionary dream is of a world in which people relate to each other in 'wonder', with the confidence not only to let down their defences but to show a truly imaginative, non-programmatic politeness towards each other. Paradise represents a gently-smiling world of human flourishing whose inhabitants encourage each other in ascertaining the existence of God, which invites reading as a figure for exploring a divine or beatific side to life! At least on the surface, this utopian vision of a society that would have removed the violence from human interactions even to the point of transforming everyday language (so that smiles 'envelop' rather than are 'wrenched from' us) could scarcely be further removed from the ostensible eulogy of brutes analysed in Chapter 1.

Genet then shifts to a more sober analysis of the 'will to dominate' that explains why such a society is likely to remain virtual:

> Nous ne pourrons rien vous dire, et les nombreux dialectes parlés ne sont pas en cause — mais rien vous dire de vrai car toutes nos paroles sont la projection sur les autres hommes de notre volonté de domination. Depuis longtemps — est-ce depuis toujours? — cette volonté de domination sous-tend les rapports des hommes, dans le monde entier, et elle se confond assez exactement avec les ordres hiérarchiques, sociaux ou religieux, avec les pouvoirs politiques et policiers, avec les situations qui opposent, dans toutes leurs confrontations, capitalisme et prolétariat, enfin, et ceci est plus fortement ressenti depuis plusieurs années dans les rapports entre les pays colonialistes et les colonisés. (GNT 6.20)

> [We can't say anything, and not because of any difference in spoken dialect — we can't say anything true because all our words project onto other men our will to dominate. Fo so long — has it been forever? — that will to dominate has underpinned relations between men, throughout the entire world, and it overlaps nearly exactly with the social or religious hierarchical orders, the political powers, the police, the opposing situations that confront capitalism and the proletariat with each other, and for a number of years this has been even more strongly felt in the relations between colonial countries and the colonised.]

This document reveals Genet as Nietzschean revolutionary: the root problem is the 'volonté de domination' that he sees as a universal determinant of human relations. By clarifying that his inability to elucidate the matter is not a problem of translation from one language to another, he stresses that it is not specific to any one culture but common to all, just as the shift from a 'long time' to 'forever' posits that it has always shaped human interactions. Moreover, the plural pronoun 'we' includes himself and his own words in the structure he deplores. Therefore capitalism per se is not the original enemy; along with colonialism, it is a subset of a greater set of hierarchical orders, all structured on the common basis of an original 'mépris' [contempt] that makes it possible for a man to view another man as lesser, inferior, and that excludes the possibility of any real exchange between them:

Pas même une réflexion, beaucoup moins qu'une réflexion, quelque chose comme un léger égarement nous indique que nous passons à côté d'une vie plus réelle: les échanges sont impossibles. Les pouvoirs de dominer — soit la force brutale ou le mépris qui rend invisible celui qu'on méprise — que détiennent certains hommes ou certains groupes, sont tels, qu'ils créent en nous une sorte de vertige dont on espère se délivrer en créant sur le même mode mis à une autre échelle, de semblables rapports avec d'autres hommes, qui eux-mêmes... La délégation d'un acte brutal — je ne parle même pas d'injustice tant il va de soi que tout acte de supériorité méprisante détruit toute justice — en une série d'actes de même nature, contamine la vie du monde entier. Ou bien nous sommes vulnérables physiquement et notre mépris est silencieux ou à peine murmurant, ou nous sommes armés et nous exigeons des autres la déférence et l'humilité. (GNT 6.20)

[It's not a reflection, it's much less than a reflection, it's rather something like a slight distraction that tells us we are missing out on a more real life: exchange is impossible. The power to dominate — whether brute force or the contempt that makes the one we despise invisible — held by certain men or certain groups is such that it creates a kind of vertigo in us from which we hope to escape by creating similar relations, in the same mode on a different scale, with other men, who in turn... The delegation of a brutal act — I'm not even going to talk of injustice, it is so obvious that every instance of contemptuous superiority destroys all justice — to a series of acts of the same kind contaminates the life of the entire world. Either we are physically vulnerable and our scorn is silent or scarcely murmured, or we are armed and we insist on deference and humility from others.]

Rather than injustice producing brutality (as in classic Marxist theory), here injustice derives from a more fundamental tendency to brutality. In retrospect, the analysis of brutality that we saw dominate Genet's early work takes on an innately political colouring: the ability to disregard — and invisibilise — another human being as less than oneself becomes not just a lamentable structure at the level of individual relationships but the condition of possibility of all systems of injustice. Hence Genet's gloomy assessment of its ascendancy:

Il semble que je me propose de dénoncer — une fois de plus et plus mal — ce que les révolutions n'ont pas réussi à détruire, ce qui subsiste, ce qui subsistera peut-être toujours dans chaque homme: la volonté de dominer et la force — ou plutôt non, pas la force, la sottise de mépriser.

On espérait que c'est d'abord en opérant au niveau de la lutte de classe et des inégalités économiques, que les révolutions viendraient à bout de ce qui, semble-t-il, est ressenti de plus en plus, avec la plus grande acuité. En aucun pays la révolution socialiste n'a été menée de façon à diminuer l'injure que l'on fait à tout homme en exerçant contre lui un acte ou une parole d'autorité qui ne suppose pas chez lui la contre-partie d'une réponse possible d'une aussi grande autorité. C'est derrière un mur très opaque que les hommes se retranchent quand ils commettent contre l'homme une agression. (GNT 6.20)

[It seems that what I am criticising — again and less well — is what revolutions have never managed to destroy, what persists, what will perhaps always persist in every man: the will to dominate, and the ability — or rather no, not the ability, the stupidity to despise.

It was hoped, by operating first at the level of the class struggle and economic inequality, that revolutions would manage to overcome something that seems to be resented more and more, ever more keenly. No country has ever carried out a socialist revolution in such a way as to diminish the injury caused to a man by being the object of an act or word of authority that doesn't suppose in return the possibility of a response of equal authority. Men take refuge behind a very opaque wall when they display aggression towards other men.]

The apparent universality of the will to dominate and the failure of the class struggle to mitigate its effects not only explain its resistance to any revolution to date but also suggest a profound pessimism about the likelihood of revolutionary progress in the future. Nonetheless, there are hints that its supremacy may not be unassailable: 'It *seems* that', 'what will *perhaps* always persist'. In fact, Genet goes on to propose that the resentment produced by situations of subordination is growing and spreading:

Pourtant ces situations sont ressenties de plus en plus, aigües, et de moins en moins localisées. Non seulement les hommes veulent s'en défaire afin de gagner une indépendance, mais parce qu'ils ont compris que toute vie véritable n'est possible qu'à partir de cela, et des richesses sont promises, des richesses contre la pacotille. (GNT 6.20)

[However, these situations are increasingly, and acutely, resented, and are less and less confined. Men wish to get rid of them not only to win their independence, but also because they have understood that a true life is possible only that way, holding out the promise of riches, riches rather than worthless rubbish.]

The assertion that an intellectual shift has taken place ('ils ont compris') introduces a note of optimism that links the vision of the promised riches on which the passage ends back to its lyrical beginning. The idea that a future might be possible in which men would relate to the other as a source of wonder rather than an adversary to be mastered shows that this most adversarial of writers dreamed at least in some part of himself that a utopian world in which men would not seek to dominate each other was possible.

★   ★   ★   ★   ★

Differences between what Genet says in public and what he explores in the unpublished archival documents are also to be found in his evolving attitude towards the contribution that art can make to the revolutionary struggle. In his public pronouncements, Genet appears sceptical about the effectiveness of anything other than 'direct action' to achieve political change. In the May Day Speech given in Yale to the rally in support of Bobby Seale, he calls on his predominantly white audience no longer to be content with action aiming only to transform social structures at a symbolic level: 'Il faudrait peut-être en finir avec les symboles, comme substitution à un acte révolutionnaire' [It may be necessary to have done with symbols and symbolic gestures as a substitution for a revolutionary act] (*ED*, 50; *DE*, 37). In words he will later import verbatim into the interview he gave Michèle Manceaux on his return from the US, he continues:

Les symboles renvoient à une action qui a eu lieu, non à une action qui sera, puisque toute action qui se fait (je parle des actions révolutionnaires) ne peut s'aider sérieusement d'exemples déjà connus. Ainsi tous les actes révolutionnaires ont une fraîcheur de commencement de monde. Mais un geste ou un ensemble de gestes symboliques sont idéalistes en ce sens qu'ils comblent les hommes qui les accomplissent ou qui adoptent le symbole, les empêchent de réaliser des actes réels, au pouvoir irréversible. Je crois qu'une attitude symbolique est, à la fois, la bonne conscience libérale et une situation qui fait croire que tout a été tenté pour la révolution. Il vaut mieux accomplir des actes réels et apparemment de peu d'envergure que des manifestations théâtrales et vaines.

[Symbols refer to an action that has taken place, not to one that will take place, since every action that is accomplished (I'm speaking of revolutionary actions) cannot make any serious use of already known examples. That is why all revolutionary acts have about them a freshness that is like the beginning of the world. But a symbolic gesture or set of gestures is idealistic in the sense that it satisfies those who make it or who adopt the symbol and prevents them from carrying real acts that have an irreversible power. I think we can say that a symbolic attitude is both the good conscience of the liberal and a situation that makes it possible to believe that every effort has been made for the revolution. It is much better to carry out real acts on a seemingly small scale than to indulge in vain and theatrical manifestations.] (*ED*, 50; *DE*, 37)

While revolutionary activity is always inventive in the sense that it envisages a state of affairs that precisely does not (yet) exist, Genet nonetheless proposes an apparently binary opposition between a symbolic gesture and a 'real act'. Only political action in the narrow traditional sense counts as revolutionary.

Genet's views as expressed in his later discussion with Fichte about revolution reiterate this distrust of the idea that action seeking to have a symbolic impact is equivalent to a political struggle. When asked if Matisse was a revolutionary artist, his first response is to query the very appropriateness of the concept of a cultural or artistic revolution, musing that the 'concept révolutionnaire' [revolutionary concept] is inseparable from that of violence. He develops several ways in which the artistic process is different from that of revolution. Whereas the work of art demands a loss of the sense of self, '[e]n face d'événements subversifs, mon "moi", mon "moi social", est au contraire comblé de plus en plus, même, il est gonflé de plus en plus' [confronted with subversive events, my 'ego' or my 'self,' my 'social self,' is on the contrary more and more filled, more and more inflated] (*ED*, 146; *DE*, 123). Moreover, unlike in revolution, the artistic process does not place the artist's body at risk. Above all, Genet challenges the idea that art produces liberation, arguing rather that more probably the opposite is true, that a 'libération des esprits' [liberation of minds] is a necessary precursor in order for the kind of innovation he brought in his books, or Sade brought at the end of the eighteenth century, to take shape (*ED*, 148; *DE*, 125).

Later in the interview, Genet develops this distinction between artistic and political revolutions with a nuance relevant to his involvement with the Panthers. Initially, he again rejects the very premise of an artistic revolution:

Ce qu'on appelle révolutions poétiques ou artistiques ne sont pas exactement des révolutions. Je ne crois pas qu'elles changent l'ordre du monde. Elles ne changent pas non plus la vision qu'on a du monde. Elles affinent la vision, elles la complètent, elles la rendent plus complexe, mais elles ne la transforment pas du tout au tout, comme une révolution sociale ou politique.

[What are referred to as poetic or artistic revolutions are not exactly revolutions. I don't believe they change the order of the world. Nor do they change the vision we have of the world. They refine vision, they complete it, they make it more complex, but they don't entirely transform it, the way a social or political revolution does.] (*ED*, 152; *DE*, 128)

However, he subsequently accepts the notion of an artistic revolution, shifting his focus to the asynchronous relationship between artistic and political revolutions:

Comme je vous l'ai dit, les révolutions politiques correspondent rarement, je pourrais dire ne correspondent jamais, avec les révolutions artistiques. Quand les révolutionnaires réussissent un changement total de société, ils se trouvent en face de ce problème-ci: donner une expression, exprimer d'une façon aussi adéquate que possible leur révolution. Il me semble que tous les révolutionnaires se servent des moyens les plus académiques de la société qu'ils viennent de renverser ou qu'ils se proposent de renverser. [...] Et alors, ils imitent les académismes, ils imitent la peinture officielle, l'architecture officielle, la musique officielle. C'est longtemps après qu'ils envisagent une révolution dite culturelle et alors ils font quelquefois appel non plus à l'académisme mais à la tradition et à des formes neuves pour utiliser la tradition.

[As I said, political revolutions rarely, I might say never, correspond to artistic revolutions. When revolutionaries succeed in completely changing a society, they find themselves faced with a problem: how to give expression, how to express their evolution as adequately as possible. It seems to me that revolutionaries make use of the most academic means they can find within the society they have just overturned or plan to overturn. [...] And then they imitate the academic styles, they imitate official painting, official architecture, official music. It's only much later that they envisage revolution as a cultural revolution, and then they sometimes appeal not to academic styles but to tradition and to new forms in which tradition can be used.] (*ED*, 152; *DE*, 128)

Rather than seeing the struggle for political transformation and the artistic struggle for a new expression as distinct and unrelated, the last sentence of this quotation posits a continuity between them, as evident in the use of the same pronoun ('ils') used earlier for 'all revolutionaries'. The claim here is that revolutionaries first change society, then imitate its culture... and *then* transform it culturally. This conclusion contradicts the position adopted earlier in the interview (that political change and artistic innovation are mutually exclusive) and subsequently rearticulated via a list of examples: 1) at the time of the Commune, Courbet, 'le seul artiste qui se soit mis au service de la revolution comme artiste et à la fois comme révolutionnaire' [the only artist who put himself in the service of a revolution as an artist and the same time as a revolutionary], although a very good painter, is not someone 'qui a nié la peinture de son temps' [who negated the painting of his age]; 2) Hugo, although deeply affected by the Commune, was not changed by it as a writer; 3) similarly, 1848 did not bring about a change in Baudelaire's poetry, however enthused by it he may have been; 4) 1848 did affect Flaubert — but Flaubert was not in favour of the revolution (*ED*, 153; *DE*, 129). Genet's overall position throughout the interview is thus that the transformations achievable by art cannot be considered revolutionary. Yet the fact that in the above quotation he constructs a category of revolutionary that serves both political and cultural transformation, albeit at different times, bears witness to a conflicting belief that art can serve the revolution. Moreover, when asked by Fichte if either Danton or Saint-Just constituted an exception to the rule that political and cultural revolutions never go together, his immediate response raises the possibility that cultural innovation can have a revolutionary potential. He accepts that Saint-Just may have produced 'une expression révolutionnaire, c'est-à-dire une façon nouvelle de sentir le monde et de l'exprimer' [a revolutionary expression, that is, a new way of feeling and experiencing the world and a new way of expressing it] (*ED*, 152; *DE*, 129). Contrary to his prior insistence that it is inaccurate to describe a cultural change as revolutionary, Genet delivers his own definition of what such a change would be with no hesitation: changing how the world is felt and expressed constitutes a revolutionary act.

The archive in the Fonds Genet contains evidence to suggest that, at least at the time of his involvement with the Panthers, he was more persuaded that art has the power to transform the world than the interview with Fichte indicates. In particular, 'Situation actuelle: le mouvement des Panthères Noires' includes a lengthy description of his attempts to persuade 'Massai' (Ray 'Masai' Hewitt, the Panthers' Minister of Education) that art has a crucial role to play in the revolution:

> Il faudra reprendre avec Massai ces longues discussions, où il refuse d'accorder à l'œuvre d'art son pouvoir révolutionnaire quand l'œuvre n'est pas au service immédiat de la révolution politique, c'est à dire une révolution en actes visibles. Si, parallèle à l'entreprise révolutionnaire, exigeant la réflexion politique, le passage à l'action et le courage s'il le faut pour défier la mort, si, dis-je, la sensibilité n'est pas développée dans tous les domaines, on en arrivera vite à réaliser une révolution froide, portant seulement sur les institutions et non sur les hommes. S'appeler 'Frère, Sœur ou camarade' n'est pas suffisant. (GNT 6.2)

> [I would need to continue with Massai our long discussions, when he refuses to grant the work of art any revolutionary power when the work is not directly in the service of the political revolution, that is, a revolution in visible acts. If, in parallel with the revolutionary project demanding political thought, the shift to action and, if necessary, the courage to risk death, if, I say, a new mode of feeling is not developed in all spheres, we will quickly have made do with a cold revolution, with bearing only on institutions and not on men. Calling ourselves 'Brother, Sister or comrade' will not be enough.]

Far from dismissing the idea of an artistic revolution, Genet here argues for its necessity: a revolution that does not transform 'la sensibilité', or modes of feeling, create 'a new way of feeling the world', one that limits itself to the overhaul of institutions and neglects to foster change at the most affective, embodied level of human experience, is incomplete.

The role of art in revolution, then, is not an instrumental one; insofar as art is the expression of a new, personal sensibility, it plays an intrinsically transformative part in society. The need for the revolutionary project to include a cultural front is further complicated at a different level, in that this cultural assault is led as much from the inside as the outside:

> Au moment même où le projet révolutionnaire commence, il doit porter sur tous les domaines bourgeois. Il existe un impérialisme culturel qui doit être mis en question et détruit, mais à l'intérieur de lui, il est indispensable de savoir que certaines œuvres, qui furent amenées par la bourgeoisie, appartiennent déjà au projet révolutionnaire. Je ne crois pas qu'il faille détruire Mozart, qui est indestructible, mais je sais que c'est la préservation de Mozart qui permettra une sensibilité plus grande, et que cette sensibilité nous mettra au fait d'explorations musicales nouvelles. Il est bien entendu que Mozart est pris ici comme symbole. Mais on peut se demander si nous 'entendons' vraiment Mozart, que lorsqu'il sera passé dans le camp de la révolution. Et encore, si l'exercice de la sensibilité ne doit pas accompagner, en quelque sorte la doubler, toute entreprise révolutionnaire exigeant la violence?
>
> Je n'ai pas convaincu Massai. (GNT 6.2)

> [From the moment the revolutionary projects begins, it must bear on all spheres of bourgeois existence. There is a cultural imperialism that needs to be questioned and destroyed, but within that, it is crucial to be aware that certain works, brought about by the bourgeoisie, nonetheless belong to the revolutionary project. We should not destroy Mozart, who anyway is indestructible, but I do know that by preserving Mozart we will enable a greater sensibility, and that sensibility will open us up to new musical explorations. Of course here Mozart is taken as a symbol. But we can ask if we really only 'hear' Mozart when he's gone into the revolutionary camp. And further, if practising a new mode of feeling should not accompany, or double, any revolutionary enterprise requiring violence?
>
> I didn't convince Massai.]

'Some works' contributed by the bourgeoisie have revolutionary potential. Whereas political revolution is waged by those excluded from power, artistic revolutions bear witness to a tension within the bourgeoisie. Genet's choice of example is key to the interpretation of the passage. While he does not make explicit the grounds on which he selects Mozart as the symbol of an artist who contributed to the revolutionary project, the fact that music is the artistic medium most free of ideological content strongly indicates that it relates not to his beliefs but to his exceptional achievements as a composer. The subset of works that belong to the revolutionary project are those that transform how their medium will henceforward be practised: music that negates music, in the way for example that Genet sees Rembrandt as negating the painting that preceded him (unlike Courbet, as above). Genet seems to propose here that the art most innovative in artistic terms is also the most revolutionary in political terms. The end of the quotation situates Mozart squarely in the camp of revolution: for Genet, insofar as art is a shake-up by the bourgeoisie of the bourgeois social order (its modes of feeling), it constitutes an attack by the bourgeoisie on its own interests.

The notion that art which facilitates a new mode of feeling is intrinsically revolutionary has echoes of the ideas associated with the *Tel Quel* group around that time, notably as developed by Kristeva in *La Révolution du langage poétique*, with the difference that for Genet the subversive dimension is by no means limited to avant-garde art. Yet he brings a further perspective of his own to bear, arguing that artistic revolutions always come from a position of cultural capital. Another document extensively develops the idea that a certain level of cultural capital is essential in order to bring about cultural change, specifically in relation to the students' audacity in May '68:

> Pour inventer des trucs nouveaux — images, litotes, mots-[*illisible*], mots nouveaux, élisions, — enfin des trucs qui permettent à la phrase d'en dire plus long et plus nombreux qu'en permet sa grammaire, il faut s'appuyer sur une culture officielle qui s'appuie — en le reniant — sur le pouvoir politique et le pouvoir économique.
>
> Le mois de mai 1968 eut tant d'audace parce que les étudiants l'avaient transformé en révolution parodique: ils pouvaient le faire, ces enfants de la bourgeoisie qui faisaient la cour aux ouvriers d'usine d'une main et de l'autre citaient les meilleures pages de *L'Éducation sentimentale*. Protégés par leur culture et leur origine ils pouvaient pirouetter sans danger des flics circuits. (GNT 6.34)

> [To invent new tricks — images, litotes, new words, elisions — tricks that enable a sentence to say and mean more than its grammar allows, we have to draw on official culture that in turn draws on — while denying — political power and economic power.
>
> May 1968 was so audacious because the students transformed it into a parodic revolution: they could do that, those children of the bourgeoise who on the one hand lectured the factory workers and on the other quoted the best pages of *The Sentimental Education*. Protected by their culture and their origins, they could pirouette away unharmed from the gathered cops.]

To the extent that inventiveness and audacity involve overturning the uses of language sanctioned by 'official' culture, itself an expression of dominant political and economic interests, familiarity with the culture to be transformed is a prequisite for any would-be revolutionary cultural intervention; only those already confident of their position in relation to cultural norms will dare to challenge them. A social revolution will look initially to seek legitimacy by burnishing its cultural credentials; only when it no longer feels the need to prove its artistic judgment will it dare to challenge its conventions. That is why social and artistic revolutions do not occur simultaneously:

> Une révolution sociale est trop peu assurée. Elle invite le style académique de la société qu'elle vient de détruire. Elle veut être digne de ce qu'elle croit être la culture. Elle n'ose pas inventer. Elle paraît bête. Plus tard elle osera peut-être inventer des trucs nouveaux: c'est que les artistes se révolteront contre la nouvelle société, qu'ils s'appuieront sur elle, bref la contesteront et qu'elle, bonne fille, les protégera. La littérature [...] même révoltée, sera complice de l'ensemble social puisque sans lui elle ne pourrait pas inventer des trucs nouveaux. Paul Klee savait très bien peindre. Webern connaissait la gamme chromatique, Giacometti aurait pu sculpter comme un membre de l'Académie des Beaux Arts.
>
> [*Biffé:*] Une certaine certitude de culture, appuyée sur un pouvoir politique

et économique, est indispensable pour accomplir une œuvre d'art audacieuse: elle est donc complice, même quand elle s'insurge. (GNT 6.34)

[A social revolution is not sure of itself. It invites the academic style of the society it has just overturned. It wants to be worthy of what it believes culture to be. It doesn't dare to invent. It seems stupid. Later on it may dare to invent new things: that is because artists will rebel against the new society, draw on it, in brief challenge it and in turn it, good girl that it is, will protect them. Literature [...] even in revolt, is complicit with the social setup because it needs it to make new inventions. Paul Klee knew perfectly well how to paint. Webern knew the chromatic scale, Giacometti could have sculpted like a member of the Academy of Fine Arts.

[*Crossed out:*] A certain cultural knowledge, drawing on political and economic power, is necessary in order to achieve an audacious work of art: art is thus complicit, even when insurgent.]

'*Later on* a revolution may dare to invent new things': there is necessarily a temporal gap between a shift in political power and its artistic expression because the new elite must appropriate cultural norms before it can transform them. The difference between political and artistic revolutionaries is thus that the latter seek to overturn an order in which they are themselves invested. For Genet, whereas political revolutionaries seek to overturn an order from which they are excluded — a view perhaps consistent with Genet's re-evaluation of the lumpenproletariat's revolutionary potential but one which entirely fails to take into account the fact that (political) revolutionaries have typically belonged to the bourgeoisie — art is an inside job: it unavoidably depends on the prior accumulation of cultural capital. Art is politically at odds with itself, simultaneously inherently transformative and inherently 'complicit'. Art is the social order's betrayal of itself.

This perspective inevitably raises questions about how Genet positions himself within this framework. For, at least on the surface, his own case goes directly against the schema he proposes: whereas he argues that revolutionaries need to acquire a stake in the social order before they can innovate culturally, artistic creation gave Genet a stake in society... and left him with an abiding feeling of betrayal for the rest of his life. It seems plausible that his resistance to the idea that art has a transformative potential is related to his own experience, notably the fact that his extraordinary success as an artist and the freedom that it afforded him in both physical and financial terms starkly put an end to his own existence as a social outcast. He does not reflect further on his personal circumstances in the archival documents elaborating his ideas; the only other observations of relevance are to be found in his 1982 interview with Bertrand Poirot-Delpech when he distinguishes his situation from that of Céline:

Premièrement, ce que j'avais à dire à l'ennemi, il fallait le dire dans sa langue, pas dans la langue étrangère qu'aurait été l'argot. Seul un Céline pouvait le faire. Il fallait être un docteur, médecin des pauvres, Bardamu, pour oser écrire l'argot. Lui, il a pu changer le français bien correct de sa première thèse de médecine en un argot, avec des points de suspension, etc.

Le détenu que j'étais ne pouvait pas faire ça.

[First of all, what I had to say to the enemy had to be said in his language, not in a foreign language, which slang would have been. Only someone like Céline could do that. It took a learned man, a doctor to the poor, Bardamu, to dare to write in slang. He was able to change the perfectly correct French of his first medical thesis into slang, with the three dots, etc.

I was a prisoner, I couldn't do that.] (*ED*, 229; *DE*, 196)

The idea that Céline's social integration made possible an audacity that a marginal figure such as a prison inmate could not envisage certainly corresponds to Genet's schema. However, the emphasis on the socio-economic privilege Céline enjoyed as a doctor, rather than on his status as a cultural figure, posits an identity of the cultural elite with the social elite that simply does not obtain in Genet's own case. All the evidence suggests that Genet was supremely confident about the artistic value of his work from the beginning of his writing career, and in no sense felt himself to be at a disadvantage in terms of his appreciation of culture.[21] If his status as a convict was determining, it was surely less because of a lack of audacity on his part than from a belief that his audacity would be construed by the reader as ignorance.

While Genet's personal trajectory may appear to contradict his theory, his suspicion that art serves at least as much to perpetuate the social order as to transform it thus bears echoes of his own experience. A sense of the difficulty of avoiding complicity in the system can be traced in his preoccupation with the danger of recuperation. In particular, a series of jotted notes show him defining a revolutionary action precisely as one that cannot be re-integrated by the social order:

Dans une action révolutionnaire, les actes sont irréversibles, et ils ne peuvent pas être récupérés par la Société contre laquelle ils se font.

C'est à dire que la société ne peut jamais accepter comme bons pour elle, ces actes. Dans le jeu de la révolution russe, dont vous parlez, la Société peut s'en amuser et le tolérer.

L'action révolutionnaire se distingue en ceci qu'elle engendre d'autres actes révolutionnaires.

Le Romantisme et la Révolution

Les Légendes révolutionnaires suscitent des actes révolutionnaires.

Y a-t-il un autre rapport entre l'illusion révolutionnaire et la Révolution? La recherche d'un style révolutionnaire en Amérique où il n'y a pas de modèle révolutionnaire, est une recherche d'un caractère révolutionnaire. (GNT 6.6)

[In a revolutionary action, acts are irreversible, and they cannot be recuperated by the Society they counter.

That means that society can never accept those acts as good for it. In the game of the Russian revolution that you mention, Society can enjoy it and tolerate it.

What distinguishes revolutionary action is that it generates other revolutionary acts.

Romanticism and Revolution

Revolutionary Legends give rise to revolutionary acts.

Is there another relation between revolutionary illusion and Revolution? The search for a revolutionary style in America where there is no revolutionary model is revolutionary in nature.]

This opening passage is underpinned by the general idea that revolutionary action has revolutionary consequences: it would therefore not be in contradiction with itself. Yet a sequence of displacements creates a conceptual slippage. Both revolutionary 'action' and revolutionary 'legends' are stated to give rise to revolutionary 'acts', suggesting that the legends form part of the action. Yet legend then gives way to 'illusion', a term with primary connotations of error rather than mythical grandeur; if legend is mere illusion, its impact is surely unlikely to be profoundly revolutionary. Moreover, the passage continues by flatly contradicting itself:

> Non. Les légendes révolutionnaires nourrissent, entretiennent, exaltent d'autres révolutions, mais elles ne sont pas à l'origine (je crois) d'un 'commencement' révolutionnaire. Elles ne sont pas un début.
>
> L'illusion révolutionnaire est dangereuse. Elle risque, dans les meilleurs cas, de pervertir l'idée révolutionnaire, ou un début d'acte révolutionnaire. C'est sans doute ce qui s'est passé en mai 68 où les étudiants ont pris des poses ouvriéristes, trotskystes, anarchistes, etc. C'est un peu comme si un mécanicien, ne connaissant pas la mécanique, s'essayait aux postures déjà enregistrées des mécaniciens, au lieu d'étudier patiemment la mécanique.
>
> Le style révolutionnaire des Panthères a précédé le contenu révolutionnaire.
>
> Le contenu actuel du moment des Panthères et le style, forment l'avenir de la révolution?
>
> Dans une certaine mesure, ils sont contraints de rester fidèles à cette image d'eux-mêmes, et pourtant, moi, je vois les efforts pour dépasser cette forme pour lui redonner un contenu, surtout théorique, vraiment révolutionnaire. Mais cela ils sont obligés de le faire eux-mêmes. Non seulement personne ne les aide, mais tout le monde les empêche d'y parvenir. Ils sont le couteau, les autres organisations le beurre, qui s'efforce de couper le couteau. (GNT 6.6)

> [No. Revolutionary legends nourish, maintain, exalt other revolutions, but they are not (I think) an origin that 'starts' a revolution. They are not a beginning.
>
> Revolutionary illusion is dangerous. It risks, at best, perverting the revolutionary idea, or the beginning of a revolutionary action. That is doubtless what happened in May '68 when the students postured as workers, trotskyites, anarchists, etc. It's a little as if a mechanic, without knowing anything about mechanics, tried out the already recorded poses of mechanics rather than patiently studying mechanics.
>
> The Panthers' revolutionary style preceded its revolutionary content.
>
> The Panthers' content at this moment and their style are the future of the revolution?
>
> To a certain extent, they are forced to remain faithful to that image of themselves, yet I see the efforts they make to go beyond that form to give it a theoretical, truly revolutionary content. But they are obliged to do that themselves. Not only does nobody help them, but everyone prevents them from succeeding. They are the knife, the other organisations are the butter trying to cut the knife.]

The text is in effect less an explanation than an oscillation between conflicting views of what constitutes the revolution. Significantly, as Genet's musing continues, the relation between 'style' and 'content' emerges as the key issue, and especially the question whether a revolutionary style can precede — and above all inaugurate — a revolutionary content. The example of May '68 infers a negative answer: there is a distinctly disdainful aspect to Genet's comparison of the students to a mechanic who assumes the recognisable 'postures' adopted in such an occupation instead of patiently working through the necessary apprenticeship. This amounts to reproaching the students for assuming the style, at the expense of learning its content, not just of any trade but of one specifically where aesthetics is generally deemed of little or no consequence, and stylistic considerations wholly subordinate to factual knowledge. Ironically, Genet shifts from an expository mode of discourse to an extremely unusual image in order to convey the priority of revolutionary content over revolutionary style.

Unlike the putative revolution, Genet's writing is thus very much in contradiction with itself. The end of the quotation shows clearly that, in contrast with his dismissive attitude towards the students, it remains a genuinely open question for Genet at this time whether the Panthers' stylistic invention will lead to further revolutionary consolidation. The declarative statement that the Panthers' style preceded their content is followed by an interrogative to that effect; above all, the concessional structure of the final paragraph conveys more a desire on Genet's part to believe that the Panthers will succeed in translating the transformation they have achieved at the level of the image into a truly revolutionary content, than confidence that they will do so. In a final paradox, in the very act of privileging theory over image, Genet has recourse to a metaphor that he deploys repeatedly in the speeches he delivered in the US: 'They are the knife, the other organisations are the butter trying to cut the knife'.[22] To elaborate the power of the Panthers' theory-based assault on American institutions, he trusts more to the power of the image than to conceptual discourse.

This question whether the Panthers can convert their image into revolutionary content is substantively equivalent to the question whether revolt will be translated into revolution. Genet admires the Panthers above all because of the image they invented of what it is to be black in the US, an image of the black community in revolt:

> Les noirs tellement ignorés comme hommes, des Blancs, avaient besoin de créer pour eux-mêmes [...] une image d'eux-mêmes qui, non seulement les rassure sur leur identité mais encore qui les contraigne à aller de l'avant, c'est à dire à être conforme à cette image, à la fois visible, révolutionnaire, violente, active, capable de défier la police et l'Administration jusqu'à la mort. (GNT 6.6)

> [The blacks, ignored as men by the whites, needed to create for themselves [...] an image of themselves that would not only reassure them as to their identity but moreover force them to go further, that is, to be in conformity with that image, all at once visible, revolutionary, violent, active, capable of defying the police and the Administration to the point of death.]

The document displaying the most optimism that this image of revolt will generate real revolutionary change is a text entitled 'Les Panthères sont des hommes', a thirteen-page typescript clearly intended for publication in the press (Genet invokes at one point the 'lecteurs' [readers] of his 'article'). As might be expected from a text that has clearly been reworked at length, its rhetoric is considerably more crafted than much of the other archival material, beginning with Genet's opening conceit on the party's chosen name (originally selected by its founder, Huey Newton, because of the idea that panthers use violence only to defend themselves). Genet begins his text with a reversible assertion that will structure his argument: 'Les panthères sont des hommes. Cette extravagante affirmation, qui semble faire déborder l'anthropologue dans la zoologie, en exige une autre: les hommes sont des panthères' (GNT 5.4) [The panthers are men. This extravagant claim, that makes the anthropologist spill over into zoology, requires this other one: men are panthers]. He then uses this as a springboard to develop his main points: that the American context is one of intense, dehumanising racism that brutally squashes any internal challenge to the status quo that it cannot buy off, just as it ruthlessly uses its military and financial might to squash any external threat to American supremacy; and that the Panthers have succeeded in harnessing poetic images to specifically political ends. What he admires above all is the new image of blackness that they themselves constitute:

> On peut dire que les Black Panthers furent célèbres dès leur naissance. Ici, il y avait création d'images neuves et multiplications de signes emblématiques nouveaux, arrachés aux jungles asiatiques et africaines. Je vois cela issu d'un génie poétique profond, individuel ou commun avec toute la communauté noire américaine. Mais si leur naissance restait encore fabuleuse, leur apparition, dramatiquement admirable, devait avoir lieu, aux yeux du monde entier, sur le podium de Mexico, où nous apprenions soudainement la signification d'une image nouvelle: ce poing tendu ganté de noir. (GNT 5.4)

> [We can say that the Black Panthers have been famous since they were born. They created new images and proliferated new emblematic signs, torn from Asian and African jungles. I see that stemming from a profound poetic genius, whether individual or one common to the entire black American community. But if their birth remained fabulous, their appearance, an admirable dramatic feat, had to take place before the whole world's eyes on the podium in Mexico, where we suddenly learned the meaning of a new image: the raised fist gloved in black.]

His emphasis is on the 'new', but on a newness that displaces rather than rejects the older images that defined the black community. 'Torn from Asian and African jungles': the images the Panthers propose both reappropriate and disrupt the centuries-old association of black people with animality and wildness, giving the old fantasy a specifically political edge.[23] Indeed, in an America characterised for Genet by its affective impoverishment and failure to dream,[24] the legacy of racism is a suffering that for him is also a sign of life, a reservoir of feeling that the Panthers have succeeded in turning into a political resource:

> Il reste que cette blessure noire, toujours saignante, est le seul point sensible de l'Amérique, c'est le seul endroit où bat un Cœur.
> Il y a quelques années, ces pulsations du Cœur étaient scandées par des

> rythmes qui rattachaient encore le peuple noir au continent d'où il fut arraché. Aujourd'hui, le danseur s'immobilise. Membre du Black Panther Party, il entre avec aisance dans les développements des philosophies matérialistes. Il a mis en doute l'autorité de ses anciens maîtres, il comprend leurs calculs, et il remet en cause ce qui relevait ici d'une sorte de dogme religieux: la propriété privée. (GNT 5.4)

> [The fact remains that this black, ever-bleeding wound is America's only sensitive point, the only place where a Heart beats.
>
> A few years ago, those Heart-beats were punctuated by rhythms still connecting the black people to the continent it had been torn from. Today, the dancer is still. A member of the Black Panther Party, he enters assuredly into the developments of materialist philosophies. He has questioned the authority of his previous masters, he understands their calculations, and he challenges what amounted here to a sort of religious dogma: private property.]

The issue is not that the Panthers have rejected dance in favour of philosophy, turned away from a physical manifestation of their originary wound to a theoretical programme. What moves Genet is rather how they have harnessed the one to the other. He goes on to highlight what he considers the common origin 'de la poésie et de l'action révolutionnaire' [of poetry and revolutionary action], the impression that for the Panthers the latter is intimately, physically rooted in the former:

> Tout donne à penser que la poésie nostalgique des noirs d'Amérique, fut engrangée en eux-mêmes durant quatre siècles, et qu'elle vient de se muer en une réflexion politique qui conduit les plus audacieux à l'action révolutionnaire.
>
> Qui aura vu Bobby Seale parler, s'est rendu compte, à une certaine façon de fermer ses paupières, qu'il rentre en lui-même, immémorialement, afin de puiser dans ce fond commun de la poésie noire; il entre en communication avec le désespoir profond de son peuple et il en arrache la force intellectuelle qui permet la réflexion et l'action révolutionnaires. (GNT 5.4)

> [Everything suggests that the nostalgic poetry of Black Americans was stored up in them for four centuries, and that it has just changed into a political reflection leading the most daring of them to revolutionary action.
>
> Anyone who has seen Bobby Seale speak realised, from a certain way he has of closing his eyes, that he retreats into himself, immemorially, to draw on that common fund of black poetry; he enters into communication with his people's deep despair, wrenching from it an intellectual force that enables revolutionary reflection and action.]

Poetry and politics are both fundamentally different and inseparably linked. It is because the Panthers, no longer content merely to express it, have sought to theorise the 'deep despair' of their community that a revolutionary praxis is possible. Poetic invention on its own is not enough to bring about lasting change:

> Tout d'abord, les trouvailles un peu enfantines, par certains côtés, semblables à celles des jeunes blancs révoltés, dans ces trouvailles ils ont fait passer une réflexion politique et révolutionnaire, empêchant ainsi leur mouvement de n'être qu'une révolte désordonnée. Mais ils ont conservé les attributs de leur apparition, et ils ont su les charger d'une signification nouvelle: l'entreprise révolutionnaire. (GNT 5.4)

[First of all, they have introduced a political and revolutionary reflection into their in some respects slightly childish inventions, similar to those of rebellious young whites, thus preventing their movement from being only a disordered revolt. But they preserved the attributes they appeared with, and were able to endow them with new meaning: that of a revolutionary enterprise.]

Poetry is not enough to convert a revolt into a revolution, but it is necessary. It is because the Panthers kept a link to the pain from which they emerged, because their politics draws on the same origin as their inventiveness in forging new, vibrant images of themselves that Genet allows himself to dream that their energy will make the future a brighter place. He sees them indeed, as the document's final paean suggests, as revolutionary stars: 'Les noirs d'Amérique et singulièrement les Black Panthers, sont ce qui luit, ce qui brille intensément, ce qui brûle même, et qui fascine, dans cet ennuyeux pays' (GNT 5.4) [The American blacks, and especially the Black Panthers, are alone what gleams, shines intensely, even burns and fascinates in this tedious country].

★   ★   ★   ★   ★

The Panthers were above all 'stars' for Genet in the sense that he deemed them superb not only at forging new, assertive images of blacks claiming their rights but in using those images to gain visibility. The writer devotes considerable energy to the fact that, as quoted above, they achieved celebrity from the outset. A passage exploring their status as stars in the 'Ouvrage inédit sur les Black Panthers' reflects on the inventiveness shown by the Panthers in turning the publicity they attracted to their advantage:

> Il est possible que la situation de vedette du Black Panther Parti provoqua cette espèce de flambée inventive dès son origine, car dès son origine ils furent vedette. D'une façon artificielle sans doute puisque la télévision avait été prévenue de se trouver au Sénat de Sacramento quand les Panthers y arriveraient armés d'armes visibles, se sachant 'vus', ils ne pouvaient pas se dérober sans honte, mais il y a plus — peut-être — cette situation 'en vue' déclenchait peut-être des possibilités, par exemple un pouvoir psychique et intellectuel plus grand. Tant qu'ils furent en vedette, les Panthères ne possédaient pas le leadership révolutionnaire grâce à un snobisme journalistique, mais parce qu'ils accomplissaient des actions nouvelles, qui étaient des solutions — peut-être momentanées — à des problèmes anciens. Je crois qu'on a montré que la vedettisation — non le vedettariat — d'un individu ou d'un groupe provoque une accélération, une effervescence intellectuelle et émotionnelle: le groupe, ou l'individu est capable alors de découvertes, de nouveautés — ce qu'on appelle bêtement le quotient intellectuel, se développe.

> [It is possible that the Black Panther Party's situation as a star provoked that kind of inventive blaze from the outset, because from the outset they were a star. Doubtless artificially, since television had been warned to be at the Sacramento Senate when the Panthers arrived there, armed with visible weapons, knowing themselves to be 'seen', they could not dodge away without shame, but more than that — perhaps — this situation 'in full view' set off other possibilities, for example greater mental and intellectual prowess. For as long as they were

stars, the Panthers showed revolutionary leadership not thanks to journalistic snobbery but because they were accomplishing new actions, that were — perhaps momentary — solutions to old problems. I think it has been shown that for an individual or a group becoming a star — and not the state of being a star — brings about an acceleration, or effervescence, of mind and feeling: the group or the individual becomes more capable of discovering, inventing. What is stupidly called the intelligence quotient increases.]

The Panthers' ability to exploit media interest in them when they stormed the Capitol in Sacramento or raised their fist on the podium at the Mexican Olympics is for Genet as creative as the actual images themselves, and as such a major contributing factor in the poetic phenomenon they constituted. The distinction he makes between the process of becoming stars ('vedettisation') and the state of actual stardom ('vedettariat') is telling: the dynamism associated with the former will later be valorised in contrast with the risk associated with the stasis of the latter. At the centre of his reflection appears to be the idea, quite distinct from his usual emphasis on the solitude of the artist, that poetic invention extends to the calculation and manipulation of the work's reception. He makes a surprising analogy with some highly canonical artists: 'Rembrandt a peint ses plus belles toiles quand il était oublié, devenu inconnu: il se savait redevenir "vedette" secrètement. Franz Hals connaissait une gloire — limitée à la Hollande, mais une gloire. Mallarmé était, rue de Rennes, une "vedette"' [Rembrandt painted his most beautiful pictures when he was forgotten, had become unknown: in secret, he knew he was becoming a 'star' again. Franz Hals enjoyed some glory — limited to Holland, but glory nevertheless. In the rue de Rennes, Mallarmé was a 'star']. The suggestion is that even the most sublime artists factor in the work's impact; the poetic inevitably has a public, and hence political, dimension. Conversely, Genet wonders elsewhere in the text 'si l'acte politique — révolutionnaire — n'est pas toujours un acte poétique' [if the political — revolutionary — act isn't always a poetic act]. Just as he drew an analogy between the Panthers' publicisation of their image and that of canonical artists, so he sees a correspondence between their gestures and those of canonical revolutionaries, also marked by a theatrical 'cinéma':

A qui dira qu'il y eut du cinéma, que les Panthères eurent recours au geste plus qu'à l'acte, nous répondrons que le geste des athlètes à Mexico — refusant de saluer le drapeau et l'hymne américains, tendant le poing ganté et baissant la tête si fort qu'on voyait vibrer les tendons du cou — , le geste des Panthères occupant le Sénat de Sacramento, et d'autres gestes déclenchaient des actes. Il y eut aussi du cinéma dans la fuite de Lénine à travers l'Allemagne, dans sa disparition de Petersbourg, dans sa réapparition: du cinéma dans la vie de Mao et dans celles de Lumumba et de Guévara. Les révolutions proposent beaucoup d'images.

[To whose who will say that they were acting, that the Panthers preferred gesture to action, we will reply that the athletes' gesture in Mexico (refusing to salute the American flag and national anthem, raising their gloved fists and bowing their heads so low that the tendons of the neck could be seen vibrating), the Panthers' gesture in occupying the Sacramento Senate, and other gestures launched acts. There was also playing to the crowd in Lenin's flight across Germany, disappearance from St Petersburg and reappearance; similarly in Mao's life and that of Lumumba and Guevara. Revolutions present many images.]

In this text as in 'Les Panthères sont des hommes', Genet sees revolutionary success in the fact that the Panthers' (poetic) gestures sparked further 'acts'. Yet whereas the earlier text stressed the heightened political awareness and reflexion that the gestures generated, this later (1972) text concentrates on the gestures themselves. He predicts that history will judge that the Panthers 'ont vaincu non par leur politique mais par la poésie' [conquered not by their politics but by their poetry], and even describes them as a 'phénomène poétique mais non politique' (poetic but not political phenomenon). With time, Genet comes to see the Panthers' deftness at public relations as a poetic rather than political resource.

Praising the Panthers' political praxis for its harnessing of a poetic dimension is nonetheless by no means equivalent to suggesting that poetry is a substitute for politics (or vice versa). Indeed, from the beginning of his relations with them Genet suspects that the very element he distinguishes as a major strength may also make them vulnerable. His piece 'Situation actuelle' [Current Situation] warns with remarkable prescience of the risk attendant on the Panthers' success in promoting powerful images. When, decades previously, Genet had explored the seductions of photography in his exploration of the link between image and power in *Le Balcon* and *Elle*, his emphasis had been on the political implications of the substitutability of image and reality. His concern for the Panthers involves the dangers arising from the glorification or idealisation of the origin of the image rather than the workings of the actual image itself:[25]

> Un des dangers qui nous guette tous, et aussi les Panthers, c'est la capitalisation de notre nom et de notre image. Je crois qu'il est temps de refuser que les moyens d'information ne servent qu'à nous, à notre célébrité — temporaire il est vrai. Il faut dominer ces images, se servir d'eux, mais n'être pas leur esclave. Pourtant, il a une telle fascination que nous nous laissons aller, et la pente est si douce et l'exaltation si grande quand nous réussissons à avoir la vedette. (GNT 6.2)

> [One of the dangers lying in wait for us all, including the Panthers, is the capitalisation of our name and image. I think it is time to refuse that the media should serve us alone, our celebrity — even if the latter is only temporary. We must dominate these images, use them, but not be their slave. However, it has such a capacity to fascinate us that we go along with it, and the slope is so sweet and there is such a great feeling of exaltation when we succeed in being in the limelight.]

Two aspects of this quotation are particularly thought-provoking. First, what kind of 'nous' is at stake in this generality in which Genet includes the Panthers only as an afterthought? Those seeking to revolutionise the world, or rather everyone with a recognisable face or name? The writer's warning to the Panthers not to succumb to narcissism is as likely an expression of his own ambivalence towards the fame that his success brought him, as of his concern that his fame may overshadow the message he seeks to convey. Second, this attention to the message is inseparable from the question of genre, in terms of the context specific to the 'moyens d'information'. The danger for the Panthers of becoming a victim of their own publicity is a corollary of their success in instrumentalising the mass media in their struggle via their exploitation of both television and, especially, journalism in the form of the publication of a weekly paper, *The Black Panther*, which at its peak attained a circulation of 300,000.

In 'Situation actuelle', Genet explicitly differentiates between the tameness of much of the Panthers' cultural production and the audacity of their journalism. He first levels directly at them the criticism that they often remain too respectful of the conventions of the order they wish to overturn:

> En moins de 4 ans, les Black Panthers ont suscité une très importante ressource culturelle ou, si l'on veut, ils ont su utiliser tous les moyens d'expression — journalisme, littérature, musique, dessein, cinéma — mais, et c'est un des reproches assez graves que je formule, sans avoir toujours inventé des formes nouvelles. Ils se sont souvent saisi de formes traditionnelles, blanches ou non, sans toujours se douter qu'une des fonctions de l'artiste c'est de rompre ces formes anciennes parce qu'elles ne conviennent plus à la sensibilité moderne.
>
> Cette accumulation culturelle si soudaine fut peut-être rendue nécessaire par l'absence de légendes, lointaines dans le temps, permettant que se prépare dans une nuit ancestrale, la naissance des Panthères Noires, et, peut-être conjointement, la naissance de la nation noire. (GNT 6.2)

> [In less than 4 years, the Black Panthers have created a very important cultural resource or, if you prefer, they have been able to exploit all the different modes of expression — journalism, literature, music, drawing, cinema — but, and it's one of my more serious reproaches, they did so without always inventing new forms. They often seized on traditional forms, whether white or not, without suspecting that one of the functions of the artist is to break with these old forms because they no longer suit a modern sensibility.
>
> This very sudden cultural accumulation was perhaps made necessary by the absence of legends, stretching back in time, that would have allowed the birth of the Black Panthers and, perhaps along with that, the birth of the black nation, to take shape in an ancestral night.]

Again, the need to transform modes of feeling is placed centre-stage. Genet attributes the derivative quality of the sudden proliferation of the Panthers' cultural output to its recency as a phenomenon; its conventionality arises from the absence of 'légendes' reaching back over time. In an earlier quotation, we saw Genet uncertain whether revolutionary legends on their own were sufficient to instigate further revolutionary action; here the lack of legends that cuts the Panthers off from their history is unequivocally portrayed as a weak point. While Genet does not spell out concretely which of the Panthers' cultural expressions he finds lacking in originality, his comments on Elaine Brown, the composer inter alia of the Panthers' anthem (and later leader of the party), in the 'Ouvrage inédit sur les Black Panthers' elaborate on his thinking:

> Parmi ces femmes noires, très belles, une plus belle que les autres — mais selon mes propres critères très peu partagés — Ellen [Elaine] Brown, la chanteuse. C'est elle-même qui compose la musique de ses chansons, imitée de très près

de la musique de Kurt Weil. En reniant délibérément le jazz et les spirituals, je ne suis pas sûr que les chansons d'Ellen Brown aient enrichi, ni la communauté noire ni le Parti. La chanteuse tournait une certaine difficulté à son profit: ses sortes de récitatifs pédagogiques, brechtiens étaient à la mesure de sa voix mais ils donnaient, dans le domaine musical, aux Panthères, une allure Germano-cinématographique des années 1925 et 30.

[Among these very beautiful black women, one is more beautiful than the others — at least according to my admittedly not widely shared criteria — Elaine Brown, the singer. She herself composes the music for her songs, closely copied on Kurt Weil's music. I don't think that by deliberating rejecting jazz and spirituals Elaine Brown's songs have enriched either the black community or the party. The singer turned a certain challenge to her advantage: her sort of Brechtian, pedagogical recitatives may have been worthy of her voice but, in terms of music, they gave the Panthers the feel of German cinema of the 1920s.]

Genet's critical attitude towards Brown's work seems due not merely to what he clearly considers its unexciting imitation of Kurt Weil but more importantly to its failure to engage with, and to renew, the tradition of black music available to her.[26] The contrast is striking between the disfavour with which he views her songs and his admiration for the unique tradition of black music as analysed in LeRoi Jones's *Blues People*. His judgment is simultaneously political and aesthetic: he deems Brown's lack of originality regrettable both in artistic terms and as a missed opportunity to enrich black cultural heritage.

Tradition matters enormously, then, or more precisely its absence. The fact that Genet perceived the Panthers as bereft of tradition, lacking legends that connect them to their past, may contribute to the exceptionally strong response they evoked in him. The most compelling section of the extended manuscript about the Panthers is a passage dealing with the reverberations of the brutal tearing away of the blacks from their roots in Africa and in particular the ongoing sense of loss of origin that it bequeathed them:

Afrique adorée, Afrique haïe c'est évidemment la même chose. Non deux temps ou deux faces d'un sentiment, ou tantôt l'un ou l'autre, mais un déchirement. Le passé, l'origine des blancs sont dans des livres, des récits, des mythes. On les retrouve, on les découvre en lisant, en consultant des archives. Le passé des noirs, leur origine, ou ce qu'ils croient tel est en somme proche d'eux mais dans l'espace, à cinq heures d'avion. Et s'ils y vont ils ne retrouvent pas les ancêtres qui les ont vendus ou auxquels on les a arrachés. Pourtant le lieu de la rupture est sur ce continent. Massaï a pris son nom africain de Massaï, croit-il que ses ancêtres appartenaient à ce peuple du Kenya? Un noir américain parcourant l'Afrique doit être dans la situation d'un blanc qui lirait des archives de familles truquées d'un bout à l'autre, trouées, pleines de fautes de toutes sortes, d'omissions, de rajouts, etc.

Pour les noirs américains, il y a le contact humain: je crois que je connaîtrais le même si j'allais en Afrique noire. Pourtant, c'est lié, leurs origines, leur passé, qui se poursuivent, en somme, assez près d'eux, dans l'espace: où ils peuvent aller et qu'ils ne peuvent jamais rejoindre. Il n'y eut pas d'âge d'or ni de contrée bien-heureuse.

[Adored Africa and hated Africa are obviously one and the same. Not two stages or aspects of a feeling, or sometimes the one and sometimes the other, but a tearing. The past and the origin of the whites are in books, stories, myths. They can be traced, they can be discovered in books, by consulting archives. The blacks' past, their origin, or what they believe to be such, is in fact close to them but in space, five hours away by air. And if they go there they don't find the ancestors who sold them or from whom they were wrenched. Nonetheless, the place of the rupture is on that continent. By taking his African name of Massaï, does Massaï think that his ancestors belonged to the Kenyan people? A black American travelling through Africa finds himself in the situation of a white reading family archives that are falsified from one end to another, full of holes, all kinds of faults, omissions, additions, etc.

For black Americans, there is a human contact: I think I would find the same if I went to black America. However, it's all linked, their origins, their past that in short continue close by them, in space: they can go there, but they can never connect with them. There was no golden age or happy country.]

Genet proposes overtly here that black Americans' desire to connect with their African origins is itself rooted in a pre-lapsarian fantasy of wholeness, in the desire to close up spatially the temporal wound of the centuries that divide them from their historical past. He, in contrast, is categorical that the 'tear' or 'rupture' that marks their current condition, manifest in the ambivalence of their simultaneously adoring and hating Africa, cannot be overcome by a return to the continent from which their ancestors were abducted: 'There was no golden age or happy land'. But the most interesting aspect of this paragraph is the difference he elaborates between blacks and whites. It is not that that the latter do not construct similar fantasies but rather that the stories they tell — 'books, narratives, myths' — find support in the existence of archived material. Yet Genet explicitly evokes the possibility that the archives can be faked; their merit is in the illusion that contact with historical reality is possible. The difference in relation to the past lies not between fantasy and reality, but rather in the ability to believe that one's fantasy is based on, and preserves, a direct relation to the past. *Writing* is what makes the difference. In this respect, the passage is significant for the parallel it suggests between his own case and that of black Americans, over and beyond the suggestion that he would enjoy the same human contact as them in Africa. For Genet, too, had no family archives to link him to his past. As his account decades earlier of his attempt to gain information about his origin bears witness, the only documentation that was released to him on attaining his majority was his birth certificate. *Journal du voleur* famously elaborates on how, deprived of a written history, Genet used writing to invent a genealogy, finding in his name proof of kinship with the plant *genêt* [broom] (*RP*, 1125; *TJ*, 34). Words offered him a way to trace a lineage in place of his missing parentage, or, as he phrases it, 'Réussir ma légende' [To achieve my legend] (*RP*, 1250; *TJ*, 170).

A development of this identification with black Americans can then be read in the manuscript's most striking rhetorical invention:

> La filiation avec ce qu'elle implique: transmission de caractères physiques héréditaires, système parental et même politique, complexe ou rudimentaire, la transmission orale de contes, de récits, de chants, la filiation — quand elle est

connue et à cause de leur pigmentation les noirs la connaissent — est si forte qu'il est impossible de prévoir encore ses effets. De l'abattage initial en Afrique jusqu'à sa fin au bout d'une corde du Ku-Klux-Klan, le noir n'est qu'un. Je veux dire qu'il éprouve ces quatre cents ans, comme si un individu de cet âge était passé par ce qu'ont connu un nombre assez grand d'individus: le jeune noir de quinze ans au bout de la corde c'est celui de vingt ans qu'on a amené, au fond d'une cale, en 1600. Il a tout éprouvé: les travaux, les chaînes, les caresses d'un maître blanc, plusieurs morts par lynch, des épousailles dans la nuit d'une cabane, des fuites — car il fut [*illisible*], traqué, cerné, repris, ramené — Chaque noir n'est pas fidèle par loyauté à la filiation: il ne peut pas s'en échapper. De la cale du bateau à voile, des premières plantations de coton, jusqu'à ces derniers coups sur l'échine, il vit une vie de quatre cents ans.

Le blanc venu d'Europe, généralement par décision libre, est arrivé comme individu. A sa mort d'autres individus — ses enfants — ont oublié, ou à peu près, l'immigration et sa patrie. Les Panthères en 1972 sont l'un des spasmes du nègre ferraillé en 1600. Ce n'est pas être sentimental, ou loyal, de se remémorer la filiation: par un malheur originel il est impossible de s'arracher d'elle.

[Filiation with everything it implies: the transmission of inherited physical characteristics, a parental and even political system, whether complex or rudimentary, the oral transmission of stories, tales, songs; filiation — when known, and because of their colour the blacks know it — is so important that its effects can't be foreseen. From his initial slaughter in Africa to his death at the end of the Ku-Klux-Klan's rope, the black is a single man. I mean he experiences those four hundred years as if an individual of that age had gone through what a large number of individuals had lived through: the young fifteen-year-old black at the end of the rope is the twenty-year-old transported in the depths of a hold in 1600. He experienced it all: the forced labour, the chains, the caresses of a white master, several lynchings, weddings at night in a cabin, fleeings — for he was hunted, surrounded, recaptured, taken back — No black is faithful out of loyalty to his descent: he can't escape from it. From the sailing boat's hold, from the first cotton plantations to the last blows to his back, he lives a life four hundred years long.

The white who came from Europe, generally of his own free decision, arrived as an individual. On his death other individuals — his children — forgot, or pretty much, that he had immigrated and from where. The Panthers in 1972 are a spasm of the negro chained in 1600. He is not being sentimental, or loyal, in remembering where he came from: by an original misfortune it is impossible to wrest himself away from it.]

Astonishingly, Genet portrays the collective black experience as that of an individual: the black is 'only one', like a single person who 'lives a life four hundred years long'. Telescoped into one generation, the loss of contact with their ancestors is by implication equivalent to the loss of their parents. As a brutal, untimely orphaning, that loss remains alive: in contrast with the children of white immigrants' ability to forget the past, it is impossible for the blacks not to 'remember where they came from'. The Panthers in 1972 are still grieving being violently separated from their parents in 1600. It is difficult not to read in the traumatic description of black history in this passage an analogy with Genet's separation from his own mother.

Moreover, elsewhere Genet proposes directly that the most powerful elements of the Panthers' sudden cultural proliferation involve a response to their originary uprootedness. In contrast with his reservations about the derivative nature of their artistic production, he claims that they have raised their journalism to an art. His discussion of *The Black Panther* in 'Situation actuelle' explains its effectiveness in terms of an attempt to invent a relation to the past that they can own: 'Cette absence de légendes expliquerait peut-être le recours fait par les Panthères au journalisme et aux autres formes d'information qui pour eux deviennent un art' (GNT 6.2) [This absence of legends perhaps explains the Panthers' recourse to journalism and other forms of information that become an art for them]. He elaborates in particular on its most widely circulated element, the iconic image of Huey Newton in a wicker chair, with a rifle in one hand and a lance in the other. For him, the power of the image lies in its linking of the 'monde archaïque' [archaic world] and the 'monde moderne' [modern world], both tapping into and displacing the nostalgic appeal of the lost homeland by associating the ancient weapon of the lance with the weapon of choice of contemporary America, the rifle.[27] He is especially attentive to how the materiality of the image conveys, rather than attempts to mask, the division or 'déchirement' [tearing] at the fore of the black experience as well as his own. The split between Africa and the US echoes not only in the break of the lance but also in the image's exploitation of its two colours, and in the poor quality of the paper, 'vite déchiré' [easily torn], that paradoxically makes it 'd'autant plus efficace pour le souvenir' [all the more potent for memory]. The 'chef-d'œuvre' [masterpiece] that the Panthers succeed in creating is all the more powerful a tribute to those it seeks to commemorate that it affirms its own ephemerality. Genet patently admires the newspaper as an expression of black experience as non-archivable, rather than an attempt to constitute a substitute archive or to replicate traditional forms.

It is thus the Panthers' innovative modes of political communication, and especially their journalism, that Genet considers most likely to bear revolutionary fruit. The archival documents repeatedly explore the possibility that the party's imaginative exploitation of the media and the elaboration of a 'nouvelle réflexion théorique révolutionnaire' (GNT 6.6) [new revolutionary theoretical reflection] mutually reinforce each other, the Panthers' creative expression working in tandem with the more conventional 'action directe' to further their revolutionary aims. However, Genet's confidence in the Panthers' political effectiveness appears to have been short-lived. An undated but seemingly later document comprising a single note unambiguously categorises the political contribution of the Panthers as one of revolt rather than revolution: 'Leur révolte fut un déferlement poétique. Leur art si banal!' (GNT 6.34) [Their revolt was a poetic outpouring. Their art so banal!]. The march of history was to see Genet's reservations about the dangers for the Black Panthers of becoming a victim of their own publicity largely proven true; within a few years, the party had lost its revolutionary momentum, riven by tensions arising as much from rivalry between its leading personalities as from ideological differences about its future direction. Like May 1968, the Panthers ultimately did not succeed in converting their revolt into durable revolutionary achievements. This inescapable political reality may account for much of the difference between the optimism about the possibility for revolution of the documents conserved in IMEC and the more sceptical positions Genet later adopted in his interviews. In addition to querying the very possibility of an artistic revolution with Fichte, he proclaimed himself in favour of revolt rather than revolution:

> Je ne tiens pas tellement à ce qu'il y ait une révolution. [...] La situation actuelle, les régimes actuels me permettent la révolte, mais la révolution ne me permettrait probablement pas la révolte, c'est-à-dire la révolte individuelle. [...] Mais, s'il s'agissait d'une véritable révolution, je ne pourrais peut-être pas être contre. Il y aurait adhésion et l'homme que je suis n'est pas un homme d'adhésion, c'est un homme de révolte. Mon point de vue est très égoïste. Je voudrais que le monde, mais faites bien attention à la façon dont je le dis, je voudrais que le monde ne change pas pour me permettre d'être contre le monde.

> [I'm not all that eager for there to be a revolution. [...] The current situation, the current regimes allow me to revolt, but a revolution would probably not allow me to revolt, that is, to revolt individually. [...] But if there were a real revolution, I might not be able to be against it. There would be adherence, and I am not that kind of man; I am not a man of adherence, but a man of reolt. My point of view is very egotistic. I would like for the world — now pay close attention to the way I say this — I would like for the world not to change so that I can be against the world.] (*ED*, 156; *DE*, 132)

The misfortunes of the revolutionary movements he had supported surely go some way to explaining his dramatic turnaround from his earlier intention to sign up unambiguously to socialism and the shift in his view of revolution as the objective.

There appears, then, to have been a relatively short space of time during which Genet was tempted by revolution: that is, tempted by the belief that revolt and revolution went hand in hand. I want to stress that Genet's subsequent change of heart did not involve his coming to believe that the Panthers awarded too great an importance to image over content and that they were in some sense not 'revolutionary enough'. He continued to admire them unequivocally for bringing a poetic dimension into politics through the images they invented. The shift was rather to do with his acceptance that such a challenge will always pertain more to revolt than to revolution. In the 'Ouvrage inédit sur le Black Panthers', he declares: 'Il est de la nature de l'éclair d'être fulgurant — illumination et disparition' [It's in the nature of lightning to be dazzling — illumination then disappearance]. Yet that does not mean it has no effect: 'Après le "passage" des Panthères, rien ne sera plus comme avant pour les noirs américains — et du même coup pour les blancs, en face d'eux' [After the Panthers' 'passage', nothing will be as it was before for the black Americans — and therefore for the whites across from them]. Even if the Panthers' particular revolutionary aims were not achieved, their revolt made a difference. They changed the American 'sensibilité' forever.

This period during which Genet believed — hoped? — that revolt and revolution went in tandem was also the period in which he displayed the greatest confidence in the revolutionary potential of art. As the documents analysed in this chapter show, the distinction between revolt and revolution maps onto the difference between an artistic revolution and a political one, between a practice that prioritises form or 'style' and one that prioritises 'content'; for a while, Genet saw those two practices as different but aligned. At no point, however, did he see them as mutually exclusive: he never opposes form and content. He never renounces the poetic dimension that reaches its peak in the work of art in favour of an instrumental or 'theoretical' mode of language. As argued above, he never actually made the public declaration of socialism announced in the documents quoted earlier. Similarly, his views on the value of literature did not falter; as he states in his interview with Rüdiger Wischenbart and Layla Shahid Barrada: 'Je crois que c'est vous qui m'avez demandé si je niais maintenant l'œuvre d'art. Ou l'écriture. Bien sûr que non' [I believe you're the one who asked me if I now disavowed the artwork. Or writing. Of course not] (*ED*, 280; *DE*, 242). Embracing the possibility of revolution did not entail rejecting the different potentialities of revolt.

Genet's views about the value of literature may not have changed, yet his practice certainly did. What relation exists between Genet's changing political views and his own writing? The discursive, often laborious passages quoted throughout this chapter strike a sharp contrast with the poetic density of his previous output. It is incontrovertible that, from May '68 onwards, Genet shifted in the direction of a mode of discourse that gave a much higher priority to content over style than had been the case in his earlier texts. As explained at the outset of this chapter, May '68 marked Genet's first foray into journalism; there is a clear temporal link between his newfound enthusiasm for revolution and his adoption of a journalistic mode of writing. Is it mere coincidence that Genet's laudatory comments about the Panthers' use of media date from a time when his own investment in addressing a wide audience implies a confidence that such interventions could be politically effective? Other than the 'Ouvrage inédit sur les Black Panthers', the IMEC documents analysed here all appear to be drafts of texts intended for publication in the press, like the majority of texts contained in *L'Ennemi déclaré*. This makes a difference in two important ways. Firstly, they typically constitute a far clearer attempt to communicate a particular meaning than was the case in Genet's earlier art. Contrary to the repeated assertions in his earlier essays that he says nothing, that in saying one thing he also says its opposite, the majority of the pieces written in this period seek to convey a message, to inform the reader about a specific reality, often one the reader might prefer not to acknowledge. Clarity is a new concern; in a note to himself filed at the beginning of the documentation in the box relating to the Black Panthers, Genet comments: 'Mes idées doivent être plus précises sur le B.P.P.' (GNT 6.1) [My ideas about the B.P.P. need to be more specific]. Secondly, the texts of this period not only seek to address a much wider audience but they also construct a different relationship with it. There is a conspicuous difference in this respect between the two pieces destined for publication in *Esquire* in 1968, which retain the highly adversarial tone of the incipit to *Notre-Dame-des-Fleurs*, and most of the other material. In the latter, Genet generally uses a *nous* that includes his reader, usually inferred to be white. The various texts in favour of the Panthers and the Soledad brothers and the articles published in *L'Humanité* in an attempt to encourage its readers to vote for Mitterrand in the 1974 presidential election especially adopt a markedly less antagonistic relation to the addressee, whom they expressly urge to take a particular action.

As such, it is no surprise that the critical reception of the texts contained in *L'Ennemi déclaré* has to date been dominated by their transparence relative to Genet's earlier works.[28] However, reading them alongside the unpublished IMEC documents, the reader cannot but be struck by their relative craftedness: Genet deploys a panoply of puns, images, rhythm to considerable rhetorical effect. Comparison between the archival documents and those Genet was prepared to release during his lifetime suggests that the difference between them is more a matter of emotive force than of intellectual rigour. This is further reflected in the difference between various drafts of the same document in the archive, which shows that Genet's priority in reworking them was less to strengthen the logic of the argument and the clarity of the message than to enhance their poetic effectiveness. Indeed, other comments in the note mentioned in the previous paragraph articulate this objective explicitly:

> Problèmes: Mes interventions deviennent de plus en plus mécaniques. [...]
> Il faut que la réflexion politique des Panthères passe par ma propre vie, je veux prononcer des mots vivants.
> Je m'étais promis d'utiliser seulement des arguments politiques, mais je m'aperçois que ces sortes d'argument ennuient les gens. Il me faut avoir recours à l'argument émotionnel. Et tout cela crée une confusion, un fouilli[s], une mélasse. [...]
> Nécessités de conserver, d'entretenir et d'augmenter la sensibilité. (GNT 6.1)

> [Problems: My interventions are increasingly mechanical. [...]
> The Panthers' political reflection needs to draw on my own life, I want to pronounce words that are alive.
> I had sworn only to use political arguments, but I see that those kinds of argument bore people. I need to resort to emotional argument. And all that creates a confusion, a jumble, a mishmash.
> I need to preserve, maintain and increase the degree of sensibility.]

Here, in contrast with the earlier image of the revolutionary as a careful student of mechanics, what is needed to be effective is to be less, not more, mechanical. In honing the political argument, he has lost the personal touch; the problem is a lack not of rigour or objective knowledge but of 'sensibilité'. In similar vein, in another document he jots down a reminder to make his text less categorical: 'S'arranger pour rendre de plus en plus indirecte la volonté de puissance, le détourner de son sens, etc.' (GNT 6.20) [Organise things to make the will to power more and more indirect, deflect its meaning, etc.]. In other words, his dissatisfaction with his endeavours on behalf of the Panthers — and presumably the reason why he declined to publish much of the archived material during his lifetime and why, in accordance with his wishes, it largely remains unpublished to this day — is primarily that they were not *poetic* enough.

I would argue therefore that Genet's turn to journalism cannot accurately be considered a turn to an instrumental mode of writing in which the political message is paramount. The texts from this period, published and unpublished, undoubtedly give greater weight to the message or 'content' than his earlier writings. Yet both his views about the Panthers' cultural production and the evidence of his own texts suggest that the key issue for him was to balance the political message he wanted to communicate with a poetic dimension that would *affect* his readers: that is, move them, both to feeling and to action. For a brief window he seems to have been tempted to believe that this was possible: that hard-nosed revolutionary practice ('action directe') and inspirational style could reinforce each other, that revolt and revolution could share the same time. Genet's experiments in journalism bear witness to that belief, vestiges of which can be traced as late as his articles in support of Mitterrand in 1974 or even the highly controversial 'Violence et brutalité' about the Red Army Faction in 1977. Yet even in advance of the failure of the causes he espoused, it is clear that he was acutely aware of an inherent tension between the 'poetic reflection' he wanted to promote and the poetic signature that he considered necessary to integrate but also at risk of overshadowing the cause he wanted to help.

The struggle to accommodate those conflicting demands largely accounts for Genet's relative silence during the late 1960s and 70s. The copious material coming to light as the IMEC Fonds Genet steadily grows provides clear proof that his silence was a refusal to publish, not a rejection of writing. Genet's experiments with journalistic writing appear to have led him back towards literature: all the evidence suggests that his energies through the 1970s were devoted to producing 'un grand chant révolutionnaire et romantique' [a great revolutionary and romantic song] (*ED*, 372; *DE*, 32), a designation that reinstitutes the poetic at the very heart of the project. The 1972 'Ouvrage inédit sur les Black Panthers' constitutes priceless evidence that Genet early turned his energies back to a more literary form of writing to implement his commitment to helping the party. The sole passage that reflects on its own form muses over the issues that arise from the choice of a 'récit':

> Ce récit ne me fait pas trembler, ni l'idée que je trahirai peut-être les Panthères. C'est qu'il ne s'agirait pas d'une trahison pure et simple. Qu'on lui donne le nom qu'on voudra, ce récit sera lu comme un roman, une chronique, mais il est écrit afin de rendre compte d'événements, mais en approchant autant que possible leur réalité — leur complexité. Qui lira d'abord ce livre sinon les blancs? Être vrai, ici, cela veut dire quoi? Comprendre d'abord que la vérité des noirs, au plus intime d'eux-mêmes et de nous, c'est le hirsute va et vient de nos rapports, qui sont ainsi puisque séquelles de l'esclavage. Être vrai voudrait donc dire travailler si peu que ce soit à combattre les blancs, mais en utilisant d'autres techniques que celles des Panthères.

> [This narrative doesn't make me tremble, nor does the idea that I will perhaps betray the Panthers. It's because it is not a matter of betrayal pure and simple. Whatever name is given to it, this narrative will be read as a novel, a story, but it is written to give an account of events, but by approaching their reality, their complexity, as closely as possible. First of all, who other than whites will read this book? What does being true even mean here? First of all, understanding that the blacks' truth, in the most intimate depths of them and of us, is the rough to-and-fro of our relations, which are the way they are as a consequence of slavery. Being true would therefore mean working, however slightly, to combat whites, but using different techniques from those of the Panthers.]

This quotation bears eloquent witness to the inherent tension at the heart of Genet's enterprise: the text's reception as a 'novel' inescapably works against its aim to give an 'account of events'; the need to speak with his own voice, to find 'techniques' appropriate to his specific vantage-point, cannot but betray the Panthers' reality. It shows him grappling to find a form that would be both politically and poetically 'true'.

Genet never succeeded in bringing this project to fruition. My personal opinion is that he (rightly) judged it poetically insufficient; while the text contains many interesting and some gripping passages, it never approaches the poetic density or luminosity of his earlier art. His own admonition to himself, as quoted earlier, may be instructive as to why he did not meet the challenge he had set himself: 'The Panthers' political reflection needs to draw on my own life, I want to pronounce words that are alive'. If the text fails to come alive, is it perhaps because he does not allow himself enough freedom to filter his account of the Panthers through his own life, that the writing does not engage him intimately enough? That is what changes in the final years of his life when, as we shall see in the next chapter, with *Un Captif amoureux* Genet finally produces his promised 'grand chant révolutionnaire et romantique'.

## Notes to Chapter 3

1. *La Bataille des Paravents*, ed. by Dichy and Peskine, p. 11.
2. This included speaking at fifteen or so universities. At the Cerisy-la-Salle conference on Genet held in 2000, Jacques Derrida noted with amusement that Genet, having frequently teased the philosopher for his academic trips to the US, himself ended up touring many of the most prestigious American universities.
3. Jean Genet: 'Après tout, il n'est pas impossible que la Tschécoslovaquie ait une jeunesse vraiment révolutionnaire grâce aux écoles et aux Universités Populaires mises en place par Mazaryk' [After all, it's not impossible that Czechoslovakia has a truly revolutionary youth movement thanks to the schools and popular universities set up by Masaryk] (*ED*, 30; *DE*, 19).
4. Discussion at the Cerisy-la-Salle conference; see also White, *Genet*, p. 578.
5. Similarly, in his interview with Nigel Williams, Genet repeated: 'S'ils avaient été de véritables révolutionnaires, ils n'auraient pas occupé un théâtre' [If they had been real revolutionaries, they wouldn't have occupied a theater] (*ED*, 303; *DE*, 262).
6. I have reservations also about the role played by the erotic in Genet's initial agreement to become involved. When asked by Rüdiger Wischenbart how he had selected which causes to support, Genet gave a somewhat different reply to the account he had given Fichte: 'j'ai été tout de suite vers les gens qui m'ont demandé d'intervenir' [I went immediately towards the people who asked me to intervene] (*ED*, 272; *DE*, 235). Moreover, Layla Shahid (who had asked him to accompany her to Beirut in 1982) was one of those he listed, and we know that another woman, Connie Matthews, was one of the Panthers who requested Genet for help in Paris in 1970 (White, *Genet*, p. 601). Genet's assertion to Fichte that his political activity had a sexual dimension at its origin may plausibly have been one of the statements he alludes to at the end of the interview, aimed more at creating a certain effect than at telling the truth.
7. At a personal level, Genet's investment in politics seems to have played a crucial role in overcoming the severe depression that afflicted him following Abdallah's suicide and in giving him a new purpose in life. In the preparatory notes for 'Quatre heures à Chatila' archived in IMEC, one page features only the words: 'Quelle sottise! Je n'ai jamais aidé les Palestiniens. Ils m'ont aidé à vivre' [What idiocy! I never helped the Palestinians. They helped me to live] (GNT 5.18).

8. In 1968 Genet had accepted a commission to travel to the Democratic Convention in Chicago to write a piece for the widely-read US magazine *Esquire* on condition that they would also publish another piece on the Vietnam War. Furious when the magazine refused to publish the second article because of its violence, Genet tore up both originals. Reconstructions of the French texts are published as an annex of *L'Ennemi déclaré*, 'Les Membres de l'Assemblée' (*ED*, 309-19) and 'Un salut aux cent mille étoiles' (*ED*, 321-28). For an analysis of these pieces, see Mairéad Hanrahan, 'Le Cru et les cuisses: écrire à l'adresse de l'Amérique', *Études françaises*, 51.1 (2015), 29-42.

9. Page 2 contains a long crossed-out paragraph beginning 'Une des choses les plus désolantes de cette époque c'est la dépolitisation des savants' [One of the most depressing aspects of this time is the depoliticisation of scholars], an idea that recurs in several of the documents relating to the Black Panthers. Genet's increasing willingness to align himself with a set of (political) ideas seems to have gone hand in hand with a growing impatience with those who propound ideas without acknowledging any political dimension to their work.

10. Herbert Marcuse, *Eros et civilisation: contribution à Freud*, trans. by J.-G. Nény and B. Fraenkel (Paris: Minuit, 1963). Marcuse, who taught Angela Davis during his years at Brandeis University, was also an important influence on the Black Panthers. Since these documents seem to predate Genet's time with them, however, it is most likely that he was exposed to the philosopher's ideas during his 1968 trip, when he had contact with figures such as Allen Ginsberg, William Burroughs and Terry Southern, and was generally enthused by the hippie movement.

11. Genet articulates this explicitly in his interview with Fichte: 'Je n'ai pas de sentiment de culpabilité. Si on me demande (ou si je m'aperçois même sans qu'on me demande) de l'argent, je le donne très facilement, vraiment très facilement, et ça n'a pas d'importance. L'injustice est dans le monde et l'injustice n'est pas dans le monde parce que mes droits d'auteur sont relativement élevés' [I don't feel any guilt. If someone asks me for money (or if I notice, even without being asked), I give it away very easily, really very easily, it doesn't matter to me. There is injustice in the world, but whatever injustice is in the world isn't there because my royalties are relatively high] (*ED*, 168; *DE*, 143).

12. See Bobby Seale, *Seize the Time: Story of the Black Panther Party and Huey P. Newton* (Baltimore, MD: Black Classic Press, 1991), p. 63. For other accounts of the Black Panthers, see David Hilliard and Lewis Cole, *This Side of Glory: The Autobiography of David Hilliard and the Story of the Black Panther Party* (Toronto: Little, Brown & Co., 1993); Elaine Brown, *A Taste of Power: A Black Woman's Story* (New York: Doubleday, 1992); and Bobby Seale and Stephen Shames, *Power to the People: The World of the Black Panthers* (New York: Abrams, 2016).

13. Kwame Ture (formerly Stokely Carmichael) and Charles V. Hamilton, *Black Power: The Politics of Liberation in America* [1967] (New York: Vintage/Random House, 1992).

14. Genet would have been able to access both *Black Power* and LeRoi Jones's *Blues People* in French translation from 1968; see Stokely Carmichael and Charles V. Hamilton, *Le Black Power: pour une politique de libération aux États-Unis*, trans. by Odile Pidoux (Paris: Payot, 1968); and LeRoi Jones, *Le Peuple du Blues: la musique noire dans l'Amérique blanche*, trans. by Jacqueline Bernard (Paris: Gallimard, 1968).

15. See, for example, White, *Genet*, pp. 626 & 665.

16. Ibid., p. 638.

17. Ture and Hamilton, *Black Power*, p. 84.

18. The extent to which Genet respected this rule in private as well as in public is less clear. In the long manuscript, he recounts attending a meeting to debate whether to claim that imprisoned Panthers were prisoners of war: 'Je fus probablement le seul à m'y opposer' [I was probably the only one to speak against].

19. See also GNT 6.2; *ED*, 84/*DE*, 67 and *CA*, 63/*PL*, 49.

20. He nonetheless situates himself more specifically in relation to revolutionary theory in a document about the Black Panthers than in the material relating to his 'declaration' of socialism analysed earlier. Towards the end of GNT 6.6, he formulates a response if asked about the kind of socialism he espoused as follows: 'Il est encore trop tôt pour le définir avec une certitude dogmatique. Le socialisme prendra la forme que les traditions populaires lui donnent, en faisant

confiance aux possibilités créatrices des masses populaires. Mais on peut déjà chercher des formules et des applications chez Marx, Engels, Lénine, Staline, Mao, Ho-Chi-Min, Castro, Max Weber. | On ne doit pas refuser un autre courant plus libertaire qui passerait par Fourier, Trotsky, Bakounine, Proudhon, par la personnalité dualiste de Lénine théoricien, mais dansant dans la neige en 17 parce que les Soviets avaient tenu un jour de plus que la Commune de Paris, par la personnalité romantique mais active de Guevara, par les mouvements anarchistes français et espagnols, par Rosa Luxembourg et Liebknecht, par le mouvement chaleureux des Panthères complétant les 10 points théoriques du Parti de Black Panthers' [It is still too early to define it with any dogmatic certainty. Socialism will take the form given by popular traditions, trusting to the creative possibilities of the masses. But formulas and applications can already be found in Marx, Engels, Lenin, Stalin, Mao, Ho-Chi-Min, Castro, Max Weber. | We shouldn't reject a more libertarian current taking in Fourier, Trotsky, Bakunin, Proudhon, the dualist personality of Lenin the theorist who nonetheless danced in the snow in 17 because the Soviets had lasted a day longer than the Paris Commune, the romantic but active personality of Guevara, the French and Spanish anarchist movements, Rosa Luxembourg and Liebknecht, the warm movement of the Panthers completing the 10 points of the theory of the Black Panther Party.]

21. See for example his correspondence with his first publisher in *Lettres à Olga et Marc Barbezat* (Décines: L'Arbalète, 1988). See also his reported answer when asked by a judge if he understood the value of the copy of Verlaine's *Fêtes galantes* that he had stolen: 'Je n'en connais pas le prix, mais j'en connais la valeur' [I may not know its price, but I know its value].

22. Genet uses this metaphor repeatedly in the texts and speeches he prepared in the US; see for example 'Genet Emerges as an Idol of Panthers', John Darnton's report on his speech in New Haven in the *New York Times* of 1 May 1970.

23. I am intrigued to have encountered no reference whatsoever to the Négritude movement in any of the material I have had the opportunity to consult. The only attempt to identify possible precursors of the Panthers' art and ideas is the passage quoted above from GNT 6.2, where Fanon is the only Francophone figure mentioned. Yet Genet must have read Césaire and Senghor at least. Did he perhaps feel that 'Orphée noir', Sartre's preface to Senghor's *Anthologie de la poésie nègre et malgache*, was an example of a white speaking for the blacks that he was so concerned to avoid? Was he similarly wary of appearing to explain the Panthers via a Francophone lens (notwithstanding the fact that the Négritude movement explicitly drew inspiration from the Harlem Renaissance)?

24. He specifies later in the text that America, caught up in a 'délire logique' [logical delirium], 'est déjà pour nous un rêve ancien qui pèse encore sur le monde' [is already for us an ancient dream weighing on the world]. In another document he complains that the country 'a desséché la pensée: je veux dire que l'acte de penser y est réduit à la seule réflexion intellectuelle, sans permettre au rêve de se former autour de la pensée et à partir de lui' (GNT 6.7) [dried up thought: I mean that the act of thinking is reduced to mere intellectual reflection, allowing no space for a dream to form around the thought and stemming from it]; in yet another, he calls its architecture 'un délire d'où tout délire est chassé' [a delirium from which all delirium has been chased]: 'Ouverture-éclair sur l'Amérique' (GNT 5.28), published in *Europe*, 808-09 (August-September 1996), 8-11 (p. 10).

25. In his interview with Fichte, Genet's reservations about the effects produced by the widespread circulation of images are expressed even more clearly: 'Je me demande même s'il n'y a pas un phénomène de grossissement qui est dû aux moyens de transmission et de reproduction mécaniques. Il y a deux cents ans, si un homme avait fait mon portrait, il y aurait eu un portrait. Maintenant, si on fait une photographie de moi — on en tire deux cent mille, même davantage, bon, mais est-ce que j'ai plus d'importance?' [I even wonder if there isn't a phenomenon of magnification created by the processes of mechanical reproduction and transmission. Two hundred years ago, if someone drew my portrait, there would be a portrait. Now, if someone takes a photograph of me — there will be a hundred thousand of them, maybe more; okay, fine, but am I any more important?] (*ED*, 148; *DE*, 125). While it might be tempting to read an allusion to Walter Benjamin in this quotation about the political consequences of the mechanical reproduction of images, Genet's focus is on images of the author, not of the work of art itself.

26. It must be said that the only other reference to Brown in the text has an unmistakably misogynist tonality: 'En parlant d'Ellen Brown, assez prétentieuse amie de Massaï, je dis à Geronimo, montrant Ellen: "Il fait bien la cuisine" et, montrant Massaï, "Elle est très fatiguée." Tout le monde d'abord est un peu ébahi. On sait que je ne parle que quelques mots d'anglais' [Speaking of Ellen Brown, Massaï's rather pretentious friend, I said to Geronimo, pointing to Ellen: 'He cooks well' and, pointing to Massaï, 'She is very tired'. Everyone is at first a little astonished]. There is doubtless an element of irony here insofar as Genet must have been aware that his willingness to entertain gender fluidity set him apart from the Panthers as much as his lack of English. Brown would later castigate the Black Panthers for their sexism and misogyny in her memoir *A Taste of Power*.

27. The image of Newton indeed achieved widespread reproduction within the US. The Panthers later produced it as a poster and circulated it widely at the protests to free both himself and Bobby Seale organised in the early 1970s; see for example the inside cover of Shames and Seale's *Power to the People*, or the page of photos opposite page 243 of Hilliard and Cole's *This Side of Glory*.

28. For a rare consideration of Genet's rhetoric in *L'Ennemi déclaré*, see Nathalie Fredette, 'Genet politique, l'ultime engagement', *Études françaises*, 29.2 (1993), 83-102.

# CHAPTER 4

❖

# Revolution and Religion

Genet's experience of walking through the streets and alleyways of Shatila on 19 September 1982 and seeing with his own eyes the evidence of the atrocities committed there over the previous three days affected him profoundly. His immediate response was to write: he took an early flight back to Paris where he produced 'Quatre heures à Chatila' during the month of October (*ED*, 406; *DE*, 370).[1] But the shock of witnessing the aftermath of the massacre perpetrated in the camps also appears to have provided a catalyst for a more sustained return to writing. He had never reworked the draft manuscript about the Panthers into a form he considered publishable; similarly, although ostensibly committed from 1971 to writing a book about the Palestinians commissioned by Yasser Arafat, he will later dismiss the agreement as a matter of 'politesses' [courtesies] that neither the leader of the PLO nor he himself really believed (*CA*, 126; *PL*, 105). In 1983, however, he embarked on the project that was to result in his first major work since *Les Paravents*. From then until his death in 1986, he produced the posthumously-published *Un Captif amoureux* whose proofs he was correcting when he died. At three separate moments within the text, the narrator dates its genesis back to Shatila and the urge to testify to the plight of the Palestinians. The use of the term *reportage* in the last of these, in the closing passage of the book, proposes a continuity with the journalistic texts examined in the previous chapter: 'Je fus, dès le milieu de 1983, assez libre pour commencer à rédiger mes souvenirs qui devraient être lus comme un reportage' [By the middle of 1983 I was free enough to start to write my *souvenirs*, which were meant to be read as reporting] (*CA*, 503; *PL*, 429). Yet *Un Captif amoureux* involves at most a highly unusual form of reporting. The most striking aspect of the book is the intensely personal, poetic approach that Genet adopts in order to write about what he calls the 'Palestinian revolution'.

This chapter investigates what is at stake in the text's idiosyncratic form, both as an account of a specific historico-political reality and in terms of its implications for Genet's own position. In particular, it seeks to explore the link between religion and revolution. This is not just because religion is a key factor in the conflict in the Middle East; it is also because Genet is interested in religion as a communitarian, and hence intrinsically political, organisation. An archival note makes an explicit link between religion and revolt:

> Il y a peut-être ceci, que toutes les grandes religions, à leur origine, sont nées dans la révolte contre un pouvoir, ont sécrété des mythes, non afin de mieux

être adaptées, mais parce que toute révolte suscite des mythes. La révolte organisée, soit parce qu'elle a réussi, soit parce que le pouvoir s'empare du mythe, le confisque, le détourne de sa fin première [...]. Il n'est pas impossible qu'en recherchant les vertus de l'origine, la religion retourne, redevienne la révolte qui l'a fait naître.[2]

[There is also perhaps that all the great religions were originally born out of revolt against a power, they secreted myths not to be better adapted but because all revolt gives rise to myths. Organised revolt, either because it succeeds or because power takes hold of myth, confiscates myth, deflects it from its primary purpose [...]. It is not impossible that in exploring the virtues of the origin, religion turns around and becomes again the revolt that gave it birth.]

For Genet, religion is intrinsically rooted in revolt: it is the myth produced by an 'organised' revolt, which in context appears to mean a revolt that has shifted from attacking power to exercising it. In other words, religion is a revolt that has lost its revolutionary direction: it seals the end of the revolt in which it originates. As we shall see, not only does *Un Captif amoureux* muse at length on the question of the origin of religion and of religion as origin but the writer's attempt to tell the truth about the Palestinians turns out to be inseparable from, or unachievable without, a confrontation with his own origins. Before I turn to this, however, it is indispensable to address the most controversial current debate relating to Genet's politics, which is also a matter of religion: the allegations that he was profoundly antisemitic.

★　★　★　★　★

In Chapter 1, I discussed the accusations of fascism levelled against Genet on the basis of his novels, especially *Pompes funèbres*. For both Jablonka and Marty, those accusations are closely bound up with the belief that Genet was predisposed to sympathy with the Nazis by an antisemitism whose traces can be found throughout his work. It is self-evident that all allegations of antisemitism need to be taken very seriously; any racism on Genet's part should be recognised as such and vigorously challenged. The allegations depend, however, on a novel conception of antisemitism. My concern is both to do justice to Genet's work, by examining whether the accusations are justified, and to explore the value of displacing the notion of antisemitism such that it no longer corresponds to the common interpretation of the term.

Jablonka and Marty both distinguish the antisemitism they perceive in Genet's work from what is usually understood by that term. Neither accuse him of a form of racism. For Jablonka, who does not examine *Un Captif amoureux*, 'les questions raciales l'indiffèrent, contrairement à un Céline, un Rebatet, un Drieu ou un Brasillach' [racial questions are a matter of indifference to him, unlike Céline, Rebatet, Drieu or Brasillach] (*VIJG*, 210). Jablonka in fact assumes Genet's antisemitism rather than seeks to demonstrate it; the aim of his book is to establish Genet's sympathy for fascism. For this reason, the following discussion will focus rather on Marty's arguments. Marty, who discusses Genet in two different books,

*Bref séjour à Jérusalem* (2003) and *Jean Genet, post-scriptum* (2006), similarly sees Genet as different, indeed unique, coining the idea of an 'antisémitisme métaphysique' (*BSJ*, 176) [metaphysical antisemitism] to define the phenomenon he extrapolates from Genet's writing: 'Aux yeux de Genet le juif est le Bien, parce qu'il est le Bien absolu et que l'antisémitisme de Genet est une angoisse du Bien, une angoisse à l'égard du Bien' (*BSJ*, 95) [In Genet's eyes the Jew stands for Good, because he is the absolute Good and Genet's antisemitism is an anguish about Good, an anguish in relation to Good].[3] Although he differentiates this 'metaphysical' antisemitism from an 'ordinary' or political antisemitism, he explores it as manifested via two defining historical experiences. The first of these was the advent of Nazism, and in particular Hitler: 'Si Hitler est le Mal, alors les juifs sont le Bien' (*BSJ*, 102) [If Hitler is Evil, then the Jews are Good]. The second was Genet's engagement with the Palestinians: 'On l'a nommée Chatila, mais, cette rencontre avec le monde juif est plus largement nouée à l'univers palestinien' (*BSJ*, 107) [It has been called Shatila, but this encounter with the Jewish world is more broadly linked to the Palestinian universe]. As the title 'Genet à Chatila' suggests, the section of *Bref séjour à Jérusalem* devoted to the writer deals primarily with the latter of these; it is only in his later book that Marty develops in detail an argument about Genet's interest in Nazism. The arguments themselves also differ considerably from book to book. As we saw in Chapter 1, the argument about Hitler in *Jean Genet, post-scriptum* focuses on the question of castration: 'l'angoisse à l'égard du Bien recoupe largement l'angoisse et le déni à l'égard de la castration' (*JGP*, 100) [the anguish in relation to Good largely overlaps with the anguish and denial in relation to castration]. There, Marty clearly relates the anguish about Good to the Jew's status as a victim: 'au lieu de procéder d'une révolte contre les dominants, les bourgeois d'autrefois, la violence de Genet a pour objet paradoxal et pour point de départ l'être-victime de l'Autre' (*JGP*, 35) [instead of proceeding from a revolt against the dominant, the bourgeois of early times, Genet's violence is paradoxically aimed against and derives from the victimhood of the Other]. (I argued in Chapter 1 that Genet's work shows to the contrary that his enemy is always the powerful.) However, it is considerably less clear in the first book what exactly Marty means by the notion of a metaphysical anguish in relation to Good and how this produces 'une ontologie morale de l'être-juif' (*BSJ*, 110) [a moral ontology of being-Jewish].

Marty states that Genet's experience in Shatila for the first time 'semble suspendre en lui ce qui à nos yeux le définit ontologiquement, l'angoisse à l'égard du Bien' (*BSJ*, 122) [appears to suspend in him what in our eyes defines him ontologically, anguish in relation to Good]. He claims that for the first time the writer seems tempted by the position of a 'témoin positif' (*BSJ*, 123) [positive witness]: in contrast with his celebration of Oradour, he shifts to passionately attacking Shatila; and he is unprecedentedly attracted by an image of Good, the couple who in his memory epitomises the Palestinian revolution, the young fighter Hamza and his mother. The word 'semble' in the above quotation is central: for Marty, the 'positivity' of Genet's discourse is misleading. He posits that, unlike the earlier massacre, Genet is disgusted by Shatila because it is, 'comme événement politique, un événement politique juif qui ne peut donc pas à ce titre s'ouvrir à la positivité du Mal' (*BSJ*, 146) [as a political event, a Jewish political event that therefore cannot by rights open onto the positivity of Evil]. And, in a passage to which I shall shortly return, he claims that Hamza is important as a figure who recalls the Nazis, rather than because of the couple he forms with his mother. In this perspective, Genet's apparent affection and concern for the Palestinians are in reality attributable to the fact that they are in conflict with the Jews. The basic gist of Marty's argument is that, rather than Genet's hostility to Israel deriving from his sympathy for the Palestinians, his support for the latter is motivated by a stronger hatred of the Jews and of Israel. In other words, the predominant current in Genet's psychical life was this 'anguish in relation to Good' that became crystallised in the figure of the Jew. Hence Marty's notion of a 'metaphysical' antisemitism, one hostile to the Jews not on racial grounds but because of their 'vocation':

> La cible première est donc le peuple juif, le peuple le plus 'ténébreux', dont le tort, contrairement à ce qu'énonce le racisme antisémite de Bloy ou de Céline, ne tient pas à sa prétendue nature raciale (puanteur, laideur, orientalité bâtarde, etc.), mais à sa *vocation*. (*BSJ*, 156)

> [The primary target is thus the Jewish people, the 'darkest' people, whose fault, contrary to the view expressed in the antisemitic racism of Bloy or Céline, lies not in its pretended racial nature (stink, ugliness, illegitimate orientality, etc.), but in its *vocation*.]

Marty bases this claim on a passage in *Un Captif amoureux* that he returns to several times:

> Si elle ne se fût battue contre le peuple qui me paraissait le plus ténébreux, celui dont l'origine se voulait à l'Origine, qui proclamait avoir été et vouloir demeurer l'Origine, le peuple qui se désignait Nuit des Temps, la révolution palestinienne m'eût-elle, avec tant de force, attiré? En me posant cette question, je crois donner la réponse. Qu'elle se découpât sur un fond de Nuit des Commencements — et cela, éternellement — la révolution palestinienne cessait d'être un combat habituel pour une terre volée, elle était une lutte métaphysique. Imposant au monde entier sa morale et ses mythes, Israël se confondait avec le Pouvoir. Il était le Pouvoir.

> [Would the Palestinian revolution have exercised such a strong fascination on me if it hadn't been fought against what seemed to me the darkest of people? — a people whose beginning claimed to be *the* Beginning, who claimed that they were, and meant to remain, the Beginning, who said they belonged to the Dawn of Time? To ask the question is, I think, to answer it. Taking place against the background of the dawn of Beginnings, the Palestinian revolution was no ordinary battle to recover stolen land: it was a metaphysical struggle. Israel, imposing its morals and myths on the whole world, saw itself as identical with Power. It was Power.] (*CA*, 198; *PL*, 166)

This quotation from *Un Captif amoureux* is in my view the single example, of all those Marty uses, that can clearly be deemed an expression of hostility on Genet's part towards the Jews, rather than towards Israel, and Marty's contribution is of value in drawing attention to an aspect of Genet's imaginary that had hitherto been overlooked. The second section of this chapter will therefore incorporate an investigation of Genet's attitude towards this 'vocation'. So as not to muddy the waters about the one area in which there are real grounds for debate, I will first recall the basic respects in which Genet's speech and actions do not correspond to any common understanding of antisemitism, as for example in the bench-mark reference definition of the International Holocaust Remembrance Alliance, and outline some of the most egregious flaws in Marty's overall arguments.[4]

Firstly, Genet does not generalise about the Jews or describe them in stereotypical terms (as victims, misers or a worldwide conspiracy wielding disproportionate power in finance, etc.). Indeed, they scarcely feature in his work before 'Quatre heures à Chatila': over the whole of his first five prose texts, there are only eight inscriptions of the word *juif* or *juive*, none of which are derogatory or suggest any metaphysical anguish in context. His writing does not suggest that he was hostile to the Jews, let alone that hatred of them was the dominant strand of his psychical investment.[5] It never claims that the Jews share negative characteristics; on the contrary, the few passages of *Un Captif amoureux* that pay any sustained attention to Jewish characters focus rather on their individual inventiveness. These all without exception concern members of the Israeli Defence Forces whom Genet respects for their ability to adopt an appearance of weakness in order to disarm and hence vanquish their enemy. His admiration is patent for the 'Fou' [Madman], a beggar speaking perfect Arabic whose eccentric behaviour — roaming around with a lantern at night, singing unintelligibly and stinking strongly, with the result that people avoided coming hear him — enabled him to reconnoitre the Palestinian neighbourhoods of Beirut without arousing suspicion, until he was spotted in the tank leading the Israeli invasion of West Beirut on 15 September 1982, wearing the uniform of an a colonel in the Israeli army (*CA*, 200; *PL*, 168). Genet is even more impressed by the six soldiers who succeeded in getting close enough to kill three important members of Fatah, by dressing up as pairs of homosexual hippies in drag:

> Le rire intérieur des travestis qui n'ont cessé de se sentir virils correspondait peut-être à la terreur des vrais travestis qui redoutent d'être découverts à cause de leurs voix papotant non comme celles des femmes mais qui se veulent indépendantes, comme leurs gestes d'ailleurs, des voix sans support. Au contraire les six Israéliens bouclés ne devaient oublier qu'ils étaient des hommes, musclés afin de se battre, entraînés à tuer. Toute l'étrangeté de leur situation venait de la douceur, de la délicatesse féminine de leurs gestes qui, d'un moment à l'autre, avec précision, deviendraient gestes de tueurs, pas de tueuses. [...] Arranger un pli de l'écharpe, rire dans l'aigu et soudainement se débarrasser des oripeaux, redevenir le guerrier dont le but est de tuer. Et aller vraiment tuer, non comme au dernier acte d'un drame très applaudi, tuer et laisser des morts. Je me demande s'il n'est pas doux de se glisser dans la tendre féminité et difficile de s'en dépêtrer pour une action criminelle. Mais l'héroïsme était là aussi.

> [The inward laugh of transvestites who never ceased feeling like men may have echoed the terror of real transvestites, afraid of being found out through their voices and gestures and using all their efforts to disguise them. But the six Israelis couldn't afford to forget for an instant that they were men, trained to

kill and with muscles meant for fighting. The strangeness of their situation lay in the gentle feminine delicacy of their movements, and their transformation from one moment to the next into the precise gestures of murderers — not murderesses. [...] The youths had to be able to arrange the fold of a scarf and give a high-pitched laugh, then whip off the glad rags and become warriors whose one object was to kill. Really kill. Not as in the last act of a play, to applause, but for real, with dead bodies. I wonder if it isn't comparatively easy and pleasant to slip into tender femininity, and hard to throw it off to commit a crime. But heroism was involved there too.] (CA, 221-22; PL, 185-86)

Strength and weakness go hand in hand: as in Genet's early novels, the most virile are also the most feminine. As ever, his writing is multi-layered: the men disguise themselves not as women, but as transvestites; the sexual difference that interests Genet here is the difference between 'false' and 'real' transvestites, between *transvestite* transvestites and 'real' ones. The transvestism remains a superficial phenomenon to the extent that the soldiers cannot forget they are men, knowing they will need to strip off the disguise in due course. However, the stability of the distinction between real and fake transvestites dissolves in the writing when Genet explicitly wonders if the soldiers' heroism consists not in the macho murdering but in doffing the disguise, renouncing the instability that, however instrumental their motivation may have been in performing it, they nonetheless enjoyed. The Israeli soldiers' 'heroism' — a term on which Genet reflects at length throughout *Un Captif amoureux* — lies in a double aptitude for loss: in their ability to surrender their virility, and then to relinquish the femininity they invented. Far from caricatural or serving to homogenise the Jews as a race apart, Genet's few Jewish characters are depicted in terms that echo his earlier view of the human condition in general and hence work to challenge rather than advocate the idea that Jews are intrinsically different from other people. His impatience with all forms of essentialising or racialising discourse, including antisemitism, is particularly evident in his response to a Palestinian friend's linking of the terms 'Arabism' and 'Arabness': 'Je ne nie pas l'arabisme qui est l'appartenance à une communauté religieuse et linguistique. Mais quand vous me parlez d'arabité je vous répondrai par quoi? Latinité, francité? Et Israël judéité?' [I don't reject 'Arabism,' which means belonging to a certain religious and linguistic community. But what about 'Arabness'? Can we talk about Latinness and Frenchness too? And for Israel Judeity?] (CA, 412; PL, 352).

Secondly, Genet does not judge Israel by a standard different from that used for other nation states; in fact, he does not explicitly challenge the right to exist in principle of a homeland for the Jews. Marty's assertion that the writer 'partage évidemment le point de vue négatif de Proust sur la création de l'État d'Israël' (BSJ, 99) [obviously shares Proust's negative point of view about the creation of the State of Israel] is perplexing, as there is no mention of the foundation of the state in either his works or his interviews. Even in *Journal du voleur*, written in 1947-48, there is no trace of either pro- or anti-Zionist arguments, indicating that he was not engaged with the Jewish national question at the time. The hostility expressed towards Israel in *Un Captif amoureux* directly concerns the dispossession of the Palestinians that resulted from the establishment of Israel. Moreover, Genet has no illusions about the reality of the geo-political situation in which the Palestinians find themselves.

He by no means deems Israel their principal enemy: 'Voici peut-être, en ordre ascendant, ceux qui furent les ennemis des Palestiniens: Bédouins, Tcherkesses, roi Hussein, féodaux arabes, foi islamique, Israël, Europe, Amérique, Haute Banque' [These were the Palestinians' enemies, in order of importance: the Bedouin, the Circassians, King Hussein, the feudal Arabs, the Muslim religion, Israel, Europe, America, the Big Banks] (*CA*, 143; *PL*, 120). His most direct and caustic criticism is reserved for the Palestinian elites, in particular the 'grandes familles' descended directly from the Prophet:

> Elles laissèrent des enfants révoltés mais rarement contre les privilèges — je note qu'aucune famille *chérifa* descendant du Prophète, ne payait l'impôt. Les familles plébéiennes mais riches, si — : titres, terres, argent, (il est encore à remarquer qu'aucun héritier ne refusa l'héritage aussi impudique en fût l'origine, né de la plus évidente imposture); les descendants s'émurent quand *leurs* paysans, devenus guerriers, se firent massacrer par des hommes à qui ils n'appartenaient pas, les Juifs et les Bédouins d'Hussein. [...]
> Les Grandes Familles s'offusquèrent quand les Juifs blessèrent leurs fermiers, peut-être par patriotisme, compassion, préfiguration de ce qui arrivera, mais surtout quelqu'un d'étranger venait de toucher à ce qu'ils possédaient.
>
> [They left offspring who were rebellious, but rarely against privilege. It's worth noting that no *ashraf* family — that is one descended from the Prophet — paid taxes, though wealthy plebian families did. Whether it consisted of office, land or money, no heir ever refused a legacy, however shameless its origin — not even if it derived from the most blatant imposture. The descendants were furious when 'their' peasants, now become fighters, got themselves masssacred by men they didn't belong to — the Jews, or Hussein's Bedouin. [...]
> The Leading Families took umbrage when their farmers were injured by the Jews, perhaps out of patriotism, perhaps out of pity, perhaps with a premonition. But chiefly because a stranger had interfered with something that was theirs.] (*CA*, 341; *PL*, 290-91)

Genet thus sees the Palestinian 'problem' no more in national than he does in racial terms. His support for the Palestinians is not identitarian in nature but relates rather to their situation; he is as exercised by the economically-privileged Palestinians as he is by American capitalists or Israel. This quotation's scathing attitude towards those who consider other people as 'property' echoes Genet's own explanation for the strength of his sympathy for the Palestinians. As he elaborates in 'Quatre heures à Chatila', his support for their struggle is due to their lack of property, and in particular their homelessness:

> Le choix que l'on fait d'une communauté privilégiée, en dehors de la naissance alors que l'appartenance à ce peuple est native, ce choix s'opère par la grâce d'une adhésion non raisonnée, non que la justice n'y ait sa part, mais cette justice et toute la défense de cette communauté se font en vertu d'un attrait sentimental, peut-être même sensible, sensuel; je suis français, mais entièrement, sans jugement, je défends les Palestiniens. Ils ont le droit pour eux puisque je les aime. Mais les aimerais-je si l'injustice n'en faisait pas un peuple vagabond?
>
> [If someone chooses a particular community outside of his birth — whereas to belong to this people one must be born into it — this choice is based on

an irrational affinity; not that justice has no part in it, but this justice and the entire defense of this community take place because of an attraction that is sentimental, or perhaps sensitive or sensual. I am French, but I defend the Palestinians entirely, without judgment. They are in the right because I love them. But would I love them if injustice had not made them a wandering people?] (*ED*, 254; *PL*, 218)

What sets the Palestinians apart for Genet is the fact that they have been dispossessed of their land. They are his 'chosen people', that is, the people to whom he is attached by choice rather than by birth. But as the parallel with the Jews implicit in the term suggests, there is nothing exclusive or essential about the privilege he awards them. The analogy with his own situation scarcely needs restating: he repeatedly refers to himself as a 'vagabond' not only in *Journal du voleur* but throughout the texts collected in *L'Ennemi déclaré*.[6] Within *Un Captif amoureux* Genet also characterises the Jews on two separate occasions as 'vagabonds': he describes the promise of the Promised Land to Abraham and Moses as given 'à un vagabond venu à pied de Chaldée, à un autre venu d'Égypte' [to one vagabond who'd walked all the way from Chaldea and another who'd come from Egypt] (*CA*, 331; *PL*, 282), and again later describes the Jews as 'la descendance d'un vagabond' [the descendants of a vagabond] (*CA*, 497; *PL*, 424). Genet claims exceptionality for the Palestinians on the basis of a quality which is neither unique nor proper to them; he specifically likes the Palestinians for a situation analogous to that of the Jews prior to the existence of Israel. Furthermore, his support is contingent on their *not* achieving national self-determination. It is clear from his interview with Rüdiger Wischenbart and Layla Shahid Barrada that his sympathy will last only as long as their revolt is ongoing: 'Écoutez: le jour où les Palestiniens seront institutionnalisés, je ne serai plus de leur côté. Le jour où les Palestiniens deviendront une nation comme une autre nation, je ne serai plus là' [Listen: the day the Palestinians become an institution, I will no longer be on their side. The day the Palestinians become a nation like other nations, I won't be there anymore] (*ED*, 282; *PL*, 244). For Genet, the enemy is as much nationhood as a particular nation; he supports the Palestinian struggle less as a national struggle against Israel than as an *anti-national* one.

Thirdly, Genet neither denied the Holocaust nor voiced satisfaction that it took place. On the contrary, when asked by Bertrand Poirot-Delpech if his pleasure at Hitler's defeat of France extended to the genocide carried out in the camps, he answers that he was not aware of it at the time:

> B.P.-D: *Et ce qu'il faisait, les camps d'extermination par exemple, c'était marrant aussi?*
>
> G.: D'abord, vraiment, je ne le savais pas. Mais il s'agit de la France, il ne s'agit pas du peuple allemand ou du peuple juif, ou des peuples communistes qui pouvaient être massacrés par Hitler. Il s'agissait de la correction donnée par l'armée allemande à l'armée française.
>
> [B.P.-D: *And the other things he did, the extermination camps, that was amusing too?*
>
> G.: First, really, I didn't know about that. But what I'm talking about is France, not the German people or the Jewish people, or the communist people

that Hitler massacred. It was a question of the corrective the German army gave
to the french army.] (*ED*, 232; *DE*, 200)

To my knowledge, nobody disputes Genet's claim that he was unaware during the
war of the Nazis' plans to exterminate the Jews; he certainly did not hold back
elsewhere from declaring extremely controversial positions. His expressions of
support for Hitler after the war, when the Nazis' genocidal policies had become
common knowledge, are more controversial. Both Jablonka and Marty argue that
there is evidence he approved of the massacres of the Jews in the camps. Their
claims are based on a quotation from 'L'Enfant criminel', the highly contentious
text written for radio in 1949 lamenting the closure of Mettray and other reform
schools and claiming the children treasured the cruelty they suffered there. In
an undoubtedly shocking and offensive passage, Genet makes a link between the
torture inflicted by the French penal system and the concentration camps:

> Sous l'action de la chaleur la plante s'est développée. Puisqu'elle fut semée
> par les bourgeois qui firent les prisons de pierre, avec leurs gardiens de chair
> et d'esprit, je me réjouis de voir enfin le semeur dévoré. Ces braves gens
> applaudissaient, qui sont aujourd'hui un nom doré sur le marbre, quand nous
> passions menottes aux poignets et qu'un flic nous bourrait les côtes. Une seule
> chiquenaude de leurs gendarmes fut vivifiée par le sang brûlant des héros du
> nord, elle s'est développée jusqu'à devenir une plante merveilleuse de beauté,
> de tact et d'adresse, une rose dont les pétales tordus, retroussés, montrant le
> rouge et le rose sous un soleil d'enfer se nomment de noms terribles: Maïdanek,
> Belsen, Auschwitz, Mauthausen, Dora. Je tire mon chapeau. (*OC*, IV, 389)

> [Under the action of heat the plant developed. Since it was sown by the
> bourgeois who made the stone prisons, with their wardens of flesh and mind,
> I am delighted to see the sower at last devoured. Those good people, today a
> gilded name on marble, applauded when we passed by, handcuffed, with a cop
> flogging our ribs. A single flick by their policemen was invigorated by the
> burning blood of the northern heroes, it developed into a plant wondrous with
> beauty, tact and deftness, a rose whose twisted, distorted petals showing red and
> pink beneath a hellish sun have terrible names: Maïdanek, Belsen, Auschwitz,
> Mauthausen, Dora. I take my hat off.]

For Jablonka, this passage is where 'le raisonnement de Genet devient proprement
antisémite' (*VIJG*, 250) [Genet's reasoning becomes properly antisemitic]; Marty
also relies on it to argue that the privileged target of Genet's animosity is the
Jew (*JGP*, 33-37). Its disproportionate comparison between the cruelty suffered
by the inmates of French prisons and the atrocities committed in the camps is
unquestionably outrageous, and the effect produced can certainly be judged an
insult to the memory of those who died in the latter. Nonetheless, the fact remains
that it never mentions the Jews. The two critics' accusations rest on the assumption
that any reference to the concentration camps — including those, like Mauthausen
and Dora, that were not built as extermination camps and incarcerated relatively
few Jews — essentially constitutes a reference to the Holocaust. But while in 1949
the existence of the extermination camps was certainly widely known, that does
not in itself suffice to subsume the concentration camps under the genocide and

show that Genet rejoiced specifically at the murder of the Jews. On the contrary, the explicit, denotative meaning of Genet's words indicates that his admiration for the Nazis specifically concerns their brutality against his fellow Frenchmen.[7] As we saw in Chapter 1, it is indubitably irresponsible on Genet's part to endorse Nazi monstrosity in this or any other way. Nonetheless, the pleasure he expresses derives explicitly from the fact that the cruelty is directed towards his compatriots: 'I am delighted to see the sower at last devoured'. Just after the war, in *Réflexions sur la question juive* Sartre had famously analysed antisemitism as a 'passion'.[8] To the extent that a recurrent pattern can be taken as the symptom of a visceral investment, Genet's praise for the Nazis shows hatred for the French, not for the Jews. However disturbing this passage may be for its celebration of cruelty, the textual evidence invalidates the idea that Genet's approval of Hitler is motivated by antisemitism and automatically implies approval for the Holocaust.

Marty's arguments have already been challenged by others on a range of grounds, both substantive and methodological: the implications of his distinction between a 'metaphysical' and a 'political' antisemitism; his confusion of anti-Zionism with antisemitism; his selective use of evidence and failure to note material on record that counters his claims; quotation out of context, etc.[9] Rather than rehearse all these arguments again, the following makes a number of criticisms relating specifically to Marty's interpretation of *Un Captif amoureux*. The first concerns the overarching thesis of *Bref séjour à Jérusalem*: the claim of a longstanding antisemitism that necessarily involves the 'relativisation du peuple palestinian' (*BSJ*, 156) [relativisation of the Palestinian people]. As outlined earlier, Marty reads the enthusiasm evinced by Genet in his later writings about the Palestinians as a displaced antisemitism; from his viewpoint, the Jews are a more significant and originary other for the writer than the Palestinians, and *Un Captif amoureux* is primarily an expression of hatred towards Israel rather than an account of what makes the Palestinians special. As its title reflects, most of the discussion in 'Genet à Chatila', the section of *Bref séjour* dealing with Genet, concentrates on the writer's second 'encounter with the Jewish world' via the Palestinians; only five pages deal with Hitler and the period of Nazism. However, those five pages play a crucial role in anchoring Marty's argument, both in *Bref séjour* and subsequently in *Jean Genet, post-scriptum*. Marty in effect infers Genet's antisemitism from his admiration for Hitler:

> Il est probable que les juifs ne sont inauguralement apparus dans l'univers imaginaire de Genet — il n'y a pas de raisons qu'il en soit autrement — que par la médiation du nazisme, du Mal, et, sans doute n'est-ce que par voie de conséquence et que par cette médiation négative, qu'ils se sont identifiés au 'Bien'. (*BSJ*, 102)

> [The Jews probably only came to feature in Genet's imaginary universe — there is no reason to believe otherwise — via the mediation of Nazism, of Evil, and it's doubtless only as a result of that and of that negative mediation that they were identified with 'Good'.]

As he acknowledges, Genet scarcely mentions the Jews in his works written during the war or shortly afterwards (*BSJ*, 108). This includes *Pompes funèbres*, the book containing the representation of Hitler on which so much of Marty's case rests. Of the eight inscriptions of the word 'Jew' in the novels mentioned earlier, only two occur in *Pompes funèbres*, and neither in a context related to Hitler. Nonetheless, Marty's inference becomes the basis of a circular argument in relation to the later writings. Notwithstanding the absence of any textual link in *Pompes funèbres* between Hitler and the Jews, his claim that Genet's later attachment to the Palestinians is fundamentally antisemitic depends on the idea that it reawakens an 'antisémitisme antérieur' [earlier antisemitism]. He rests his case on Genet's mention of Germany in *Un Captif amoureux* in a passage describing his return to Ajloun in 1984 in the hope of finding Hamza and his mother again, fourteen years after he spent a momentous night in their house. Genet senses something German about the decor of the house to which he is taken that suggests he has found the right place, as he knows Hamza had spent time in Germany in the intervening period:

> Je ne sais encore en quoi cette maison palestinienne, dans le camp d'Irbid était aussi allemande. Ce que j'écris je ne l'ai pas pensé par raisonnement mais éprouvé d'un coup comme on éprouve la non-maturité d'une pomme avant de la cueillir, quand on voit le vert et même avant de l'avoir vu. La maison n'était pas construite avec des éléments venus de la Forêt-Noire, mais entre elle, entre plutôt sa vue et la sonorité du mot Allemagne je pressentis l'accord qui allait, plus profondément que je ne l'ai dit; j'y pressentis celui qui s'établit maintenant quand on parle d'eux: Allemagne et Grand Mufti de Jérusalem.

> [I still don't know how, but that Palestinian house in the cap at Irbid had something German about it. I didn't reason about this. I experienced it directly, as you know an apple is unripe before you pick it, just from its colour, or even wihout looking at it. The house wasn't built with materials from the Black Forest, but I sensed a parallel between it, or rather between the sight of it and the sound of the word Germany. Perhaps I even had a presentiment of the present-day link between Germany and the Grand Mufti of Jerusalem.] (*CA*, 471; *PL*, 401)

According to Marty, Genet's association of Germany with the Grand Mufti of Jerusalem transforms not just Hamza's mother's house but the entire 'espace palestinian' into a 'mise en abyme de l'espace nazi' (*BSJ*, 138). He reads the Mufti as a figure of the 'collaboration des Palestiniens avec le nazisme' [collaboration between the Palestinians and Nazism] to which he attributes their attraction for Genet; and Hamza, the emblem of the Palestinian struggle, is revealed as 'l'une de ces poupées nazies que Genet évoquait dans *Pompes funèbres*' (*BSJ*, 138) [one of the Nazi dolls that Genet evoked in *Funeral Rites*]. But this interpretation of Genet's meaning is extremely tendentious. Firstly, Marty fails to take into account the fact that it is only on Genet's return to the Irbid camp that the link between Germany and the Mufti strikes him. Yet Hamza and his mother have haunted him for the previous fourteen years, prior to Hamza's time in Germany and the emergence of any German influence on the decor. During that time, Hamza figured in Genet's imagination — to the writer's own perplexity, as we shall explore — as part of the couple he forms with his mother. The idea that the dominant factor in the fascination Hamza holds for him is that he crystallises an image of triumphant antisemitism is frankly nonsensical. In addition, the assumption that Genet's association of Germany with the Grand Mufti unambiguously betokens hostility to the Jews rather than to Israel is highly problematic. Mohammed Amin al-Husseini, the Mufti during the Second World War who attempted to secure Hitler's backing for Arab independence and support for the movement opposing the establishment of a Jewish state, is indeed infamous for his collaboration with the Nazi regime. But there is, to say the very least, a controversy about whether he was motivated by Arab nationalism or antisemitism.[10] Genet presents the link between Germany and the Mufti as an intuition on which he does not elaborate; there is nothing in the passage to indicate that he saw the Mufti as a proponent of antisemitism rather than as a vocal and visible leader of anti-Zionism. This is why the idea of a prior antisemitism on Genet's part is so crucial to Marty's argument:

> On suppose alors ceci: l'antisémitisme antérieur de Genet, celui qui s'accompagnait d'une métaphysique du Mal, d'une fascination exaltée pour Hitler et pour Oradour, n'a pas été aboli. Il n'est pas devenu un antisionisme politique nourri par la positivité d'une cause liée à une métaphysique du Bien. La superposition de la figure du nazisme à l'espace palestinien, la réminiscence involontaire du passé nazi, jusque-là forclos, vient hanter un combat qui semblait reposer sur un discours voué à la communauté palestinienne. (*BSJ*, 139)

> [So we can presume this: Genet's earlier antisemitism, accompanied by a metaphysics of Evil and a heightened fascination with Hitler and Oradour, has not been abolished. It did not become a political anti-Zionism supported positively by a cause linked to a metaphysics of Good. In superposing the figure of Nazism over the Palestinian space, the involuntary memory of the Nazi past, hitherto forclosed, comes to haunt a fight that seemed to rest on a discourse concerned with the Palestinian community.]

The assumption of a prior, longstanding antisemitism in Genet's imagination is needed to lend credence to the claim that Genet's siding with the Palestinians against Israel is a manifestation of antisemitism rather than a 'political anti-Zionism'. Yet Marty has advanced no basis on which to support that assumption. The argument that Genet's apparent support for the Palestinian struggle is haunted by a more primordial hatred of the Jews remains ungrounded in any evidence.

A related, and even more crucial, point concerns what exactly is at stake in the very notion of a 'metaphysical antisemitism'. When, early in his book, Marty announces that he will elaborate on Genet's production of an 'ontologie morale de l'être-juif', the reader understands that this will elucidate the 'metaphysical' aspect of his putative antisemitism. Yet the ontology he develops is in fact the 'ontologie morale d'Israël' (*BSG*, 152) [moral ontology of Israel]. The metaphysical antisemitism he alleges in fact involves Genet's hostility towards Israel, 'comme entité métaphysique incarnée par ce nom même' [as a metaphysical entity incarnated by that very name), 'unique personnage de l'histoire' [the unique character of the story] (*BSJ*, 152). It is Israel that Marty recognises as Genet's enemy; it is in that enmity that he finds evidence of antisemitism. His slippage from antagonism towards the Jews to antagonism towards the country is clearest in relation to the passage identified earlier as the most troubling and most warranting investigation. Marty finishes the paragraph following his analysis of that quotation (where he asserts that Genet abhors the 'Jewish people' for their 'vocation' rather than their race) with the words: 'C'est la proclamation même d'Israël, c'est donc son nom et la proclamation de son nom que Genet souhaite anéantir' (BSJ, 157) [It's the very proclamation of Israel, therefore its name and the proclamation of its name, that Genet wants to obliterate].

Marty's case for Genet's antisemitism thus hinges on considering the country Israel as a 'metaphysical entity'. This is clearly dubious in a number of repects. First, in relation to Genet: opposition to Israel and its policies is not the same as antisemitism; insofar as it is on the grounds of Genet's hostility to Israel that he is alleged to be antisemitic, Marty's case is deeply flawed. But the confusion of anti-Zionism and antisemitism has implications also for Marty's own project. It is disingenuous of him to suggest that he is making a metaphysical rather than a political argument. Far from abstracting a philosophical question from a political one, it is a highly political stance to frame opposition to Israel as a form of antisemitism, with the concomitant implication that hostility to its treatment of the Palestinians has no basis other than irrational hatred and prejudice.

Marty's partisanship is especially visible in the attempt to place Israel in the position of the powerless, or victim. As quoted above, in the same paragraph where Genet wonders if he is hostile to the Jewish people, the writer explicitly situates Israel on the side of power: 'Israël se confondait avec le Pouvoir. Il était le Pouvoir'. Yet when Marty invokes this unequivocal statement, he immediately turns it around to place Israel rather in a position of relative weakness:

> Israël est le Pouvoir. Or si Genet n'est jamais avec le Pouvoir, s'il est toujours contre lui, ce n'est pas parce qu'il est du côté des 'pauvres', c'est qu'il est du côté de l'hyper-pouvoir, du côté de l'hyper-puissance, du côté de la domination absolue, de la dureté, de l'arme, des grenades que les gamins arabes exhibent comme de 'doubles ou quadruples monstrueux testicules', de ces soldats palestiniens 'en armes, ornés par elles, costumés léopard, bérets rouges sur l'œil, tels enfin que chacun paraissait non seulement la transfiguration de mes fantasmes mais leur matérialisation m'attendant là, devant moi, et, comme s'ils m'étaient offerts'. (BSJ, 141)

> [Israel is Power. Now, if Genet is never with Power, is always against it, it is not because he is on the side of the 'poor', it is because he is on the side of hyper-power, hyper-potency, the side of absolute domination, hardness, weapons, the grenades that Arab boys show off like 'double or quadruple monstrous testicles', of the Palestinian soldiers 'decorated with guns, in leopard-spotted uniforms and red berets tilted over their eyes, each not merely a transfiguration but also a materialization of my fantasies, there before me, as if offered to me.]

Astonishingly, to contend that Israel represents the victim, later the 'scapegoat', rather than the powerful element in the Israeli-Palestinian relationship, Marty simply substitutes a hierarchy of 'hyperpower/power' for the usual hierarchy of powerful/powerless. The same mode of argument by mere assertion that Marty used to construct Genet's representation of Hitler as a glorification of the powerful and hatred of the victim is again deployed here. Most importantly, he quotes extremely selectively from Genet in order to create the opposite impression of what Genet actually said. In Genet's text, the assertion that Israel 'était le Pouvoir' is followed by the sentence: 'La vue seule des pauvres fusils des feddayin montrait cette distance incommensurable entre les deux armements: d'un côté peu de morts ni de blessures graves, de l'autre l'anéantissement accepté et voulu par les nations européennes et arabes' [The mere sight of the fedayeen's meagre guns showed the immeasurable distance there was between the two forces: on the one hand just a few dead and wounded; on the other annihilation, accepted and even desired by Europe and Arab countries] (*CA*, 198-99; *PL*, 166). Genet unequivocally emphasises Israel's military superiority over the Palestinians, in sharp contrast with the quotation Marty imports from an entirely different context in the book, involving a comparison between the Fedayeen and the Black Panthers (*CA*, 244; *PL*, 205).

Once more, the substantive question of Genet's positioning in relation to instances of power, as analysed in Chapter 1, is the core issue. According to Marty, Genet's animosity towards Israel stems from his hatred of the weak while his love for the Palestinians is a function of their 'hyperpowerful' position, their 'domination' over their merely 'powerful' enemy. That interpretation is massively at odds with the evidence of *Un Captif amoureux*. The text does not merely repeatedly recognise Israel's military superiority, as in the quotation truncated above. Israel's military advantage extends to the domain of rhetoric, as Genet muses in a discussion of the relative power of the graffiti scrawled on the buildings of Paris, including the Opera Garnier, during a visit by Jordan's King Hussein:

> Le bulbe vert-de-gris, me dit-on, fut la chose et peut-être la seule qu'il [Hussein] vit, où les capitales géantes, peintes en blanc: PALESTINE VAINCRA étaient dessinées. [...] Mais à ce PALESTINE VAINCRA, j'eus l'occasion, vingt fois ou plus, aux environs de l'Opéra ou ailleurs, de lire sur les murs gris de Paris, les bombages rapides, discrets, presque timides, de la réplique israélienne: *Israël vivra*. [...] La force, immensément plus grande, de cette réponse — et non réplique — où mieux, à l'affirmation limitée du *vaincra*, l'affirmation presque éternelle du *vivra*. Dans le simple domaine rhétorique Israël, dans la demi-nuit parisienne, par ses bombages furtifs, allait, je l'ai dit, immensément loin.
>
> [I've been told the grey-green dome was the first and perhaps the only thing he saw: it had 'PALESTINE WILL OVERCOME' painted on it in huge white letters. [...] But twenty times or more on the grey walls of Paris, near the Opera and elsewhere, I saw Israel's answer to that message. Sprayed on hastily, unobtrusively, almost shyly, it read: 'Israel will live.' [...] How immensely more forceful was this response! — response rather than answer. Or rather, what a contrast between the limited declaration of 'will overcome' and the almost eternal claim of 'will live.' Simply in the field of rhetoric, in the twilight of Paris, Israel and its furtive sprayings went immensely far.] (*CA*, 90-91; *PL*, 74-75)

Secondly, the association of the Fedayeen with their weapons — glossed by Marty as adulation of their domination — is explained by Genet rather in terms of the image, as the word 'ornés' in Marty's borrowed quotation exemplifies. In contrast with his reluctant admiration for the inventive ruthlessness of the Israeli army, he focuses on the dangers of their adolescent posing with their rifles, 'sans se douter

que cette pose en elle-même était une menace érotique ou mortelle, ou les deux'
[not suspecting this attitude was in itself either an erotic or a mortal threat, or both]
(*CA*, 103; *PL*, 85). Above all, Marty fails to take account of the fact that *Un Captif
amoureux* is haunted throughout by the failure of the Palestinian revolution. Just as
Genet only gave voice to his delight at France's humiliation when it was over, he
expressed his enchantment at the Palestinian revolution at a time when he believed
its peak had passed:

> Car elle fut une fête, cette révolte palestinienne, sur les rives orientales du
> Jourdain. Une fête qui dura neuf mois. Si quelqu'un a connu la liberté de Paris
> au mois de mai 1968, qu'il ajoute une élégance du corps, une politesse de tous
> à l'égard de chacun, mais surtout qu'il compare, car les feddayin étaient armés.

> [For it was a party, the Palestinian revolt on the banks of the Jordan. A party
> that lasted nine months. To get an idea of what it was like, anyone who tasted
> the freedom that reigned in Paris in May 1968 has only to add physical elegance
> and universal courtesy. But the fedayeen were armed.] (*CA*, 334; *PL*, 285)

The passage where he most clearly outlines what was distinctive about the revolution
is also where he most concisely expresses his view that it was doomed to failure:

> De plus haut que moi-même quand je la contemplais, la révolution palestinienne
> ne fut jamais désir de territoires, presque terrains perdus, jardins potagers ou
> vergers sans clôture, mais un grand mouvement de révolte d'une contestation
> cadastrale jusqu'aux limites du monde islamique, non seulement limites
> territoriales mais révision et probablement négation d'une théologie aussi
> endormeuse qu'un berceau breton. Le rêve, mais pas encore la décision des
> feddayin était sensible de faire basculer les vingt-deux peuples arabes, aller
> au-delà afin de faire naître chez tous des sourires, enfantés d'abord et vite idiots.
> Les munitions des feddayin s'épuisaient. L'Amérique, première visée, inventait
> des merveilles. Croyant aller tête altière la révolution palestinienne coulait à pic.

> [When I looked at the Palestinian revolution from a viewpoint higher than
> my own, it was never desire for territory, for land more or less derelict and
> unfenced kitchen gardens and orchards, but a great movement of revolt, a
> challenge over rights which reached to the limits of Islam, not only involving
> territorial boundaries but also calling for a revision, probably even a rejection,
> of a theology as soporific as a Breton cradle. The dream, but not yet the declared
> aim, of the fedayeen was clear: to do away with the twenty-two Arab nations
> and leave everyone wreathed in smiles, childlike at first but soon foolish.
> But they were running out of ammunition and their main target, America,
> was endlessly resourceful. Thinking to walk tall, the Palesine revolution was
> sinking fast.] (*CA*, 123; *PL*, 103)

Far from a celebration of the Palestinians' 'domination' over Israel, *Un Captif
amoureux* is a nostalgic reminiscence of a movement of revolt against a more
powerful enemy.

In pride of place here is America but, to return to the question of whether Genet
is antisemitic, how important is it that another enemy, Israel, is also a Jewish state?
To what extent is the 'negation of a theology', be it Islamic or Judaic, a key factor
in Genet's support for the Palestinians? What is the specific role of religion in all

this? Not only is Marty's argument that Genet is driven by a fascistic enjoyment at the Palestinians' triumphalist domination over a weaker opponent profoundly unconvincing, but the case he makes does not actually address the association that led Genet himself to wonder if there is an antisemitic element to his support for the uprising: the fact that it is targeted against the people 'dont l'origine se voulait à l'Origine, qui proclamait avoir été et vouloir demeurer l'Origine'. Nor does Marty engage with the most extraordinary aspect of *Un Captif amoureux* as testimony to an armed battle: Genet's choice of an image of tender solicitude as the emblem of the Palestinian revolution. I now turn to explore the link between these questions.

★　★　★　★　★

Divided into two parts entitled 'Souvenirs I' and 'Souvenirs II', *Un Captif amoureux* presents as a book of memories. Although not defined generically by any paratextual indication, the genre to which it corresponds most closely is the memoir.[11] As the term's French etymology signals, the defining characteristic of the memoir is that it constitutes an account of events from the perspective of the author's remembered experience. It can have a predominantly historical or autobiographical focus depending on whether it focuses on external matters or the author's own life. What makes *Un Captif amoureux* unusual is the unprecedented and intriguing relationship that it weaves between these two dimensions. The first of the passages in which the writer attributes a role to Shatila in having motivated him to write the text suggests that the historical dimension is paramount insofar as the book derives primarily from a desire to bear witness to a reality outside of himself:

> Après les tueries de Sabra et de Chatila en septembre 1982 certains Palestiniens me demandèrent d'écrire mes souvenirs. [...]
> — Dis exactement ce que tu as vu, ce que tu as entendu. Essaye d'expliquer pourquoi tu es resté si longtemps avec nous. Pourquoi tu es venu et si l'on veut accidentel. Tu es venu pour huit jours, pourquoi es-tu demeuré deux ans. En août 1983 j'en commençai la rédaction, tout entier revenu dans les années 70, je voyais remonter jusqu'à 83 mes souvenirs. Aidé par ces nombreux acteurs, ou témoins des faits que je rapporte je me précipitai dans la mémoire. C'est alors que je connus la fraîcheur de n'être plus en France. Elle fut lointaine et très rétrécie. L'auriculaire le plus petit des feddayin occupait plus de place que l'Europe entière et la France fut un souvenir lointain de ma première jeunesse.

> [After the massacres at Sabra and Chatila in September 1982 some of the Palestinians asked me to write my memoirs. [...]
> — 'Put down exactly what you saw and heard. Try to explain why you stayed with us so long. Why you came. You intended to stay for a week. Why did you stay for two years?' I started writing in August 1983, went right back to the 1970s, and found my memories carrying me on to 1983. I plunged in, helped by the many people who took part in or witnessed the events I recorded. Being abroad helped me see things afresh: France seemed far away, and shrunk very small. One fedayee's little finger seemed bigger than the whole of Europe, and France just a distant recollection of my childhood.] (*CA*, 330-31; *PL*, 282)

According to this narrative, *Un Captif amoureux* originated as a work of testimony, an attempt to provide an external record of what the author saw and heard. Although Sabra and Shatila provided the initial jolt that set him writing, he scarcely mentions them; most of the text concerns the time he spent in the refugee camps and on the military bases of the Fedayeen in 1970–72. The book roams through both space and time, as he announces near the beginning:

> Les titres de parties de ce livre portent les mots de souvenirs, je dois conduire le lecteur selon un va-et-vient dans le temps et bien sûr dans l'espace. L'espace sera la planète, le temps, plutôt celui qui passa de 1970 à l'année 1984.

> [The titles of the parts of this book carry the words 'Souvenirs', and I will lead the reader back and forth in time as well as, inevitably, in space. The space will be the whole world, the time chiefly the period between 1970 and 1984.] (*CA*, 49; *PL*, 38)

This timespan is that of Genet's involvement with the Palestinian revolution, from his first visit to Jordan in 1970 to his return there in 1984. He plunges into his memories, but without going back very far in time. The autobiographical dimension of this memoir is therefore dramatically different from what might be expected of a man in his seventies, diagnosed with a terminal cancer and deeply aware of his approaching death. With one exception, of which more later, the book does not evoke memories of Genet's childhood or youth. Far from looking back over his life and exploring the early experiences that formed him, his focus is his engagement in the recent past with what he reiterates, in the final paragraphs of the text, is a reality 'hors de moi, existant par et pour elle-même' [outside me, existing in and for itself] (*CA*, 503; *PL*, 430).[12]

As an account of the Palestinian revolution, however, the most striking aspect of *Un Captif amoureux* is its intensely personal, subjective nature. It focuses not on external events recognised as being of political or historical importance, but on memories of particular conversations and interactions with individual Palestinians. Moreover, the text seems haphazard and lacking in structure, as the narrator shifts repeatedly between places and times. Genet time and again foregrounds that no chronicler can lay claim to objectivity. The book is haunted by its author's awareness that his rendering of what he saw and heard is inescapably shaped by the fact that it was *his* eyes and ears that mediated the experience:

> Les métamorphoses d'un fait en mots, signes, série de mots, séries de signes et de mots, sont d'autres faits qui ne restituent jamais le premier à partir duquel je vais transcrire. Cette vérité première je dois la dire afin de me mettre en garde moi-même. S'il ne s'agit que de commune morale, mentir ou non serait sans importance à mes yeux, je dois dire pourtant que ce sont *mes yeux, mon regard*, qui ont *vu* ce que j'ai cru décrire, *mes oreilles* entendu. La forme que j'ai donnée dès le commencement au récit n'eut jamais pour but d'informer le lecteur réellement de ce que fut la révolution palestinienne. La construction même, l'organisation, la disposition du récit, sans vouloir délibérément *trahir* ce que furent les faits, arrangent la narration de telle sorte qu'apparaîtra probablement que je fus le témoin peut-être privilégié, ou l'ordonnateur?

> [By transforming a fact into words, characters, series of words, series of characters and words, you create other facts that can never recreate the original

one. I state this basic truth to put myself on my guard. If it's only a question of ordinary morality, I don't care whether someone's lying or telling the truth. But I must stress that it's my eyes that saw what I thought I was describing, and my ears that heard it. The form I adopted from the beginning for this account was never designed to tell the reader what the Palestinian revolution was really like. The construction, organization and layout of the book, without deliberately intending to *betray* the facts, manage the narrative in such a way that it will probably seem that I was a privileged witness or even a manipulator?] (*CA*, 416; *PL*, 355)

At issue is more than the inevitable gap between an event and its representation, the fact that history is always conditioned and constrained by the language used in its construction. Genet is interested in the singular position of the witness, as it impacts on both the form and the content of the testimony provided. Especially, the form of his text bears witness to the witness not as neutral or objective observer but as *body*: as a set of eyes and ears that determine the spatial perspective from which events are perceived, but also as an entity existing in time and subject to an unconscious, whose perception of events is structured, more unknowingly than deliberately, by its experience to date. The passage continues:

> Ce que je rapporte était peut-être aussi ce que j'ai vécu et pourtant différent car une continuité avait fondu le disparate de mon existence dans la continuité de la vie palestinienne, mais pas sans me laisser des aperçus, des traces, quelquefois des coupures avec ma vie antérieure, de sorte que les événements de celle-ci étaient si forts qu'à certains moments je devais m'en éveiller: je vivais un rêve, duquel je deviens le maître aujourd'hui, en reconstituant les images qu'on lit, en les assemblant. A ce point du reste que je me demande parfois si je n'ai pas vécu cette vie de telle façon que j'en ordonnerais les épisodes selon le désordre apparent des images d'un rêve.
>
> Mais tant de mots afin de dire: *ceci est ma révolution palestinienne* récitée dans l'ordre que j'ai choisi. A côté de la mienne il y a l'autre, probablement les autres.
>
> Vouloir penser la révolution serait l'équivalent, au réveil de vouloir la logique dans l'incohérence des images rêvées.

> [What I recount may well be what I experienced, but it was different in that the disparateness of my own existence had merged into the continuity of Palestinian life, though still leaving me with traces, glimpses of, sometimes severances from, my former life. Sometimes events from this former life became so vivid I had to wake myself up: I was living a dream, which I am able to control now by reconstructing and assembling its various images. Sometimes I wonder whether I didn't live that life especially so that I might arrange its episodes in the same seeming disorder as the images in a dream.
>
> All these words to say, this is *my* Palestinian revolution, told in my own chosen order. As well as mine there is the other, probably many others.
>
> Trying to think the revolution is like waking up and trying to see logic in the incoherence of the dreamed images.] (*CA*, 416; *PL*, 355)

Although an eyewitness account of the Palestinian revolution, *Un Captif amoureux* is therefore fundamentally shaped — both in form and content — by its author's previous existence, notwithstanding the near total lack of direct reference to his life prior to 1970. The difficulty of separating out the part played by Genet himself from the external reality he seeks to render echoes in the difficulty of distinguishing between dreaming and waking. 'Les événements de *celle-ci* étaient si forts qu'à certains moments je devais m'en éveiller': if, in accordance with common usage, 'celle-ci' refers to the last-mentioned relevant noun (here the narrator's 'vie antérieure' as distinct from 'la vie palestinienne'), the narrator's personal memories are the dream from which he awakens. But the following sentence displaces the apparent opposition between one life and another. If to 'live a dream' means to live so intensely it seems like a dream, surely the vivid experience that Genet is reconstituting via the images he presents concerns rather his time with the Palestinians? In other words, the crucial distinction in the passage is the difference not between dreaming and living but rather between dreaming and writing. The question is less whether *Un Captif amoureux* betrays the external reality of the revolution (as we shall see, he believes any account of it must necessarily do so) than whether it is sufficiently faithful to the dream he lived. In writing, he becomes 'master' of the dream, a term at odds with the disorder or incoherence that defines the latter. Writing is not the same as dreaming. The best it can do to render dreaming is to ensure that the order it imposes at least recalls the disorder of a dream.

*Un Captif amoureux*, then, is not a failed attempt to 'think' the revolution.[13] What appears to the reader as a lack of organisation is a singular, oneiric, very personal order. Just as the 'incoherence of the dreamed images' cannot be reduced to any logical explanation, the text's disconnected, fragmentary structure serves as a reminder that the revolution fundamentally exceeds Genet's perspective on it. If, as he says, the aim of the book is not to tell the reader what the Palestinian revolution was really like, the question arises about the kind of contribution it makes to the Palestinians' political struggle. What kind of witnessing is at stake? What kind of truth does it tell? And what role do his memories play in the telling of that truth? Earlier, I quoted his line that his memories should be read as a 'reportage'. Yet elsewhere, he explicitly demarcates his book from journalistic accounts of the revolution that to him seemed the opposite or negation of the reality he had experienced:

> Dans le journal chaque détail en creux avait une correspondance en relief dans le réel, et du moindre au plus effronté. Autant avouer qu'en restant avec eux je restais, et je ne sais pas comment, de quelle autre façon, le dire, dans mon propre souvenir. Par cette phrase peut-être enfantine je ne prétends pas avoir vécu et me souvenant d'elles, des vies antérieures, ma phrase dit aussi clairement que je le puis que la révolte palestinienne était parmi mes plus anciens souvenirs. 'Le Coran est éternel, incréé, consubstantiel à Dieu'. Sauf ce mot, 'Dieu', leur révolte était éternelle, incréée, consubstantielle à moi-même. Était-ce assez révéler l'importance que je donne aux souvenirs?

> [Every negative detail in the newspaper, from the slightest to the boldest, had a positive counterpart in reality. I might as well admit that by staying with them I was staying — I don't know how, how else, to put it — in my own memory. By that rather childish expression I don't mean I lived and remembered previous lives. I'm saying as clearly as I can that the Palestinian revolt was among my

oldest memories. 'The Koran is eternal, uncreated, consubstantial with God.' Apart from the word 'God,' their revolt was eternal, uncreated, consubstantial with me. Is that enough to show how important I think memories are?] (*CA*, 288; *PL*, 243-44)

This precisely-worded, puzzling quotation raises several key issues. Primary among them is the question of origins: since the relatively recent, external event of the Palestinian revolt is paradoxically one of Genet's oldest memories, he recognises it as equivalent to his own beginnings, the origins of the man he has become.[14] In addition, his comparison of his attachment to the Palestinians to the link between the Qu'ran and God suggests that his adhesion to their cause has a religious structure. It is a uniquely Islamic belief that the word of God is 'uncreated' since, as an attribute of God, there cannot have been a time when it did not exist. The quotation thus signals that, at least in this respect (and unlike in Judeo-Christianity?), Islam has a non-logocentric structure: the Qu'ran is not the subsequent incarnation of a pre-existent, abstract, transcendental entity. The word 'consubstantiel' further troubles the idea of a pre-existent, unitary origin, in that the term is used to denote the common substance of the three hypostases of the Christian Trinity: God the Father, God the Son and God the Holy Spirit. In the Palestinian revolution, Genet encounters an otherness that he remembers as an essential part of himself; an origin simultaneously integral to his sense of himself *and* irreducibly different. This consubstantiality is the common element that his relation to the Palestinians shares with the religious relation of the Qu'ran to God. Except, as he specifies, that in his case there is no God: 'Sauf ce mot, "Dieu"'. He relates to the Palestinian revolution as though to God, but without God. But to what extent is a religious structure without a God still a religious structure?

Religion shapes Genet's relationship to the Palestinians in a further way. Just as he found in the foreignness of the Palestinians a memory of himself, he is perplexed to find that the image that best figures the revolution is a foreign, Christian image. The memory that affected him most was the night he spent in the house of the young fighter, Hamza, and his mother. The span of the 'souvenirs' covered by the book, 1970-84, is the length of the time Genet knew them; Part I culminates in the description of the night he spent in their house, which he recalls as the highpoint of his 1970 sojourn in Jordan; the climax of Part II is the contact he succeeds in making again with them fourteen years later, once he had launched into writing the book. Genet was deeply touched by the hospitable welcome afforded him by Hamza's mother who, when told he was not a believer, immediately offered him food notwithstanding the fact that it was Ramadan, and before dawn, as he slept in Hamza's bed while the young man was away at combat, brought him the coffee she usually prepared for her son. For one night, Genet found himself in the position of a son being cared for by a mother:

> Puisqu'il était cette nuit au combat, dans sa chambre et sur son lit je tenais la place et peut-être le rôle du fils. Pour une nuit et le temps d'un acte simple cependant nombreux, un vieillard plus âgé qu'elle devenait le fils de la mère car 'j'étais avant qu'elle ne fût'. Plus jeune que moi, durant cette action familière — familiale? — elle fut, demeurant celle de Hamza, ma mère.

[Because he was fighting that night, I'd taken the son's place and perhaps played his part in his room and his bed. For one night and for the duration of one simple but oft-repeated act, a man older than she was herself became the mother's son. For 'before she was made, I was.' Though younger than me, during that familiar act she was my mother as well as Hamza's.] (*CA*, 230-31; *PL*, 193)

The experience is by no means 'simple' in Genet's reconstruction of it: not only as a son is he older than his mother, but in taking Hamza's place he is less replacing the younger man than gaining him as well as his mother, acquiring a mother-son dyad. The importance of the impact that this encounter with Hamza and his mother had on Genet is difficult to exaggerate. To his own puzzlement, he finds in the couple that they form the most powerful encapsulation of his experience with the Palestinians. Writing the text does not resolve the puzzle; in its closing paragraphs, he underlines that he still does not understand why such a personal and transcultural image as the couple of a mother and a son best conveys what the Palestinian revolution means for him:

> Le couple mère-fils est aussi en France et n'importe où. Ai-je éclairé ce couple d'une lumière qui m'était propre, faisant d'eux non des étrangers que j'observais mais un couple issu de moi et que mon habileté à la rêverie aura plaqué sur deux Palestiniens, le fils et sa mère, un peu à la dérive dans une bataille en Jordanie?
>
> Tout ce que j'ai dit, écrit, se passa, mais pourquoi ce couple est-il tout ce qui me reste de *profond*, de la révolution palestinienne?
>
> [The pair made up by mother and son is to be found in France and everywhere else. Was it a light of my own that I threw on them, so that instead of being strangers whom I was observing they became a couple of my own creation? An image of my own that my penchant for day-dreaming had projected on to two Palestinians, mother and son, adrift in the midst of a battle in Jordan?
>
> All I've said and written happened. But why is it that this couple is the only really profound memory I have of the Palestinian revolution?] (*CA*, 503-04; *PL*, 430)

He is in equal measure certain that the couple channels a truth about the revolution, and uncertain as to whether the key to its significance lies within himself or outside. Having numbered the Palestinian revolution among his own originary memories, here he wonders if he is the origin of the external story he wants to tell.

Throughout the book, he explores this conundrum via reference to the pietà, as many critics have noted. Notably, in a discussion of the text's radical literariness Michel Deguy considers the best example of the poetic inventiveness that distinguishes Genet's last work to be his use of the image: 'le meilleur [exemple] eût été peut-être celui de la *pietà*, grande image chrétienne qui traverse le livre, du corps du fils barrant la Mère et déployant l'étendue, et qui l'unifie' [the best example would perhaps be that of the *pietà*, the great Christian image running through the book of the son's body over the Mother, marking out space, and unifying it].[15] It is scarcely a surprise that the image and the question of who tends to a (son's) dead body should resonate with Genet, given his lack of ties of filiation and awareness of his own impending death. Yet in the book's most developed reflection on the pietà and its history, the writer in fact distinguishes the image of mother and son that imprinted itself so powerfully on his memory from historical representations of the pietà:

> Dans ce monde, langue, population, profils, animaux, plantes, territoires qui respiraient un air islamique, le groupe qui s'imposait à moi était celui de *mater dolorosa*. La mère et le fils; non tels que les artistes chrétiens les ont représentés — peints ou sculptés dans le marbre ou le bois, le fils mort, allongé sur les genoux de la mère plus jeune que le cadavre décrucifié — mais toujours l'un ou l'une veillant sur l'autre.

> [Amid that world, that language, that people, those faces, those animals, plants and lands all exuding the spirit of Islam, what preoccupied me was a group embodying the image of the *mater dolorosa*. The mother and son, but not as Christian artists have depicted them, painted or sculpted in marble or wood, with the dead son lying across the knees of a mother younger than the son de-crucified, but one of them always protecting the other.] (*CA*, 241-42; *PL*, 203)

In contrast with the traditional focus on the son's death, the image of mother and son that haunts Genet is one of reciprocal care and protection: 'Chacun étant la cuirasse de l'autre, trop faible, trop humain' [Each was the armour of the other, who otherwise would have been too weak, too human] (*CA*, 242; *PL*, 203). It is the bond between mother and son, his perception of an uninterrupted exchange between the two, that Genet finds profoundly affecting. Moreover, the pietà is not the only mother-son image. Genet refers to other images of the couple of the Virgin and her son that again underline the reciprocity of the mother-son relationship, and undermine the representation of the mother as clearcut origin of the son. He has recourse to the Black Madonna of Montserrat to illustrate how Hamza and his mother each defer to the other:

> Veuve très forte, la mère armée exactement comme son fils, elle-même chef de famille, déléguait mais en souriant, à chaque micro-seconde, ses pouvoirs de chef à Hamza qui, en agissant selon Fatah, mais secrètement conduit par elle, laissait sa mère régner. Repensons, à elle, revoyons la Vierge Noire de Montserrat montrant, exhibant son fils plus fort qu'elle-même, la précédant afin qu'elle fût, mais l'enfant afin qu'il demeurât.

> [She was a widow, but very strong; a mother armed exactly like her son; and in fact the head of the family. But every microsecond she smilingly delegated her powers to Hamza. And he, while taking orders from Fatah, left her in command and was secretly guided by her. Remember the Black Virgin of Montserrat, showing her son as greater than herself, as taking precedence of her so that she might exist, and of the child so that he might live for ever.] (*CA*, 228; *PL*, 191)[16]

In his account, the element these different mother-son couples have in common is the fluidity that makes it impossible to determine who comes first, either in authority or in age, just as in the previous quotation he found himself the son of a mother younger than himself. As man and as baby, the son is cared for by a mother whom he protects and precedes. Which is the origin of the other? Moreover, this image of an uncertain origin itself has an uncertain origin. Just as we saw him specify that the mother-son couple is not unique to France, his own country of origin, Genet suggests that Christianity has succeeded in imposing the pietà as the origin of an image that in fact existed previously and in many different parts of the world. Its apparent cultural specificity masks an appropriation:

Mais qui fut premier: le groupe souvent nommé *Pietà*, de la Vierge et de son divin Fils, ou plus haut dans le temps et ailleurs qu'en Europe, Judée et Palestine? Aux Indes, par exemple, mais alors peut-être en tout homme, et faut-il tant se préserver de l'inceste s'il eut lieu, à l'insu du Père, dans la confusion des rêveries de la mère et du fils. Cela aurait peu d'importance mais le mystère est grand ici: le sceau de la Révolution palestinienne ne me fut jamais un héros palestinien, une victoire (celle de Karameh par exemple) mais l'apparition presque incongrue de ce couple: Hamza et sa mère, et c'est ce couple que je voulus car, en quelque sorte, je l'aurai découpé à ma mesure dans un continuum temps-espace-appartenance nationale, familiale, parentale, et si bien découpé de tout le monde auquel il se rattache naturellement que j'en isolai les deux composantes que je pouvais agréger — la mère et l'un des fils — écartant comme par mégarde les deux autres fils, la fille, le gendre, probablement une famille, une tribu, et même un peuple car je ne suis plus sûr d'être attentif aujourd'hui aux nuits de la Révolution, comme je l'étais en 1970. Mais n'étais-je pas déjà à la recherche du sceau de la Révolution, le sceau comme il est dit dans le Coran de Mohammed, le sceau des Prophètes?

Ce n'était pas tout. Ce groupe, tant de fois répété, profondément chrétien, symbole de la douleur inconsolable d'une mère dont le fils était Dieu, comment pouvait-il m'apparaître, et si vite, avec la vitesse d'un coup de foudre, le symbole de la résistance palestinienne, ce qui serait assez explicable, mais au contraire *'que cette révolte eut lieu afin que me hantât ce couple'*?

[Which came first, the group often known as a *Pietà*, depicting the Virgin Mary and her divine Son, or some other image farther back in time and in some place other than Europe, Judea or Palestine? In India, perhaps. Or perhaps rather in every man. And should so many precautions be taken against incest, if it was committed, unknown to the Father, in the intermingled dreams of mother and son? Perhaps it's not very important, but it is very strange, that for me the seal, the emblem of the Palestinian Revolution was never a Palestinian hero or a victory like Karameh, but that almost incongruous apparition: Hamza and his mother. That was the couple I needed, for in a way I'd cut it out to suit myself, cut it out from a continuum that included time, space, and all connections with country, family and kin. I'd made a good job of detaching it from the universe to which it naturally belonged, selecting just the two elements I could assimilate — the mother and one of the sons — and imperiously discarding the two other sons, the daughter, the son-in-law, and probably also a family, a tribe, perhaps a whole people. For, as to the latter, I'm not sure I feel as strongly now about the nights of the Revolution as I did in 1970. But perhaps even then I was looking for the Revolution's emblem and seal, as in the seal of the Prophets in the Koran.

That wasn't all. That this oft-repeated, profoundly Christian couple, symbolizing the inconsolable grief of a mother whose son was God, could appear to me like a bolt from the blue as a symbol of the Palestinian resistance, would be understandable enough, but why on the contrary did it also strike me *'that the revolt took place in order that this couple should haunt me?'*] (*CA*, 242–43; *PL*, 203–04)

The enigma for Genet is not simply whether the pietà is the most successful expression of a universal fantasy (or at least a fantasy shared by 'every man'). The mystery that fascinates him is why an experience should best be conveyed via an 'incongruous' or evidently inappropriate image: why a 'profoundly Christian' symbol should represent for him the 'seal' of the Palestinian revolution. He is clearly dissatisfied with the most obvious, orientalising, explanation: that he is drawn to an image that seems out of place in relation to the predominantly Muslim Palestinians because it relates to his own (Christian) origins.[17] His repeated use of the word *sceau*, a term that itself seems slightly incongruous when first used (as hallmark or emblem in 'sceau de la Révolution palestinienne'), deserves attention in this respect. The reference to its use in the Qur'an at the end of the paragraph explicitly inscribes the question of religious difference. But the explicit analogy Genet makes between his use of the term and how it is used in the Qur'an merits attention. Surah 33, v. 40 says that 'Mohammed is not the father of any man among you, but he is the messenger of Allah and the Seal of the Prophets'. This is generally taken to mean the last of the prophets: there could be no need for prophets after Mohammed because his message brought the earlier teaching of the Jewish and Christian religions to fulfilment or culmination. As supreme prophet, he set the seal on prophecy, crystallised it in its final form. Genet's comparison thus makes of an image of origins a source of finality. It raises the question not only why he should find in a Christian image the most truthful representation of the Palestinians, but also how his image affects, concludes, the revolution it captures.

The uncertainty of the origin in effect goes in tandem with an uncertain end. ' "*Cette révolte eut lieu afin que me hantât ce couple*" ': the uncertainty of cause and effect is such that Genet goes so far as to wonder if the very purpose of the revolution was its effect on him. This ties in with a number of wider uncertainties about his engagement with the Palestinians. From its opening paragraph, *Un Captif amoureux* not only asks if the gaps between the words on the white page contain more reality than the 'minuscules signes noirs' [tiny black characters] that set out to account for 'la réalité du temps passé auprès — et non avec eux — les Palestiniens' [the reality of time spent among — not with — the Palestinians], but also wonders if the words were written 'afin que disparaisse cette réalité' [in order for that reality to disappear] (*CA*, 11; *PL*, 5). Genet is deeply aware that the memorialist may serve the interest of his own glory more than that of those he seeks to commemorate:

Puisque tout peuple, toute famille a son barde, sans trop l'avouer le mémorialiste voudrait être son propre barde et c'est en lui-même que se joue ce drame infinitésimal mais jamais achevé: Homère aurait-il écrit ou récité *L'Iliade* sans Achille en colère, ou de la colère d'Achille que saurions-nous sans Homère?

[Since each people, each family has its own bard, the writer of memoirs, although he doesn't advertise the fact, wants to be *his* own bard: it's within himself that his tiny, never-finished drama takes place. Would Homer have written or recited the *Iliad* without Achilles' wrath? But what would we know about Achilles' wrath without Homer?] (*CA*, 59; *PL*, 46-47)

Genet's focus is once more the aporetic nature of the origin: we can never know if Achilles created Homer or Homer created Achilles. His choice of illustrative example is also overdetermined in a way relevant to this discussion. In his interview with Fichte, Genet recognises a religious dimension to Homer's writing in the *Iliad* as distinct from the *Odyssey* (*ED*, 145; *DE*, 122), and recognised that it could be, and was, exploited for ritual purposes, which he defines as the 'reconnaissance d'une transcendance' [recognition of a transcendence]. But he stresses that, as a literary mode of expression, it is not itself a rite or ritual: 'Pendant les Panathénées, on récitait officiellement *l'Iliade*. Mais *l'Iliade* en elle-même n'est ni rituelle ni sacramentelle. C'est un poème' [During the Panathenæa, the *Iliad* was recited officially. But the *Iliad* itself is neither a ritual nor a sacrament. It's a poem] (*ED*, 161; *DE*, 137). For Genet, a poem can be religious without being transcendental. The poem, in other words, does not serve a God. To the extent that it generates, or bears witness to, a spiritual relation without a guarantor, it functions rather as an affirmation of chance. In another passage, Genet invokes, not Mallarmé, but Claudel — 'the most religious of French poets', and thus of all poets the one whose work might most reasonably be expected to recognise a transcendent being — in support of the distinction he makes between religion, or belief in a 'Dieu-Un', and the celebration of chance:

> Je ne croyais pas en Dieu. L'idée de hasard, combinaison aléatoire de faits, combine même d'événements, d'astres, d'êtres, devant à eux-mêmes ce qu'ils sont, et cette *idée* me paraissait plus élégante et rigolote que celle d'un Dieu-Un. Le poids de la foi écrase quand le hasard allège et rit. Il rend joyeux et curieux, donc souriant. S'il n'a pas accepté de le savoir clairement, le plus croyant des poètes français, Claudel l'a mieux dit : '*les jubilations du hasard*'. Un tel blasphème dans une telle carrure! Sans le hasard, le Japon tout sourires et rires serait-il où il est, comme il l'est, sans les pets incalculables des volcans?
>
> [I didn't believe in God. The idea of chance, a random combination of facts — a trick, even, of events, stars and beings owing their existence to themselves — such an idea seemed to me more pleasing and amusing than the idea of One God. The weight of religion crushes; chance brings lightness and laughter. It makes you cheerful and curious; it makes you smile. Claudel, the most religious of French poets, though he wouldn't acknowledge he knew it, expressed it the best when he wrote of 'the jubilations of chance.' Such blasphemy from such a block! And would Japan be what it is and where it is if it weren't for chance and the incalculable farts of the volcanoes?] (*CA*, 426; *PL*, 363)

The abrupt shift at the end of this quotation to Japan, determined in this instance by its chance geography but featuring throughout the book more broadly as the predominant example of a non-Western culture, is telling: the difference between 'faith' and 'chance' maps onto the difference not between religion and atheism but between monotheism, with its exclusive attitude towards the origin, its insistence that its God alone exists, and its others.

Those others are themselves plural in *Un Captif amoureux*, including both atheism and polytheism. Genet's non-belief ('I didn't believe in God') does not involve a hostility towards religion in general; what matters for him is one's attitude towards one's origins, not whether one believes them to be human or divine. In his interview with Antoine Bourseiller, he singles out the Ancient Greeks for an irreverence towards their gods precisely inconceivable in the three main monotheistic religions:

> C'était, et c'est, le seul pays au monde où le peuple a pu vénérer, honorer ses dieux et se foutre d'eux. Ce que le peuple grec a fait à l'égard de l'Olympe, jamais les Juifs n'auraient osé et n'oseraient le faire encore pour Yahvé, aucun Chrétien n'oserait le faire pour le Crucifié, aucun Musulman pour Allah. Les grecs ont pu se moquer à la fois d'eux-mêmes et se moquer de leurs dieux. Je trouve ça épatant.

> [It was, it is, the only country in the world where the people were able to venerate, to honor their gods, and also not to give a damn about them. What the Greek people did in relation to Olympus, the Jews would never have dared and would still never dare to do for Yahweh, no Christian would dare to do for the Crucified, no Muslim for Allah. The Greeks were able at the same time to mock themselves and to mock their gods. That to me is astounding.] (*ED*, 218; *DE*, 187)

In *Un Captif amoureux*, he explicitly privileges paganism over atheism:

> Le mot paganisme sonne comme un défi lancé à toute société. Du moralisme chrétien le mot athée est trop proche, chrétien mais d'un Christ réduit à l'unique épine de sa couronne royale et divine; le paganisme fait le païen s'enfoncer dans les siècles des siècles, auxquels on donne le sobriquet de 'nuit des temps', celle où Dieu n'existait pas encore. Une espèce d'ivresse et de générosité permet au païen d'aborder toute chose aussi respectueusement que toute autre et que soi-même sans s'avilir. Aborder. Peut-être contempler.

> [The word paganism sounds a challenge to any society. The word atheist is too close to Christian moralism, or at least the kind that reduces Christ solely to the thorn in His kingly and godly crown. But paganism puts the unbeliever back amid the so-called 'mists of time,' when God didn't yet exist. A sort of intoxication and magnanimity allows a pagan to approach everything, himself included, with equal respect and without undue humility. To approach, and perhaps to contemplate.] (*CA*, 53; *PL*, 41)

Ironically (given that paganism is generally considered to be a Christian projection), for Genet paganism is more radically different from Christianity than atheism, seemingly because it is non-exclusive. To the extent that atheism opposes reason to faith, it mirrors the Christianity it denies in operating a reduction to a single element. In contrast, paganism — a word itself with two irreducible meanings: not believing in (the true) God, believing in (many) false Gods — allows both 'ivresse' and 'générosité'. Genet glosses it as a tolerant mode of existence, one able not only to admit the existence of others' gods, but to entertain a non-hierarchical relation to alterity. The difference in tolerance between paganism and Christianity is foregrounded at the beginning of the book, when a priest categorically rejects Genet's account of having witnessed two different religious processions on Good

Friday, a sombre Catholic one led by the priest and another, more joyful, one preceded by a banner with an image of the Virgin: 'Non, ce que vous appelez deuxième cortège et Vierge n'existaient pas' [No. What you refer to as the second procession and the Virgin Mary — they were no such thing] (*CA*, 17; *PL*, 10). Genet later discovers from a Benedictine friar that there had indeed been two processions, and that what he had taken for an image of the Virgin had in fact been an image of the Pole Star. Just as Genet will later signal that the pietà had equivalents in other cultures, the image of the Virgin Mary as Star of the Sea draws on pagan antecedents: 'l'image de la dame n'était ni virginale ni chrétienne, mais apportée par les anté-islamiques peuple de la mer. Son origine étant païenne, les marins lui rendaient un culte depuis des millénaires' [the image of the lady was neither virginal nor Christian but belonged to the pre-Islamic 'Peoples of the Sea'. Her origins were pagan, and she'd been worshipped by sailors for thousands of years] (*CA*, 18; *PL*, 11). The first priest's angry refusal even to acknowledge the existence of the other procession emphasises not just Christianity's dismissive attitude towards other religions but its monopolisation of religious space. A monopolisation, however, that imposed its own cost; Genet muses that the more joyous 'pagan' procession was a sign of 'le triomphe aujourd'hui vendredi du paganisme sur la religion du Fils' [the triumph of paganism over the religion of the Son] (*CA*, 18; *PL*, 11).

Paganism therefore mixes 'intoxication and magnanimity': unlike Christianity, it is generous; unlike atheism, it makes place for affect. As such, it represents the kind of religion most compatible with revolution. Because revolution involves achieving emancipation at a holistic level, as we saw in Chapter 3, and not merely 'l'interprétation correcte et la pratique d'une idéologie qui se donne presque comme transcendance' [the approved interpretation and application of some transcendental ideology], the movements that Genet finds revolutionary are not simply atheistic:

> Si le marxisme-léninisme est par autorité athée, des mouvements révolutionnaires comme les Panthères et les Palestiniens ne semblent pas l'être: leur but secret plus ou moins, c'est peut-être de lentement user Dieu, le rendre plat, exsangue, oublié, transparent jusqu'à l'effacement total.

> [While Marxism-Leninism is officially atheist, revolutionary movements like those of the Panthers and the Palestinians seem not to be; their more or less secret goal may be to wear God down, slowly flatten Him out until He's so drained of blood and transparent as not to be at all.] (*CA*, 62; *PL*, 49)[18]

For Genet, these movements have a religious dimension, albeit not a conventional, deferential one; God is recognised, but as a figure of privilege to be exploited, not an object of worship to be respected. In a still more astonishing metaphor, Genet paints the Palestinians' recourse to both Islam and Marxism as a marriage:

> Il y a tant de façons d'être mariés. Mais ce qui me paraissait étrange c'était [...] les jeux de ce curieux manège: l'islam avec le marxisme. En théorie tout y était contradictoire: Coran et *Capital* se haïssaient, cependant une harmonie, sensible à tous, semblait résulter de ces deux divagations. Qui donnait par générosité semblait l'avoir fait par justice, après lecture intelligente du livre allemand. Nous naviguions en pleine folie, avec vitesse et lenteur, un Dieu cognait du front le front bombé de Marx qui le niait.

[There are so many ways of being married. But what struck me as really strange [...] were the doings of that curious trip: Islam and Marxism. In theory everything about it was incompatible: the Koran and *Das Kapital* were foes, yet harmony seemed to result from their contradictions. Anyone giving out of generosity seemed to have done so out of a love of justice resulting from an intelligent reading of the German tome. We sailed along madly, sometimes slowly, sometimes fast, with God always bumping into the domed forehead of Marx who denied him.] (*CA*, 125; *PL*, 105)

The link between Islam and Marxism is disconcerting not just as an example of marriage but for the turbulent conception of marriage that Genet elaborates. Their couple forms not a *ménage* [household, domestic arrangement] but, unexpectedly, its paronym *manège*: a merry-go-round or fairground ride. Their relationship is one of hatred rather than love; far from stable, both are 'divagations': ravings or wanderings. What clearly enthuses Genet is the Palestinians' eclectic mingling of two ideologies that are sworn enemies of each other: when neither is respected as authority, religion and revolution can work in concert, generate a 'harmony' from their very divergence.

In addition, Genet finds in the Palestinians' practice of Islam a degree of proximity to polytheistic religions that sets it apart from Judaism and Christianity. The Fedayeens' ablutions remind him of ritualistic bathing in the Ganges, creating the impression that 'la forêt mahométane était peuplée de bouddhas debout', or even of pagan ceremonies:

> Où que coulât ou croupît un peu d'eau c'était une source, et debout devant elle, la nuit tombant, moins qu'au Maroc l'islam ici à chaque foulée butait contre le paganisme. Ici même où les croyances chrétiennes sont blasphèmes au Dieu, solitaire, comme le vice du même nom, le paganisme apporte un peu de nuit à midi, de soleil dans l'obscur, un peu de mousse, une humidité venue par capillarité du Jourdain, causant ce rhume des foins à la fée qui veille et tousse, sa baguette à la main. Humidité qui laisse la trace d'un pied d'homme.

> [Wherever there was a drop of flowing or standing water there was a spring: here (though less than in Morocco) Islam stumbled over paganism at every step. Here, where Christian beliefs are held to blaspheme a god as solitary as the vice to which the same adjective is applied, paganism provides a touch of darkness at noon, of sunlight in shadow, a little moss, a touch of dampness drawn up from the Jordan, causing the watching, coughing fairy with the magic wand to catch hayfever. A dampness that leaves behind it the print of a human foot.] (*CA*, 142; *PL*, 119)

The Fedayeen's receptiveness to the alternative resource of pagan beliefs finds an echo in their relation to chance, posited above as the alternative to a single, commanding origin. One of the book's most memorable scenes is the game of cards Genet witnesses the Fedayeen playing but without cards, since Islam bans games of chance:

> Le jeu de cartes, qui n'avait existé que par les gestes scandaleusement réalistes des feddayin — ils avaient joué à jouer, sans cartes, sans les as ni les valets, sans les Bâtons ni les Épées sans dame ni roi, le jeu de cartes me rappelait que toutes

les activités des Palestiniens ressemblaient à la fête d'Obon où seul manquait, exigeant cette solennité — fût-elle dans le sourire — celui qui ne doit pas apparaître.

[The game of cards, which only existed because of the shockingly realistic gestures of the fedayeen — they'd played at playing, without any cards, without aces or knaves, clubs or spades, kings or queens — reminded me that all the Palestinians' activities were like the Obon feast, where the only one absent, yet imposing solemnity — even if in smiles — on the ceremony in his honor, was the one who must not appear.] (CA, 40; PL, 30)

Again, a Japanese reference concretises the relation to chance earlier opposed to worship of the 'Dieu-Un'. Obon is the Japanese feast — Genet also calls it a 'jeu', or game — during which people return to their ancestral haunts to honour their forebears, and by their gestures include the dead among the living. 'Partout était Obon le mort japonais inexistant, et le jeu de cartes sans cartes' [Everywhere Obon, the non-existent dead Japanese, and the card-game without cards] (CA, 133; PL, 111): the simultaneous respect for the invisible and lack of deference towards the origin that Genet sees as integral both to Obon and to the Palestinians' card-game delights him. He sees in the Fedayeen's invention of a game that simultaneously obeys and defies the Islamic prohibition a challenge to belief in an all-powerful God. In a passage that compares the gesture of rolling dice to that of Zeus abducting Ganymede, he muses on the anxiety to which the very existence of the ban testifies:

Les cartes avaient probablement la fonction du jeu de dés. On sait l'habileté des joueurs chacun cachant aux autres le sien, Zeus décidant de la partie. 'Que Dieu ne joue pas aux dés avec le monde', écrite en français la phrase ne signifie pas grand-chose puisque si Dieu Est, par définition Il Est Tout, le jeu de dés comme le reste du monde. Le hasard porte alors le nom de Providence, passez muscade. Quand le Coran déclare péchés les jeux de hasard, l'interdit semble un palliatif, un détournement de phrase afin d'écarter des joueurs la question qui rôde aux abords: Dieu décide-t-il du résultat de la partie, alors il m'a choisi, et pourquoi moi? Que l'angoisse me saisisse on me comprendra. Ou le hasard l'a-t-il fait à sa place, le hasard fut plus prompt que Dieu? Dieu fut-il par hasard?

[It was probably the same with the cards as with dice. The players try to be clever and conceal their hands from each other, but Zeus decides on the outcome. 'God does not play at dice with the world:' in French, the saying doesn't mean much since if God is, He is by definition Everything, the game of dice along with all the rest. So hey presto, chance's name is Providence. When the Koran declares games of chance sinful, the prohibition sounds like a makeshift attempt, a perversion of words, to stop the gamblers asking the lurking question: If God decides the result of the game, then if I win it's because he's chosen me, but why me? It's only natural I should be anguished. Or if it was chance and not God that made me win, is chance swifter than God? Did God come to exist by chance?] (CA, 337; PL, 287)

Just as Genet sees Islam in some respects close to paganism, the analogy between Einstein's famous line and the Qur'an proposes that atheism is not necessarily immune to the structure of the religion it denies. While Einstein did not believe in God, his assertion that God does not play dice with the universe was a rejection of the central idea of quantum mechanics that randomness was at the heart of natural laws; perturbed by the idea, he sought ways to rationalise it away until he died.[19] Genet similarly interprets the Qur'an's ban on games of chance not as an expression of confidence in the distinction between good and evil but as a symptomatic ploy to keep God at a safe distance from the question of chance. Both, in other words, are profoundly resistant to the idea of chance that enchants Genet.

Yet in its very prohibition, Islam at least registers chance as a force. In contrast, nothing mitigates for Genet the repressiveness of Judeo-Christianity. In a key passage of which several drafts exist, it becomes clear that the monotheism whose crushing effect he distinguished from the jubilant liberation of a celebration of randomness as the only source of order is more properly, more narrowly, Western monotheism.[20] The passage describes an experience that happened, not without significance, on a flight to Japan; Genet recalls having the sensation that he was being stripped clean of Judeo-Christian morality when the air hostess wished the passengers 'Sayonara':

> A partir de ce mot, je fus attentif à la manière dont s'enlevait par lambeaux de mon corps au risque de me laisser nu et blanc la noire et certainement épaisse morale judéo-chrétienne. Ma passivité m'étonnait. L'opération se faisait sur moi [...]. Un peu plus tard il me sembla que 'Sayonara' [...] était sur mon corps malheureux — malheureux car il avait soutenu un siège dégradant contre cette morale judéo-chrétienne — la première touche de ouate qui allait me démaquiller tout à fait, selon que je l'ai déjà dit, me laisser blanc et nu. Cette délivrance que j'avais supposée longue, lente, harassante, en profondeur ce qui veut dire menée comme avec un scalpel, commençait par une sorte de jeu — un mot [...] fut le léger début d'un nettoyage qui ne porterait que sur la surface de moi-même, pourtant me délivrerait de cette morale plus gluante que corrosive. Plutôt que par une intervention chirurgicale, toujours un peu solennelle, j'aurais dû penser qu'elle se déferait grâce à un savon décapant. Rien n'était intérieur. Je me levai pourtant afin d'aller chier à l'arrière de l'avion, espérant me libérer d'un ver solitaire long de trois mille ans.

> [The word made me feel my body being stripped bit by bit of a thick black layer of Judeo-Christian morality, until it was left naked and white. I was amazed at my own passivity. The operation was being done to me [...]. A little while later it seemed to me that 'Sayonara' [...] was the first touch of cottonwool that was going to cleanse my wretched body — wretched because of the long degrading siege it had had to withstand from Judeo-Christian ethics — leaving me white and naked. This deliverance, which I'd expected to be lengthy, irksome and deep, as if carried out with a scalpel, began with a sort of game — a word [...] was the start for me of a clean-up that, while only superficial, would free me from a moral system that clung to the skin rather than burned into the flesh. I ought to have realized before that it would be got rid of not by a solemn surgical operation but by the application of good strong soap. My inside wasn't affected. Nevertheless I got up to go and have a crap in the rear of the plane, hoping to get rid of a tapeworm three thousand years long.] (CA, 65–66; PL, 52–53)[21]

Here Genet suggests that it was relatively easy to divest himself of the Judeo-Christian morality he found so oppressive. The specification that it involved merely cleaning makeup away rather than surgery equates the change with transvestism rather than transsexualism, positing a link between his change of religious identity and the motif of gender-transitioning developed throughout the text. The passage clearly associates 'Judeo-Christian' morality not with the Jews but with the West in general: Genet specifies that the plane was departing from a 'longitude occidentale' [western longitude] towards 'la partie orientale du globe' [the eastern part of the globe]. His hostility is directed as much towards the 'Christian' as the 'Judeo' element; as he states subsequently, 'L'église catholique étant aussi le pouvoir autant que la morale biblique, je faisais des représentants de ces deux superpuissances mes ennemis' [As the Catholic Church was the incarnation of authority and Biblical morality, I saw any representative of those superpowers as my enemy] (*CA*, 235; *PL*, 197). Indeed, Catholicism is his primary enemy. He defines his atheism as a rejection of his religion of origin; when Hamza asks him about his religious identity, Genet answers: 'Aucune religion. Mais si tu y tiens, catholique' [No religion. But if you insist, Catholic] (*CA*, 216; *PL*, 181). And it is the Catholic church he blames for the deathly, zombie-like state to which he felt reduced prior to the new lease of life that began for him in 1970: 'Les souvenirs que je rapporte sont peut-être les ornements dont on pare encore mon cadavre, ce que j'écris ne pouvant servir personne mais ce cadavre de moi-même certainement tué par l'église catholique, très doucement le paganisme lui rendra hommage' [Perhaps the memories I record are mere draperies with which my corpse is still being decked. Perhaps what I write is no use to anyone. But the cadaver of myself, most certainly killed by the catholic Church, will receive quiet homage from paganism] (*CA*, 260; *PL*, 219). Catholicism and paganism are the religious forces most opposed to each other.

In the book's final pages, Genet returns to the idea that he has managed to separate himself entirely from the West and, especially, that a previous existence is easy to efface:

> Quand un dessin présente trop de défauts, le peintre l'efface et les deux ou trois coups de gomme laissent parfaitement blanc le papier Canson; ainsi la France et l'Europe gommées, ce blanc devant moi, qui avait contenu autrefois la France et l'Europe, devint un espace de liberté sur lequel la Palestine que j'avais vécue s'inscrirait, mais avec des retouches qui me parurent graves. Comme l'Algérie, comme d'autres pays, oubliant la révolution dans le monde arabe, elle ne songeait qu'au territoire sur lequel un vingt-deuxième État naîtrait, apportant avec lui ce qu'on exige d'un nouveau venu: l'Ordre, la Loi. Cette révolte si longtemps hors la loi, aspirait-elle à devenir loi dont le Ciel serait l'Europe? J'ai essayé de dire ce qu'elle devint; mais rendue pour moi *terra incognita*, l'Europe fut gommée.

> [When a drawing has too many mistakes in it an artist rubs it out. Two or three rubs with the eraser and the paper's blank again. With France and Europe rubbed out I was faced with a blank space of liberty that was to be filled with Palestine as I experienced it, but with revisions that worried me. Like Algeria and other countries that forgot the revolution in the Arab world, my Palestine thought only of the territory out of which a twenty-second state might be born, bringing with it the law and order expected of a newcome. But did this revolt, that had been an outlaw for so long, really want a law that would have Europe for its Heaven? I've tried to say what happened to it, but for me Europe had become *terra incognita*, and I'd had to leave it out.] (*CA*, 502; *PL*, 429)

The Western space from which Genet relishes having distanced himself is primarily that of France and Europe. But France and Europe are not replaced by the Palestinians. By the time of writing, Genet is suspicious that their revolution has, like the Algerian War of Independence, become a struggle like any other to impose a particular order. He fears that they, too, have succumbed to the order they sought to overcome; that their revolt is no longer 'alive':

> La lutte métaphysique, impossible de l'ignorer, se poursuit entre les morales judaïques et les valeurs, — ce dernier mot accepté aussi dans son sens monétaire puisqu'il est vrai quelques Palestiniens sont devenus très riches, — et les valeurs de Fatha ou des autres composantes de l'O.L.P. où les plus sûres sentent le numéraire; entre les valeurs judaïques, dis-je, et les révoltes vivantes.

> [The metaphysical struggle goes on, impossible to ignore it, between Jewish morality and the values — using the word in its monetary sense as well, since a few Palestinians have got rich — the values of Fatah and other elements in the PLO. Between the values of Judaism and those of living revolutions.] (*CA*, 448; *PL*, 381)

The crucial 'metaphysical' distinction for Genet is not the line that divides the Jews from Christian Europe (as in the tradition of antisemitism that culminated in the Nazi genocide); it lies for him in the struggle between the 'judaic values' that continue to determine Catholicism and 'living revolts'.

★　★　★　★　★

Until now, I have focused on Genet's discourse about religion in *Un Captif amoureux*, showing how the hostility that Marty interprets as antisemitic is in fact the sign of a broader enmity towards Judeo-Christianity. For Genet, the Judeo-Christian hierarchical, deferential relation towards God, and enforcement of obedience towards the oppressive Law underpinning that hierarchy, are inseparable from Europe's success in establishing and consolidating its privileged position within the world. But his book devotes considerably more energy to celebrating 'living revolt', epitomised for him in the Palestinian Revolution, than to criticising respect for authority.

The revolt that Genet recognises in the Palestinian movement for liberation, and that attracts him so powerfully to their cause, is distinguished by a markedly different narrative of beginnings from the monotheistic privileging of a single, exclusive origin. The Palestinians are no different from any other people in looking to genealogy to validate the claims underpinning their revolt:

> Ce que je vis d'abord c'était que 'chaque peuple', afin de justifier plus fortement sa révolte, cherchait au plus profond du temps sa singularité; sous chaque révolte se découvraient des profondeurs généalogiques dont la vigueur n'était pas dans ses branches encore virtuelles mais ses racines, si bien que les révoltes surgissant un peu partout sur terre semblaient célébrer une sorte d'immense culte des morts. On déterra des mots, des phrases, des langues entières.

> [What I saw first was that every 'nation,' the better to justify its rebellion in the present, sought proof of its own singularity in the distant past. Every

uprising revealed some deep genealogy whose strength was not in its almost non-existent branches but in its roots, so that the rebellions springing forth everywere seemed to be celebrating some sort of cult of the dead. Words, phrases, whole languages were disinterred.] (*CA*, 48; *PL*, 37)

However, different peoples have recourse to genealogical tracing in very different ways. In the context of this quotation, it is interesting to note the similarity between Genet's hostility to monotheism's insistence on a single, exclusive origin and Deleuze and Guattari's critique of 'arborescence': that is, a structure modelled on the genealogical tree, with a rectilinear, uni-directional path from single root or origin to the branches into which the trunk will divide.[22] In contrast, this quotation's description of the quest for the origin is notable for its non-arborescent structure. Far from a unitary root, revolt draws on a wide range of revolutionary (and non-revolutionary) precursors; the dead to whom the Palestinians pay homage (in the actual examples of words and sentences cited just before) involve figures as diverse as Guevara, Abd el-Kader, Stalin, Churchill and Roosevelt. The overall pattern revealed by the network of revolutionary roots — 'springing forth everywhere' — is that of a horizontal, multiple, non-hierarchical spreading: a structure akin to the rhizomatic model that Deleuze and Guattari opposed to the arborescent. Genet uses the figure of the mole to mark the contrast between a struggle for peoplehood that defines itself in relation to others, and the attempt to excavate a single origin that he associates with the Zionist project:

> La génération la plus jeune était composée d'hommes-taupes. Après deux mille ans à la surface du globe, après des voyages à cheval, à pied, par mer, par galeries souterraines, revenir en un endroit où ici et là surgissent les taupinières, rechercher les résidus d'un temple, les retrouver, quel exemple! L'inélégance, non de la recherche seule, mais de l'identification d'un peuple avec un autre, racines et branches, me paraissait — outre bien sûr l'incertain du résultat — d'une vulgarité parisienne, mondaine. Car c'est bien une paresse, qui veut croire que la noblesse se découvre dans l'ascendance nobiliaire. Les Palestiniens, quand je les connus, échappaient à cette misère. Le danger eût été qu'ils voient en Israël un surmoi.

> [The youngest generation were a lot of moles. What an example, after two thousand years of travelling the earth's surface on horseback, on foot or by sea, to go back and burrow among molehills for the remains of some temple! Not only the search itself but also the wholesale identifying of one people with another, root and branch, struck me as undignified, a pretentious vulgarity worthy of Paris. It's a form of laziness to think nobility is proved by ancestry, and when I knew them the Palestinians didn't go in for it. The danger then was that they might see Israel as a sort of super-ego.] (*CA*, 48; *PL*, 37)

The reference to the 'two thousand years' suggests that the 'moles' include those attracted by the Zionist project. What Genet finds distasteful ('inelegant') is the focus on identifying and reclaiming a single spatial point of origin, and the concomitant privileging of a single line of descent that this entails. The contrast is striking with his enthusiasm for the Palestinians' embrace of the many strata contributing to their identity:

> Longtemps avant d'être feddayin le peuple était palestinien, c'est-à-dire que
> son soubassement était fait de ce qu'il demeure d'une forêt détruite où ne
> mouraient toujours pas les troncs de deux dizaines d'arbres généalogiques dont
> les dernières branches sont encore vertes, les premières ayant mille cinq cents
> ans au moins, peut-être plus, chrétiennes et monophysites sous Byzance, juives
> avant, musulmanes enfin.
>
> [Long before they were fedayeen the people were Palestinians. The nation arose
> out of the remains of a forest — a couple of dozen family trees that wouldn't
> die, and whose last branches were still green. The most ancient family trees
> were at least fifteen hundred years old, perhaps more. They had been Christian
> and Monophysite under Byzantium; Jewish before that; Muslim since.] (*CA*,
> 180; *PL*, 151)

Genet highlights the diversity of connections relating the Palestinians to their
past: not only are there twenty different genealogies that trace the Palestinian
great families back to Mohammed (elsewhere he quotes an instance where a single
family has two family trees, *CA*, 342; *PL*, 291), but that beginning is in fact the
continuation of a long previous Christian and Jewish history.

The metaphor of a forest of trees that would not die is a figure of life clinging
on in spite of destruction that constitutes a motif significant both rhetorically and
politically throughout *Un Captif amoureux*. Trees literally form the backdrop to
Genet's memories of the Palestinians, as the writer himself notes: 'Les arbres, je
me relis, sont évoqués souvent. C'est qu'ils sont loin. Il y a quinze ans, aujourd'hui
probablement sciés' [I see I often mention trees. That's because it was a long time
ago, fifteen years, and they've probably been cut down by now] (*CA*, 134; *PL*, 112).
He claims to have been conscious of their fragility already at the time of his first
visit:

> Tout était en arbres, en bois, avec des feuilles jaunes attachées aux branches
> par un pétiole très fin mais vrai, pourtant la forêt d'Ajloun était si fragile
> qu'elle m'apparut plutôt comme certaines armatures qui vont disparaître quand
> l'immeuble sera bien maçonné. Immatérielle, elle était plutôt une esquisse de
> forêt, une forêt improvisée avec n'importe quelles feuilles, mais parcourue de
> soldats si beaux qu'ils apportaient avec eux la paix.
>
> [Everything was covered with trees, with yellow leaves attached to the branches
> by a fine yet real stalk, but the forest itself looked as frail to me as a scaffolding
> that vanishes when a building's finished. It was insubstantial, more like a sketch
> of a forest, a makeshift forest with any old leaves, but sheltering soldiers so
> beautiful to look at they filled it with peace.] (*CA*, 134; *PL*, 113)

Politically speaking, Genet's emphasis on the fragility of the forest through which
the Fedayeen move is highly charged. The precarity of the trees associated with
the Palestinians stands in stark opposition to one of the most successful, and
most bitterly resented, justifications of Israeli appropriation of the land previously
inhabited by Palestinians: the narrative that, beginning with the Yishuv (Jewish
immigration to Palestine prior to 1948), Jewish settlement in the territory had
'made the desert bloom'. The success of this narrative depended on the idea that
Palestine was largely unpopulated — a 'land without people for a people without

a land', as the famous Zionist slogan has it — with large uncultivated areas that could accommodate substantial numbers of immigrants. While it was not until the research of the Israeli New Historians in the 1980s that the academic credibility of this idea was thoroughly undermined, it was already under intense challenge by the time Genet was writing his book.[23] Genet was keenly aware of Israel's rhetorical victory in shaping the narrative so effectively in its favour: 'Les longues élégies sur Israël; la seule démocratie du Moyen-Orient; le désert arrosé, fertilisé, arboré, où chaque pommier ou bouleau portait un nom' [The long rhapsodies about Israel; the congratulations on being the only democracy in the Middle East; tales of how the desert had been irrigated, fertilized and planted and each apple and birch tree given a name] (CA, 199; PL, 166). As this summary shows, he was also sensitive to the political implications of the policy of massive afforestation embarked on by the Jewish National Fund (JNF) following the establishment of the state. Recent research has highlighted how this policy was heavily over-determined: in addition to its agricultural purpose (the cultivation of trees), it constituted a site of memory, with thousands of trees planted in memory of the victims of the Holocaust.[24] As Nur Masalha argues, it further symbolised the success of the European Zionist project in 'striking roots' in the land of the Jews' ancestors.[25] But it was also a key tool, along with toponymic renaming, deployed in order 'to de-Arabise Palestine and erase traces of the destroyed Palestinian villages'.[26] The JNF forests were planted over the remnants of many deserted villages whose names no longer appear on any official documentation; the trees previously cultivated by the Arab farmers (olive, fig, carob) were cut down and replaced with pine and cypress trees that had the effect of Europeanising the landscape and reiterating the settlers' cultural claim to the land.[27]

In a passage that explicitly references the Palestinian film-maker Michel Khleifi's 1985 documentary *Ma'loul Celebrates Its Destruction*, Genet signals how the growth of the forest obliterates the remains of the earlier Palestinian village:

> Les affiches, les placards publicitaires dans les journaux incitant les touristes à visiter Israël vantent surtout les plantations d'arbres dans le désert. Aussi fortiche que Shakespeare, Eretz Israël fit avancer des forêts. L'une d'elles s'arrêta sur le village de Maaloul près de Nazareth. Les maisons des Palestiniens, d'abord minées, explosèrent comme c'était l'usage de l'époque. Une forêt y continua sa croissance. Avec les ongles, en grattant un peu au pied des arbres, les fondations, les caves, seraient à fleur de sol. Israël, à chaque anniversaire de ce qu'il fête sous le nom de Libération, vient regarder ses arbres croître, où chacun porte le nom de celui qui le planta. Les anciens habitants du village ou leurs descendants palestiniens, tous arabes musulmans, y viennent aussi, pique-niquer. Les premiers, qui furent les derniers, rient et sont ivres. Les derniers qui étaient les premiers racontent qui ils étaient. Comme ils peuvent et en quelques heures, beaucoup moins de temps que n'en ont les morts Obon au Japon, ils font revivre le village décédé. Aux jeunes ils précisent un détail, puis un autre; croyant se souvenir, ils embellissent, donc inventent un village si riant, si gai, si éloigné de leur tristesse que tous en deviennent encore plus tristes, et peu à peu, à mesure que ce nouveau village imaginaire prend vie, leur tristesse s'en va. [...] Ainsi l'État bien réel d'Israël se connaît doublé d'une survie fantomatique.

[Posters and magazine advertisements exhorting tourists to visit Israel are especially proud of the trees that have been planted in the desert. Eretz Israel is as good as Shakespeare at making forests move. One of them stopped at the village of Maaloul, near Nazareth. The houses of the Palestinians were mined and blown up — the usual practice at the time — and the forest swept on. If you scratched the ground under the trees you'd find the cellars and foundations. On every anniversay of what's known as the Liberation, Israel comes and sees how the trees are getting on. Each tree bears the name of the person who planted it. The former inhabitants of the village, or their Palestinian descendants, come here too, to picnic. The first, who were last, laugh and get drunk. The last, who were first, describe what they used to be like. For a few hours — much less time than the Obon dead are allowed in Japan — they do their best to bring the dead village to life again. They tell the young people about one detail after another. Thinking they're remembering, they actually improve on the facts and invent a village so cheerful and happy and far from their present sadness it only makes it worse. But gradually, as the imaginary village comes to life, the sadness disappears, and young and old make awkward attempts to dance their ancient dances. [...] And so the very real state of Israel finds itself shadowed by a ghostly survival.] (*CA*, 409-10; *PL*, 348-49)

The trees that commemorate their Israeli planters are simultaneously what make the existence of the preceding inhabitants of the village invisible. Just as the first can also be last, so the same place that on the one hand is celebrated as evidence of Israel's flourishing on the other signifies the destruction of the Palestinians' community. Yet although the community has been destroyed, the Palestinians recreate it in memory. In their return to their place of origin (again like that of Obon), they bring the dead alive again. The analogy with *Macbeth* that Genet invokes at the beginning of the paragraph finds its own double at the end: as well as making forests move, Israel, 'shadowed by a ghostly survival', is haunted by the ghost of the life it killed, Banquo to its Macbeth.

This image of survival after destruction, a tenuous existence maintained against all odds, is emblematic of Genet's conception of the Palestinians' 'living revolt'. In a refusal of the narrative that Israel had made the desert bloom, the trees that prevail in his memory are associated with the Fedayeen, as noted above. This is clearly evident in one of the most lyrical passages of *Un Captif amoureux*, which is also where he sets out most explicitly what is at stake for him in writing the text:

Personne ni rien, aucune technique du récit ne diront ce que furent les six mois imposés aux feddayin dans les montagnes de Jérash et d'Ajloun, surtout dès les premières semaines, avant que commencent les grands vents, les grands froids. Donner un compte rendu des événements, établir la chronologie, les réussites et les erreurs des feddayin, l'air du temps, la couleur du ciel, de la terre et des arbres, je pourrai les dire mais jamais faire éprouver cette légère ébriété, la démarche au-dessus de la poussière et des feuilles mortes, l'éclat des yeux, la transparence des rapports non seulement entre feddayin mais entre eux et les chefs. [...] Tout, tous, sous les arbres étaient frémissants, rieurs, émerveillés par une vie si nouvelle pour tous, aussi pour moi, et dans ces frémissements quelque chose d'étrangement fixe, aux aguets, réservé, protégé comme quelqu'un qui épie sans rien dire. Tous étaient à tous. Chacun était en lui-même, non saoul, mais seul. Et peut-être non. En somme souriants et hagards. La région jordanienne où ils s'étaient repliés — je peux utiliser les mots enfuis ou repliés selon certaines dates — le bonheur sous les arbres était si grand qu'aux yeux des privilégiés du monde arabe la révolution palestinienne passait pour une simple fronde.

[No one, nothing, no narrative technique can ever tell what they were like — those six months the fedayeen went through in the mountains of Jerash and Ajloun. Especially the first few weeks, before it got really windy and cold. I could give an account of events, indicate times and dates, describe the fedayeen's successes and mistakes, the weather, the colour of the sky and the earth and the trees. I could do all that, but I could never convey the faint intoxication, the feeling of walking on but not touching the dust and leaves, the shining eyes, the complete openness of the relations not only between the fedayeen themselves but also between them and their leaders. [...] There under the trees everything and everyone was quivering, laughing, filled with wonder at a life so new to them, and to me too. Yet in the quivering there was something strangely still alert, reserved, hidden, as in someone silently on the watch. Everyone belonged to everyone else, yet each was alone in himself. Or perhaps not. Anyway, both smiling and strained. The part of Jordan they'd fallen back on — I use the words retreat or fall back according to the date — was wooded. And they were so happy there under the trees that in the eyes of the privileged of the Arab world the Palestinian revolution seemed like a foray into the woods.] (*CA*, 302–03; *PL*, 256)

The importance of this paragraph, asserting that his attempt to bear witness to the Palestinians seeks not to state or describe but rather to 'faire éprouver' [convey the feeling of] what life was like for the Fedayeen, echoes in the fact that it is the only part of *Un Captif amoureux* recycled from 'Quatre heures à Chatila'. It closely reproduces the beginning of the earlier text's opening section, itself a late addition describing the Fedayeen rather than the camps, and introducing a bucolic tone that dramatically affects the impression created on first contact with the text.[28] Genet makes few changes to the recycled version, but significantly those he does make relate disproportionately to trees. The words 'et des feuilles mortes' after 'poussière' are a new addition, as is the entire final description of the happiness under the trees that gave the revolution the appearance of 'une simple fronde'. The play in French on the double meaning of the homonym *fronde* is unmistakable: the revolution is indeed a 'révolte vivante', both revolt and foliage.

Along with trees, the main metaphorical thread Genet uses to associate the Palestinians' revolt with aliveness is that of water, literally as well as figuratively the vital substance, without which no form of life is possible. 'Wherever there was a drop of flowing or standing water there was a spring': the Fedayeen's openness and inclusivity not only brought a pagan tinge to their practice of Islam, as we saw earlier; it made any drop of water into a 'source', a word which in French means both 'origin' and 'spring' or 'stream'. Genet explicitly compares the origins of their revolution to those of the Amazon:

Ce qui fut à l'origine de la résistance je ne peux pas l'expliquer, il faut constater que des centaines d'années ne suffisent pas pour l'écrasement définitif d'un peuple: la source de la révolte est peut-être cachée, aussi obscure, aussi souterraine que celle de l'Amazone. Où sont les sources de la Révolution Palestinienne? Quel géographe va les chercher? mais l'eau qui en sort est vraiment nouvelle, et peut-être féconde?

[I can't explain how the resistance arose. But it's clear a few hundred years aren't enough to crush a people out of existence. The source of the revolt may be hidden as dark and as deep as that of the Amazon. Where is it? What geographer will go in search of it? But the water that flows from it is new, and may be fruitful.] (*CA*, 280; *PL*, 236-37)

As with the molehills, Genet's emphasis is on the plurality of the origin; like a river, the Palestinian Revolution has multiple, invisible sources. But what does it mean for water itself to be 'féconde' (as distinct from being necessary for land to be fertile)? It is clear that the novelty Genet expresses via the link between the Palestinians and water in no way concerns an instrumental use of the latter. This becomes evident in relation to the stream that features in his memories of one of the scenes that most affected him, the improvised concert he witnessed of three young combatants singing, sometimes in unison, sometimes in turn, in a playfully rivalrous attempt to outperform each other. The polyphonic structure not only allowed the difference between the voices to be heard; the pauses as one voice took over from another also 'laissaient filtrer la voix d'un ruisseau' [allowed the voice of a stream to filter through] (*CA*, 56; *PL*, 44) that Genet recalls as just as active a participant in the concert as the young singers who enchanted him. To his dismay, on his return to Jordan in 1984 he discovers the stream now 'canalisé en trois tuyaux, et complètement silencieux. Ce ruisseau, servait à conduire son eau près des plants de salades et de choux-fleurs' [channelled now through three pipes, and completely silent. The stream was being used to irrigate beds of lettuces and cauliflowers] (*CA*, 249; *PL*, 209). The shift from water-as-song to water-as-irrigation encapsulates the failure of the revolution in its most distinctive aspect, its comprehensive revolt against institutionalised ownership of any kind. Similarly, Genet has recourse to a lexicon of water to describe the dramatic alteration that he notes in Hamza's mother on his second encounter with her, fourteen years after the memorable night when she welcomed him unreservedly:

D'où avait pu venir à la mère tant de sécheresse et de méfiance? La sécheresse étant obscurément pensée comme un ruisseau à sec, dans quelle source sèche aurait-elle pris son cours? La métaphore ne valait rien. Aucune image ne pourra rendre compte mieux ni aussi bien que les mots 'sec' et 'sécheresse'. Il y a en eux une absence de tout ce qui évoque le courant, un liquide en mouvement, une eau qui coule, partant d'un point afin d'irriguer une périphérie; au contraire, tout en eux comme en la mère est fixe, immobile, sec enfin. [...] Joyeuse autrefois dans la défense au fusil comme dans sa fierté du fils; aujourd'hui tarie.

[Where could all the mother's coldness, dryness and mistrust have come from? From what dried up stream? But the metaphor didn't help. No image applied so well as the words 'dry' and 'dryness' themselves. In them there's an absence of anything suggesting a flow, a liquid in movement, a water spreading out from a point to irrigate its surrounds; on the contrary, everything in those two words is fixed and motionless, as in the mother, dry. [...] She'd been gay before defending her cause with her gun and proud of her son. Now she had stopped flowing.] (*CA*, 485-86; *PL*, 414)

The writing conspicuously draws attention to its own choice of words: no longer a source of movement, flow, life, the mother is now so dry that the metaphor of the 'ruisseau à sec', or dried-up stream, is inapt to describe her. So dry, in fact, that it seems that any metaphor will fail; what appears to be at stake is less the difference in meaning between some words and others than the difference between an 'image' and words that do not move, that is between metaphor and a denotative use of language, between 'evoking' and 'saying'. Is Genet suggesting that, insofar as metaphor necessarily implies a verbal displacement, insofar as its mode of operation is intrinsically fluid, slippery, it is by definition inappropriate to render the still aridity that saddens him in the mother? Yet the end of the passage quietly reintroduces the metaphor he had earlier rejected: the mother is 'tarie', herself a dried-up stream. In his own practice of writing, in other words, Genet aligns himself not with what the mother has become but with the joyful, living, moving experience that had so delighted him fourteen years earlier.

*Un Captif amoureux* is in effect a paean to the Palestinian revolution as source: it bears witness to Genet's enchantment not only at the Palestinians' embrace of a plurality of origins but at the origin as plurality: at the budding, emergent aspect of their struggle and the vital, joyful maternity that go in tandem together in his recollection. The powerful impression Hamza's mother originally made on the writer was emblematic of his experience of the revolution generally as a heady series of unexpected motherings. For example, he specifies that the commanders' attitude towards the young Fedayeen was more maternal than warlike: 'Des activités vraiment maternelles, que je n'ose pas nommer féminines obligeaient les responsables à considérer les jeunes soldats [...] comme autant de fils ou de chéris et non de subordonnés comme le veut encore l'Occident' [Truly motherly, that I don't dare to call feminine, duties made the leaders look on the young soldiers [...] as sons or dear ones rather than subordinates, as is still the way in the West] (*CA*, 346; *PL*, 295). The Palestinian revolution gave rise to mothers in the most unexpected of places. Hence, in a typical Genetian twist, the *ruisseau* is more *mère* [mother] than *mer* [sea]. Genet's nostalgia for the mother's lost fluidity echoes a wistfulness on the part of his friend Abou Omar (Hanna Mikhail) for a freedom earlier enjoyed by the PLO: 'Mer internationale aujourd'hui Fatah était un très petit ruisseau en 1964. Mais le petit ruisseau était libre, la mer est parcourue d'une flotte américaine et soviétique' [Fatah, an international ocean now, was only a little stream then. But the stream was free, and the ocean is patrolled by an American and Soviet fleet] (*CA*, 370; *PL*, 315). Later, Genet adapts his friend's image, all the more poignant in the light of the latter's drowning during the 1976 Lebanese civil war, in order to insist on the dangers of the geopolitical realities facing the Palestinians and condemning their revolution to be less a revolt than a *noyade* [drowning]:

Je date de ce moment la certitude d'un naufrage et dans une eau qui serait noire. Tout alors me paraîtra se dérouler sous l'eau, sous les vagues. Aussi désespérée qu'un homme tombé à la mer et qui ne sait pas nager, la révolution palestinienne fera entre deux eaux la gesticulation inefficace qui fut peut-être celle d'Abou Omar se noyant.

[I date from that moment my certainty of a shipwreck to come, and in murky waters. Everything would seem to happen under the waves. The Palestinian revolution, desperate as a man who falls in the sea and can't swim, would make the same useless gesture as Abu Omar may have made when he was drowning.] (*CA*, 436; *PL*, 371-72)

In contradistinction to this overwhelming body of water threatening a dark future, the spring is figured as life-giving. Even more precious than the springs that give rise to the Amazon are the water-sources of the desert, as is evident in a passage where again in Genet's writing can be read a reflection on its own operation. Genet cites an old 'plaisanterie', or jest, repeated by the Fedayeen: 'Faire confiance au désert, afin qu'on y retrouve nos sources' [Trust the desert to give us back our sources]. The wit lies in the pithy expression of a double, contradictory meaning: the desert can be trusted to preserve anything it holds because of its dryness, but the 'sources' that one might most wish to locate there are its springs of water. Genet then, bizarrely, proposes to 'compléter ce bizarre apophtegme' [complete this strange saying] by the following sentence: 'Apprenons de Marx les causes et les déboires de la révolution industrielle en Angleterre, attendons du désert qu'il conserve nos sources' [Study Marx for the causes and failures of the English Industrial revolution, and let the desert preserve our sources] (*CA*, 175; *PL*, 147). The notion of completion suggests that the first saying finds an expanded, fuller version in Genet's reformulation, yet the effect of the latter is if anything more cryptic than that of the former. Its division into two parallel parts ('Apprenons [...], attendons'), the second of which offers a condensed form of the aphorism, suggests that the complement is to be found in the first part. Yet the analogy at the level of meaning announced by the formal parallel remains opaque, to say the least. How does Marx's explanation of the industrial revolution mirror the desert's preservation of its sources? Does the explanation of the causes of the revolution keep them intact or make them available for exploitation? Does the example of Marx add a political supplement to the (non-political) truth expressed in the aphorism or rather highlight a pre-existing political dimension? The very opacity of the meaning of the comparison casts into relief the contrast in form between the first saying and Genet's reworking. The latter is strikingly unaphoristic: both less humorous and more laboured than the original. But that is perhaps the point. The 'completed' version is arid: the attempt to achieve a totality is dull, lifeless. For Genet, only the source is exuberant, a word which, etymologically, means 'fertile'.

Figured as 'fronde', as 'source', the Palestinian revolution does not merely aim at a new beginning; it is already imbued with the fresh life it seeks to foment. *Un Captif amoureux* is above all a love-letter to the vitality and creativity of the Palestinians; as we have seen, Genet is much less interested in their victories or possible future achievements than in their subversion of authority, embrace of the random and generosity of spirit. I want to suggest that this view of the Palestinian revolution as a living revolt, as a revolt by life itself, is determining for the very shape of the book, the elusive 'form' to which Genet repeatedly alludes. To do this, I shall turn to a scene of synecdochal importance for the book as a whole. It is placed immediately following the distinction between 'judaic values' and 'living revolts', and involves the only memory from the writer's early life included in *Un Captif amoureux*. Genet justifies its inclusion in terms of a playful obedience to the rules of genre: 'Puisque le mot souvenir est écrit dans le titre de ce livre, il faut par gaieté accepter le jeu de littérature mémoriale et remonter au jour quelques faits' [As I am writing this book in the form of 'Souvenirs', I must cheerfully accept the rules of memoir writing and dredge up a few facts] (*CA*, 449; *PL*, 382). Yet the scene is by no means of secondary or accessory importance; rather than a matter of conforming to generic convention, it is arguably at the origin of Genet's choice of the memoir genre. The memory deals with his experience in Syria when he was just eighteen years old, newly recruited to the French army direct from Mettray. Notwithstanding his lack of either expertise or experience, he was placed in charge of a team of older Arabs to construct fortifications for a cannon. Once erected and the cannon installed, his superior gave the order to fire a shot:

> Très lentement, presque trop doucement afin de m'épargner, afin que je n'en croie pas mes yeux, une toile d'araignée apparut. Doucement la tourelle se fissura, frissonna je crois, et j'en fus certain, s'écrasa, devint gravats, le noble canon de marine tangua, retrouvant sur cette colline de sable tout naturellement le mouvement qu'il avait sur son torpilleur par mer démontée; un peu de ce mouvement de tangage qu'ont encore quelques contrôleurs tyroliens dans les tournants des trains, et cela seulement rappelle que l'Autriche eut un port, Trieste, et des mers, toutes les Mers.

> [Very slowly, almost too gently, as if to spare me from believing my own eyes, a spider's web appeared. Slowly the tower cracked; trembled, I think; and certainly collapsed into rubble, the noble naval gun pitched and tossed, reverting naturally to its motion back on its torpedo boat in a raging sea; with something of the movement of Tyrolean ticket collectors as their trains go round bends in the rails, and that is a reminder that Austria once had a port, Trieste, and seas, ruled all the Seas.] (*CA*, 453; *PL*, 386)

The scene is that of an attack on power, in effect if not in intention: instead of reinforcing French military might, the young Genet's actions served to undermine it. Most noteworthy of all is Genet's representation of the scene of destruction as a scene of life. The fracturing of the cement that renders the weapon unusable is depicted as an organic creation: 'a spider's web appeared'. At the same time it animates the cannon, brings it to life. That animation in turn creates a further set of connections: the long sentence itself pitches backward and forward like the movement it describes, tracing a web of links between land and sea, between boats and trains, between Austria and Italy. Between death and life: the repetition of the word *mer*, ending the paragraph with 'toutes les Mers', links the destruction of the weapon to the mother. This unexpected connection to the mother was adumbrated a few paragraphs earlier, when Genet mused, 'Existe-t-il des livres ou un seul livre, une seule page, sur la formation la nuit, dans l'obscurité, des toiles d'araignées?' [Are there any books, is there one book or even a single page on how spiders' webs are formed, at night, in the dark?] before answering: 'Il existe un livre italien décrivant l'Italie du Sud et la Sicile en évoquant Ariane ou Ariadne pendue au bout d'un fil de la Vierge' [there is a book in Italian about southern Italy and Sicily which talks about Ariane or Ariadne hanging on to the end of a cobweb] (*CA*, 452; *PL*, 385). The use of the synonym for cobweb, *fil de la Vierge*, which in the plural (*fils de la Vierge*) is a homonym for 'the Virgin's son', unmistakably associates this boyhood memory with the mother-son figure that he sees as emblematic of the Palestinian revolution.

Genet's question as to whether a book exists about the weaving of spiders' webs inevitably invites us to consider whether and how *Un Captif amoureux* itself constitutes such a book. In shape, a spider's web exemplifies the rhizomatic structure that Deleuze and Guattari oppose to the linear arborescent model, a non-hierarchical multiplicity of contiguous and contingent rather than causal connections. For Genet too, this structure appears to carry a specifically political significance. He deems his experience with the cannon, the only distant memory incorporated into his book, a precursor of his support for the revolution, claiming that 'ce minuscule, grotesque mais monumental naufrage' [tiny, grotesque but monumental shipwreck] (*CA*, 453; *PL*, 386) prepared him to become the friend of the Palestinians. From what follows, it seems that his chance experience was formative, not in the sense that it altered the course of his future behaviour but rather in that it was a particular experience of connectivity that destined him to feel a connection to those whom he recognises as open to such an experience. 'L'arbre est filiation, mais le rhizome est alliance, uniquement d'alliance', in Deleuze and Guattari's formulation.[29] Genet is affected by the web he remembers: caught up in it, connected by it to the Palestinians. Hence the planar, strangely flattened nature of his relationship with them; just as he recognised their revolution as one of his oldest memories, so his early memory continues to exert an influence in the present. But he is affected also in the sense of moved; as he elaborates, his experience of their struggle revives something archaic in him, touches him intimately:

> Le fait palestinien seul me fit écrire ce livre, mais pourquoi ai-je si bien adhéré à la logique apparemment folle de cette guerre, je ne le trouve qu'en ceci, rappelant ce qui m'est précieux, c'est-à-dire l'une ou l'autre de mes prisons, un peu de mousse, quelques tiges de foin, peut-être des fleurs des champs soulevant une chape de béton ou une dalle de granit, ou, mais ce sera le seul luxe que je m'accorde, deux ou trois églantines sur un buisson épineux et sec.
>
> Que la prison fût solide, les blocs de granit assemblés par le plus fort ciment et encore par des joints de fer forgé, et de fissures inattendues, provoquées par l'eau de pluie, une graine, un seul rayon de soleil, et un brin d'herbe avaient déjà disloqué les blocs de granit, le bien était fait, je veux dire la prison ruinée.

> [It was the Palestinian phenomenon that made me write this book, but why did I stick so closely to the obviously crazy logic of that war? I can only explain it by remembering what I value: one or another of my prisons, a patch of moss, a few bits of hay, perhaps some wild flowers pushing up a slab of concrete or granite paving-stone. Or, the only luxury I'll allow myself, two or three dog roses growing on a gaunt and thorny bush.

The prison was strong, its blocks of granite stuck together with the strongest possible cement and also with iron clamps; there were strange cracks caused by the rain. But one seed, one ray of sunlight or blade of grass was enough to shift the granite. The thing was done, the prison destroyed.] (*CA*, 453-54; *PL*, 386)

The political vision channelled here — the idea that the fissure or gap may hold the power to disable a massive monument; that the weak are more powerful than the powerful — dates far back in Genet's writing, echoing the undermining of hierarchy explored in relation to his novels in Chapter 1.[30] What is new is the association between the fissure and the emergence of new life, the idea that the tiniest, most elementary sign of life is enough to undermine the most powerful edifice. In the following pages, Genet repeatedly deploys the image of moss and lichen to convey the Palestinians' capacity to survive and, especially, to create new life:

Mousse, lichen, herbe, quelques églantines capables de soulever des dalles de granit rouge étaient l'image du peuple palestinien qui sortait un peu partout des fissures... Car s'il me faudra dire pourquoi j'allai avec les feddayin, que j'en arrive à cette ultime raison: par jeu. Le hasard m'aida beaucoup.

[Moss, lichen, grass, a few dog roses capable of pushing up through red granite were an image of the Palestinian people breaking out everywhere through the cracks... If I have to say why I went with the fedayeen, I find the ultimate explanation is that I went for fun. Chance helped a lot.] (*CA*, 455; *PL*, 388)

Comme les mousses d'abord, les lichens ce début de vie apparaissait dans les fissures d'un pan de mur resté vertical, dans la rainure à peine visible de deux dalles de calcaire, des graminées, des gamins près des hommes, dans les femmes les lézardes avaient germé. Tous ici naquirent des fissures du béton. Ils y apportaient ce que j'avais cru arraché pour toujours par les Bédouins de Hussein, par les aviateurs de Dayan et par les précautions de la Banque Mondiale ou World Bank: la lumière des dents et des yeux, avec le tremblement.

[Like moss or lichen these beginnings of life would appear in the cracks of a ruined wall, in the almost invisble groove on a paving stone, grasses had sprouted in the cracks in men and women and children too. They were all born out of cracks in the concrete. They still had what I'd thought had been destroyed for ever by Hussein's Bedouin, Dayan's pilots and the precautions of the World Bank: the light of their teeth and eyes, trembling.] (*CA*, 460; *PL*, 391-92)

L'image, mais où cette matrice se trouvait-elle en moi? dans la fissure d'une dalle de granit ou de béton un peu de mousse avait germé. Quelques spores, des racines d'un jeune figuier soulevèrent les dalles, doucement ou durement, et les fragmenteraient; cette image était en face de moi, non avec netteté, mais dans le même flou où m'apparaissaient autrefois, mentalement, la borne-fontaine.

[There was an image, but where in me did it originate? in a crack in a block of granite or concrete a tuft of moss had sprouted. A few spores or the roots of a fig tree would prise up, softly or strongly, the paving-stones. And shatter them. This image was before me, not clear, but dim like the mental picture I'd had in the past of the tap in the wall.] (*CA*, 485; *PL*, 414)

The extended metaphor renders the Palestinians' revolt as indeed living, alive, constituting a rebellion by life at its most elementary against the forces of destruction. At issue is not merely their survival in the face of adversity but their continued aliveness and their embrace of a chance, sporadic existence. Nothing is further from the idea that the value of a human life is determined by the family one descends from, or from the rootedness of one's ancestors in a particular place, than the random, haphazard, structureless existence in the cracks of a harsh world forced on the Palestinians by political necessity. Nothing is more precious for Genet than the life that takes root tenaciously, against the odds, in the most inhospitable of places and shines not in the glitter of jewels or gold but in 'la lumière des dents et des yeux, avec le tremblement'.

The fissuring and proliferation that Genet remembers towards the end of his text thus function as an image of what he values most about the experience of the Palestinians that he had the opportunity to share: the affirmation of life at its most irreducible, at its most elementary, an affirmation that constitutes at least as fundamental an aspect of their revolution as the armed revolt against authority. The image thematises a structure that furthermore echoes throughout *Un Captif amoureux* in the very form of the book. For Genet's valorisation of life as chance germination, as new beginning, extends to every level of his writing. It is visible at micro level, in the signature hallmark of the chains of signification that reproduce themselves sporadically throughout his text, rooting aimlessly here and there with no apparent logic. And it is replicated at the macro level of the narrative. The book's purposeless, apparently disorganised, meandering is a carefully-crafted rhetorical practice to inscribe or convey the embrace of the sporadic, the haphazard, the accidental that he posits discursively as the other of Judeo-Christian morality. The very shape of *Un Captif amoureux*, a contrived shape that creates the illusion of the accidental, aligns it with the 'living revolts' that inspire its author.

★   ★   ★   ★   ★

The writing of Genet's last text therefore does not support Marty's claim that his work is driven by antisemitism. Far from using the Palestinians to channel more original and profound negative feelings and attitudes towards the Jews, *Un Captif amoureux* variously and repeatedly inscribes Genet's delight at the vital force they exhibit in the most precarious of circumstances. Far from eulogising a fascistic 'hyperpower', it celebrates both in form and in content what the writer perceives as an inclusive life-force. A life-force situated not in any individual but in the relations between them, best exemplified in the couple formed by Hamza and his mother, forming a web of connections that reaches beyond them. Via another image of fibrous, organic tissue, Genet connects their relationship both to himself and to his book:

> Que cette existence de Hamza avec sa mère — ou plus exactement leur rapport mère-fils et fils-responsable — se poursuivît en moi au point d'y vivre une vie autonome aussi libre qu'un organe envahisseur, un fibrome multipliant son audace et ses pousses, me semblait de l'ordre de la vie animale et de la végétation

des tropiques; que ce couple en moi poursuivît son destin ne m'effaroucha pas puisqu'il y symbolisait la résistance, au moins cette résistance qui avait pris forme dans mon discours et mes pensées sur elle.

[That the existence of Hamza and his mother — or more precisely their mother-son and son-chief relationship — should have come to live a life of its own inside me, independent as an invading organ or a developing fibroid, seemed to me as natural as similar phenomena in the animal kingdom or in tropical vegetation. It didn't worry me that this pair's destiny should continue within me in this way, because their fate symbolized the resistance, at least as it had come to seem to me in my thoughts.] (*CA*, 345; *PL*, 294)

A 'fibrome multipliant son audace et ses pousses' is Genet's emblem of the Palestinian revolution, that is, *his* Palestinian revolution, the resistance that had both shaped and been shaped by his words about it.

Marty is correct, on the other hand, that *Un Captif amoureux* contains a hostile reflection on the Jewish religion. But that animosity is part of a wider hostility towards Judeo-Christianity; it is directed not towards a figure of the Other but towards Genet's own origins, his own culture, that of France and the West more generally. Genet's writing has always been outrageous and offensive, but not about the Jews; the regular butt of his antagonism is French authority. Moreover, insofar as the book explores that hostility, it is to convey Genet's detachment from it rather than investment in it; the converse of his revelling in the web that connects him to the Palestinians is the relief he feels at the unravelling or erasure of his links to Europe ('l'Europe fut gommée'). It is not clear, therefore, if it is of any other than polemical value to label his hostility to Judeo-Christianity as antisemitism when it is accompanied by none of the discourses that represent the Jews as an inferior or hateful race, let alone any action directed against the Jews. It does not shed any light on the complexities of Genet's singular case to classify him in the same category as racists with whom he has nothing in common. More importantly, doing so runs the risk of blunting our understanding of antisemitism today, in a context where it is increasingly imperative to be able to identify and call out the very real threat posed by its alarming resurgence. It is only possible to confuse Genet's stance with those who harbour prejudice or hatred towards the Jews by ignoring or bracketing the most distinctive feature of his writing: its relentless attack on hierarchies of all kinds, including, above all, the idea that any person's life is worth more than that of another.

I began this chapter by foregrounding the role of religion in Genet's conception of revolution. Religion provides an unexpectedly productive lens through which to analyse Genet's relationship to the Palestinians. This is not because of their religion; Genet's total lack of interest in any form of Islamic revolution can be seen in the absence of any reference to the Iranian revolution anywhere in his writings. What he responds to in the Palestinians' practice of religion is in fact its eclecticism: their cheerful drawing on the incompatible doctrines of Marxism and Islam in a way that entirely undermines the doctrinaire aspect of both missions; the insouciance they show to religious authority; their proximity to paganism. But he also admires the fact that their revolt is potentially religious, that is, it is not *yet* religious. If successful, it runs the danger of becoming a religion, a dogma, like any other. But in 1970 the revolution had the energy of religious belief without its exclusivity.

Above all, there is a religious dimension to Genet's own engagement with the Palestinians in the sense that the word 'religion' derives from the Latin *religare*, to tie, bind together. *Un Captif amoureux* leaves no doubt that Genet was attached to the Palestinians, as to the Black Panthers, in a way he had never experienced in his earlier life. But if he loves them as his community, it is as one to which he does not belong. He feels connected to them because their struggle evokes in him a memory of his own: a revolt against authority, an assertion of an indomitable will to live in the face of greater odds. But he knows their struggle is not his, and his primary concern in writing his book is to bear witness to that struggle in a way that does not mask their voice with his, does not enclose them in a monument in which they would no longer breathe. His hope — I would say his achievement — in *Un Captif amoureux* is to craft an interstitial, weblike text in whose fissures he provides space for some lichen and some moss to survive, even to grow.

## Notes to Chapter 4

1. 'Quatre heures à Chatila' was published on 1 January 1983: *Revue d'études palestiniennes*, 6 (1983), 3-19.
2. This note, stored in Box 5 of the Fonds Genet, is jotted on the front cover of an empty *fémina* note-pad whose back contains calculations sums of money given to 'Jaky' (presumably Jackie Maglia) up to 1984, suggesting it was contemporaneous with the writing of *Un Captif amoureux*.
3. Marty's views generated numerous rebuttals on several grounds; see especially René de Ceccaty, 'Jean Genet antisémite? Sur une tenace rumeur', *Critique*, 714 (2006), 895-911; Alain David, 'Derrida avec Levinas: "Entre lui et moi dans l'affection et la confiance partagée"', *Le Magazine Littéraire*, 419 (April 2003), 30-34; Albert Dichy, 'Genet est resté en marge, tout en étant au centre', in *Jean Genet: un écrivain sous haute surveillance*, Le Monde Hors-série, Une vie, une œuvre (Paris: Le Monde, 2016), pp. 56-63; and 'Il prend sur lui le Mal de ses personnages', *Le Monde des livres*, 4 April 2003 (repr. in *Jean Genet: un écrivain sous haute surveillance*, pp. 90-91); Sylvain Dreyer, 'Controverse: Jean Genet, l'antisémitisme en question', *Esprit*, 310 (2004), 191-201; Gene A. Plunka, 'Jean Genet's Anti-Semitism: Fact or Fiction?', *French Review*, 76.3 (2003), 507-19; Hill, *Radical Indecision*, pp. 310-16; and Camille Toffoli, 'La Question de l'antisémitisme chez Jean Genet: un débat sur le "sens du monde". Autour de la réception critique d'*Un Captif amoureux*', *Postures*, 24, (2016) <http://revuepostures.com/fr/articles/toffoli-24> [accessed 21 November 2019].
4. For the IHRA's working definition of antisemitism, including a non-exhaustive list of examples of words and behaviour that qualify as such, see <https://www.holocaustremembrance.com/working-definition-antisemitism> [accessed 24 January 2023]. For a recent discussion surrounding issues of definition, see Deborah Lipstadt, *Antisemitism: Here and Now* (New York: Schocken, 2019).
5. Nor is there convincing anecdotal evidence from Genet's life, as distinct from his writing, that he had antisemitic attitudes. Marty derives considerable rhetorical effect from opening his discussion of Genet with a quotation from Sartre that Jablonka also uses: 'Genet est antisémite. Ou plutôt, il joue à l'être' [Genet is antisemitic. Or rather, he plays at being it] (Sartre, *Saint Genet*, p. 230 n., quoted in *BSJ*, 91, and *VIJG*, 273). While the substance of Sartre's argument is in fact that Genet is *not* antisemitic, the discussions of both Marty and Jablonka privilege the first sentence quoted above at the expense of the second, treating it as a more accurate reflection of Sartre's view; for example, Marty later claims that Sartre had 'aucun doute' [no doubt] that Genet was antisemitic (*JGP*, 43). Both critics seek to discount Sartre's distinction between

Genet and antisemites such as Céline, Drieu La Rochelle etc. as an attempt to neutralise an accusation in which he really believed. Rather than the somewhat convoluted arguments they bring forward to support the idea that the first part of the quotation merits greater confidence than the second, it seems more plausible that the reason why Sartre differentiated between Genet and Céline is simply the one he gave: that he did not consider Genet's words or actions those of an antisemite. The fact that others who knew Genet personally such as Jacques Derrida, himself a Jew, and Juan Goytisolo (who for example has had no hesitation in recognising that Genet's private discourse was sometimes misogynist) have forcefully refuted the allegation of his antisemitism adds further weight to this probability.

6. See for example *ED*, 47, 56, 286; *DE*, 34, 43, 247.

7. On this point, see also de Ceccaty's extensive discussion in 'Jean Genet antisémite? Sur une tenace rumeur', p. 900. Moreover, Jablonka himself quotes a page that Genet excised from *Journal du voleur* (quoted in White, *Genet*, p. 281) in which Genet specifically attributes his pleasure at the idea of Dachau to the suffering undergone there by communist members of the resistance that had shunned him in prison (White, *Genet*, p. 281).

8. Jean-Paul Sartre, *Réflexions sur la question juive* [1946] (Paris: Gallimard/Nrf, 1954), p. 10.

9. See n. 3 above.

10. See for example Robert Fisk, *The Great War for Civilisation: The Conquest of the Middle East* (New York: Alfred A. Knopf, 2006); James L. Gelvin, *The Israel-Palestine Conflict: One Hundred Years of War* (Cambridge: Cambridge University Press, 2005); Walter Laqueur and Barry M. Rubin, *The Israel-Arab Reader: A Documentary History of the Middle East Conflict* (London & New York: Penguin Books, 2001); Henry Laurens, *Une mission sacrée de civilisation: la question de Palestine* (Paris: Fayard, 2002); Philip Mattar, *The Mufti of Jerusalem: Al-Hajj Amin al-Husayni and the Palestinian National Movement* (New York: Columbia University Press, 1992); and Benny Morris, *1948: A History of the First Arab-Israeli War* (New Haven, CT: Yale University Press, 2008).

11. For a discussion of the text's critical reception in generic terms, see Pierre-Marie Héron, '*Un Captif amoureux* et le genre des mémoires', *Littérature*, 159 (September 2010), 53–63.

12. Moreover, even the exceptions are unusual in an autobiographical context insofar as they focus, not on what was distinctive about Genet's early life, but rather on how it was not unusual. For example, his brief allusion to his 'abandon à l'Assistance publique' [being abandoned to social security] and 'enfance chez des paysans' [childhood among peasants] claims that there was nothing exceptional about them (*CA*, 205; *PL*, 172).

13. I differ strongly here from Simon Critchley's reading of *Un Captif amoureux* as a 'book of *flawed* memory, a flaw that is caused by the failure of writing itself': *Ethics, Politics, Subjectivity: Essays on Derrida, Levinas and Contemporary French Thought* (London & New York: Verso, 1999), p. 36. For Critchley, Genet's book represents a dramatic reversal of Genet's previous positions, inscribing the author's 'frustration at not being able to relate facts as they happened' (p. 33) and 'proclaiming the triumph of truth over art' (p. 39), a formulation that firmly situates 'truth' outside the kind of (subjective) experience to which Genet's text, and art more generally, so successfully bears witness. He argues that the book is evidence of a 'redemptive moment of transcendence' in which the earlier exploration of the potential of textuality is subordinated to 'a writing of the truth of what lies outside of writing' (p. 47). Even more surprisingly, he not only goes on to propose that in subordinating writing to everything Genet had previously sought to undermine, the writer 'becomes Hegel' and 'privileges love, family, home, property, community and divinity' (p. 47) but appears to consider such a normalisation a mark of unquestionable political progress. In contrast, as will become clear in this chapter, I see Genet's book as a (powerful) exploitation of what writing can, rather than cannot, achieve. For a developed critique of Critchley's analysis, see Hill, *Radical Indecision*, pp. 303–06.

14. In his discussion of the links between fantasy and community in *Un Captif amoureux*, Scott Durham reads this quotation in similar terms as 'an alternative origin for the world [...], a point of view on the world that he had not yet occupied, but which had always remained virtual within him': *Phantom Communities: The Simulacrum and the Limits of Postmodernism* (Stanford, CA: Stanford University Press, 1998), p. 159.

15. Michel Deguy, 'La Pietà de Jean Genet', in *Jean Genet et son lecteur: autour de la réception critique de*

*Journal du voleur et Un Captif amoureux*, ed. by Agnès Fontvieille-Cordani et Dominique Carlat (Saint-Étienne: Publications de l'Université de Saint-Étienne, 2010), pp. 149-54 (p. 152).

16. Genet voiced a similar fantasy more than forty years earlier in his first novel, *Notre-Dames-des-Fleurs*: 'Être la mère humaine d'une divinité est un état plus troublant que celui de divinité. La mère de Jésus dut avoir des émotions incomparables en portant son fils, puis en vivant, en dormant côte à côte avec un fils qui était Dieu — c'est-à-dire tout et elle-même avec — qui pouvait faire que le monde ne fût pas, que sa mère, que lui-même ne fussent pas, un Dieu à qui il fallait bien préparer, comme Joséphine à Marie, le jaune brouet de maïs' [To be the human mother of a divinity is a more disturbing state than that of divinity. The Mother of Jesus must have had incomparable emotions while carrying her son, and later, while living and sleeping side by side with a son who was God — that is, everything and herself as well — who could make the world not be, His Mother, Himself not be, a God for whom she had to prepare, as Josephine did for Marie, the yellow corn mush] (*RP*, 194-95; *OLF*, 263).

17. For an account of Genet's avoidance of an orientalising optic in *Un Captif amoureux*, see Edward J. Hughes, *Writing Marginality in Modern French Literature: From Loti to Genet* (Cambridge: Cambridge University Press, 2001), pp. 135-65.

18. While the Black Panthers were certainly influenced by Malcolm X and the Nation of Islam, its leaders were in fact profoundly atheistic.

19. Einstein later insisted that he had used God as a metaphor: 'I do not believe in a personal God and I have never denied this but have expressed it clearly. If something is in me which can be called religious then it is the unbounded admiration for the structure of the world so far as our science can reveal it', cited in *Albert Einstein: The Human Side, New Glimpses from his Archives*, ed. by Helen Dukas and Banesh Hoffmann (Princeton, NJ: Princeton University Press, 1989), p. 43.

20. In addition to drafts held in IMEC, a version nearly identical to that of *Un Captif amoureux* was published in Jean Genet, *La Sentence, suivi de J'étais et je n'étais pas* (Paris: Gallimard, 2010).

21. For a more detailed analysis of this passage, see my 'Espèces de travestissements et travestissement de l'espèce dans l'écriture de Genet'.

22. Gilles Deleuze and Félix Guattari, *Mille plateaux* (Paris: Minuit, 1980).

23. See for example Alan George, ' "Making the Desert Bloom": A Myth Examined', *Journal of Palestine Studies*, 8.2 (Winter 1979), 88-100.

24. Amos Elon, *The Israelis: Founders and Sons* (London: Penguin, 1983), p. 200.

25. Nur Masalha, *The Palestine Nakba: Decolonising History, Narrating the Subaltern, Reclaiming Memory* (London & New York: Zed Books, 2012), p. 120.

26. Ibid., pp. 121-22.

27. Ibid., p. 127.

28. See the 'Notice' to 'Quatre heures à Chatila' (*ED*, 406; *DE*, 370).

29. Deleuze and Guattari, *Mille plateaux*, p. 36.

30. The link between this political vision and Genet's revised views about eroticism in 'Ce qui est resté d'un Rembrandt...' is particularly evident. The power of the fissures to undermine the most monumental edifice is strongly reminiscent of the earlier text's account of the de-eroticisation entailed by no longer being able to believe that a powerful male body was the sign of an individuality immune to castration, untouched by the 'blessure' or wound. In the words of its hesitant conclusion: 'Un sexe érigé, congestionné et vibrant, dressé dans un fourré de poils noirs et bouclés, puis ce qui les continue: les cuisses épaisses, puis le torse, le corps entier, les mains, les pouces, puis le cou, les lèvres, les dents, le nez, les cheveux, enfin les yeux qui appellent comme pour un sauvetage ou un anéantissement les fureurs amoureuses, et tout cela luttant contre le si fragile regard capable peut-être de détruire cette Toute-Puissance?' [An erect phallus, congested and vibrating, standing in a thicket of curly black hairs, and after that: thick thighs, then the torso, the whole body, the hands, the thumbs, then the neck, the lips, the teeth, the nose, the hair, finally the eyes that summon amorous furies as if for a rescue or an annihilation, and all that struggling against this so fragile look capable perhaps of destroying this All-Power?] (*OC*, IV, 31; *FA*, 101-02).

# AFTERWORD

❖

It seems fitting to end with an Afterword, which by definition comes 'after' the whole of which simultaneously it forms part, since the continual emphasis throughout this book has been on how Genet's texts are constantly at odds with themselves. One major reason the overall argument is structured on the basis of genre is because a constitutive insufficiency of any identity, an inherent lack of identity to itself, appears particularly obvious in his practice of genre. As the different chapters have sought to show, his writing never leaves intact the genre it borrows: his novels are intrinsically hybrid forms; his theatre calls attention to an outside always in excess of what it can integrate; his later journalistic writings bear witness to a fundamental contradiction undermining the straightforwardness of the message they convey; *Un Captif amoureux* profoundly challenges the generic conventions of the memoir. The aim of this book has been to explore the political implications of that troubling of generic identity, and its links with the tension between poetry and politics — between the urge to create something beautiful irrespective of external constraints, and the desire to affect the very real world in which those constraints materialise — that I have argued characterises Genet's writing from the outset.

Genre, then, is out of joint in Genet. The expression has fortuitous connotations in that the political credentials of out-of-jointedness are today well established in political philosophy. In his first sustained engagement with Marxism, Derrida famously borrowed the line from *Hamlet*, 'The time is out of joint' (1.5), to formulate his notion of 'hantologie' [hauntology] and the temporal disjunction that he discerned at the heart of political discourse.[1] Throughout, my book has repeatedly shown how generic disjunction in Genet finds a parallel not only in temporal disjunction but in the widespread, one might even say compulsive, undermining of identity at every level possible: gender, race, religion, etc. It finds echoes across his *œuvre* in instances as diverse as his insistence, for example, that Chartres Cathedral, that masterpiece of French Latinity, is a foreign creation whose closest analogy is to be found literally poles apart, in the Sanctuary of Nara in Japan;[2] or, still more thought-provokingly, his proposal that for Giacometti 'une ligne est un homme' [a line is a man].[3] Above all, it is mirrored in the pervasive, comprehensive destabilisation of the identity of the word that we have seen Genet's writing practise at the most minute, microtextual level. Nearly forty years after his death, an Afterword therefore seems to offer the ideal place to raise the question of Genet's timeliness, that is to ask how timely Genet's systemic out-of-jointedness may be today.

The world is now, inescapably, a very different place from the 1970s when the struggle by the Palestinian Fedayeen moved Genet as a fresh, joyful explosion of revolutionary fervour, let alone decades previously while he was writing his novels, a time when, notwithstanding France's comparatively progressive record of legislation in relation to sexuality, homosexuality remained forcefully repressed with only extremely rare symbolic representation. Yet in my view such shifts in the fortunes of the collective identities Genet treated in his work — for the worse in the case of the Palestinians, for the better in terms of increasing sexual emancipation — have rather little effect on the resonance and relevance that his work holds for us. For Genet's singularity does not lie in his promotion of a 'minority' perspective.[4] As we saw, he stands only with 'l'homme seul' [solitary man]; the sole collectives he even partially supports are those — the Palestinians and Black Americans — to which he does not belong. Indeed, as Leo Bersani has argued, '[n]early all his works relentlessly, floridly, celebrate homosexuality, and yet he is the least "gay-affirmative" gay writer' there may be.[5] And if Hélène Cixous influentially deemed this uniquely homosexual man a shining example of 'écriture féminine' [feminine writing], it was not because of any homology between the condition of gay men and that of women but rather because of a generous porosity at the level of his writing that was in no sense straightforwardly determined by its author's identity.[6]

I want to suggest that the enduring political value of the message of Genet's work lies less in what he says about any particular identity than in what he suggests of identity more universally: that it is fundamentally a heterogeneous, always provisional construct. Hence, doubtless, one reason why Jacques Derrida has been such a major reference-point in my argument; it is worth restating that it was in showing relentlessly time and time again that a concept was not identical to itself that deconstruction's challenge to the metaphysics of presence revolutionised philosophy in the late 1960s and 70s. Superficially, the message that the very idea that an identity can ever be at one with itself is a wish rather than a reality may seem redundant today, at least in liberal democracies where young people declare unprecedented levels of tolerance of fluidity in relation to issues such as gender or sexuality. Nevertheless, that increase in tolerance is not replicated in many of the authoritarian regimes in which a high proportion of the world's population live their lives. And within Western democracies too, the tolerance for people to practise the gender or sexuality they choose has not yet been accompanied by a comprehensive overturning of the old orthodoxy that identity is exclusionary: that a self is defined by boundaries designed to keep otherness at bay. As Julia Kristeva has argued, such a conception of identity is intrinsically violent;[7] its effects continue to be seen not only in the ongoing tragedy of the Israeli-Palestinian conflict but in the vitriolic arguments about identity that persist even among many motivated by societal injustice, notably in the increasingly polarised debates opposing some proponents of trans rights and some gender-critical feminists; it is arguably evident also in the alarming rise in dissatisfaction with democracy expressed by younger generations across the globe.[8] In that respect, Genet's message — that all identity, majority or minority, is at odds with itself, that the self is inherently heterogeneous — is as timely, as vital, as ever.

But I want to stress also that there is a political dimension to the demands Genet's texts make on us. His destabilisation of the categories by which we divide people from each other echoes in the need to engage with his writing not as a vehicle of content or ideas but as a practice that involves not immediately understanding, not knowing, not being categorical. Reading Genet involves — needs — a constant alertness to the possibility that what the text says may not be identical to the meaning it conveys. It involves accepting that reading is a negotiation with a material body and surrendering to the need for that encounter to be attentive rather than teleological or instrumental in order for it to be productive, a requirement that thereby sets the reader at odds with societal practice in general. Reading Genet takes — needs — time; Genet's dissidence lies also in the different practice of time his texts require of the reader, time experienced or valued as something other than a means to an end. But therein also perhaps lies his timeliness: does reading him not remind us that literature at its greatest is always a dissident practice?

## Notes to the Afterword

1. Jacques Derrida, *Spectres de Marx* (Paris: Galilée, 1993); *Specters of Marx*, trans. by Peggy Kamuf (London & New York: Routledge, 1994).
2. Genet, 'Cathédrale de Chartres' (*ED*, 191-97).
3. Genet, 'L'Atelier d'Alberto Giacometti' (*OC*, v, 60).
4. See, for example, Didier Eribon, *Une morale du minoritaire: variations sur un thème de Jean Genet* (Paris: Fayard, 2001).
5. Leo Bersani, *Homos* (Harvard, MA, & London: Harvard University Press, 1995), pp. 160-61.
6. Hélène Cixous, 'Le Rire de la méduse', p. 42; 'The Laugh of the Medusa', p. 879.
7. See for example Julia Kristeva, *Étrangers à nous-mêmes* (Paris: Gallimard/Folio, 1991); *Strangers to Ourselves*, trans. by Leon S. Roudiez (New York: Columbia University Press, 1991).
8. See <https://www.cam.ac.uk/system/files/youth_and_satisfaction_with_democracy.pdf> [accessed 30 January 2023].

# BIBLIOGRAPHY

❖

BEARDSWORTH, RICHARD, *Derrida and the Political* (London: Routledge, 1996)

—— 'The Irony of Deconstruction and the Example of Marx', in *The Politics of Deconstruction: Jacques Derrida and the Other of Philosophy*, ed. by Martin McQuillan (London: Pluto Press, 2007), pp. 212-34

BENNINGTON, GEOFFREY, *Legislations: The Politics of Deconstruction* (London: Verso, 1994)

BERGER, ANNE, *The Queer Turn in Feminism: Identities, Sexualities and the Theater of Gender*, trans. by Catherine Porter (New York: Fordham University Press, 2014)

BERMEL, ALBERT, 'Society as a Brothel: Genet's Satire in *The Balcony*', *Modern Drama*, 19.3 (1976), 265-80

BERSANI, LEO, *Homos* (Harvard, MA, & London: Harvard University Press, 1995)

BROWN, ELAINE, *A Taste of Power: A Black Woman's Story* (New York: Doubleday, 1992)

BRUETON, JOANNE, *Geometry and Jean Genet: Shaping the Subject* (Cambridge: Legenda, 2022)

CARMICHAEL, STOKELY, and CHARLES V. HAMILTON, *Le Black Power: pour une politique de libération aux États-Unis*, trans. by Odile Pidoux (Paris: Payot, 1968)

CECCATY, RENÉ DE, 'Jean Genet antisémite? Sur une tenace rumeur', *Critique*, 714 (2006), 895-911

CHEAH, PHENG, and SUZANNE GERLACH, eds, *Derrida and the Time of the Political* (Durham, NC: Duke University Press, 2009)

CHESNEAU, ALBERT C., 'Idée de révolution et principe de réversibilité dans *Le Balcon* et *Les Nègres* de Jean Genet,' *PMLA*, 88.5 (1973), 1137-45

CHIESA, LORENZO, 'The First Gram of *Jouissance*: Lacan on Genet's *Le Balcon*', *The Comparatist*, 39 (2015), 6-21

CIXOUS, HÉLÈNE, 'Le Rire de la méduse', *Arc*, 45 (1975), 39-54

—— 'The Laugh of the Medusa', trans. by Keith Cohen and Paula Cohen, *Signs*, 1.4 (Summer 1976), 875-93

CIXOUS, HÉLÈNE, and CATHERINE CLÉMENT, *La Jeune Née* (Paris: 10/18, 1975)

COE, RICHARD, *The Vision of Jean Genet* (London: Owen, 1968)

CORVIN, MICHEL, and ALBERT DICHY, 'Notice', in *Les Bonnes* (TC, 1041)

CRITCHLEY, SIMON, *Ethics, Politics, Subjectivity: Essays on Derrida, Levinas and Contemporary French Thought* (London & New York: Verso, 1999)

DARNTON, JOHN, 'Genet Emerges as an Idol of Panthers', *New York Times*, 1 May 1970

DAVID, ALAIN, 'Derrida avec Levinas: "Entre lui et moi dans l'affection et la confiance partagée"', *Le Magazine Littéraire*, 419 (April 2003), 30-34

DEGUY, MICHEL, 'La Pietà de Jean Genet', in *Jean Genet et son lecteur: autour de la réception critique de Journal du voleur et Un Captif amoureux*, ed. by Agnès Fontvieille-Cordani et Dominique Carlat (Saint-Étienne: Publications de l'Université de Saint-Étienne, 2010), pp. 149-54

DELEUZE, GILLES, and FÉLIX GUATTARI, *Mille plateaux* (Paris: Minuit, 1980)

DERRIDA, JACQUES, 'Fors: les mots angles de Nicolas Abraham et Maria Torok', in Nicolas Abraham and Maria Torok, *Cryptonymie: le verbier de l'homme aux loups* (Paris: Aubier Flammarion, 1976), pp. 9-73

—— *Glas: que reste-t-il du savoir absolu?* [1974] (Paris: Denoël, 1981)

—— *Glas*, trans. by John P. Leavey, Jr., and Richard Rand (Lincoln & London: University of Nebraska Press, 1986)

—— *Spectres de Marx* (Paris: Galilée, 1993)

—— *Specters of Marx*, trans. by Peggy Kamuf (London & New York: Routledge, 1994)

DICHY, ALBERT, 'Genet est resté en marge, tout en étant au centre', in *Jean Genet: un écrivain sous haute surveillance*, Le Monde Hors-série, Une vie, une œuvre (Paris: Le Monde, 2016), pp. 56-63

—— 'Il prend sur lui le Mal de ses personnages', *Le Monde des livres*, 4 April 2003; repr. in *Jean Genet: un écrivain sous haute surveillance*, Le Monde Hors-série, Une vie, une œuvre (Paris: Le Monde, 2016), pp. 90-91

DICHY, ALBERT, and LYNDA BELLITY PESKINE, eds, *La Bataille des Paravents* (Paris: Théâtre de l'Odéon, 1986)

DIDI-HUBERMAN, GEORGES, *Images malgré tout* (Paris: Minuit, 2003)

DREYER, SYLVAIN, 'Controverse: Jean Genet, l'antisémitisme en question', *Esprit*, 310 (2004), 191-201

DUFF, DAVID, 'Intertextuality versus Genre Theory: Bakhtin, Kristeva and the Question of Genre', *Paragraph*, 25.1 (2002), 54-73

DUKAS, HELEN, and BANESH HOFFMANN, eds, *Albert Einstein: The Human Side, New Glimpses from his Archives* (Princeton, NJ: Princeton University Press, 1989)

DURHAM, SCOTT, *Phantom Communities: The Simulacrum and the Limits of Postmodernism* (Stanford, CA: Stanford University Press, 1998)

EKOTTO, FRIEDA, *Race and Sex Across the French Atlantic: The Color of Black in Literary, Philosophical and Theater Discourse* (Lanham, MD: Lexington Books, 2011)

ELON, AMOS, *The Israelis: Founders and Sons* (London: Penguin, 1983)

ERIBON, DIDIER, *Une morale du minoritaire: variations sur un thème de Jean Genet* (Paris: Fayard, 2001)

ESSLIN, MARTIN, *The Theatre of the Absurd* (New York: Anchor Books, 1971)

FEDERMAN, RAYMOND, 'Jean Genet ou le théâtre de la haine', *Esprit*, n.s. 391.4 (1970), 697-713

FINBURGH, CLARE, 'Genet and the Problem with Postmodernity', in *Jean Genet: Performance and Politics*, ed. by Clare Finburgh, Carl Lavery and Maria Shevtsova (Basingstoke & New York: Palgrave-Macmillan, 2006), pp. 78-102

—— 'Speech Without Acts: Politics and Speech-Act Theory in Genet's *The Balcony*,' *Paragraph*, 27.2 (2004), 113-29

FISK, ROBERT, *The Great War for Civilisation: The Conquest of the Middle East* (New York: Alfred A. Knopf, 2006)

FREDETTE, NATHALIE, 'Genet politique, l'ultime engagement', *Études françaises*, 29.2 (1993), 83-102

FREUD, SIGMUND, 'Fetishism' [1927], in *Collected Papers*, 5 vols (London: Hogarth and Institute of Psycho-Analysis, 1924-50), v, 198-204

GELVIN, JAMES L., *The Israel-Palestine Conflict: One Hundred Years of War* (Cambridge: Cambridge University Press, 2005)

GENET, JEAN, *The Balcony*, trans. by Barbara Writing and Terry Hands (London: Faber & Faber, 1991)

—— *L'Ennemi déclaré*, ed. by Albert Dichy (Paris: Gallimard, 1991)

—— *The Declared Enemy, Texts and Interviews*, trans. by Jeff Fort (Stanford, CA: Stanford University Press, 2004)

—— *Fragments of the Artwork*, trans. by Charlotte Mandell (Stanford, CA: Stanford University Press, 2003)

——*Funeral Rites*, trans. by Bernard Frechtman (London: Panther, 1971)
——*Letters to Roger Blin*, trans. by Richard Seaver (New York: Grove Press, 1969)
——*Lettres à Olga et Marc Barbezat* (Décines: L'Arbalète, 1988)
——*The Maids*, trans. by Bernard Frechtman [1953] (London: Faber & Faber, 2009)
——*Miracle of the Rose*, trans. by Bernard Frechtman (London: Penguin, 1971)
——*Œuvres complètes*, 6 vols (Paris: Gallimard, 1952–79)
——*Our Lady of the Flowers*, trans. by Bernard Frechtman (London: Panther, 1966)
——'Ouverture-éclair sur l'Amérique', *Europe*, 808-09 (August-September 1996), 8-11
——*Poèmes* (Décines: Marc Barbezat/L'Arbalète, 1948)
——*Prisoner of Love*, trans. by Barbara Bray (New York: New York Review Books, 2003)
——'Quatre heures à Chatila', *Revue d'études palestiniennes*, 6 (1983), 3-19
——*Romans et poèmes*, ed. by Emmanuelle Lambert and Gilles Philippe with Albert Dichy, Bibliothèque de la Pléiade (Paris: Gallimard, 2021)
——*La Sentence, suivi de J'étais et je n'étais pas* (Paris: Gallimard, 2010)
——*Théâtre complet*, ed. by Michel Corvin and Albert Dichy, Bibliothèque de la Pléiade (Paris: Gallimard, 2002)
——*The Thief's Journal*, trans. by Bernard Frechtman (London: Penguin, 1967)
——*Un Captif amoureux* (Paris: Gallimard, 1986)
GEORGE, ALAN, '"Making the Desert Bloom": A Myth Examined', *Journal of Palestine Studies*, 8.2 (Winter 1979), 88-100
GOLDMANN, LUCIEN, *Structures mentales et création culturelle* (Paris: Anthropos, 1970)
——'Une pièce réaliste: *Le Balcon* de Jean Genet', *Les Temps modernes*, 171 (1960), 1885-96
HANRAHAN, MAIRÉAD, 'Le Cru et les cuisses: écrire à l'adresse de l'Amérique', *Études françaises*, 51.1 (2015), 29-42
——'Double Signature', in *Resounding Glas*, ed. by Mairéad Hanrahan, Martin McQuillan and Simon Morgan Wortham (Edinburgh: Edinburgh University Press, 2016) (= special issue of *Paragraph*, 39.2 (2016)), 165-86
——'Espèces de travestissements et travestissement de l'espèce dans l'écriture de Genet', *Modern Language Notes*, 128.4 (September 2013), 917-34
——*Lire Genet: une poétique de la différence* (Montréal: Presses de l'Université de Montréal; Lyon: Presses Universitaires de Lyon, 1997)
——'Une écriture retorse: la réponse de Genet à ses juges', *French Studies*, 68.4 (October 2014), 510-25
HANRAHAN, MAIRÉAD, SIMON MORGAN WORTHAM and MARTIN McQUILLAN, eds, *Resounding Glas* (Edinburgh: Edinburgh University Press, 2016) (= special issue of *Paragraph*, 39.2 (2016))
HARTMAN, GEOFFREY, *Saving the Text* (Baltimore, MD: Johns Hopkins University Press, 1982)
HÉRON, PIERRE-MARIE, '*Un Captif amoureux* et le genre des mémoires', *Littérature*, 159 (September 2010), 53-63
HILL, LESLIE, *Radical Indecision: Barthes, Blanchot, Derrida and the Future of Criticism* (Notre Dame, IN: University of Notre Dame Press, 2010)
HILLIARD, DAVID, and LEWIS COLE, *This Side of Glory: The Autobiography of David Hilliard and the Story of the Black Panther Party* (Toronto: Little, Brown & Co., 1993)
HUGHES, EDWARD J., *Writing Marginality in Modern French Literature: From Loti to Genet* (Cambridge: Cambridge University Press, 2001)
JABLONKA, IVAN, *Les Vérités inavouables de Jean Genet* (Paris: Seuil, 2004)
JAMESON, FREDERIC, *The Political Unconscious* [1981], Routledge Classics (Abingdon: Routledge, 2002)
JONES, LEROI, *Le Peuple du Blues: la musique noire dans l'Amérique blanche*, trans. by Jacqueline Bernard (Paris: Gallimard, 1968)

KANT, IMMANUEL, *Critique of Judgement*, trans. by James Creed Meredith, rev. and ed. by Nicholas Walker (Oxford: Oxford University Press, 2007)

KILLEEN, MARIE-CHANTAL, 'Pour une lecture girardienne des *Bonnes* de Genet', *French Studies*, 58.4 (2004), 485–98

KRISTEVA, JULIA, *Étrangers à nous-mêmes* (Paris: Gallimard/Folio, 1991)

——*Strangers to Ourselves*, trans. by Leon S. Roudiez (New York: Columbia University Press, 1991)

LACAN, JACQUES, *Le Séminaire Livre V: Les Formations de l'inconscient*, ed. by Jacques-Alain Miller (Paris: Seuil, 1998)

LANE, CHRISTOPHER, 'The Voided Role: On Genet', *Modern Language Notes*, 112.5 (1997), 876–908

LAQUEUR, WALTER, and BARRY M. RUBIN, *The Israel-Arab Reader: A Documentary History of the Middle East Conflict* (London & New York: Penguin Books, 2001)

LAROCHE, HADRIEN, *Le Dernier Genet* (Paris: Seuil, 1997)

——*The Last Genet*, trans. by David Homel (Vancouver: Arsenal Pulp Press, 2010)

LAURENS, HENRY, *Une mission sacrée de civilisation: la question de Palestine* (Paris: Fayard, 2002)

LAVERY, CARL, *The Politics of Jean Genet's Late Theatre: Spaces of Revolution* (Manchester: Manchester University Press, 2010)

LIPSTADT, DEBORAH, *Antisemitism: Here and Now* (New York: Schocken, 2019)

LUCEY, MICHAEL, 'Genet's *Notre-Dame-des-Fleurs*: Fantasy and Sexual Identity,' in *Genet: In the Language of the Enemy*, ed. by Scott Durham (= special issue of *Yale French Studies*, 91 (1997)), 80–102

——*Someone: The Pragmatics of Misfit Sexualities, from Colette to Hervé Guibert* (Chicago & London: University of Chicago Press, 2019), pp. 85–108

McQUILLAN, MARTIN, ed., *The Politics of Deconstruction: Jacques Derrida and the Other of Philosophy* (London: Pluto, 2007)

MARCUSE, HERBERT, *Eros et civilisation: contribution à Freud*, trans. by J.-G. Nény and B. Fraenkel (Paris: Minuit, 1963)

MARTY, ÉRIC, *Bref séjour à Jérusalem* (Paris: Gallimard/L'Infini, 2003)

——*Jean Genet, post-scriptum* (Paris: Verdier, 2006)

MASALHA, NUR, *The Palestine Nakba: Decolonising History, Narrating the Subaltern, Reclaiming Memory* (London & New York: Zed Books, 2012)

MATTAR, PHILIP, *The Mufti of Jerusalem: Al-Hajj Amin al-Husayni and the Palestinian National Movement* (New York: Columbia University Press, 1992)

MILLETT, KATE, *Sexual Politics* [1969] (London: Virago, 1977)

MORALY, JEAN-BERNARD, *Le Maître fou* (Paris: Nizet, 2009)

MORRIS, BENNY, *1948: A History of the First Arab-Israeli War* (New Haven, CT: Yale University Press, 2008)

NEVEUX, OLIVIER, *Le Théâtre de Jean Genet* (Lausanne: Ides et Calendes, 2016)

NOTTET-CHEDEVILLE, ÉLISE, 'Les Poèmes de Jean Genet: la subversion comme style?' (unpublished doctoral thesis, Sorbonne Université, 2020)

PENNEY, JAMES, 'The Phallus Unveiled: Lacan, Badiou and the Comedic Moment in Genet's *The Balcony*', *Paragraph*, 42.2 (2019), 170–87

PHENG CHEAH and SUZANNE GUERLAC, eds, *Derrida and the Time of the Political* (Durham, NC: Duke University Press, 2009)

PLUNKA, GENE A., 'Jean Genet's Anti-Semitism: Fact or Fiction?', *French Review*, 76.3 (2003), 507–19

——*The Rites of Passage of Jean Genet: The Art and Aesthetics of Risk Taking* (Rutherford, NJ: Fairleigh Dickinson University Press; London: Associated University Presses, 1992)

PUCCIANI, ORESTE, 'Tragedy, Genet and *The Maids*', *Tulane Drama Review*, 7.3 (1963), 42–59

RANCIÈRE, JACQUES, *La Mésentente: politique et philosophie* (Paris: Galilée, 1995)

ROUSSO, HENRY, *Le Syndrome de Vichy* (Paris: Seuil, 1987)

RUNNING-JOHNSON, CYNTHIA, 'Genet's "Excessive" Double: Reading *Les Bonnes* through Irigaray and Cixous', *French Review*, 63.6 (1990), 959–66

SARTRE, JEAN-PAUL, *Réflexions sur la question juive* [1946] (Paris: Gallimard/Nrf, 1954)

—— *Saint Genet: comédien et martyr* (Paris: Gallimard, 1952)

SAVONA, JEANNETTE, *Jean Genet* (New York: Grove Press, 1983)

SEALE, BOBBY, *Seize the Time: Story of the Black Panther Party and Huey P. Newton* (Baltimore, MD: Black Classic Press, 1991)

SEALE, BOBBY, and STEPHEN SHAMES, *Power to the People: The World of the Black Panthers* (New York: Abrams, 2016)

SOHLICH, W. F., 'Genet's *The Blacks* and *The Screens*: Dialectic of Refusal and Revolutionary Consciousness', *Comparative Drama*, 10.3 (1976), 216–34

STEPHENS, ELIZABETH, *Queer Writing: Homoeroticism in Jean Genet's Fiction* (Basingstoke: Palgrave Macmillan, 2009)

STEWART, HARRY E., and ROB ROY MACGREGOR, *Jean Genet: From Fascism to Nihilism* (New York & Berlin: Lang, 1993)

THODY, PHILIP, *Jean Genet: A Study of His Novels and Plays* [1968] (New York: Stein & Day, 1970)

TODOROV, TSVETAN, *Face à l'extrême* (Paris: Points, 1994)

TOFFOLI, CAMILLE, 'La Question de l'antisémitisme chez Jean Genet: un débat sur le "sens du monde". Autour de la réception critique d'*Un Captif amoureux*', *Postures*, 24 (2016) <http://revuepostures.com/fr/articles/toffoli-24> [accessed 21 November 2019]

TURE, KWAME (formerly STOKELY CARMICHAEL), and CHARLES V. HAMILTON, *Black Power: The Politics of Liberation in America* [1967] (New York: Vintage/Random House, 1992)

WALKER, DAVID, *Outrage and Insight: Modern French Writers and the Fait Divers* (Oxford & Washington, DC: Berg, 1995)

—— 'Revolution and Revisions in Genet's *Le Balcon*', *Modern Language Review*, 79.4 (1984), 817–30

WEBB, RICHARD, 'Ritual, Theatre and Jean Genet's *The Blacks*', *Theatre Journal*, 31.4 (1979), 443–59

WEBER, SAMUEL, 'Double Take: Acting and Writing in Genet's "L'Étrange Mot de..."', in *Genet: In the Language of the Enemy*, ed. by Scott Durham (= special issue of *Yale French Studies*, 91 (1997)), 28–48

WHITE, EDMUND, *Genet* (London: Chatto & Windus, 1993)

# INDEX

❖

www.ingramcontent.com/pod-product-compliance
Lightning Source LLC
Chambersburg PA
CBHW080542090426
42734CB00016B/3179